Interdisciplinary perspectives on modern history

Editors
Robert Fogel and Stephan Thernstrom

Cradle of the middle class:
the family in Oneida County, New York,
1790–1865

Frontispiece is the seal of the Utica Building Association, 1820 (Oneida Historical Society, Utica, N.Y.)

Cradle of the middle class

The family in Oneida County, New York, 1790–1865

MARY P. RYAN

Department of History
University of California, Irvine

The right of the
University of Cambridge
to print and sell
all manner of books
was granted by
Henry VIII in 1534.
The University has printed
and published continuously
since 1584.

CAMBRIDGE UNIVERSITY PRESS

Cambridge
New York   Port Chester   Melbourne   Sydney

Published by the Press Syndicate of the University of Cambridge
The Pitt Building, Trumpington Street, Cambridge CB2 1RP
40 West 20th Street, New York, NY 10011, USA
10 Stamford Road, Oakleigh, Melbourne 3166, Australia

First published 1981
First paperback edition 1983
Reprinted 1984, 1985, 1986, 1987, 1988, 1989

Printed in the United States of America

Library of Congress Cataloging in Publication Data
Ryan, Mary P
Cradle of the middle class.
(Interdisciplinary perspectives on modern history)
Bibliography: p.
Includes index.
1. Family—New York (State)—Oneida Co.—History.
2. Middle classes—New York (State)—Oneida Co.—
History. I. Title. II. Series.
HQ555.N7R9   306.8'0974'62   80–18460

ISBN 0 521 23200 7 hard covers
ISBN 0 521 27403 6 paperback

Portions of Chapter 2 have appeared in *American
Quarterly*, Volume XXX, no. 5, Winter 1978, portions of
Chapter 3 have appeared in *Feminist Studies*, Volume 5,
no. Spring 1979.

PATRICK H. RYAN   IN MEMORIAM

Contents

x   Contents

Preface

This book has grown in the shifting, sluggish style of an amoeba. It has changed its shape considerably and more than once over the years, yet it remains recognizable as the same species of scholarship. It even contains a few cells of a doctoral dissertation completed almost a decade ago. That initial study of the literature written about the family between 1830 and 1860 attempted to identify the relationship between a popular preoccupation with domesticity and concurrent changes in the organization of the American economy and social structure. The basic axis of change, as I first dimly saw it, tilted the ideological center of family life from an authoritative father to a loving mother, from household production to the socialization of children. I succeeded in linking domestic ideas to social change only in a highly abstract and synchronic fashion, however – by little more than the crude assertion that the early stages of industrial capitalism sponsored a sharpened division between the worlds of work and home, male and female, and private and public life.

Thus the ink was hardly dry on that dissertation when I determined that its subject matter deserved a more penetrating mode of analysis. In order to explore these changes in family and gender at the level of concrete historical processes, and infuse them with some sense of human agency, I had to undertake something more than a reading of published literature. At about this time the fortuitous appearance of a handful of ethnographic studies of early American communities suggested a sounder research design. By narrowing their historical compass to the range of a single community, the new social historians had uncovered patterns of everyday social life in local records that were far more resonant and variegated than the products of remote publishing firms. Their research techniques seemed ideally suited to the history of the family and gender. First of all, the small, out-of-the-way archives they mined seemed to contain ample evidence of a private life that might expose the experience of heretofore anonymous and secluded populations, perhaps even such reticent historical subjects as women and children. Second, the community study could serve as a laboratory of social history, an experimental context chosen to reflect a specified set of social and economic changes, such as the halting process of American industrialization. Finally, this localized ethnographic approach promised to open up an avenue to total history, if only at a microcosmic level. Within its finite boundaries at least, the family could be charted through the whole web of social relations that surrounded and penetrated it. In sum, a community study seemed a sound start along the trail of family and gender in antebellum America.

This new trail led ultimately to Utica and Oneida County, New York. Although hardly the nineteenth-century equivalent of "Middletown," Utica and its environs recommended themselves for analysis for a variety of reasons. The region replicated a process of historical development that characterized many American communities in the antebellum era, that is, rapid advancement from a sparsely populated frontier through a bustling stage of small-scale commercial capitalism and on toward industrialization. At the same time, it was the site of a unique if not idiosyncratic cultural and social history. It was Oneida County's colorful history as part of the "Burned-Over District" that first captured my attention. In the decades before the Civil War the region was set aflame with evangelical religion and reforming zeal. As the men and women of west-central New York flocked to revivals, joined a plethora of voluntary associations, and lent their support to a variety of reform movements, they also bespoke their domestic concerns and enacted a complex range of gender and familial roles. In other words, the Burned-Over District stood out among other antebellum regions because of the multitude of social innovations enacted by its citizenry and a consequent wealth of historical evidence about the private lives of the local populus. I surmised that its archives would contain something more than the arid statistics about occupation and mobility that dominated so many studies of nineteenth-century towns and cities.

Of all the towns in the Burned-Over District, Utica in the county of Oneida proved to be especially appropriate for a study of the family. It was a regional publishing center and the portal through which countless volumes of literature on domestic subjects sped their way through the Burned-Over District and beyond. One set of such publications especially piqued my curiosity. Two of the first American mothers' magazines bore Utica imprints and traced their origins to one of the city's first, but least studied, reform movements, the maternal associations. In these congregations of mothers, founded in the 1820s and devoted to cultivating grace in

the souls of young children, I discerned the keystone to the transformation of family and gender in antebellum America. Clues like
these led me to a veritable treasure trove of historical sources. The
local history collection at Utica's public library welcomed me with
family manuals, schoolbooks, and novellas, all steeped in domestic
details. Across the street at the Oneida Historical Society I found
family letters, diaries, and records of reform societies, all containing titillating revelations about private life. The rectories of local
churches yielded worn leather volumes full of testimony to the intricate relationship between religion and kinship. Finally, as luck
would have it, I even came upon the membership list of Utica's first
maternal association, almost by accident, in the New York State
Library in Albany.

Yet for all this wealth and variety of documents, the archives of
Oneida County were on one score very stingy. Rarely did they record the experience of the immigrant and non-Protestant population, which at midcentury accounted for approximately 40% of
Utica's residents. Not even my persistent supplications to local
priests, Catholic social workers, and the officers of Irish and German fraternal associations yielded more than a few shards of evidence about the immigrant population that comprised the lower
ranks of the city's social structure. Thus, reluctantly and at a very
late date, I excised from my manuscript most references to lower-
class immigrant families.

The narrowed focus was justified on more than pragmatic
grounds. It served to spotlight a major historical process that underpinned the whole frenetic history of family and gender in antebellum Oneida County – the emergence of a definable middle class. It
soon became clear that many innovations in family practice, attitudes, and relations emanated from a select segment of the region's
shifting social structure, namely, the farmers, artisans, and shopkeepers buffeted by the intensified competition and instability of a
rapidly growing marketplace. By midcentury these new domestic
patterns had jelled into a sequence of strategies whereby parents
might secure for their children comfortable middle-range occupations, especially within a growing white-collar class. In other
words, this history of the family and society assumed yet another
shape: It had become a chronicle of the formation of a new American middle class. This aspect of American social history is still yet
dimly understood; it begs further research and portends more
amoeboid developments in the study of family and class.

Throughout the twists and turns in my research, I have been sustained by a number of institutions and many colleagues and friends. A Rockefeller Foundation Humanities Fellowship financed a year of uninterrupted research, during which time I incurred debts to the staffs of numerous archives, including the American Antiquarian Society, the Baker Library of the Harvard Business School, the New York Historical Society, the New York Public Library, the New York State Library, and the Utica Public Library. I am especially grateful to Douglas Preston and Francis Cunningham for introducing me to the rich collections of the Oneida Historical Society and to Deborah Gardner who conducted me on a tour of Oneida County's antebellum architecture. Finally, my thanks go to those residents of Utica, Whitesboro, and New Hartford, New York, who welcomed me into their churches, homes, and attic archives.

During the quantitative phase of my research, I was absolutely dependent on the assistance of others. The Newberry Library's Summer Institute on Community and Family History gave me the courage to tackle this facet of my research in the first place, and Michael Haines patiently and generously guided me through the snares of analyzing the New York State Census. The State University of New York at Binghamton helped me to fund the work of a team of graduate students, among them David Brooks, Barbara Goldstein, Richard Holmes, and Susan Weber, who toiled at minimal wages preparing the data for computerized analysis. Paula Petrik and Glenna Potts assisted with the footnotes and bibliography as well. Ruth Keen cleaned and polished the writing. Finally, nary a statistic nor a table could have been generated without the cheerful, efficient labor of my research assistant, Chinnah Mithrasekaran.

In its final form, this book has been dramatically improved and clarified by the criticisms of my fellow historians Stuart Blumin, Thomas Dublin, Clyde Griffin, Paul Johnson, Michael Katz, Kenneth Lockridge, Kathryn Kish Sklar, Daniel Scott Smith, and Carroll Smith-Rosenberg, who read the manuscript and offered extensive invaluable suggestions for revision. Steven Fraser of Cambridge University Press and series editor Stephan Thernstrom provided astute editorial advice along with detailed comments on the manuscript. Through the course of this project I was sustained and inspired by fellow editors of the journal *Feminist Studies,* especially Judith Stacey and Judith Walkowitz, and by my friend Zillah Eisenstein. Finally, I thank Richard Busacca for the special intensity and exhilaration of his criticism and his companionship.

Irvine, California   Mary P. Ryan
November 1980

Introduction: locating domesticity

Among all the graceful and gauche nineteenth-century objects stored in the museum of the Oneida Historical Society in Utica, New York, is a heavy brass implement impressed with the seal of the Building Association and dated 1820. Etched on the antique metal is the figure of a stocky carpenter and an equally robust female companion whose arms are crudely raised above the simple outlines of a small family dwelling. Utica's builders took the time to carve some whimsical ornamentation into this symbol of their craft. Greek revival cornices, pillars, and a picket fence give a homey, personal touch to this two-story, single-gable house, replicas of which can still be found hidden away along the congested streets of downtown Utica and scattered throughout the countryside of central New York State. The house is also framed by two cornucopias overflowing with fruits. This prosaic icon would seem to betoken a kind of domestic awakening among the carpenters and joiners of this small but bustling town. Here, preserved in solid brass, are some bucolic symbols of home life, created by a usually inarticulate and anonymous class of nineteenth-century Americans.

Historians and archivists might have some difficulty cataloguing this charming but curious artifact. The carpenters' rendition of domesticity does not fit very neatly into existent classifications and chronologies of American family history. Yes, volumes have been written about a nineteenth-century cult of domesticity, and numerous studies indicate that the typical family of the era was small enough to fit into a house drawn to the scale of the model of the Building Association. Yet the date, the class origin, and the gender imagery of this particular domestic icon all seem confusing and somehow out of place. The sense of "home sweet home" conveyed by this artifact is more germane to the period after 1830 and is commonly associated with Victorian ladies rather than artisans. The hefty physique, flowing garments, and androgynous characteristics of both the male and the female figures also seem to contradict the gender stereotypes one would expect to find in a nineteenth-century museum of family history. Yet this brass seal is not an anomaly. It is as valid and suggestive a document of family history as can be found in any antebellum archive. The following pages will establish a context for such documents, explore their meaning, and argue that they are central to our understanding of the history of the American family.

Until very recently, historians and social theorists could offer only the most general directions about how to locate the origins and meaning of domesticity in nineteenth-century Utica. Sociology posted an imprecise road sign that pointed to some functional connections between "industrial society" and "the modern family." The standard hypothesis, argued most forcefully by Talcott Parsons in the 1950s, contended that large extended households were decimated into small, "isolated, nuclear families" by the process of industrialization. According to Parsons, the modern family was typified by expressive emotional and psychological functions and its remoteness from society, politics, and production. Such an ideal type of family organization might also be read in the imagery of the Utica Building Association. Yet the schema of economic development that accompanies Parsons's theory, that of "industrial society," hardly seems appropriate to Utica, New York, in 1820, whose carpenters' shops and other handcrafts could hardly be dignified, or demeaned, by the term *factory*. To confuse things further, recent historians, led by Peter Laslett and his Cambridge group, have argued that industrialization did not noticeably alter either the mean size or the modal structure of households. More perplexing still is the discovery by Michael Anderson that industrialization in England could actually enlarge, extend, and increase the domestic interdependency of working-class families. Joan Scott and Louise Tilly have carried this argument even further and charted the many integral connections between households, factories, economics, and the labor force that endured throughout the nineteenth century and extended across the continent. In sum, the functionalist association between industrialization and the rise of the small nuclear family does not promise a very helpful or specific clue to the study of nineteenth-century American households.[1]

This does not mean, however, that the family is an immutable institution. Rather, this recent literature challenges historians to devise more accurate measures of family change than the size and structure of households and to link these changes to more refined typologies of economic and social development than to merely the broad term *industrialization*. Again taking the lead from European historians, we can now identify myriad family characteristics, such as kin associations, inheritance patterns, marriage rules, and domestic affections, that vary markedly according to time and place. We need only turn to Philippe Ariès's classic account of the evolution of childhood, Lawrence Stone's erudite tripartite typology of family change between 1500 and 1800, Edward Shorter's jaunty description of a revolution in sentiment, or David Levine's painstaking local analysis of the family and nascent capitalism to discover an array of family changes that accompany the long-term transformation from feudalism to advanced capitalism.[2]

This last decade of highly productive historical scholarship has also advanced our knowledge of the family in America. American scholars have been particularly resourceful and successful in recovering the history of colonial families. Building on the work of Edmund S. Morgan and employing the interdisciplinary techniques of the new social history, John Demos has provided a detailed portrait of the New England family. In *A Little Commonwealth* Demos pictured early American households whose expansive social functions and organic ties to the community pose a dramatic contrast to the cozy bungalow embossed on the seal of the Utica Building Association. Philip Greven's *Four Generations*, published, like *A Little Commonwealth*, in 1970, identified the economic and demographic factors that would ultimately fracture that institution and send American family history into a new phase. Subsequent inquiries into the history of the American family have not, however, picked up where Demos and Greven left off or followed where European historians such as Stone or Levine led. Rather, studies of the American family in the nineteenth century have tended to proceed from a distinctive perspective. Urban studies in which analyses of census records play a premier methodological role provide the setting for this second stage of American family history, which exhibits itself in a wealth of journal articles and segments of important monographs such as Michael Katz's study of Hamilton, Ontario. These statistical tabulations of the structure, size, and employment patterns of nineteenth-century families stand apart from the chatty wills and record books of New England towns, divided by a century of largely uncharted historiographic territory. There are a few studies in between – Bernard Farber's monograph on Salem, Massachusetts, in 1800, Daniel Scott Smith's demographic portrait of Hingham, Massachusetts, and Herbert Gutman's analysis of the kinship of slavery – but no one has illuminated the precise family transformations that might connect the early American farm family to the nineteenth-century urban household. Our picture of the latter, furthermore, still suffers from the flatness peculiar to narrowly quantitative history that fails to take cognizance of the affective, normative, and experiential aspects of family life; it is like the raw outlines of the model house of the Building Association with none of its evocative domestic trim.[3]

Fortunately, quantitative social historians have not been alone in their exploration of family history over the last decade. Energized by quite another historical objective, that of assaulting a wall of ignorance about the sex that has been so often veiled in domestic privacy, historians of American women have also penetrated into the domains of family history. Women's history is highly complementary to the new social history of the family. It tends to specialize in the analysis of literary documents rather than statistics, pays more attention to the nineteenth century than to the colonial period, and focuses on mothers and daughters rather than fathers and sons. As a consequence, historians of women have been able to expose some special dynamics in nineteenth-century family history. First of all, a careful reading of the nineteenth-century literature on femininity has revealed a significant escalation in the volume and intensity of domestic sentiments. This cult of domesticity is too effusive in the celebration of an intensely privatized home to be effaced by assertions of the changeless structure and persistent economic functions of nineteenth-century households. Second, historians of nineteenth-century women have exposed gender divisions that cut through society and introduced a new emotional complexity into American households. By illuminating a woman's "world of love and ritual" and devising the concept of homosocial bonding, Carroll Smith-Rosenberg has challenged family historians to examine more intently the shifting emotional dimensions and sexual alliances within families. It should be noted, however, that homosocial bonds and the segregated women's culture they circumscribed were not deferred to by the heterosocial imagery of the Utica Building Association in 1820. Having illuminated the feminine emotive and cultural elements in family history, women's historians still need to pay heed to the new family historians and link the changing image and experience of women to a larger social and economic context.[4]

That artifact from the Oneida Historical Society seems to denote a moment in family history that stands squarely in the middle of this scholarly lacuna, somewhere between the seventeenth-century farm and the nineteenth-century city, between the "little commonwealth" and the cult of domesticity, between Puritan fathers and Victorian ladies, between the new social history and the history of women. By coming to terms with that document of domesticity – with a product of the artisan culture of a small New York town in the middle period of American history – it will be possible to explore a crucial turning point in the history of the American family.

To follow up on this intriguing archeological clue, it is necessary at the outset to fully describe the site where it was found, its economic, cultural, and class context. Oneida County, New York, was chosen as the location of this historical exploration because it promised to harbor many such resonant documents. Between 1790 and 1865, Oneida County, and particularly its southeastern corner where the Sauguoit Creek joins the Mohawk River, experienced some pivotal social and economic transformations. By midcentury, Utica, the commercial center of the region, had grown from a frontier trading post into a small city of twenty-two thousand people with a variegated urban economy. The city's social and economic structure was very much like the other middle-sized cities of the era, places such as Poughkeepsie and Kingston in New York or northward in Hamilton, Ontario. All these cities, described respectively by the historians Sally and Clyde Griffen, Stuart Blumin, and Michael Katz, shared Utica's basic economic organization, wherein a few large steam-powered factories coexisted with many small craftsmen and shopkeepers and a growing number of salaried white-collar workers. Like Utica, these cities were characterized by rapid population growth, a high level of transience, voluminous social mobility (in upward, downward, and horizontal directions), and a massive influx of immigrants from abroad. Much of the fluid social and economic life of nineteenth-century America was caught up in the constant movement in, around, and out of cities like these.[5]

The nineteenth-century city, at the same time, was not an isolated, exactly bounded social and economic space. It was inextricably connected, as Diane Lindstrom's study of the Philadelphia area has demonstrated, to a whole regional network of smaller and larger places, of farmlands, villages, and major centers of national and international distribution. Thus the appropriate context for nineteenth-century community history is not a single local political unit but a complex of interrelated economic sites. The basic components of such an interdependent economic network can be found within a small radius of Oneida County, New York, in the agricultural district of Whitestown, its precocious commercial stepchild, Utica, and its industrial offshoot, New York Mills. By the middle of the nineteenth century the economic life of Oneida County had been inte-

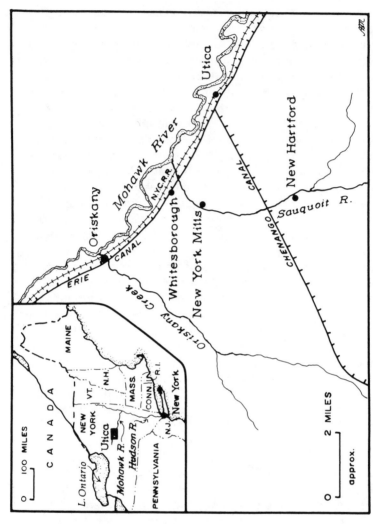

Utica, New York – detail from map 29, *An Atlas of the State of New York*, David S. Burr (Ithaca, 1839); redrawn by Adrienne Morgan.

grated into a national and international market system whose regional focal point was now the city of New York. This regional network that centered around Utica and maintained some measure of economic autonomy early in the century will set the serpentine boundaries of this study.[6]

The individual units of the regional economy, Whitestown, New York Mills, and Utica, also represent the stages in a developmental sequence, a sequence that is far more complicated than the linear notion of industrialization. On the one hand, the brief period that followed on the European settlement of Upstate New York recapitulated changes in material life that had initially taken millennia. On the other, the nineteenth-century residents of the region seemed to inch slowly and haltingly from small-scale capitalist agriculture toward an industrial city. What follows then is a close-up picture of a broad economic transformation as seen through the telescopic lens of local history.

Neolithic and feudal relics could still be found along the Mohawk River in the eighteenth century, when the decree of an English king converted the hunting ground of the Oneida Indians into a royal fief. King George granted New York's governor William Cosby a generous slice of Indian land, eleven miles in length and six miles wide, from which the latter hoped to reap a handsome income in quitrents. American patriots had other designs on Cosby's Manor, however, and after the Revolution a veteran of the New York campaign, Hugh White, returned to settle his name and his family on fifteen hundred choice acres along the Sauquoit Creek. Whitestown was soon a thriving agricultural settlement producing a variety of foodstuffs for domestic consumption and for exchange within the regional market. The agrarian economy swiftly became specialized enough to support a number of processing plants – saw and flour mills, tanneries, distilleries, and carding factories. These manufactories were still primitive operations. They processed local grains, hides, and wool, distributed them within a five- or six-mile radius and conducted much of their exchange by barter. Those farmers' sons and daughters who produced wool in the Oneida Manufacturing Society, for example, were paid in yarn, room and board, and merchandise from the company stores. According to the local weekly, the *Whitestown Gazette*, even the most modish commodity available on the frontier, patent medicine, could be exchanged for "country produce."[7]

Within this rudimentary exchange economy, however, some merchants found opportunities for more sophisticated and specialized marketing. A few miles west of the town center of Whitesborough, where two bridges crossed the Mohawk, John Post's general store and Moses Bagg's hostelry were doing a bustling business by 1800. When three turnpikes met in front of Bagg's door in 1805, the boom was on in the newly incorporated village of Utica. By 1817, when the village broke off from Whitestown to form an independent township, the population numbered nearly three thousand inhabitants, most of whom earned their livelihoods as shopkeepers, merchants, and handcraftsmen. As the construction on the Erie Canal stretched westward, reaching Utica in 1820 and Lake Erie in 1825, the town's population tripled and its shopkeepers and artisans flourished. One local craftsman enscribed the boosterism of the canal era on a piece of china in 1824: "Utica, a village in the State of New York, thirty years since a wilderness, now inferior to none in the Eastern Section of the State in Population, Wealth, Commercial enterprise, active industry and civil improvement."[8]

The hubris of Utica's citizens would become deflated during the next two decades, and dreams of becoming the capital of the Empire State were never to be realized. Still, as the mercantile and manufacturing center of the county, the city continued to thrive. The years before 1845 are marked off in the city's history as a particularly energetic and volatile epoch in the history of small-scale American capitalism. When Utica drew up its first city charter in 1832, its nine thousand residents were busily conducting the commercial operations of Oneida and the surrounding counties. A typical edition of the *Utica Observer* in the early 1840s advertised the wares of more than a hundred different specialty shops, hawking everything from fine-ground flour to colorful ginghams and shimmering looking glasses. The financial apparatus necessary to this expanded commerce – banks, insurance companies, law offices – grew apace. At the same time, however, it was the manufacturing segment of Utica's economy that expanded most rapidly during the canal era. The largest single mode of employment, accounting for 45% of the occupations listed in the city directories, was provided by the skilled crafts.[9] Most of these carpenters, shoemakers, wheelwrights, blacksmiths, and wallpaper hangers were either self-employed master artisans or apprentices and employees of small mechanic shops. As late as 1850, 3 out of 4 firms employed fewer than ten workers. The modal shop counted only two or three workers, who relied on their own skill and muscle rather than horse, water, or steam power.

Despite the limited scale and mechanization of local production,

Uticans were, by their own standards, resolutely and enthusiastically capitalists. Nearly every newspaper advertised the sale of "capital stock." Sunday sermons spoke of the "moral capital of clean living," and the local sleuths employed by the Mercantile Agency went around town assessing the "capital resources" of everyone from bank presidents to saloonkeepers. The only economic term more popular than *capital* was the word *cash*. Beginning in the 1830s local merchants lured the farmers on market day with such slogans as "cash for wool" and "wheat for cash." Once a local farmer had converted his produce into currency he was a welcome customer in many a shop. He or his wife could walk into William Stacy's Domestic Staple and Fancy Goods Store, for example, and choose from some forty-six varieties of cloth, ribbons, and sewing paraphernalia, all "at the lowest prices." Another merchant placed this guileless announcement of the cash economy in a Utica paper: "Money Wanted." Countless others appended the label "Cash System" to their business cards, denoting a fundamental transformation in the organization of material life in Oneida County.

The greatest stocks of capital and the reins of the cash economy were in the hands of a few elite families, those lawyers and merchants of Genesee Street who sat on the boards of directors of the city's four banks. Yet large numbers of lowlier citizens participated actively in the advance of capitalism in Oneida County. For example, the stockholders of the Utica Bank in 1830 included some twenty-eight farmers and about an equal number of artisans. By 1840 Whitestown farmers were engaged in frenetic production for the cash market; their dairy products alone were valued at almost $80,000. These farmers had been eager to invest in industry as well. As early as 1809 they became subscribers to the stock of the Oneida Manufacturing Society, along with their pastor, James Carnahan, whose modernity on all other scores would seem somewhat to the rear of Cotton Mather's. In sum, the virgin soil of Oneida County was quickly planted with the seeds of profit and improvement. By 1845 the spirit of cash and capital had run riot over Whitestown's farms and along Utica's streets, involving the middle ranks of the social structure – farmers, artisans, and shopkeepers – as well as lawyers, bankers, and industrialists.[10]

The only bona fide industrialist in the region before 1845 was Benjamin Walcott, owner and president of the New York Mills Company. Walcott arrived in Oneida County in 1825, bringing with him the expertise and financial contacts of an experienced Rhode Island textile manufacturer. By 1845 the Walcott family, in collaboration with the elite of Utica, had organized farmers' sons, daughters, and widows into the factory village of New York Mills, the tenth largest producer of cotton yarn in the United States. It was not until 1845 that Utica's capitalist city fathers had cause to consider the assets of industrial production. A broadside appearing in that year noted that the frontier had passed Utica by, as had the Erie Canal; Utica could no longer expect to grow merely on the strength of its agricultural hinterland. The local economists were indeed correct; in fact, as early as 1820 the rural population had reached 75% of its 1940 level. In order to forestall economic stagnation, Utica's business leaders invited the local citizenry to purchase stock in a textile factory to be powered by steam and located within the city proper. With the opening of the Utica Cotton Works, the urban-industrial stage of local economic development was inaugurated. Soon three more textile factories opened their doors to some twelve hundred workers after making an investment totaling more than $500,000. In the 1860s a large garment industry and a major shoe factory, both, like the textile industry, products of the age of rails and steam rather than canals, further augmented the industrial sector of Utica's economy. As a consequence, the average size of manufacturing establishments more than tripled, to a mean of 37.3 workers. Again Utica began to change and to grow, reaching a population of more than twenty thousand by the Civil War and employing many men and women who had recently immigrated from England, Ireland, and Germany.[11]

Still, the industrial proletariat constituted only a small portion of the local population as of 1865. As Bruce Laurie, Theodore Hershberg, and George Alter have noted of Philadelphia during the same period, highly mechanized production still coexisted with small artisan shops.[12] The expansion of the population of wage earners, furthermore, created an enlarged market for local commerce, and the volume and scale of retailing increased accordingly. These larger factories and department stores also created more jobs for salaried white-collar workers, the managers, salesmen, and clerks who would become a new middle class. Utica and Oneida County had changed remarkably in seventy years. This latest, increasingly industrial stage of capitalist development was built, however, upon layers of economic activity that had survived from the past. To slice through the local economic terrain at any given moment is to expose these multiple and interlaced strata of agriculture, commerce, urban services, and industry.

For analytical purposes, however, this complicated, seamless economic history will be interrupted at two points. The approximate date of 1820 will demark that point when diversified agricultural production lost hegemony to the small-scale merchandisers and manufacturers enamored of cash and capital. By around 1850 the dominance of artisans and shopkeepers was challenged, in turn, by the more massive mercantile and manufacturing firms of an embryonic industrial era. The geographical focus of the study will shift concurrently from rural Whitestown to the city of Utica. It was about midway through this sequence of regional economic development and at a very volatile point not too far along in the rise of industrial capitalism that the builders and joiners of Oneida County deposited that quaint document of domesticity in the local historical record.

Although the location of this study is representative of economic changes that occurred throughout America during the nineteenth century, Utica, Whitestown, and New York Mills do not conform to any bland notion of average or typical American communities. This region, especially during the period between 1825 and 1845, was far too turbulent for that dubious honor. The special vitality of Oneida County's history is responsible for its prior claim to historical attention as the easternmost section of what Whitney Cross called the "Burned-Over District." It was in Oneida County, New York, that Charles Grandison Finney first practiced those "new measures" that have come to identify the modern evangelical tradition. It was in Oneida County, and preeminently Whitestown and Utica, that the fires of revivalism kindled a fervent campaign to rid the world of intemperance, slavery, prostitution, profanity, Sabbath breaking, and nearly every sin a seventh-generation Puritan-turned-Victorian was capable of imagining.[13]

American scholars have begun to apply the concepts and methods of the new social history to the analysis of the events that Cross recounted a generation ago. In his pathbreaking study of the Second Great Awakening in Rochester, New York, Paul E. Johnson has argued that evangelical religion was a kind of ideological cover for more fundamental shifts in class relations. His thesis has two facets. First, he maintains that Rochester's emergent industrial capitalists employed the sanction of Protestant religion, the injunctions to be hardworking, honest, and frugal, as a means of disciplining their labor force. Second, Johnson interprets the preponderance of shopkeepers and artisans among revival converts as evidence that evangelism also served as a mode of self-definition for the middle ranks of the population. Evangelical religion, in Johnson's estimation, can also be seen as the "moral imperative around which the northern middle class became a class." Based on the analysis of another evangelical site, the mill towns of Pennsylvania, Anthony Wallace adds credence to the first facet of Johnson's interpretation, that revivals consolidated the cultural hegemony of industrialists over their workers. Both these historians, and both variants of class analysis, offer suggestive and insightful but still incomplete explanations of the social history of revivalism in antebellum America.[14]

A closer look at the Second Great Awakening indicates that the history of class and religion was hopelessly entangled with questions of family and gender. The religious controversy of the Burned-Over District was ignited in the first decade of the nineteenth century and centered around such issues as the religious status of the offspring of church members and the role of women in public worship. The roster of converts during the revivals that followed was laced with common surnames and dominated by female Christian names. The copious reform movements that ensued in the wake of revivals enacted yet another family pageant. Temperance literature, for example, was soaked in domestic images – of degenerate wives, prodigal sons, and, of course, that most pathetic victim of demon rum, the gentle waiflike daughter who waits the requisite ten nights outside a barroom. The organization of temperance suggests that society was being reorganized along the lines of age and sex; segregated groups of young men filed out of their families and into the Cadets of Temperance, and mothers and sisters congregated outside the home in groups like the Martha Washington Total Abstinence Society. At the same time, revivals and reform movements seemed to conspire to draw family members together again on a new basis; mothers were especially active in the evangelical churches and moral reform societies where they took particular concern to convert and to rehabilitate their own sons, daughters, and husbands.

In Utica, in other words, the pressure for moral regeneration was exerted within and around families as much as across classes. The interpretation of revivals as the actions of the elite meting out social control over their employees would make most sense in the village of New York Mills, where the paternalistic Benjamin Walcott encouraged his workers to join evangelical churches. But class differences were not this sharp in the major centers of the Second Great Awakening, in the agricultural regions like Whitestown and the commercial towns like Utica. The farmers, artisans, and shopkeepers of Oneida County were struggling to maintain and improve themselves as small-scale independent businessmen. Conversely, hardly a laborer could be found in the ranks of the evangelicals, and the richest manufacturer among them was merely a prosperous and enterprising hat maker. There is ample reason to entertain the hypothesis, then, that those who joined the evangelical churches and reform crusades along the route of the Erie Canal were responding to the inducements of their kin as much as of their employers and were often involved in an exercise in "self-control" rather than "social control."

This less hierarchical interpretation of the social relations of the Burned-Over District also seems more consistent with the demography and age structure of the region. The towns along the canal, like the revival churches and the reform societies, were inundated with youthful migrants between 1820 and the mid-1840s. Many of the young men would find their first jobs as apprentices, clerks, and junior partners in small retail stores. They were, in other words, only beginning to find positions for themselves in the urban social structure. Given the formative period in their life cycles, and the relatively fluid social structure of the canal era, they might have been attracted to revivals and reform groups as forums through which they could experiment with new values and social relationships. In the process they became acquainted with novel ideas about the family and gender. It is not unreasonable, then, to entertain another hypothesis: That much of the frenzy of the Burned-Over District was created by young men and women from farm, artisan, and shopkeeping families who were struggling to find a comfortable place for themselves within a changing social and economic structure.

The central characters in the religious, social, and family drama of the Second Great Awakening were neither industrialists nor proletarians but occupants of intermediate, middle-level social ranks located somewhere in the vast undifferentiated status category Americans call the middle class. This class is largely a residual category in American historiography, the assumed, but largely unexamined, context for much of the writing about popular culture and reform movements. Its social identity is further muted by association with a long Anglo-Saxon lineage within a nation of continuous immigration and ethnic diversity. Historians have hardly begun to analyze middle Americans as a class unto themselves. Burton Bledstein has done yeoman service by charting the educational and cultural history of the nineteenth-century middle class.[15] Yet the social and occupational characteristics of this class remain unspecified. The new social historians, who have the tools with which to undertake this research, have been preoccupied with the elite and the working class and treat what lies in between as the unstable terrain of mobility studies.

Consequently, the class context for the Second Great Awakening and the family history of Oneida County, New York, remains nebulous, and its social historians are sorely wanting in theoretical direction. The best guide to the study of the American middle class was written almost thirty years ago by C. Wright Mills. In his classic, *White Collar*, Mills gave some needed occupational specificity to the term *middle class*. Mills classified the owners and operators of small independent retail and productive enterprises, chiefly farmers, artisans, and shopkeepers, as the older middle class. He designated white-collar workers – salaried managers and professionals, retail clerks, and office workers – as the new middle class. Mills also set up a historical dynamic within the middle class. By the mid-nineteenth century the new middle class had begun to supplant the old; by Mills's estimate, four-fifths of American workers were self-employed in the early nineteenth century and only 1 in 3 by 1870. Mills also acknowledged that the middle-range occupations constituted a peculiar and tenuous class, whose human links were fragile and evanescent. Occupants of middle-class jobs were notably lacking in the class solidarity evidenced by either trade unions or cabals of large businessmen. As Mills put it, "The white collar people slipped quietly into modern society. Whatever history they have had is a history without events; whatever common interests they have do not lead to unity; whatever future they have will not be of their own making."[16]

Analysis of the events that transpired in antebellum Oneida County may retrieve these middle Americans from historical limbo. Utica's old middle class was neither without a history nor bereft of a collective identity. The "middling sort" participated actively in a major historical event, the Second Great Awakening, and formed many groups like the Building Association, which in turn articulated a social and cultural self-image, if only that of an emblem on a brass seal. Often, however, they chose images of private family life as their class insignia. This peculiarly isolated and privatized identity began to evolve within the old middle class of a largely pre-industrial capitalist town. By the time Utica industrialized, the middle class had withdrawn from association into the secluded social space that Mills described. At the same time, the middle range of Utica occupations had come to include a growing number of clerks,

professionals, and managers, that is, members of the new middle
class. The occupational base of the middle class seemed to be
changing at the same time that its domestic consciousness grew
more powerful. In other words, Oneida County and Utica, New
York, take us via religion and reform to an intricate historical juncture between family and class. It elicits a final hypothesis: Early in
the nineteenth century the American middle class molded its distinctive identity around domestic values and family practices. At
any rate, it is this intuition, this kernal of a reinterpretation of the
making of the modern family that this book seeks to elaborate.

Thus the pivotal turn in family ideology that dates from the early
nineteenth century seems to have occurred at a busy intersection of
American history, where structural changes in the household, economics, and class were entangled with the idiosyncratic episodes of
evangelism and reform that gave the Burned-Over District its
name. The task of disentangling these complex relationships required some deviation from the standard practices of family historians. It was necessary to trespass beyond the simplest boundaries
of family history, the walls of a single dwelling unit and the bonds
of kinship. First of all, examination of the basic biological relationships that constitute traditional family status, the differences in age
and sex, were found to extend outside the household into schools,
reform associations, clubs, and women's networks. Second, the
central functions of the modern family – the socialization of children, the care and feeding of the population, the development of
personality, the regulation of sexuality – all take shape in a larger
social universe and, theoretically at least, can be transferred outside
the conjugal unit. These tasks, whereby people, rather than goods,
are created, are encompassed in the term *social reproduction*, which
sets the wider conceptual boundaries of the subject matter of this
book.[17] Finally, age, gender, family – the relations of social reproduction – were seen to operate as causal as well as derivative forces
in the shaping of society, politics, and economics. This book will
focus on one manifestation of this dynamic relationship, the role
played by changes in social reproduction in the making of an American middle class.

This process, which will be recounted according to the uneven
pulsations of Oneida County history, has been constrained into
five roughly chronological chapters. The first, focusing on rural
Whitestown, approximately between 1790 and 1820, will describe
the volatile, inherently temporary phenomenon of the frontier farm
family. The transformation of family, age, and gender that neces-

sarily ensued as the second generation reached maturity will be demonstrated in the next chapter, which analyzes the cycle of religious revivals extending from 1813 to 1838. Chapter 3 will examine similar transformations in the relations of the sexes and age groups as they worked themselves out in the more secular arena of voluntary associations and moral reform groups between 1825 and 1845. These three chapters taken together describe a particularly exuberant period in local family history. First the frontier and then the rapid growth of the regional market during the canal era created the conditions in which a variety of liminal social and family forms could take shape.

Chapters 4 and 5 speak to a more subdued stage in local history, when Oneida County and Utica were banished to the sidelines of American social history around 1850. As Utica moved slowly and rather staidly toward the industrial era, its families seemed to settle down into more predictable patterns. At this point the demographic focus of the study will narrow in on native-born men and women, most of whom had been born within New York State and maintained personal or generational continuity with the era of canals, revivals, and reforms. The majority of native-born males of Utica would find nonmanual or skilled jobs for themselves and their progeny, either in the ranks of the old middling sort, artisans and shopkeepers, or in the occupations of the newer, white-collar middle class. Chapter 4 will explore the family strategies that contributed to the creation and maintenance of such middle-class status. Whereas Chapter 4 is organized according to the timing of the life cycle and gives more attention to males, Chapter 5 focuses on females and examines gender divisions that cut a deep slash through the middle-class household and through society itself.

These five chapters in the history of Oneida County, New York, attempt to speak to more than idiosyncratic local experience. They are elements in a community study, aptly described by Conrad Arensberg as a "device for coming to grips with social and psychological fact in the raw. It is a tool of social science, not a subject matter."[18] This tool is particularly useful for the study of the family, an institution and historical process that can be made visible only through intense, specific analysis at a local level. Narrow focus on a single region and set of communities also exposes the exact and concrete links between the family and other social forms. The study of Oneida County, in other words, can lay bare private experience along with the delicate tentacles that link the family to society and the economy; neither phenomenon is clearly manifest at the national level. Beneath these raw details of local history are social and historical structures that have existed in many other times and locations. First of all, the local history of Oneida County was grafted upon a stratum of social change that occurred at about the same time in many cities of the northeastern United States and was general enough to sustain a common, widely circulated middle-class ideology of the family. Second, there occurred at other times and in other places around the globe analogous transitions, from simple agriculture to widening markets and toward early industrial capitalism: from frontier to town to city. Beneath the detailed account that follows, in sum, lurk larger patterned relations between family, gender, and social change.

It cannot be denied, at the same time, that this route along the back roads and narrow streets of Oneida County, New York, leads the historian to some unique manifestations of family history. But this should not offend those who refuse to equate empirical reality with some colorless mean or average. Recent community studies, most notably Paul Boyer and Stephen Nissenbaum's work on Salem village witchcraft, have proven that a single quite extraordinary town can, like a biography writ large, illuminate, enliven, and give a human dimension to our understanding of general social conditions and developments. In addition, a carefully chosen town is like one of Hegel's world historical individuals: It can initiate as well as represent historical change. It is not too farfetched to grant Oneida County, New York, such a grandiose role. It was there that the Second Great Awakening began its most creative phase; it was there that American abolitionists fought some of their first and most ferocious battles. It was there that the first mother's magazines, propagators of novel ideas about the relations of age and sex, were written and published. Finally in Utica, New York, ordinary artisans embossed on a brass seal one of the earliest icons of American domesticity. Thus Oneida County was one medium through which a variety of changes in the family and society made their way into the broader channels of American history.

1 Family, community, and the frontier generation, 1790–1820

When Hugh White left Middletown, Connecticut, to settle the New York frontier township that would bear his name, he broke with a long family tradition. Five Hugh Whites before him had lived in Connecticut, reaching back in one direct line to the founding of the colony in 1636. Whitestown's founder was himself the father of ten children, one of whom was named Hugh. This strong sense of family must have pressed heavily on the mind of Hugh White, the sixth, when he left for New York in 1784, for he was no lone pioneer or footloose adventurer. Within a year he had settled five sons, two daughters, and three daughters-in-law on a fifteen-hundred-acre tract of wilderness surrounding his homestead. Only two married daughters stayed behind in Connecticut. His eldest son, Daniel, was given the honored place on a large farmstead nearest his father's dwelling house. It would appear that the process of migration had changed the location, but not damaged the integrity nor diminished the strength, of a tenacious New England lineage.[1]

Hugh White's arrangements for his family could well have been made in seventeenth-century New England. They closely resemble the kinship organization that Philip Greven discovered in the first generation of Andover, Massachusetts, and called a modified extended family. The White family could, with some modifications resulting largely from the wealth of land available in America, also fit roughly into the scheme of family organization delineated in the last century by Frederic Le Play. The Whites' pattern of landowning, kinship, and inheritance also resembles the stem family that Le Play, as well as contemporary scholars like Lutz Berkner, identified as a basic structure of peasant society. The stem family, whose identifying feature is the settlement of at least one son on the father's farm, has also been traced through the wills of colonial New England by John Waters. In other words, Hugh White's personal supervision of an intergenerational family economy and his extraordinary efforts to settle his family on contiguous landholdings hark back even further than six generations to an old European agrarian tradition.[2]

The Hugh White family was not a lone and eccentric survivor of

18

this ancient kinship system. Before the third decade of the nineteenth century, the approximate concluding date of this chapter,
the outlines of a distinctive family pattern could be discerned in the
general vicinity of Hugh White's homestead. At first glance it appears to be made in the very image of the first settlers' great-great-
grandparents. Almost 90% of the pioneer families of Whitestown
came from Connecticut or Massachusetts. An equal proportion remained simple farmers. Most of these would bequeath their homesteads to one of their children, and many others would settle additional children on nearby farms. This chapter will document the
manner in which settlers from New England created a corporate
family economy, a domestic system of production that bound family members together, like a single body, in the common enterprise
of subsistence. With it came a set of ideas about the family, an inner
structure of households, and a placement of family in society that
seems, at first glance, like "the little commonwealth" reincarnate.

But the origins of this family system are actually more convoluted
and more interesting than the simple lineal survival of colonial or
peasant customs. They germinated in that American amalgam of
uprooting and settlement, innovation and conservation, past and
future, that is called the frontier. Family life on the New York frontier was, first of all, very different from the contemporaneous experience of New Englanders. Few of Hugh White's former neighbors
back in Connecticut had succeeded in preserving their own family
lines into the sixth and seventh generations. Where in the dense
settlement of Connecticut in the revolutionary era, after all, could a
father find fifteen-hundred unimproved acres on which to settle
five sons? If the towns of Andover and Hingham, Massachusetts,
are at all representative of New England, then families as early as
the fourth generation had taken measures to prevent the emergency
White faced when his children came of age and in need of farmland.[3] Fewer and fewer of them were as profligate as Hugh White,
who fathered ten candidates for succession to the family farm.

Nonetheless, Hugh White of Whitestown was a man of his times,
who commingled his seemingly archaic family practices with many
more current notions. His frontier homestead was not an unques-
tioned ancestral patrimony, nor the grant of a colonial town meeting, but an outright, individual purchase. The business transactions that established the White homestead were learned in a
Connecticut that had long been given over to market agriculture
and land speculation. Reproduced on the New York frontier, that
commercial system gave a distinct lay to the land; it created a patch-

work of detached farms and dwelling units rather than a dense nucleated New England village. Hugh White came to his freely purchased fifteen-hundred acres with other modern ambitions. He was
fully schooled in setting up water-powered sawmills and chose his
homesite accordingly, on the banks of the turbulent Sauquoit
Creek.[4] His farm, like those of his fellow pioneers, was planted on
frontier land but would be fertilized by eighteenth-century agricultural practices. This blending of past and present with the glisten-
ing future possibilities of a new land gave a distinctive frontier
identity to the households of Whitestown.

It must be borne in mind, however, that a frontier is by definition temporary, doomed to extinction probably within the space of
a generation. The frontier family, then, is necessarily an ephemeral,
perhaps a paradoxical, institution. It is the essence of the family to
link together at least two generations, parents and children. By the
time the children of youthful pioneers came of age, however, they
would inherit a settled community rather than the wilderness recalled by their fathers and mothers. The sons and daughters of the
first settlers could not expect to duplicate the family arrangements
of their parents or the domestic conditions under which they themselves had been reared. The frontier family, in other words, by virtue of the intergenerational nature of the family and the inevitable
brevity of the pioneer epoch, is an inherently evanescent historical
phenomenon. The potential for conflict and change gently quaked
beneath the foundation of the New England families who occupied
the New York frontier. When the sons and daughters born of the
first settlers came of age, these contradictions would rise to the surface of family and social life.

I will return to the harbingers of change at the end of this chapter
and examine them more thoroughly in the next. For the time being,
the families of the New England migrants themselves are the subject of this chapter. Unfortunately, because of the paucity of vital
statistics, they cannot be neatly arranged into actual generations
that exactly reconstitute the biological succession of parents and
children. The frontier generation is defined here in vaguer historical terms as, roughly, those men and women who put down
roots and reared families before the exhaustion of open farmland
in 1820.

To explore the family history of the American frontier between
1790 and 1820 is to encounter multiple layers of social experience,
which, in their complexity, surpass the theories of Frederick Jackson Turner. There was, first of all, the openness and roughhewn

freedom of the wilderness. This stage of the frontier was quickly superseded, as any aficionado of American Westerns knows full well, by the efforts of pioneer settlers to build a functioning, stable community on the new land. During this second stage the traditions acquired behind the frontier were sifted and winnowed by the exigencies of occupying the new territory. Finally, when these frontier developments are refracted through the full family cycle, they take on an especially ephemeral, illusive, and dialectical character. In the very process of reproducing themselves the pioneers filled up the wide-open spaces and built a community of households, thereby destroying the conditions that had given their families their evanescent frontier identity.

The frontier household economy

The earliest stage of social life on the frontier was essentially a prefamilial epoch. The demographic profile of Whitestown even in 1790 was not conducive to a stable, pervasive family order. In Oneida County at that date there were more than 150 men for every 100 women (Table A.1). The relative paucity of females and the consequent retardation of family formation were partially responsible for whatever semblance of the "wild West" that existed on the New York frontier. This stage of the frontier was about to end when Hugh White arrived in 1784 to wrest the land from the Iroquois and a few squatters, fur traders, and seasoned Indian fighters. Whitestown folklore offers only slight anecdotal homage to this era. The wife of John Post, proprietor of the first trading post at Old Fort Schuyler, exemplified the local mythology. She was renowned for the guile with which she tamed the violent passions of a famed Indian chief inflamed by her husband's "fire water."[5] A far more civilized world had grown up around Old Fort Schuyler by the time Post's store and livelihood were destroyed by fire in 1807. Yet remnants of frontier openness and family laxity continued beyond this time and were disclosed in the local press by recurring advertisements for runaway servants, wives, and children. Almost every issue of the *Whitestown Gazette* contained a notice such as this dated January 8, 1803: "Eloped from my bed and board my wife Peggy without any just reason. All persons are forbid harboring or trusting her on my account, on penalty of the law." Countless notices to this effect suggested that many a rugged individualist, including some of the female gender, found release from the bonds of family and social propriety on the New York frontier.

The primitive economy and fluid social circumstances also made it relatively easy to transgress against the economic authority of the male household head. At least some women briefly evaded their husbands' surveillance as they "ran around town incurring debts." One early settler in the Oneida County township of Western was the victim of a total domestic coup in 1822 when he advised the readers of the Utica paper: "This is to forbid all persons harboring or trusting any of my family on my account as I will pay no debts of their contracting after this date." Frontier conditions also allowed husbands to escape from family responsibilities. One Daniel Owner acquired an informal frontier divorce on what appeared to be the flimsiest of grounds: He notified the readers of the *Columbian Gazette* that his wife, Mary, "has conducted herself in an unbecoming manner which renders it unfit that I should live with her any more." Other frontier divorces, presumably more reciprocal, were phrased like this: "Whereas some unhappy differences have lately arisen between me Joseph Eaton and Rebeckah my wife we have mutually agreed to live separate."[6] However phrased, these cases of divorce and elopement from the household testify to abundant frontier opportunities to break free of family constraints.

The dawn of the nineteenth century was to bring a more domesticated social life to Whitestown. After more than doubling in 1790s, local population growth diminished markedly and soon stabilized at around five thousand persons (Table A.2). The demographic profile in 1810 reflected the hearty growth of the first settlers' families. The sex ratio had evened off by 1800, when there were only 108 men for every 100 women (Table A.1). Concomitantly, the frontier was overrun with boys and girls of native birth, with children under ten years of age accounting for 37.3% of Whitestown's population. Men and women and children lived together in households that sheltered six persons on the average (Tables A.3 and A.4). Society had been created largely from the natural growth of the region's first families, nearly 90% of which were headed by migrants from New England. By 1820, when hardly an unimproved acre could be found within the boundaries of Whitestown, the wilderness had been transformed into one dense fabric of households.

Whitestown's first settlers employed the language of Puritan social theory to articulate their ideal of social organization. Local publications conceptualized the social system as a trilogy of overlapping and parallel structures – "our families, societies, and churches." The family was not only on a par with the church but also analogous in organization and function. Whitestown's first religious congregations looked to households as their chief allies in creating a Christian community. Injunctions to practice "family worship" were found in the sermons and didactic writings of Baptists, Presbyterians, and Methodists alike. In the session records and church trials of each sect an array of accusations of "neglect of family prayer" testify to the seriousness of the family's religious function. When the First Presbyterian Society was founded in 1794, its members pledged "to maintain family and secret prayer"; as late as March 4, 1828, no fewer than three parishioners were brought under church discipline for "neglect of sabbath and family worship." The meetinghouse and the private hearth were judged equally essential to the practice of religion, and on the frontier they were often interchangeable. The first meeting of the Presbyterians took place in the home of Hugh White; the Baptist congregation met in the dwelling house of his neighbor Amos Wetmore. Nor were political institutions remote from the religious sphere: The town charters of both Utica and Whitestown enforced the regulation of the sabbath.

These three institutions – family, state, and church – also formed the interlocking components of Whitestown's system of caring for the poor. The church's role in providing for the physical welfare of the disadvantaged was articulated in the articles of church government of the First Baptist Society of Deerfield (just north of Utica). In 1800 these rural Baptists pledged "that we will take care of the poor of our community as necessary for subsistence and not cast them upon the mercy of the public; yet not excluding application to the public fund for their relief in certain cases of extreme indigence." The Whitestown Baptist Church enacted the customary procedure when they learned that their "Sister Lawrence" was in needy circumstances. The deacons visited this widow and "inquired as may be necessary concerning her temporal circumstances and bid her such advice relative to the support of her family as may be deemed proper."[7] The secular authorities played a parallel and intersecting role with families and churches. The case of Mrs. Startman of Utica's Presbyterian Church is particularly interesting on this score. "Mr. White reported that the town poor master would not extend relief to Mrs. Startman and family without the liberty of binding out her children." The church granted Mrs. Startman a small amount of supplies to allow her to support herself and keep her family intact.[8]

The actions of both the town and the church, in binding out children and the granting of relief, were supplementary to a basically household method of providing for the dependent population of Whitestown. Neither required an independent agency or institution, be it an orphanage or a welfare bureau, to intercede in the relations of family, church, and town. Both relied on the household, either that of a subsidized widow or the one to which a dependent child might be bound out, as the basic location of this social service. The aged as well as widows and orphans could be accommodated within this system. The Oneida County court ruling in the case of Archibald Murray illustrated this procedure: Murray's son David was commanded to support his aging father in order to avoid expense for the town.[9]

This same combination of New England traditions and frontier exigencies determined that a whole array of social tasks would be delegated to the family. A system of free schools supported by property taxes was not established in New York State until 1840. No public provision whatsoever was made for education in Whitestown until 1812. The pioneer generation relied on a few private schools as the only supplements to the domestic education of children, servants, and apprentices. The scarcity of school buildings, indeed of any public buildings, made the dwelling unit the almost monopolistic center of community life. The private home was the center of government until 1807 when a federal-style Town Hall was constructed on Main Street in Whitesborough, the village center of early Whitestown. Until then, when citizens were called, New England style, to a public meeting ("The freeholders of Whitestown are hereby notified that the Annual Town Meeting will beholden . . ."), they would assemble as they did in 1789, "at the house of Captain Daniel C. White" or "in Hugh White's barn." Much of what passed for "public" entertainment and amusement in early Whitestown also transpired within the households of individual residents. A few grocery stores, public houses, and hotels were the chief centers of socializing outside the family circle. Even these institutions had a markedly domestic flavor. One of Utica's first historians recalled how visitors to Bagg's Hotel sat down together at a common table presided over by the proprietor and his wife.

In sum, everyday socializing, like worship, welfare, and most every aspect of social reproduction, was conducted largely within the household unit. The central integral place of the household in a tripartite social order composed of church, state, and family seemed to replicate the social system idealized by Puritan social theorists and honored in practice in seventeenth-century New England. Local frontier conditions undoubtedly reinforced this tradition. The primitive economy and the scarcity of both money and labor would not allow for a more refined and specialized institutional or political structure. Certainly the tax collector's revenue for Whitestown in 1800, amounting to the grand sum of $40, was not about to support a more complex system of public services. At the same time, the New York frontier may actually have tilted the balance of social power in the direction of individual households, which in the first generation of settlement waxed in the commodious circumstances of relatively large homesteads set at some distance from neighbors, churches, and meetinghouses.

Above all else, the households of Whitestown gathered strength and coherence from their function within the frontier economy. Between 1790 and 1820 the household was the principal, almost solitary place of production within the township. Advertisements placed in the *Whitestown Gazette* before 1800 describe a paltry stock of commercial goods, largely imported spices, liquors, and luxury goods that could not be produced locally. In exchange for these goods the area farmers were invited to barter a wide variety of objects: bark, rags, lye, butter, potash, to name but a few. The local miller and first settler, Ezra Wetmore, accepted payment in labor as well as kind – a few hours' sawing, for example, or a half day of carting. The converse of this limited exchange system was near self-sufficiency within individual farm households. The agricultural fairs of Oneida County honored everything from butter to bonnets "produced in the family of the owner." In 1810 Oneida County was one of New York State's largest producers of domestic cottons and linens. Whitestown families produced more than twelve thousand yards of cloth, according to the census of 1820, or more than forty yards of flannel, cotton, or linen per household.[10]

Because the farmer's abode was a place of production, it housed laborers as well as relatives. The two were often but not always one and the same. Local newspapers were filled with notices of runaway apprentices and servants well into the 1830s. These indentured farm workers were of both sexes and as young as eight years of age. More than 15% of the households visited by the Reverend John Frost contained unrelated workers, whose family status was designated by such terms as *servants, apprentices,* or *bound boys* (Table A.5). A few were slaves, identified by servile equivalent "black boy" or "black girl." Several other households sheltered persons with anomalous titles like "a girl who lives with them," "a girl taken in to bring up." These may have been former wards of the town or orphaned members of the church. In either case they would be expected to work for their board. Only a tiny minority, twenty individuals residing in four households, worked outside their dwellings, apparently in the cotton factory. Thus the household workshop often acquired a complex labor force. Newton Mann, for example, lived and worked with his wife, Abigail, and their three children as well as "John Denny, a bound boy," and "Sarah West, a black girl." Mann's neighbor Daniel Ashby and his wife and four children were joined by three apprentices and two "young ladies brought up by Mr. Ashby."[11]

Sons and daughters were not exempted from the laborious duties of running the family economy. In fact, they were taught even as infants to conceive of themselves as workers as well as children. A local publication called *Rhymes for the Nursery* proffered daughters the negative model of "Idle Mary":

> The little girl who will not sew,
> Should neither be allow'd to play.

The same early example of children's literature directed little boys to this identity:

> I'm a little husbandman
> Work and labor hard I can.[12]

Parents conceived of their children as their own flesh, blood, and labor supply. One local farmer who promised $5 for the "arrest and delivery" of his runaway son did not describe the escape as a case of running away from home but simply as: "Left my employment, my son Patrick."[13] Indeed, as one local wag saw it, a large brood of children was one of the foremost "signs of a prosperous farmer." "When a farmer is seen marrying young, it shows Providence helps those who help themselves and that in future he will have 'helps' of more kinds than one."[14] The reliability of this familial source of labor is indicated in the diary of a fourteen-year-old girl named Hannah Gilbert. Her journal for 1816 was little more than a work record that noted her regular employment at preserving, sewing, child care, and housecleaning, interspersed with the most erratic school attendance in the winter months. A summer's day for Hannah and her sister might go like this: "We baked, ironed, churned and twisted. In the afternoon took tea at Grandmama's. In the evening, Susan, Eliza Eels and I had fun."[15]

The delegation of these relatively simple chores to daughters no doubt freed Mrs. Gilbert and other women like her to perform the more skilled and supervisory roles of the farmer's wife. Certainly the farmer expected as much, even in the supposedly more romantic stages of courtship. On the occasion of the 1818 agricultural fair, one local swain was moved to write some doggerel on the productive abilities of women. As a correspondent to the *Utica Patriot and Patrol*, he rose to the heights of punning on this theme:

> Ye maidens young who learn to spin and reel
> Know that the Fair by farmers shall be prized
> And that the Man is cold who does not feel
> A worsted suit is not to be despised.

Indeed, men's expectations, women's behavior, and the whole supporting culture concurred in regarding the frontier wife as preeminently a worker in a home economy.[16] This consensus was illustrated in the testimony of a Sarah Blackmore, who was accused of intemperance before a local church. She admitted that "for want of food" she drank too much but defended herself by saying that she was "never so much under the influence of liquor as to be incapacitated for business."[17]

The centrality of productive economic roles within the relations of maid and suitor, husband and wife, parent and child, found more prosaic representation in the wills of Whitestown farmers. For example, John Bellinger contrived in his last testament to perpetuate a union of workers as well as a family. His will stated that three daughters could reside with their brother in the ancestral homestead until each reached the age of eighteen. Thereafter, however, Bellinger stipulated that shelter within the parental household would be contingent upon each child's continuing efforts to support and maintain the common economy. The typical organization of this corporate household economy is exemplified by the will of Frederick Bowman, probated in 1824. Bowman's three daughters were each bequeathed the sum of $100 and a featherbed. The farm was conveyed to his son Adam on the condition that he support his widowed mother. By means of these bequests Bowman preserved the integrity of the family corporation, which passed on to his son, provided for the support of his widow, and repaid the labor of his unmarried daughters out of his movable and more readily expendable property. Bowman's neighbors commonly employed similar strategies to preserve the organic nature of their family enterprises.[18]

Most Whitestown patriarchs assumed, first of all, that a wife's economic identity was fully incorporated into the family business. Accordingly, 55% of the wills probated in Whitestown before 1825 made reference to the rights of dower (Table B.1). The typical farmer followed the procedure customary to seventeenth-century colonists as they returned one-third of their estates to their wives.

That the reference to dower was more than a legal anachronism is witnessed by the will of Septa Barnard, probated in the 1830s. Mr. Barnard granted his wife "all the cloth which she has made since her said marriage to me." Many wives were not granted title to the products of their own labor or their most intimate furnishings and personal apparel until after their husbands' deaths. Even in widowhood, few wives earned full, independent title to family property. One in five bequests to wives contained the conditioning clause "for her natural life" (Table B.1). Another 30% employed the phrase "in her widowhood" to prevent wives from directing the transfer of any remaining family property to the second generation. Typically then, the widow remained tied to the family economy whose leadership had already passed on to one of her children.[19]

Some of Whitestown's first settlers sought to bind not only their wives but also the entire second generation to this corporate property. Consider the elaborate plans sketched out in the will of Orre Hovey. Hovey's will included a map of his "messuage and tenements" overlaid with an intricate patchwork of land allotments for his two sons and three daughters. As if these interwoven legacies did not integrate his children's property quite tightly enough, Hovey added a final provision: That all the tools and farm utensils must be held in common by his offspring. Hovey's extraordinary precautions differed from the wills of his neighbors in detail but not intent. Most Whitestown farmers made some provision for each of their children, usually allocating land to sons and cash or household goods to daughters. Although these complicated legacies cannot be converted into precise and easily comparable monetary terms, they nonetheless seem to suggest a pattern of inequality based on age, sex, accident, and idiosyncracy. Indeed, only 10% of the early wills employed an outright standard of equality in making bequests to children (Table B.2).[20] The convoluted pattern of the typical will seems designed to achieve two at times contradictory parental goals: to ensure that the ancestral homestead would pass on relatively intact to a second generation and at the same time to encourage all offspring to branch off into their own home economies.

The first of these objectives was met by granting the father's farm to one male heir. In a few cases the favored child was selected on the basis of age. As late as 1857, Whitestown's Jonathan Halsey singled out his "eldest son," John, as the owner of "the farm on which I now live, called the homestead." In a will probated more than forty years earlier, a farmer named Eli Butler chose the youngest of his sons to carry on the parental farm economy. Most wills, however, remained mute on the subject of age and failed to define either primo- or ultimo-geniture as the preferred practice. These wills were often simple reiterations of previous land grants, affirming a son's right to "the farm on which he now lives." By the time of his death in 1812, Eli Butler had already situated his three oldest sons on their own farms, leaving only his youngest son to fall heir to his father's farm. To prosperous farmers like Butler, at least, the dual objectives of maintaining the original family farm and providing for all sons could be fulfilled without overt discrimination on the basis of age.[21]

There is ample evidence that Whitestown's settlers had no such compunctions about sexual discrimination among their heirs. About one-third of the bequests to women were clearly of lesser value than their brothers' legacies. Sometimes the pattern of discrimination was exact and incisive. Amos Miller, for example, whose will was probated in 1806, devised an intricate strategy for inequality: He divided his estate into thirteen equal parts and then distributed two-thirteenths to each of his five sons, leaving one-thirteenth to each of his three daughters. In the relative absence of cash legacies, few wills could outline such an exact pattern of sexual inequality. A daughter's legacy most often took the form of a small amount of cash, household goods, or livestock, whose value was clearly less than the acreage accruing to her brothers. This difference in kind, the allocation of land to men and movable property to women, was as significant as the variation in the dollar value of the bequests to sons and to daughters. It confirmed the patrilocal nature of the corporate family economy: Whitestown's fathers provided their sons with the wherewithal for establishing a conjugal economy, often on or near the parental farm, whereas the daughters were expected to locate on the more remote farmlands of their husbands.[22]

Title to the family farm, on the other hand, was not merely the result of paternal largess. It was almost always accompanied by the proviso that the chosen heir care for a widowed mother or younger brothers and sisters. In other words, the successor to the parental homestead was held responsible for supervising the corporate economy during the closing stages of the family life cycle. This responsibility entailed first and foremost the maintenance and support of the widowed mother. Sons were enjoined to provide their aging and dependent mothers with firewood, orchards, gardens, barns, and often a space in their dwelling house. The will of

Thomas Thornton made the status of his widow painfully clear: It granted her the "use and improvement of the Northwest room. Also the north bedroom and the pantry or closet adjoining the said room and privileges of using the oven in the kitchen for baking. Also, one half of the kitchen cellar. Also the use of the front yard and one fourth part of the piece of land now occupied for a garden." Another widow was bequeathed half a barn, "full use of the fourth front room of the dwelling house, with a right to use the kitchen." These women would live out their lives in the carefully partitioned spaces of a household economy controlled by their children.[23]

These wills also indicate that inheritance of the family farm often created an extended household, when widowed mothers were promised a place of residence in homes bequeathed to their married children. Other wills suggest that elderly fathers opened their homes to a third generation even before their deaths. This was the purport of one clause in the will of Thomas Wharron, who bequeathed to his wife "all the household furniture now in the north room now occupied by us." Many other wills rewarded married sons and daughters for having boarded their aging parents. The consignment of an elderly couple to the back rooms of a farmhouse that had passed into a son's ownership is reminiscent of the practice of stem households in peasant Europe. This seemingly archaic domestic pattern had assumed significant proportions in Whitestown during the first quarter of the nineteenth century. When the Reverend John Frost of the First Presbyterian Society made a census of his parishioners between 1813 and 1816, he found an elderly couple or single grandparent residing in 1 in every 15 households. This is a remarkably high figure, given the fact that only 14% of Whitestown's residents were more than forty-five years of age (Tables A.3 and A.5). The U.S. census taken in 1810 gave further substance to the case for extended ties in this agricultural setting. Based on the clustering of surnames on the census list, nearly 12% of the residents of Oneida County lived adjacent to their kinfolk. So high an incidence of stem family structure, such close proximity to kin, and the large size of Whitestown's households were all reminiscent of seventeenth-century New England.[24]

The family structure of Whitestown, New York, should not be seen, however, simply as testimony to the tenacity of either peasant or Puritan culture. Such customs as the stem family, the right of dower, and deed by will were rooted in the frontier agrarian economy. The availability of relatively plentiful land at the turn of the century allowed fathers to provide nearby farms for their sons. At the same time, the primitive nature of the market discouraged the conversion of family property into cash or fluid assets that would allow the family members to collect their separate inheritances and disperse. The same conditions made it practical to support aging parents in the households of one of their several sons. The extended structure of these Whitestown houses is one muted consequence, a brief generational extension, of the corporate family economy. It inhered in the basic material asset of Whitestown families, the common productive property of the land. It would endure as long as that property remained the central, abundant, indivisible, and largely self-sufficient base of local production.

The corporate family economy wove together all ages and sexes in the incessant and inescapable interdependency of making a living on the new land. Rooted in the common means of survival in a new settlement, those organic relationships were ingrained in the habits and expectations of local farmers and intertwined themselves with a full generational cycle. Occasionally these norms were articulated by the local printers. They were expressed, for example, in a poem entitled "My Mother," which bore an 1815 Utica imprint. It began with the celebration of maternal nurture:

> Who fed me from her gentle breast?
> And hushed me in her arms best?
> And on my cheek sweet kisses prest?
> My mother.

This image of infant dependency is not extraordinary (although Victorian readers a few decades hence might find its sensuality a bit too explicit). What clearly identifies this children's literature as an expression of the family economy are the following lines:

> When thou are feeble, old, and grey
> My healthy arms shall be thy stay
> And I will soothe thy pains away
> My mother.[25]

The young reader of this and other poems like it was advised of the reciprocal responsibilities of the family, including those obligations that would not fall due until much later in his or her life cycle, when parents had grown "feeble, old, and grey." This sense of interdependency within family units and over generational time, whether recited by a child or written into an old man's will, is the hallmark of a corporate family economy.

Patriarchy within and between households

The organic nature of this way of making a living should not be construed, however, as some bucolic idyll in family history. For the family economy to function efficiently , it had to employ discipline and regulation rather than rely on automatic harmony and love. In fact, most early writing on domestic subjects employed a much sterner rhetoric: It spoke of government, authority, and submission, rather than of love. The writings of Isaac Watts, which went through almost annual editions in early Oneida County, are typical of this genre of family literature. One verse from Watts's *Divine Songs Attempted in Easy Language for the Use of Children* seems to belie the subtitle of the volume:

> Have you not heard what dreadful plagues
> Are threaten'd by the Lord,
> To him that breaks his father's Law,
> Or mocks his mother's word?[26]

Not only children but servants and wives as well were held to this standard of obedience, and often in the same intimidating tones. Patriarchal family government died very slowly on the New York frontier, at least among the distant progeny of the English dissenting sects. A Methodist periodical presented a full-scale blueprint for patriarchy in 1826. The Reverend Richard Treffey began his treatise on the assumption that "it will of course be understood that we refer, in our observations upon these subjects especially to a father, master, or head of a family; one who is placed by providence in a state of authority over his domestics." Treffey went on to assert that "all government originated in patriarchal authority and families contain the rudiments of empire."[27]

This imperial rhetoric was something more than a remote analogy drawn between the family and the state. If anything, the etymology proceeded from the family to politics and not vice versa. After all, every reader of *The New England Primer*, first issued in Utica in 1810, knew the imperative of the fifth commandment: "I will fear God. I will honor my father and mother. I will obey my superiors." The relations of subordination within the family were the source and standard for a social hierarchy that extended to "superiors" throughout the community. Obedience to the household head was deemed essential to the good order of society, for only one decisive and unchallenged person could link the family to church and town. Appeals for town meetings, communal work, ecclesiastical elections, all were issued to adult male heads of households. The other members of the population – wives, children, servants, dependent relatives – were, to use Treffey's term, *domestics* whose social identity was confined within the household.

The subordination of "domestics" was particularly clear and decisive in matters of economics. The male head was put in charge of economic relations, including exchange outside the home. Debts were recorded in the account books of local merchants under the name of the husband and father – even expenditures for bonnets and ribbons. The Oneida County agricultural fair distributed awards on the same basis; even prizes for needlework went to men on the grounds that a domestic manufacture was any item "produced in the household of the owner." The patriarchal economic order could convert even women and children into a species of property. Such was the import of the idiom for runaway wives and servants: They were "stolen" from the household head. In politics, economics, and the law, the male household head remained the only enfranchised individual within the family. The logic and justice of this arrangement would remain acceptable to the people of Whitestown throughout the frontier era.[28]

Within the household itself, a more complicated, but no more democratic, set of social relationships held sway. The *Young Christian's Guide*, published in Utica in 1819, enjoined the reader to "be always submissive and dutiful to my parents, treating them uniformly, with reverence and affection." A servant was advised by his master to "be always reconciled with my position; obedient to those I serve; endeavoring to promote their interest; and to be faithful in all that is committed to my trust." Only among brothers and sisters were the strictures of authority and obedience suspended. Here the obligation was to "treat with marks of affection, those to whom I am so nearly related." But even these relations were not without their vitriol, at least in the dour perception of the Old Testament and Isaac Watts. His words might resonate through the ranks of the stem family:

> The devil tempts one mother's son
> To rage against another;
> So wicked Cain was hurried on
> Till he had kill'd his brother.

Aware of the potential for conflict in the generational life of a little economy, the early writers and publicists of the New York frontier placed their trust in a system of authority and obedience as the most reliable basis for a well-ordered family.[29]

Authority and obedience also characterized the relations of husband and wife. An obituary dated 1811 offered as the highest accolade to a good wife the testimony that she was "always obedient." Ten years later, the Methodist woman was instructed to "acknowledge the superiority of her husband in all the distinctions which the Bible requires." Included among these distinctions was Paul's sentencing of women to silence.[30] An early pamphlet entitled "A Dialogue Between a Missionary and a Man and His Wife upon the Duty of Prayer" demonstrates the depths of Whitestown's traditional attitudes toward women. The frontier missionary was unsuccessful in convincing either of his hearers, the fictional "Mr. and Mrs. P.," that women had the most minimal rights of self-expression. Mrs. P. never led the family in prayer, not even during the absence of the household head, for she and her husband agreed that "it does not belong to a woman to pray before her family." To do so would be to "usurp authority" over the patriarch.[31] More direct evidence of patriarchal authority and wifely submission is found in John Frost's report on the visit he paid the families of Whitestown between 1813 and 1816. Three women confessed to Frost that their husbands had probibited them from attending church meetings and baptizing their children. As Hannah Story recounted it, her husband Enoch threatened to desert her if she should leave her children to attend church. Certainly this kind of intimidation was not characteristic of all conjugal relations. The Young Christian's Guide, for example, spoke of the relations of husbands and wives as one of "peculiar tenderness and affection" and as an "endearing bond."[32] Still, the fact remains that Whitestown's first generation continued to construe even this most intimate of family relations in the hierarchical fashion of their Puritan forefathers. In their writings about marital relations they chose to articulate the standard of authority and submission and underplay the reciprocal emotional bonds between family members.

When not indifferent or oblivious, Whitestown writers were suspicious of the emotional dimensions of family relationships. Ministers cited scripture to condemn domestic affections that bordered on idolatry: "He that loveth father or mother more than me, is not worthy of me: and he that loveth son or daughter more than me is not worthy of me." The second clause of this quotation from Matthew identified an issue particularly worrisome to early Whitestown writers and publishers. Noah Webster, in a Utica imprint of 1806, frowned on those who "encouraged their children in a thousand familiarities, which render them ridiculous and by diminishing the respect which is due to their age and station destroy all their authority." At the same time that Webster eschewed "too rigid a maxim of age" and would ameliorate "the rigor of the parental discipline," he feared that excessive parental affection would undermine the basis of family and social order. Those first settlers who purchased a family library in the bookstores of Utica carried this ideal of government rather than of love into their rural homesteads. As Webster put it, the ideal father "should maintain his authority; but it should be like the mild dominion of a limited monarch, and not the iron rule of an austere tyrant."[33]

It is unlikely that most Whitestown farmers ruled their families in conscious conformity to the standard of benevolent monarchy. Yet this system of domestic authority was structurally consistent with the corporate family economy. The multiple functions and diverse population that inhabited the crowded quarters of the frontier farmhouse had to be ordered in a deliberate and decisive manner. To order such households required what Webster called "regulations of behavior" or what a local Presbyterian editor referred to as "The Rules of this Family." Both emphasized the formal rights and duties, the code of politeness, and the quiet disposition necessary to keep a "miniature society" in good running order. All household members had best be as prudent and watchful as Isaac Watts's model youth:

> I would be subject ev're hour
> To parent and to ruler too
> Pay honor and obedience due
> In ev're word would truth preserve
> Nor let one act from justice swerve.[34]

The rewards for such behavior would come only over the long haul of the life cycle as sons and daughters finally rose to the status of head or mistress of their own households. Even then, a formal regimen was often required to ensure domestic harmony. Why else would the wills of Whitestown stipulate an heir's right-of-way through his brothers' orchard or formally grant a widowed mother freedom to use one-half of her son's barn?

The best direct evidence of the actual day-to-day operations of this family system comes from the detailed testimony of church trials. In most cases, these documents report infractions against the model of good family government. The alacrity with which Whitestown's Baptists, Methodists, and Presbyterians brought these offenders to trial, however, indicates the seriousness and pervasiveness of the New England way of family governance. Perhaps the commonest offense against family propriety was sexual in nature, and every church brought its parishioners, and not infrequently its elders, deacons, and even ministers, into the court on the charge of adultery. But ecclesiastical meddling in family affairs did not stop there. Cases of domestic violence, for example, were brought before the clerical tribunals of all denominations. The Oneida Conference of the Methodist Church was still hearing these cases in 1844 when one H. H. Winter was called to account for "laying violent hands upon his wife."[35] Relatively minor lapses in domestic propriety could warrant a rebuke or excommunication. The Whitestown Presbyterians charged Seth Wilson, for example, with "profane and obscene language before his family." In 1800 Caroline Moseley was accused of "unchristian and offensive treatment of her servant." The Whitestown congregation demanded that Mrs. Moseley make a public confession, which read as follows: "The chastisement I inflicted to those whom providence committed to my care and protection I am now dispersed to acknowledge was excessive and disproportionate to their guilt." Such were the fine distinctions by which the church modulated the relations of the household; they recognized a familial but authoritative relationship between the members of the household (composed of both "care" and "chastisement") that applied even to non-kin (to servants as much as children). The church fathers did not hesitate to intervene in those domestic relations to see that the proper balance of authority and humanity was exercised. Mrs. Caroline Moseley put this system to its severest test. She appeared in the church records at least three more times, charged with beating a black servant, slandering a neighbor, and writing a poison-pen letter to a fellow church member.[36]

The church fathers of Whitestown found their way into the most private crevices of local life. The Methodists seemed to take particular interest in the sleeping arrangements of sexual offenders. One cross-examination inquired whether two transgressors "slept in the sitting room or bedroom or whether others were on the same floor." They discovered in a second case that a man seduced his servant girl as his wife slept approximately eight feet away. In a third trial it was revealed that one of the witnesses occupied the same bed as the adulterers.[37] All this testimony comes from the long-settled rural areas of Oneida County where it seems that ordinary farmers went about their work and their play, fair and foul, in the most congested dwelling houses. This crowded and relatively undifferentiated apportionment of domestic space, as revealed by church trials and suggested by a few remaining examples of frontier architecture, had far-reaching implications for family life.

First of all, it undoubtedly conditioned the quality of sexual experience. The closed and crowded quarters described in the Methodist trials were not likely locations for lavish sexual playfulness. The very language as well as the factual reporting of the church trials portrays a different quality of sexuality. One encounter proceeded this way: The male "put his hands around her in a very unbecoming manner," and she responded with the threat, "I'll murder you if you don't let me alone." Another man unceremoniously "thrust his hand into the bed and took hold of her hand." In the session records of the local Presbyterians, sexuality was presented in a similarly stilted and limited vocabulary: "criminal intercourse," "had a connection," or "were bad together." The Methodist suspicion of sexuality extended to the prohibition of "unchaste conversation," and the Presbyterians condemned "licentious talking."[38] The crude housing, crowded sleeping arrangements, the watchful eyes of household members and church fathers certainly did not encourage spontaneous and imaginative sexual explorations. Neither was the utter absence of privacy likely to foster an intense emotional interchange between sexual partners.

These same material and social conditions could also set the stage for household conflict. The presence of servants was frequently the cause of embattled social relationships. Servants appeared in church trials both as victims of the master's violent temper and sexual predation and as accusing witnesses to the transgressions of the household head. Boarders were another frequent source of contention. The trial of Silas Bartlett, for example, was predicated on the difficulties of housing relative strangers under the same roof. One witness was called into court because he had bragged of knowing enough about one of the offending parties, his fellow boarder, to "shut the church doors against her." Yet a third boarder in the Bartlett household admitted to bitterness toward the household head, stemming from "difficulties between our wives." Before Bartlett's trial was over at least a half dozen angry plaintiffs came forth from the ranks of the accused's boarders. This potential for household conflict was once again brought to its highest form by Whitestown's incorrigible social deviant, Caroline Moseley. In 1809 Mrs. Moseley was accused of slandering Mary Flagg and her brother, former residents in her household. Mrs. Moseley had apparently kept a watchful and suspicious eye upon the Flaggs and when she observed Mary sitting in her brother's lap, she took their affectionate gestures as evidence of "carnal relations." The church tribunal was not so easily convinced that the Flaggs had committed incest, and once again Caroline Moseley confessed her mistake and pledged to be "more cautious in mentioning evil reports."[39] The fact remains that the complex and fluctuating population of the first-generation households was an ideal school for such slander.

The intergenerational extension of these households and the precarious balance of the stem family were a second source of family conflict. The transfer of family property to the second generation was the cause of one of the most complicated church trials in the history of the Whitestown's Presbyterian Society. In 1818 Mr. David Williams of the village of Sangerfield was visited by the church elders who inquired "whether he was willing to make the debt of his son Levi secure, and thus satisfy us that he did not intend to defraud him." This accusation of paternal graft involved the sum of somewhere between $120 and $220, the value of a note that David Williams had given his son in payment for services he had rendered some eight years before. In the intervening years, David Williams had made provisions for his old age, which complicated the relations between father and sons. As his other son, Othniel, bore witness, the elderly Williams gave him "a valuable consideration by engaging to support his parents during their life by notes now in possession of his father." As the family estate passed into the control of his brother, Othniel, Levi feared that his credit would not be recognized and paid. The church managed to patch up this family quarrel in the manner of the frontier economy. Othniel promised to make payments on his father's debt "from time to time" and free the aging patriarch from the charge of "a present intention to defraud his son."[40] Fraternal conflicts like this were built into the family economy and exacerbated by the primitive methods of exchange, those dubious "notes."

An extensive litigation in Utica's Presbyterian Church exposed the tensions within the stem household itself. This trial embroiled one of the founding artisans of Utica, Bildad Merrill, whose corporate family history had entered into a second generation by the date of the church trial. On November 10, 1834, a complaint was issued against Bildad's wife, Nancy, regarding the treatment of her daughter-in-law Julia.[41] A year earlier, Julia and her husband, Bildad, Jr., had moved into the household of the senior Merrills. Bildad Merrill Senior was aging rapidly and within a few months acknowledged that he was no longer capable of "getting provisions for the household." Accordingly, he transfered responsibility to his son and agreed to "pay the usual price for board and rent of the house." Thus, Bildad Merrill, reluctantly but smoothly, surrendered his role as head of the household and master printer to his son and name-sake.

Bildad's wife, Nancy, however, did not make her peace with this arrangement quite so easily. Always a cantankerous character to say the least (fifteen years earlier she allegedly had branded her husband with andirons), she now faced the frustration and ignominy of sharing her lifelong work space with her son's wife. The younger Mrs. Merrill testified: "I told the hired help that I was mistress and should direct the work. The morning after [the mother-in-law] laid violent hands on me. She came to the table in a passion and would not allow me to take tea . . . she had emptied the contents on the table when she found there was no water below with which to make tea for herself. She would not take tea from the same pot with myself." In the face of this prosaic but grating domestic contention, the church fathers determined to excommunicate Mrs. Nancy Merrill with the hope that she would reform and win readmission to the church.

In the Merrill household domestic tension reached its peak in that awkward period of the family cycle when two generations of adults shared a precarious balance of power. Many other homes undoubtedly experienced quarrels like these, as typically more than six persons, of various statuses, shared the crowded work spaces of the frontier household. The Merrill trial, for example, involved not only the two principal couples but an additional son, two more daughters-in-law, two former boarders, and a neighbor who was "in the habit of visiting." The Merrill case brought to a crescendo of conflict problems that inhered in the families of the first generation: their large size, their hospitality to a second generation, and their openness to boarders, kinsmen, servants, prying neighbors, and pious church members.

The Merrill case also illustrates the repeated intrusion of the frontier church into the private lives of families. The frequency, routineness, and casualness of these intrusions call into question whether these families were *private* institutions at all in the current meaning of the term. As a matter of fact, the frontier churches explicitly eschewed domestic privacy. Drawing on the Puritan practice of the church covenants, Baptists and Presbyterians took formal vows to violate the boundaries of the individual family. The Baptists pledged to "extend a faithful watch over all its members, also in every private relation," and to "use our influence to promote true piety and family religion."[42] John Frost, the guiding influence of the Whitesboro Presbyterian Church, exhorted his flock to "converse with our brothers [about] their private sins in a direct and public manner." Frost's reading of the Christian covenant also permitted him free access to the homes of the entire township. Between 1813 and 1816 he inquired into the private lives and personal beliefs of "all the families within the boundaries of the United Society of Whitestown," regardless of their church affiliations. As George Bethune of the Dutch Reformed Church of Utica put it more than a decade later: "It is [the minister's] office to follow you to your homes and firesides and to recommend as a friend . . . Remember the duties of the pastor are never intermitted. Chide me not therefore, if in honest zeal I press upon you in private, the same truths I recommend in public." In sum, neither family matters nor individual consciences were held sacrosanct and protected from the observation, scrutiny, and control of a community of church members.[43]

The objective of the covenant was to link Christians together in a circle of loyalty, harmony, and mutual care that was larger than the family. On a routine basis the Baptists pledged to "settle compromises respecting temporal matters (if such should arise) by submitting them to judgment of particular Brethren, of the church, or judicious neighbors." The Presbyterian pledged to "walk in brotherly love with his church to watch over and admonish the brethren to submit to government and discipline as they dispense; and to live so as to give no reasonable ground of offense." The church trial enforced all these bonds between Christian brethren. For example, one member of the Whitesborough church was called to task in 1819 for being "very impudent in conversing about the character of his neighbors" and was instructed to "make concessions immediately and endeavor to heal all the divisions which he has occasioned." Similarly, the Baptists reported happily that two quarreling parishioners "had confessed to each other and settled their controversy."[44]

This emphasis on the loving bonds between fellow Christians invites comparison with the emotional ambience prescribed for households, for the comparison of the two presents a vivid contrast, an apparent reversal of modern usages. As already noted, the literature on family relationships emphasizes notions of authority and the rigid maintenance of hierarchy; church members, on the other hand, were exhorted to regard one another as equals bound together by mutual love. The *Utica Christian Magazine* printed a treatise, "On Covenanting," in 1814, which rooted church organization "wholly in the heart" in a "holy Love" and "holy affection." A second religious periodical, the *Western Recorder,* put it this way: "But whoever loveth the Lord Jesus in sincerity is the same as our brother, our sister, and mother. For God is love."[45] The father is conspicuously absent from this metaphorical family circle, for the authority and superiority he represented was at odds with the affection attributed to mothers and the egalitarian sentiments that passed between siblings, both of which found a legitimate place in the Christian community. Furthermore, the local writers seemed relatively unconcerned about the corrosive effects of fraternal love upon the hierarchical social order. Brotherly love was, in fact, the cement of a community, the antidote to controversy and contention between neighbors. In sum, the sentiment called love was judged at least as appropriate among church members as it was within the family. Even in matters of human emotions, the first generation on the New York frontier seemed careless of the distinction between family and church and society.

This and many other peculiarities of local culture played havoc with commonplace notions of the boundary between private and public life. The terms rarely appeared in the writings of the frontier generation, and when they did, they had a uniquely circumscribed meaning. The major usage of the terms *private* and *public* was to differentiate the proper spheres of men and women. All agreed that women should not assume a position of authority or prominence in the public chambers of church or government. This did not mean, however, that women were being consigned to "privacy" as we currently use the term. They were not sentenced to insulation in the family unit. The extreme antonym of the public sphere, in religious parlance, was the "closet," where neither men nor women were expected to isolate themselves. The obituary of one prominent matron of the frontier generation praised the deceased precisely because "her religion was not confined to the closet" but exercised among her friends and neighbors as well as family. The *Young Christian's Guide* advanced this position on privacy: "To be secluded from the world, to worship God in your closet, and in our families we have already seen to be praiseworthy, but it was never intended that these should superceed the practice of public devotion." Both personal and domestic privacy, then, were to be constantly counterbalanced by attendance at those large formal assemblages designated by the term *public,* as well as by active involvement in wide but informal social circles.[46]

Beyond this, the exact meaning of these terms is very difficult to pin down. It is quite clear, however, that the family was not coterminous with some "private" sphere. A Christian's "private" or "personal" duties would include his or her everyday informal responsibilities to friends and neighbors. The *Utica Christian Repository*, for example, advised its readers in one uninterrupted phrase to minister to the souls of both "their impenitent children *and neighbors*" (emphasis added).[47] The repeated citation of the covenant responsibility to watch over the conduct of fellow church members was another "private," but hardly domestic or cloistered, duty. Finally, the dwelling unit itself was not a particularly private institution, housing as it did servants, boarders, and itinerant guests and being, at the same time, ever vulnerable to the scrutiny of neighbors and the interrogation of church elders. The distinction between privacy and public life was muted in early Whitestown. Each social category tended to dissolve in an expansive and informal community network.

Whitestown's primitive social theorists tended to downplay a second conceptual building block of society, the category of the individual. The restriction of privacy within the corporate community was not conducive to the development of an independent, autonomous, egocentric self. Indeed, communal institutions tried systematically to suppress these personality traits. The First Presbyterian Society of Whitestown seemed dedicated to the obliteration of an independent identity. It exacted shamefaced, self-abasing public confessions from its erring parishioners. Joseph Black, a church elder who committed adultery, was obliged to make an obeisant confession: "When I look back upon my conduct and consider my profession, my age, and public situation in the church, I feel that I ought to be deeply humbled before God and man." Lemuel Leavensworth acknowledged his intemperance in an even more abject demeanor: "With shame and full of guilt I appear before this church and congregation to confess my iniquity in a transaction which is known to the society and for which I have been suspended from the congregation and the church. I have nothing to speak in justification of my conduct. I was base and vile, I ought not once to be named among Christians. On account and thereof I abhor myself and am bowed down all the day long. I am sensible that by this act I have injured my character, brought disgrace on my family and given occasion to the world to speak reproachfully of that holy religion which I am a professor. For these reasons I am ashamed and deeply grieved. But above all I have sinned against God." After reciting this confession before the congregation in November 1807, Lemuel Leavensworth was welcomed "back into the fellowship of the church." In exchange for the embrace of the Christian community, he had penitently offered up a large portion of his esteem and autonomy as an individual.[48] That principle could hardly be lost on the congregation before him. The prerogatives of the individual were routinely sacrificed in order to protect the integrity of the covenanted community.

The family economy was no less hospitable to individualism. Its organic interdependence did not permit of either self-reliance or solitary employment. The organic terminology of family structure, the reference to the head, the limbs, and branches, signifies the fact that individual family members could not survive apart from the cooperative activity of the corporate whole. It was the family, moreover, that was charged with the overt repression of individualism in its young members. To this end, parents were advised to use a time-honored New England technique of socialization, will-breaking. A major local treatise on frontier childrearing, which appeared in the *Utica Christian Magazine* in 1816, was culled from a Connecticut publication. Titled "On the Education of Children," it was premised on the necessity of suppressing the child's independent desires and self-assertions. The diligent parent, it was said, could accomplish the wholesale destruction of individualism in infancy. "As soon as a child is old enough to have wishes that ought not to be gratified . . . it is time to deny him the gratification of his desires . . . Here begin; here interpose your parental authority; accustom him to be denied and to take it patiently; habituate him to submit *his* will to *yours*, and to take pleasure in gratifying *you*, as well as *himself*."[49] Similarly, local treatises on the process of conversion prescribed the utter suppression of individual initiative. The reader of the *Young Christian's Guide*, for example, was interrogated as follows: "Have you been brought to renounce all dependence on your self."[50] Thus, in yet another essential feature of family and community life, the pioneers of Whitestown seemed to have planted a New England colony on the New York frontier.

Household economies in factory villages and market towns

In fact, the traditions of the seventeenth century were so hearty that they cropped up in even the more advanced villages of the township, New York Mills, and Utica – that is, in manufacturing centers and commercial towns as well as in farmhouses. The patriarchs of Whitestown were not worried that the factory system would undermine either the home economy or the corporate community. Sober

Connecticut farmers like Amos Wetmore and his brother-in-law, the pious Utica merchant Jesse Doolittle, and even James Carnahan, the minister of the First Presbyterian Society, were stockholders in the Oneida Manufacturing Society.[51] The secular order represented by the Oneida Society for the Promotion of American Manufacturers was equally confident that industry was compatible with the family economy. An 1817 address before that body was published by another devout Presbyterian, William Williams. The author, Isaac Briggs, argued that factories would supplement the family economy by putting otherwise idle children and women to work. He estimated that forty thousand able-bodied American boys and girls could be profitably employed in the textile industry. Briggs did not express any great concern for the physical danger to these young workers, but he did feel compelled to ensure their moral protection. "From my own experience," he wrote, "I know that a course of the purest moral and religious instruction may, with great facility, be connected within these establishments, without preventing reasonable profits." Briggs casually tossed off the industrial employment of women, on the other hand, as the continuation of another honored tradition: "Wives and elder daughters of our farmers can spin and weave – for we will suppose them all very industrious."[52]

The first factories in the Whitestown wilderness proved these sanguine expectations to be essentially correct. The saw and grist mills, tanneries, and fulling mills that dotted Sauguoit Creek were all assimilated into the family economy. Farm families allocated only one stage of domestic production to the factory, that is, usually the processing rather than the production of grain, hides, and woolens. Most of the thirteen textile factories to which Whitestown farmers pointed with such pride and curiosity in 1820 spun yarn from wool and flax that had been raised and cleaned and would in turn be woven in farmhouses. In sum, the early mills of Oneida County were casually but tightly integrated with the family organization of local production. The factory system itself, moreover, was built around a domestic system of labor. The first mills of Oneida County, following the plan of Rhode Island's Samuel Slater, recruited entire families as their labor force. They sought out workers through the Utica Patriot in 1813 with the following advertisement: "A few sober and industrious families of at least five children each, over the age of eight years, are wanted at the Cotton Factory in Whitestown. Widows with large families would do well to attend this notice. Recommendations as to moral character will be expected." Even these families of mill workers, however, were imper-

fectly absorbed into capitalist economic relations: They still were
paid in kind rather than cash, still maintained an independent base
of production in their garden plots and barnyards, and still bartered
for their basic needs through their home-produced foodstuffs, their
own labor and that of their children.[53]

The family intersected with the factory at the level of capital as
well as labor. The first mills were monuments to entrepreneurial
kin networks. Cotton tycoon Seth Capron took his brother-in-law
Newton Mann as a partner in managing the Oneida Manufacturing
Society. The necessary waterpower was supplied, in return for a
share in the factory stock, by a family of farmers whose lands
fronted the Sauguoit, Amos Wetmore, his son Asher and son-in-
law William Cheever. The necessary expertise in manufacturing
was provided by Benjamin Walcott, Jr., who had to be recruited
from Rhode Island. Walcott soon married into a local family of
stockholders, the Doolittles, and would establish a lineage of entrepreneurship with the succession of his son William to the directorship of factories in both Utica and Whitestown.[54]

In 1825 Benjamin Walcott took control of the Oneida Manufacturing Society, renamed it New York Mills, and remodeled its labor

New York Mills – company town circa 1825. Architectural Archive, Munson-Williams-Proctor Institute, Utica, N.Y.

system according to the Waltham plan. Walcott constructed a "Lowell West," complete with a handsome mill surrounded by neat family cottages and one male and one female boardinghouse. From his own stately mansion in the center of this bucolic circle, Benjamin Walcott oversaw the social life of his factory community. Such paternalism did not, however, place Benjamin Walcott in patriarchal control, in loco parentis, of a mass of unchaperoned workers. Surviving work ledgers reveal that a fine network of kin relationships was superimposed upon the factory order of New York Mills. One set of employment records dating from 1827 was actually arranged into family units.[55] This ledger detailed the work experience of some twenty families, all identified by the name of the father or occasionally a widowed mother at the top of the page. The record for Peter Billington, dated March 31 to April 14, illustrates this family method of accounting. Beneath Peter Billington's name there appeared the following credits:

11 days self $8.25
2 weeks James $3.00
10¾ days Lucy $2.24
9¾ days Lucina $1.25

This pattern of precise payments for some unspecified form of labor recurs in all the family employment records. It would seem to indicate that wage differences were determined by the age and sex of each family member. The variation in the number of days worked by different family members and the seasonal fluctuations in the pattern of labor suggest that the heads of these working households had some leeway in organizing and allocating the labor time of their kin. Workers like Peter Billington could also bargain with a variety of personal skills and family assets. Billington's account, for example, also included a small payment for laying a floor on the company property. Other heads of laboring households expanded their incomes by employing their apprentices or indentured servants as well as children. Abram Camp's account for March 28, 1828, included the following entries:

Hopkins, Bill, Bound $3.20
Board of
    Louisa Hayes   3 weeks/$6
    Hannah Hayes
    Lydia Hayes

Abram Camp supervised a complicated labor system for that month. The work of one son and one apprentice, the provision of board for three other workers, and finally his own services on the watch, all combined to net him $37.21. Such versatile family management was common among the heads of working families, who typically bargained with the skills, labor, and resources of five to seven members of their households.

At first glance it may appear that the revenues that had been assembled so dexterously would pass quickly and easily out of the grasp of the household head. Each worker was assigned, after all, a specific, individual cash wage. A look at the right side of the page, however, will dispel this notion. Few payments in cash are recorded on the debit side of the work ledger. Dollars-and-cents figures seem to have been a means of computing the value of labor rather than an indication of the actual movement of cash from one pocket to another. Even as late as 1828 these workers were remunerated largely in kind, by such things as cloth, butter, groceries, food, shelter. Abram Camp, for example, received part of his monthly wages in the form of pasturage for his cows. All these payments took the form of products to be pooled and consumed within the household, not money that granted to an individual worker independent access to the marketplace. As late as 1828 then, some families managed to retain aspects of the corporate family economy even at the very vortex of industrial development.

The seeds of the corporate community as well as the family economy took root in the factory villages of Oneida County. William Walcott's plans for New York Mills, the stately factory buildings surrounded by neat workers' cottages and presided over by his own proud mansion, were little more than a paternalistic update of the New England village. Other factory villages leave a similar archeological testament to the well-ordered factory community. In the village of Clayville, just southwest of Utica, identical two-family dwelling units still encircle the millpond. They are interspersed periodically with two churches as well as the owner's mansion, the mill, the school, and the town hall, each constructed in the same solid brick with the same simple trim. Indeed, the nucleated plan of the industrial village seems a better monument to the New England way than do the dispersed farmsteads of Whitestown. The wealthy factory owner was better equipped than the pioneer farmer to execute fully the town plans of his native New England.

The factory was as tightly integrated into the communal network of the church as was the family economy. Benjamin Walcott was an elder of the First Presbyterian Church and the major benefactor of the Methodist congregation, which began to meet in a room at the cotton mill even before the machines were put in operation.[56] The names of factory workers appeared regularly in the Presbyterian session records. In 1828, for example, the First Presbyterian Society intervened in the factory work process in order to protect the "children" who worked under the supervision of Silas Bartlett. According to the accusation of Betsey and Margaret Bilington, Bartlett had ordered them to "do things which he did not care about their doing to see if they would obey or to plague them." Factory employment did not give Bartlett a license to exercise such arbitrary power: The social hegemony of the church community extended even within the factory walls and suspended the petty tyrant from communion. The village of New York Mills would retain the reputation of a community of sober New England families well into the industrial era.

The same good order and its structural underpinnings, the home economy and the Christian community, had once dominated the social life of Utica itself. It was possible to find a fully developed family economy in the workshops and stores of the busy commercial center even in the middle of the nineteenth century. Both artisans and shopkeepers held property that could be shared and inherited through the ancestral line. Both could employ wives and children within a home-based division of labor. Craftsmen and shopkeepers alike often resided in or near their workshops and stores. In fact, only 13% of those listed in the 1817 village directory identified a place of work that was clearly detached from their address.

A closer look at the early city directories indicates that many of Utica's first residents put the corporate home economy into practice. The 1837 directory, for example, revealed that 13% of those listed, most of them artisans and shopkeepers, shared a place of residence with an adult worker of the same surname. In many cases these kinsmen shared a place of work and common skills as well as a home address. For example, two members of the Camp family lived together above the firm of Merrill and Camp, Book Publishers. The co-partners, Ira Merrill, printer, and Andrew Merrill, bookbinder, shared a house a few blocks away. To further cement this family economy, the Merrills and the Camps intermarried. Extended families like these replicate the pattern Bernard Farber found in Salem in 1800: the lateral expansion of the family in order to capitalize on the skills of kinsmen and form a complex division of artisan labor.[57] The family organization of the Camps and Merrills parallels similar domestic groupings among shoemakers, silversmiths, masons, and carpenters. Occasionally, the city directory also publicized the sexual division of labor within artisan families.

The familiar pairing of a tailor and his seamstress wife is a case in point. Shopkeepers could manage these variations on the home economy as well. Witness Harry Barnard whose fancy-goods store adjoined his wife's millinery shop or the extensive Doolittle family, four members of which shared the same place of residence as well as the same dry-goods store on Whitesboro Street.

The family economies of Utica's artisans and shopkeepers were often extended to include a second generation. This domestic arrangement is detailed particularly well in the last testament of Joseph Harter who left a tannery business to his wife and children in 1863. Joseph Harter prescribed a detailed division of family labor among his survivors. He stipulated that his wife, Sophia, was to "take my place in the business and trade of said tannery and stores." She was also granted a share in the owenrship of the tannery equal to those of her children. The legacies of Harter's youngest son and daughter would be conveyed when they reached twenty-five years of age, with these provisions: that the son would "faithfully divide and employ his time, energies, skill and talents in, to, and about the said business" and that the daughter would "continue to live with my said wife and assist her in the homestead house."[58] Merchants as well as artisans had designs like these for their children. Utica's small but thriving band of hat makers illustrates the potential for establishing an artisan lineage in a commercial town. Of the six hatters listed in the first village directory, only two would remain in Utica ten years later. But these two artisans, Samuel Stocking and Levi Barnum, represented an optimistic prototype of family capitalism. Both would remain in business more than thirty years and succeed in conveying a thriving small manufactory to their sons. Barnum's shop employed no fewer than seven kinsmen, most of whom shared a nearby dwelling house.

The New England ideal of community organization also held sway in early Utica (and guaranteed the Federalists an electoral majority until 1815). In conquering Utica, the New England way had tamed not just a wilderness but the rowdy disposition of a cosmopolitan commercial town. The Massachusetts missionary John Taylor was not optimistic about the prospects for christianizing Utica when he passed through the settlement in 1802. "Utica appears to be a mixed mass of discordant materials. Here may be found people of ten or twelve different nations, and of almost all regions and sects, but the greatest part are of no religion. The world is the great object of the body of the people."[59] Despite the worldly predilections of the populace, the minority status of New En-

A view of Utica from the hotel, September 1807. Sketch by Baroness Hyde de Neuville, I. N. Phelps Stokes Collection, Print Collection, New York Public Library, Astor, Lenox and Tilden Foundations.

glanders, and the presence of an Episcopalian, a Catholic, and a Universalist church in the town, the Calvinistic congregations left their clear imprint on Utica's public life right into the canal era. Even public amusements were curtained in this Puritan stronghold. In the 1820s theatrical companies were still being driven out of town by outraged members of the First Presbyterian Church. As has already been demonstrated, the members of the parish itself were subject to communal control in many aspects of their public and private lives. The town concurred with the church in the imperative of regulating private activities in the interest of public morality. The charter of the village of Utica, drawn up in 1817, set up a system of community control that was reminiscent of Boston in 1630 or an English borough a century earlier. It enforced the sanctity of the Sabbath, established just prices, and provided for "the effective suppression of vice and immorality."[60] The charter of the town corporation tried to place the commercial life of Utica under similar constraints. It regulated the prices of grocers, victuallers, and innkeepers, and maintained an assize of bread as late as the 1830s.[61]

Thus the frontier family system had acquired both definition and breadth by the third decade of the nineteenth century. Its distinguishing characteristics could be found in the industrial village of New York Mills and the commercial town of Utica as well as in the original agricultural settlement of Whitestown. Foremost among the family's attributes was a corporate economic structure that was

based on the organization of production around the social categories of sex and age and a stem pattern of inheritance. The internal
relations and ideology of the family were colored by these economic
imperatives and gave prominence to notions of hierarchy, authority, and patriarchy rather than either warm mutual ties or the free
play of individual interests. The frontier household did not derive
its social meaning merely within the boundaries of a dwelling
house but in its placement in relation to other institutions of the
community. The Protestant church in particular, as well as the town
government, turned to the household as a basic ally in maintaining
social order. To that end neither institution hesitated to call upon
the household to perform a multitude of social functions or to intervene in family affairs. In sum, the household was not only corporate and patriarchal but also a prime unit of society. If anything,
frontier circumstances exaggerated the importance of the family in
society beyond what even a Puritan social theorist would advise.
The primitive economic organization, the limited number of established social and political institutions, and the dispersed pattern of
settlement in Upstate New York before 1820 forced men and women
to fall back on their families to meet many of their social needs.

A wide array of documentary evidence suggests that this family
system had become deeply rooted in the soil of Oneida County and
would, if Puritans and patriarchs had their way, endure into a second generation. The content of the archives and the judgment of
historians cannot, however, always be one and the same. New Englanders, and especially the Presbyterians of Oneida County, it
would seem, were compulsive record keepers who have left an imprint on written history in excess of their dominance in their own
time. The documentation of the family economy is similarly limited
and biased. Fewer than 50 wills were probated in Utica and Whitestown before 1825 and fewer than 350 before 1865. The rare member
of the pioneer generation to leave a will was almost always the
owner of substantial property, usually abundant farmland. Less affluent, more transient residents of the region, like the unchurched,
have left fewer traces in the Oneida County archives. Of their family life we can learn relatively little. At the same time, much of the
literary evidence in support of a partriarchal corporate household is
not only drawn from Presbyterian and Baptist periodicals and publishers but dates from quite late in the frontier era, from the 1810s
and 1820s. One might well ask if these writers do not protest too
loudly. Were these transplanted New Englanders merely vainly and
nostagically celebrating a family system that would be buried with the
frontier generation?

The subversion of the frontier family

By the second and third decades of the nineteenth century the corporate patriarchal family was, in fact, threatened from several quarters from within and without Whitestown farmsteads. First of all,
Whitestown's farmers were never really insulated from the social
and economic developments behind the frontier. The coloration of
New England in the eighteenth and nineteenth centuries suffused
the New York frontier. The mature culture blended with the im-
provisations of the new settlers to give a distinctly modern cast to
frontier society and family. As has already been noted, Hugh White
and his compatriots brought some newfangled economic conceptions into the wilderness – plans for gristmills, cotton factories, and
banks. Other of his Connecticut neighbors also carried some novel
notions about social organization into the new land. While still in
New Hartford, Connecticut, Whitestown's pastor, the Reverend
John Frost, had founded the first domestic missionary society of the
Congregational Church. In so doing, he not only forged an important link between New England and the frontier but also experimented with a new social institution, a "society" standing apart
from the church, the family, the town. The notion of the voluntary
association of individuals for a specific benevolent or religious purpose was just beginning to be bandied about back in New England
when "societies" began to flourish in the environs of Whitestown,
almost with the pioneers' first crops. A Whitestown Charitable Society had been formed in 1806; Baptists, Methodists, and Presbyterians had missionary societies within a decade. All were founded
so close in time to the first benevolent and religious societies of
New England that it is hard to say where along the trail of migration
they actually originated. It was in 1812 in New Haven that Lyman
Beecher called for the establishment of societies to encourage the
reform of personal morals. His sermon on the subject was printed
in Utica within the year.

The rapid proliferation of "societies" in Whitestown is one indication of the dynamic historical element of the frontier: the com-
mingling of primitive social organization with contemporary culture in such a way as to produce genuine innovations in collective
life. The goals and the ideology of the benevolent and religious societies were basically congruent with the New England way and
supportive of the family economy. They were dedicated to planting
traditional religious values on the frontier. They did, however, sit
rather awkwardly amid the covenanted communities of the church.

For example, the Oneida Bible Society, founded by Whitestown Presbyterians in 1810, presumed without ministerial status to enter any household to inquire as to the possession of a family Bible. This kind of aggressive social action was a staple of the nineteenth-century frontier life, and, like those other "self-created societies," the Federalist and Republican parties, a sure sign of the shifting balance between family and society. They represented the emergence of a new sector of social life, intermediary between the household and the corporate institutions of church and town meeting. They were poised precariously on the fragile axis between public and private life.

This novel element in social organization was identified in *The Utica Almanac* of 1810 in a list of four "Village Corporations," which included the Village Corporation, the Whitesboro Cotton Factory, the Manhattan Bank, and the Female Charitable Society. The first of these was the long-established center of public life formalized by a village charter. The next two represented the increasingly rationalized economic organization endemic to even the frontier arm of the expanding American commercial system. The last, however, represented an innovation of the frontier and a breach of the customary order of the family and the sexes. The officers of the Female Charitable Society appeared before the public independently of the household head, listed by name, and with such awesome titles as "president," "treasurer," "trustee."[62] The founder of the organization was Mrs. Sophia Clark, formerly of Hartford, Connecticut, where the first Female Charitable Society was not founded until 1809, that is, after the Whitestown group.[63] Back in Connecticut, moreover, female organizations like this could not assume such public prominance, absorbing one of the four places reserved for village corporations.

The charitable society was only the first of many such organizations to be founded by the frontier generation of women in Oneida County. Baptist cent societies (small-scale charitable enterprises) and Methodist sewing circles soon followed in the wake of this adjunct of the First Presbyterian Society of Whitestown. Most of them expanded into missionary activities in the 1810s and set up auxiliaries throughout the Western District of New York State. The Female Missionary Society of Oneida County, the offshoot of the Whitestown Charitable Society, was founded in 1814 and was the first such association in the United States to be financially independent of the male religious establishment. Despite their considerable recognition in the public press, the female societies conducted most of their activities within the more private social spaces. The societies themselves were laced with kin associations that extended from Connecticut through Oneida County. Meetings were held only four times annually, within the homes of the members. Even then a minister was often present to lead the female congregation in prayer. Female charitable and missionary societies also stayed within the bounds of the family economy, contributing their domestic productions to the charitable cause. The Whitestown Charitable Society began as a sewing circle and the missionary societies continued to receive donations in the form of home manufactures.[64] The 1816 receipts of the Hamilton Baptist Missionary Society included such things as twenty-five and two-thirds yards of broadcloth from the Fabius Female Mite Society and one pair of mittens from Sister Mary Thomas of Lisle.[65] Within the broad framework of the New England way, however, these female organizations harbored the potential to transform the relations of the sexes and to reshape the boundaries of public and private life. They did, after all, promise women a prominent social place outside the household independent of its patriarchal head.

Like the benevolent society, the nuclear family itself seemed to be subtly subversive of the balanced placement of households within the community. The parishioners of the First Presbyterian Society of Whitesboro failed to uphold one major buttress of the well-ordered households of their ancestors, that is, the customary practice of putting out their young children to labor in other households. In fact, the Reverend John Frost found what he called servants and apprentices in less than 4% of the households he visited. He used the more ambiguous term *boarder* to describe members of less than 10% of Whitestown's homes (Table A.5). This contrasts sharply with a ratio of one servant in every third household in seventeenth-century Rhode Island and an even higher rate of putting out children in Puritan England. It would seem, then, that Whitestown's families kept their children occupied in home production and by their sides through the earlier years, the traditional time of servitude in peasant cultures. If, as historians such as Alan Mcfarlane and Edmund Morgan have contended, the strategy of putting out children was designed to repress the parental indulgence that was deemed subversive to the Puritan order, then Whitestown's families, had discarded one safeguard of patriarchal control.[66] By clustering more closely together, through longer portions of the family cycle, the parents and children of Whitestown may have been forging more intimate bonds to one another than either peasant cultures or Calvinist theologians allowed.

Both these generational bonds and the frontier family system were also being undermined by demographic conditions. It would be frontier demography, in the end, that posed the most direct threat to the agrarian family order. The population dynamics of Whitestown can be compared to the frontier pattern described by Richard Easterlin. Using statistics drawn from the 1860 census, Easterlin identified a three-generation cycle of population change in frontier settlements. The pioneer generation replicated the fertility pattern of its place of origin, those densely settled territories that had already placed restraints upon family size. Their children, however, the first generation to grow up on the open land of the frontier, were not so inhibited about rearing large families. They exhibited the largely uncontrolled fertility characteristic of seventeenth-century New Englanders and other couples blessed with abundant farmlands on which to settle their sons. The rapid conquest of the American West in the nineteenth century exhausted this agricultural cornucopia by the time the third generation reached adulthood. It was this third generation that drastically reduced the rate of reproduction and completed the frontier cycle of fertility.[67]

The limited demographic data available for New York State allows for only the crudest comparison with Easterlin's findings. The aggregate statistics on age and sex compiled by state and federal censuses do indicate, however, that the women of the township were remarkably fecund between 1790 and 1810. During that period there were more than two thousand children aged zero to nine for every thousand women in the age gruop sixteen to forty-five. A fairly complete set of vital records compiled by the First Presbyterian Society of Whitestown confirms this trend. The rate of infant baptisms was extremely high through the second decade of the nineteenth century and began to descend to a lower plateau soon thereafter. Already in the 1810s, however, the overall population of Whitestown had begun to decline, as local population was siphoned off to new frontiers. Fertility rates soon fell into line with this demographic transition. The child/woman ratio for 1820 had fallen to 1,307, or by about one-third in the space of a decade. This magnitude of change is only partially accounted for by the influx of young and single mill workers. Older and married women had undoubtedly slackened their fertility as well. Those women who remained in Oneida County until 1865, when they could be included in the more accurate measurement of fertility taken by the New York State Census for that year, provide more direct evidence of a declining birthrate. Females born before 1805 gave birth to 5.1 children on the average; the cohort of women born in the following decade mothered only a mean number of 3.6 offspring. Scattered and imprecise evidence such as this does add up to a cumulative demonstration of a very craggy fertility pattern on the Whitestown frontier. A high birthrate in the first several decades of settlement was swiftly followed by a steep decline in the rate of reproduction (Tables A.6, E.1). Indeed, the Whitestown demographic record suggests a more rapid turnaround in fertility than in either colonial New England or on later frontiers. The time span between the founding of the township in 1784 and the precipitous fertility decline in the 1810s approximates the interval between two generations, not three.

This decisive shift in the fertility of Whitestown families coincided with the virtual exhaustion of the supply of unsettled land capable of supporting farm families. Between 1820 and 1825 only the trifling sum of five hundred acres of new land was put under cultivation in all of Whitestown. Once again the Whitestown farmers could consult their New England experience and find an appropriate response to this frontier predicament. Faced with the unbalanced ratio between population and land, their ancestors had put their fertility in check, first by later marriage, then by birth control (chiefly the ancient practice of coitus interruptus). Fertility control was not, however, efficient and quick enough to account for the stabilization and actual decline in the local farm population by 1820. The slack had to be taken up by other demographic responses: by outmigration, particularly of those sons who did not inherit their fathers' farms, and by late marriage, spinsterhood, or childlessness among daughters. As the frontier moved to the rich agricultural lands of the West and as the competitive advantage of New York crops declined, even the depleted ranks of Whitestown's second generaiton were pressed to find new ways of making a living, often away from the family farm.

These alternative modes of employment were also readily in evidence by the 1820s: the factories where farmers' daughters tended their spindles, the sawmills, the artisan shops, and the general stores where their sons might find vocations. By the 1820s, furthermore, a farm father could channel his son into a novel occupation through formal education at such newly founded institutions as the Utica Free Academy, Hamilton College, or the Oneida Institute. In

occupational as well as demographic and social terms, the residents
of Whitestown appeared to telescope the slow evolutionary process
of previous American history. They leapt in scarcely two generations, it seemed, from seventeenth-century New England to nineteenth-century New York.

In every sense the family would orchestrate this transformation.
Parents shifted through the old and the new to design strategies for
controlling family size and for locating their offspring in new occupations. Because of the relative isolation of households and the in-
frequency of putting out children, moreover, parents and children
of Whitestown might have experienced a heightened sense of concern about their impending separation. The precarious foundation
of the ordered hierarchy of the corporate patriarchal family was exposed as the second generation came of age. The prospect of migration might produce a calculating sense of private interests among a
farmer's sons and daughters. Education and factory labor alike
might foster psychological independence from the corporate family
and community. The seduction of the commercial network might
engender impatience with the slow rewards of the family cycle and
inheritance. This unsettled atmosphere, and the dramatic public
prominence of Christian matrons, might even inspire young
women to design their own life strategies. It was the young at any
rate who would in the 1820s be buffeted most violently by the ebb
tide of the frontier.

Two brief biographical sketches illustrate their peculiar predicament. The first comes from the poignant handwritten diary of John
Coleman who was born in 1809 and raised on his father's farm in
Whitestown.[68] Coleman began his diary on a note of subdued discontent with the family economy. "And here I will say that I do not
like farming, though I am convinced that it is the best business a
man can follow." He quickly added, "But I had to, of course, endure it till my seventeenth year when I was put to a trade with
Messrs. Danby and Maynard, printers and publishers of the *Oneida
Observer*." The transition from country to town and farm to shop
did not prove swift and smooth, not for John Coleman at any rate.
When his apprenticeship terminated two years later Coleman set
out on his own, trying to become a printer. He made five attempts
to set up shop and failed in each. In 1834 at age twenty-five he was
back on his father's farm and more discontent than ever: "I take no
peace when at my labor. My father and elder brother are scolding
me everytime they come into my presence! Everything I do is all
wrong. It is impossible to please them and I get nothing for my

labor scarcely at all." It was not until 1840 that he and his brother bought their father's grist mill and formed their independent family economy. In the case of John Coleman, the internal cohesion of the family economy had broken down in the 1820s, but no easy alternative had yet been found.

The women of his generation experienced parallel discontent. The early life of Utica's most noteworthy author, Emily Chubbuck Judson, will illustrate the woman's trials that lurked just beyond the frontier.[69] Emily Chubbuck was born in 1817 in Eaton, New York, a small village forty miles south of Utica. A mere eleven years later, she had already been evicted from the comforts of household production and was earning $1.25 a week splicing reels in the local woolen factory. The experience granted her a measure of independence and a potent foretaste of a new woman's world. Her parents allowed her to spend half her wages and "with numerous incentives to economy, I first learned the use of money." Emily's introduction to commerce and industry was not, however, without its own price. "My principle recollections during this summer are of noise and filth, bleeding hands and aching feet, and a very sad heart." Emily Chubbuck's bittersweet experience outside the home economy also instilled some noble feelings and vaulting ambitions. She occupied her mind while at work with "fantasies of inheriting money and becoming a great poetess." In actuality, Emily Chubbuck Judson would travel a long and circuitous route to a brief and relatively impecunious period of literary fame.

The uncertain prospects for the women of her generation provided material for the popular short stories Chubbuck authored in the 1840s. Writing under the name of Fanny Forrester, she described young girls who left farm families to try their hand at being milliners, mill girls, songstresses, and servants. The unfortunate among them returned home to die in the comfort of their mothers' arms; the privileged ventured off to marry factory owners, westward pioneers, or, as in Chubbuck's own case, a foreign missionary. It would appear that the imperative of leaving the corporate family of the New York frontier had entered even into the imagination of young women. Just where that path might take the daughters and sons of Whitestown farmers remained, however, very much in doubt.

In the course of their journey to adulthood, both John Coleman and Emily Chubbuck would stop to participate in the Second Great Awakening. Like so many other aspects of the New York frontier, revivalism had its roots back in New England. The Second Great

Awakening began in Connecticut in the last decade of the eighteenth century and counted some of Whitestown's first residents
among its converts. It was, however, in the southeastern corner of
Oneida County, New York, and in the 1820s, in the stomping
grounds of Charles Finney, John Coleman, and Emily Chubbuck,
that nineteenth-century evangelism would reach its full furor. It
was the explosive fusion on the maturing New York frontier of
changes in the family, gender, age structure, and society that prepared the Burned-Over District for this epochal historical event.
That unique combination of social forces might be summarized as
follows. Before 1820 the first settlers had succeeded in re-creating a
New England social organization that included the reincarnation of
such seventeenth-century institutions as the corporate family economy, a patriarchal household structure, and the covenanted religious community. These throwbacks to the days of the Puritans,
however, coexisted with the culture, economics, and society of the
eighteenth century – with habits of trade, industry, and benevolence that had been acquired east of the frontier, especially in Connecticut. The residents of Whitestown adapted these old and new
social forms in the course of a rapid transition from the primitive
home economy to a specialized trade network. At the same time,
the region seemed to telescope a major demographic transition into
a span of family time that enclosed fewer than two full generations.
This vertiginous social atmosphere attained the velocity of a hurri-
cane in the 1820s, roughly as the second generation came of age. It
found its dramatic historical expression in the Second Great Awakening, the subject of the next chapter.

2 Family in transition: the revival cycle, 1813–1838

The farmlands of Oneida County are still dotted with a few Greek Revival houses, most of them larger and more ornate than that depicted in the sketch of the Utica Building Association in 1820. They survive to testify that at least a few families resolved the contradictions of the New York frontier and managed to sustain a lineage of small farmers for generations into the future. By the fourth decade of the nineteenth century the men and women of Whitestown had made the necessary accommodations with the advances of commerce and rapid population growth, but not without a struggle. The sleepy villages of western New York did not retreat from history without one last burst of remarkable energy and creativity. A sequence of religious revivals and reform movements identified rural backwaters like Whitestown as the heartland of the Burned-Over District. Whitestown itself was crucially implicated in those epochal historical events. It was one of the first townships to be set ablaze during Charles Finney's tour in 1825. Ten years earlier Finney's future wife, Lydia Andrews, had confessed her faith in the religious center of the township, the First Presbyterian Society. The same congregation also enrolled the founders of the Oneida Female Missionary Society, which in 1824 allocated $192 to support Finney's first evangelical ministry.[1]

The Female Missionary Society was the favorite project of a group of women who resided with their lawyer- and merchant-husbands around the port on the Mohawk River in the village of Utica, within the township of Whitestown. Itself an offshoot of the Whitestown Charitable Society, the Missionary Society adopted its evangelical focus in 1814 and promptly began to set up auxiliaries throughout the evangelical route that Finney would follow during the Second Great Awakening. These matrons of Utica commandeered a key social position at the foundation and within the infrastructure of the subsequent revivals. It would take more than thirty years for the cycle of conversions to run its course. The history of evangelism proceeded in the rhythms of family time, spanning the years between 1814 and 1838, when many of the first converts saw their lastborn reach early adulthood and join the church. Throughout the entire period Utica's coterie of evangelical females also nurtured strong ties to some fictive kin, to their "beloved sisters," assembled in churches throughout Oneida County and western New York State. This chapter will recount how and why Utica's women became the central nervous system of this evangelical network, which extended far into the surrounding agricultural districts. The Female Missionary Society and similar evangelican institutions were keenly sensitive to the family tension that sparked through town and country in the early nineteenth century. We shall see how, in converting these inchoate impulses and half-conscious concerns into revival enthusiasm, these evangelicals came to terms with some more terrestrial problems as well, not the least of which was the progressive erosion of the corporate family economy.

It is no coincidence that the course of the revivals paralleled the trade routes through Oneida County. The structure of communication, the divisions of labor, and the underlying causes of evangelism all followed the contours of a regional economic network. A market in goods as well as converts had its organizational nucleus in Utica. More than 40% of Oneida County's retail establishments were located in Utica, where the professional and financial services subsidiary to commerce, chiefly law offices and banks, were also centered. The first village directory, compiled in 1817, revealed that Utica was top-heavy with ambitious merchandisers. No less than 17% of the entries in the directory boldly put forth the business cards of "merchants," often prefixed with such terms as *commission*, *auction*, and *wholesale*, which announced the voluminous scale of these enterprises (Table B.3). The largest wholesalers among them dealt in agricultural commodities such as flour or leather. By the close of the revival cycle, the forces of commerce had penetrated into every corner of Oneida County to collect and distribute agicultural products. The fields of Whitestown were soon yielding tens of thousands of bushels of wheat, corn, and potatoes annually, and its dairies produced more than three million pounds each of butter and cheese.[2] Marketing this surplus drew the farm families of Whitestown ever more closely into a commercial network whose traffic in cash, credit, and wages introduced some potentially divisive monetary interests into corporate farm families.

The families situated within Utica proper experienced the most explosive commercial fission. The demographic conditions of Utica during the canal era rivaled frontier Whitestown in their volatility. The town's population more than doubled between 1820 and 1830 and had quadrupled by 1840 (Table A.2). Instant cities like Utica

were no more hospitable to family formation than was a raw frontier. Few of Utica's newcomers, furthermore, seemed to share the
strong family loyalties of pioneers like Hugh White. Most arrived in
the busy marketplace alone, young, and unmarried. In 1820 more
than one-fifth of Utica's population was between the ages of sixteen
and twenty-six, whereas the supposedly more staid and rooted age
group of over forty-five accounted for only 7.2% of the city's residents (Table A.3). Males and females were so mismatched in numbers and in ages as to discourage or postpone the formation of families. After the years of childhood, when boys were in the majority,
females either arrived or remained in Utica in excess of their male
peers and consequently dominated every age group. The pattern of
sex and age stabilized in 1840 but with permanently unbalanced
ratios. Women outnumbered men in Utica for the remainder of the
antebellum period (Table A.1). Uticans employed a novel form of
household organization and a new terminology of residence to
identify this young, single population. In 1828 the city directory
began to employ the term *boarder*, which in that year described the
family status of no less than 28% of the employed males of Utica.

When families did form within the commercial entrepôt of Utica,
they were rarely bound together in the manner of Whitestown's
original corporate household economies. Wills probated in Utica,
even before 1825, seldom paid homage to the stem family or to the
generational continuity of the household unit of production. The
fathers of Utica were four times more likely than their counterparts
in Whitestown to provide for their children on the basis of simple
equality and outright cash grants. Uticans also preferred to regard
their widows as free economic agents; only 1 in 7 wills referred to
the practice of dower. After 1825 the vestiges of the older patterns of
inheritance all but disappeared in Utica. Discrimination on the
basis of age and sex was rarely detectable in the will books. Conversely, the majority of the wills used the phrase "share and share
alike" to underscore the simple egalitarian basis of children's bequests. The terms *free* and *simple* denoted a similar transformation
in the inheritance of wives, the majority of whom were given absolute control of their husband's full estate after 1845 (Tables B.1 and
B.2). Thus, from an early date, the families of commercial Utica had
revised the agricultural pattern of inheritance and seemed thereby
to undermine the corporate, intergenerational dimension of the
family.

This reformulation of the principles and practice of inheritance is
rooted in the shrinking size of the material base of the corporate

family economy, productive property. By 1835 less than half the household heads in Utica owned as much as the $100 in property that would subject them to taxation. Most of the citizens whose names appeared on the tax list, furthermore, owned merely a place of residence, a dwelling house rather than a place of business.[3] Even before 1825 only one of the twelve wills probated in Utica transferred a productive enterprise, a farm, shop, or store, directly to the second generation. After that date the proportion fell to less than 2%. Most residents of Utica, including the majority of those who never bothered to write a will, probably owned too little to justify a complex pattern of inheritance. Abraham Miller's short will, which was probated in 1837, made this reasoning explicit. Miller prefaced his will with a reference to "my little property" and then proceeded to grant his entire estate to his wife. If any property remained after Mrs. Miller's death it was to descend in equal portions to their four children.[4] Fathers like Miller simply did not possess the extent of productive resources that required the elaborate procedures for generational transfer once employed by the farmers of Whitestown. In this Miller was typical of the town's household heads, the majority of whom were employed in retailing, professional services, or casual labor, that is, bereft of any integral productive enterprises that could engage and unite the members of their families. Only Utica's artisans, with their family workshops, domestic division of labor, and productive resources, had the wherewithal to duplicate Whitestown's traditions of the corporate family economy.

As long as Whitestown's fathers retained their farmsteads, the corporate household economy was protected from the utter ravages of commerce. Thus in the 1820s and 1830s Whitestown still maintained allegiance to such corporate customs as dower and the stem family. At the same time, and again in opposition to the pattern in Utica, the incidence of simple equality in bequests to children declined dramatically in Whitestown. The majority of wills probated in Whitestown between 1825 and 1845 were so intricate that no clear overall pattern to the discrimination among children is discernible (Tables B.1 and B.2). This would suggest that it was becoming increasingly difficult and costly to preserve the family farm. As the supply of unimproved land dwindled and the cost of farm real estate rose, many small farmers were forced to distribute their agricultural property in an arbitary and unequal fashion, perhaps even excluding some offspring from the family patrimony. Alternatively, the profits reaped in commercial agriculture may have allowed more prosperous farmers to educate their sons or set them up in some nonagricultural business. In still other cases, Whitestown's sons and daughters might have responded directly to the enticements of market capitalism by breaking their own trails out of the agricultural family economy. Even in Whitestown, then, commerce had introduced a divisive wedge into the corporate family and opened up independent economic paths, especially for the second generation.

Similar changes were also under way in the growing industrial segment of the local economy. When Benjamin Walcott, Jr., put his new textile mill into operation in 1827, less than one-fourth of his workers were employed in family groups. The bulk were listed on the payroll by individual names and issued independent cash wages. By the end of the next decade, when New York Mills had become one of the top ten cotton manufacturers in the United States, the family system of accounting was no longer in use at all. The labor force was composed entirely of independent workers, most of them young and female. Thus the increasing differentiation of the economic network had installed, in the very center of the township of Whitestown, a system of production that seemed to repudiate the family order. One of Walcott's mills employed 250 females, 100 boys under sixteen (30 of them under twelve), and a mere 6 adult males.[5]

The increasing regional specialization of production had a decided effect on the division of household labor. Most directly, the advance of textile manufacturing coincided with a diminished domestic production of cloth. The home manufacture of textiles declined to one-fourth of its former volume between 1820 and 1835. Other aspects of domestic production were surrendered to the artisan shops of Utica, which by the 1830s were producing and selling such domestic staples as soap, candles, and medicines. The diversification of the regional economy was accomplished by the transfer of expendable labor, especially that of children, from family farms to shops and factories. Most migrants into both the factory village of New York Mills and into commercial Utica were young natives of New York State. Many of them were born in Oneida County. In other words, they were probably the sons of daughters of the first generation of farmers, the stepchildren of the family economy, whose roles in the farm household had been transferred to other segments of an increasingly complicated regional economy.[6]

Throughout the regional marketplace the corporate character of family economics was either tattered or torn asunder. Be it in Utica,

Whitestown, or New York Mills, it was the generational ties of the home economy that seemed most fragile, most vulnerable to the corrosive power of commerce. The men and women of Oneida County were not unaware of this fact. They did not express their family concerns in economistic terms, however, but rather in the language and central ideological structure of their time, that is, in an essentially religious mode of thought.

Religion in defense of patriarchy

The increasing fragility of generational bonds was greeted with particular alarm by the guardian of the old family order, the Presbyterian Church. The Presbyterians had attempted from the first to shore up the patriarchal household and had defended its bulwarks with special diligence in the 1820s against the "restless and wandering activity of youth."[7] Their church trials and those of Baptists and Methodists could keep the families of loyal church members in line but were helpless before the turbulent multitude, the "mixed mass" of the bustling canal town. By 1820 Utica supported Episcopalian, Roman Catholic, and Universalist congregations and harbored growing numbers of the unchurched and unbelieving as well. Pious Calvinists might well despair of conferring a heritage of salvation upon the sons and daughters who inhabited this heterogeneous and secular town. Their attempts to find new methods of securing these familial ties generated the liveliest era in the social and religious history of Utica and Whitestown.

The church and the family found a principal ally in this work in the local press. The early printers of Oneida County were Presbyterians almost to a man and acted as a commercial arm of the clerical establishment. They were also among the foremost exemplars of the old family order. Merrill and Camp, Book Publishers, whose own extended family economy has already been described, issued countless sermons and several periodicals, among them the *Utica Christian Magazine*, which was a major source of evangelical communication beginning in 1813. The Merrills took a new partner, Thomas Hastings, in 1824 when they began to publish a second organ of revivalism, the *Western Recorder*. Evangelism was also reported and orchestrated in a third magazine, the *Utica Christian Repository*; this too was published by founding families of the First Presbyterian Church, those of William Williams and Asahel Seward. These printers enacted the same artisan version of the family economy exemplified by Merrill and Camp. William Williams was first apprenticed to his brother-in-law, Oneida County's first printer, William McClean, and next formed a partnership with Asahel Seward. Kinship cemented this last business alliance when William's sister Martha married his new partner.[8] The body of religious literature issued by this band of Presbyterian printers supplies the earliest source of literary evidence for a major transition in the family order. From his base in Utica, the Presbyterian printer spoke to and for a population that was scattered all across western New York, as far as the turnpikes and canals could carry his little tracts and magazines.

From the first, these printers were embroiled in religious controversies that bespoke family concerns. The sectarian argument that inaugurated the lively religious history of Utica and Whitestown, the debate about infant baptism, was addressed explicitly to the generational and familial continuity of religion. The first skirmish between Baptists and Presbyterians began in a small rural village within the township of Whitestown. It was reported in a pamphlet subtitled "The Rise and Progress of a Dispute Carried on Between Certain Members of the Congregational and Baptist Churches in Sangerfield." The short piece recounted a series of discussions that took place every Wednesday night for more than six months, involving clergy and laymen from both denominations. The lively debate, conducted in local farmhouses, was described as "promiscuous discourse" and merged private and public, along with persons of both sexes and all ages, in one informal community. Much of the discussion involved arid theological matters – searches through scripture for references to baptism, the source of grace, and the moral nature of infants. But just beneath the surface lay the more earthly concerns of this excited band of farmers. The Baptist controversy posed in religious terms a question of great practical concern to parents and children, the opposition between inherited and achieved status.

The Calvinist defense of infant baptism began: "Our children are part of ourselves – God has constituted the parent the head of the family, and so it is so in nature. Would it not be inconsistent to take in the head and leave out the body. Households are saved on account of the head, whether they be infant or not, that is they are reputed and treated so." The last sentence displayed considerable carelessness about the fine points of Calvinism and the basic doctrine of predestination. The first, however, displayed an adamant commitment to an organic family and the generational extension of the Christian covenant, even on to "a thousand generations." The

Presbyterian party to the debate repeatedly asserted one defense of infant baptism, the doctrine of the Abrahamic covenant: "God does connect parents and children together in dispensing his favors; and . . . he does so in a covenant, in fulfillment of his promise to bless the seed of the righteous." The defense of this family bond generated virulent debate among the simple farmers of Sangerfield in 1803. It would still be exercising Oneida County in 1820 when another sermon printed by William Williams noted that "the bitterest spirit of party" still reigned on this issue.[9]

The source of all this excitement can be gleaned from the arguments of the Presbyterians' opponents. The exponents of the Baptist position in Sangerfield were capable of arguments like this: "I was once a Pedo-Baptist. My parents taught me that way and I received it upon their instruction. While I was a Pedo-Baptist I put forced construction on scripture." A later writer presented this filial rebellion more openly: "How small a number of those who at this day belong to the Baptist Churches, can say that their present view of the subject was early impressed upon their expanding minds by the kind instruction of a pious father; or the still more enduring solicitude of a tender mother. You will find by far the greater will say . . . they were compelled to forsake father and mother, brother, and sister, and in the face of a sneering world, were enabled to take up the cross." In short, the Baptists expounded, at least for the sake of argument, a doctrine of independence from the patriarchal household.[10] They were apparently joined in this opinion by the local Methodists. In a pamphlet dated 1812 the Reverend Elijah Norton deemed Methodism a direct threat to patriarchy. This Oneida County Presbyterian accounted a host of impudent children among the consequences of Methodism: "Some children and youth among them (as we have seen) behave themselves proudly against the ancient, and treat old men, even ministers, and parents with great contempt who hold the doctrine of election. This I have seen and experienced in a family and a public assembly also." In his paranoia about the maintenance of family authority the Reverend Mr. Norton reached the heights of hyperbole. He saw the Methodists "swarming out like the locusts, out of the pit, and like grievous wolves and roaring lions, with deadly poison among our lambs render our families, societies, and churches in pieces." As if this menagerie of mixed metaphors were not enough, Norton invoked the most extreme image of family disorder. The Methodist doctrine, he said, "has a direct tendency to kill and murder fathers and mothers."[11]

Sermons like this bespoke high-pitched anxiety among the first generation of the New York frontier about their bonds to their children. The direct descendants of the Puritans, most of whom had under the Plan of Union formed Presbyterian rather than Congregationalist parishes, perceived this threat as an assault from their sectarian rivals, Baptists and Methodists. The intensity of their reaction, however, was churned by palpable and immediate problems: the closing of the agrarian frontier, the imminent passage of the corporate family economy and covenanted community, and the portended dissolution of generational ties. In these circumstances the simple invocation of doctrine, be it the Abrahamic covenant or adult baptism, was an ineffectual and ultimately unsatisfying recourse for all the New England denominations.

Therefore, Presbyterians, Baptists, and Methodists alike began to devise more concrete methods of reinforcing parental ties to their children. In 1808 Joshua Leonard rose before the Presbyterian congregation to remind his parishioners that the lineage of grace was sealed by a covenant, an agreement with the Almighty that obliged parents to abide by their side of the bargain. Parents were sworn by the covenant to fulfill an "awesome responsibility" to train, instruct, and admonish their children in the ways of God and grace. [12] It was not mere coincidence that ministers throughout Oneida County frequently chose this theme as the text of their Sunday sermons. One of the first recommendations of the Oneida Presbytery, founded in 1808, was an annual sermon on "the privileges and obligations of the Abrahamic covenant, presenting distinctly the duty of pious parents to dedicate their infant children to God in baptism, their responsibilities in connection with their religious training and the precious grounds of expectation and confidence that if found faithful, 'saving blessing,' would follow." Not the doctrine of grace stemming from an arbitrary God but the duty of parents to educate and sanctify their children had become the crux of the pastoral message. [13]

Accordingly, infant baptism itself had primarily symbolic and monitory value. It was a rite in which parents publicly assumed and resolved to fulfill their religious responsibility to their sons and daughters. Without such a ritual, the Reverend Jabez Chadwick feared that parents would feel free to deny the Sabbath, distort scripture, and neglect family prayer. In fact, he already saw the dire consequences of parental complacency all around him on the New York frontier. He observed that many parents were "awfully insensible of the truth of this subject, and neglectful of their duty to their

children." "If they did not reform," he warned, "parents themselves would bring a curse upon their posterity, instead of a blessing." By underscoring the fine print in the Abrahamic covenant,
the clerical leadership of Oneida had arrived at a point of agreement
with their denominational rivals. The Baptists, their rhetoric of independence aside, also held parents practically responsible for the
souls of their children. One of their pamphlets ended on a familiar
note: "What an awful judgment will those unnatural parents draw
upon their heads who neglect to bring up their children in the nurture and admonitions of the Lord." The same refrain could be heard
in Methodist quarters. *The Methodist Magazine,* briefly published in
Utica, harbored its own essays on "Parental Duty and Responsibility." Indeed, the religious press of all denominations was littered
with essays on "Parental Duties" and "The Christian Education of
Children."[14]

The actual working out of the dictums of Christian education was
fraught with difficulties, especially for the descendants of Calvinists. Early writers like David Harrowar (published by Merrill and
Camp in 1815) were bold enough to invoke undiluted Calvinism in
sermons with such uninviting titles as "On the Total Depravity of
Infants." Baptism was not equivalent to salvation according to Harrowar, who was coldly unsentimental in his Calvinist purity: "If the
infants of pious people die without its attainment they must be
consigned to eternal ruin." Within the next decade some Presbyterians began slowly to work their way toward a new, less callous
child psychology. In 1813 Merrill and Camp printed this novel definition of the child's nature: "Infants are *moral agents* and possess
moral characters." This moral capacity appeared even before a child
was capable of the most rudimentary acts of reasons and the most
fundamental knowledge of Christian doctrine: It was a faculty of
the heart rather than of the mind. The precise nature of the moral
agency of infants was very vaguely illuminated. The anonymous
author spoke of "impressions on their minds, . . . accompanied
with feelings or exercises which partake of a moral quality"; he resorted to emotional rather than cognitive terms, to feelings, affections, the heart.[15]

However cloudy the concept and insubstantial the logic, the notion of the moral agency of childhood opened a wedge into Calvinism, through which parents could actively enter into the salvation
of their children. Armed with this doctrine, parents and parsons
could begin, and begin early, to secure the promises of the Abrahamic covenant. The Reverend Joshua Leonard offered the parents

of Oneida County a model of the new Christian socialization in his sermon to children published in 1808. Leonard assured his young listeners that "there are numberless pleasing instances, of children and youth of the church, whose hearts, under the pious instructions, and in answer to the effectual prayers of faithful parents, have been quickly ripened for heaven; and made thoroughly to confide in their Father's will; resigning the world not with submission only, but with pleasure." Fifteen years later, in 1823, the *Utica Christian Repository* printed a sermon that translated Leonard's ad hoc strategies for converting children into a new formulation of the relationship between the child and the church. The anonymous author offered children a secure and comfortable, indeed, almost an honored and superior, place in the Christian community. "The truths of religion which are necessary to be known to enable the soul to fix its affection on God, are so simple, so evident and so impressive, that we cannot deem them above the capacity of childhood; and there is on the contrary a less perverted state of the feelings to obstruct the acquirement of this necessary elementary knowledge in childhood than in maturer years." As the author approached close to the doctrine of infant innocence, he glimpsed the possibility of infant salvation. Ever so cautiously, he questioned the belief that "the conversion and piety of children except in very extraordinary cases was not to be expected until they arrived at the years of discretion."[16]

The Oneida County theologians had arrived at an auspicious point in the history of religion and of child psychology. They now entertained optimism about the salvation of the second generation, happy prospects that grew from the wholesome feelings of the young, rather than from the will of the Almighty. The ministry and the publishing arm of the First Presbyterian Society of Whitestown had found a means of concertedly and swiftly linking their children to their own church and the lineage of Abraham.

The religious press was more conservative about the secular aspects of childrearing, the practical matters of parental discipline, moral education, and character formation. The *Utica Christian Magazine* reprinted a Connecticut treatise, for example, which excoriated "the fashion of the times to be lenient, loose, licentious . . . out of mere *parental affection.*" This writer preferred the traditions of the seventeenth century. He reminded the Christian father that "*his* offspring, *his* darlings, are naturally perverse; that they are by nature just as bad as the children of other people; that they are possessed of the same natural temper, have the same malignant passions." With such a vision of the child's nature, parents had no recourse other than the method of discipline employed by their ancestors: "Let every parent make it his inflexible determination that he will be obeyed – *invariably* obeyed." This was little more than a reiteration of that childrearing method favored in seventeenth-century Plymouth Colony, will-breaking. This ancient childrearing regimen was still recommended to the readers of the *Western Recorder* in 1824. In an essay originating in England, lifted from a Massachusetts publication and sent into the Western District of New York by Merrill and Seward, a pious couple described the ideal method of managing children as follows: "Our will, when once announced, was the law of the house . . . We demanded an entire acquiescence in our determination whether he saw its reasonableness or not." As in the seventeenth century, this test of wills occurred at age two and left the parents victorious. This doctrine was modulated by only the most cautious praise for the use of reason and restraint of the rod. In the secular relations of parents and child, authority rather than affection still reigned supreme. Those relations were still perceived, furthermore, as elements of a patriarchal family order. In the pages of the Presbyterian, Methodist, and Baptist press, it was fathers rather than mothers who exercised supreme authority and responsibility in the education of children.[17]

Local publishers upheld this traditional hierarchy of the sexes in every aspect of family and public life. On the New York frontier, however, there were some temptations for women, like youth, to step out of their assigned place in the patriarchal order. The first minister of the Whitestown Society sounded the alert on this issue in 1808. The Reverend James Carnahan trumpeted his ire at the approach of a woman named Martha Howell, an itinerant Baptist, who had been testifying to her sect's doctrines throughout the Western District. According to Carnahan, certain churches in the neighborhood of Whitestown had even allowed her to mount the pulpit to discourse on the subject of baptism. Carnaham invoked the standard scriptural condemnation of such behavior: "She contradicts the apostle Paul who says: I suffer not a woman to teacher; but to be silent." James Carnahan unleashed the most belligerent rhetoric against the denominational rivals who sponsored this offense. "The leaders of this party are those who go bawling through our streets – baptism! baptism! baptism! in our way, or no salvation!" Carnahan's charge against the Baptists was spiced with images of sexual license: "They suffer that woman Jezebel which called herself a prophetess, to teach and to seduce the servants of the Lord." From the alarmed perspective of the leader of the Presbyterian flock in Whitestown, the Baptists were unleashing the unsavory powers of Eve and sponsoring independence among women as well as children.[18]

The details of Martha Howell's travels through Whitestown have been lost to history, but other fragments of evidence testify to such aggressive female religiosity. A short, crudely printed pamphlet entitled "A Scriptural Vindication of Female Preaching, Prophesying and Exhortation" dates from this period. The author announced herself as "Deborah Pierce of Paris, Oneida County, New York," a village just south and west of Whitestown. Deborah Pierce called upon the members of her sex to publicize their religious beliefs in no uncertain terms: "Rise up ye careless daughters, for many, many days shall ye be troubled, for ye have not harkened to the voice of God yourself."[19] It would appear that the openness of the frontier combined with the democratic tendencies of the Baptist faith had threatened to sunder the sexual hierarchy of the covenanted community. Not only did local Baptists follow female preaching, according to Carnahan, they also permitted women to participate in the church discipline, to usurp the role of the household head in the public jurisdiction of church government.

Once again a nervous Presbyterian imagination had exaggerated the extent of this subversion of the patriarchal system. The Baptists denied Carnahan's charges in the case of Martha Howell. In their estimation she had only spoken of her own personal religious experience, testifying to her own faith, "presuming neither to preach nor to teach." "Were she to attempt to teach in public," they went on, "we should immediately interpose; she has, however, no inclination for any such thing." Likewise, on the score of women's participation in church discipline, the Reverend Elias Lee described Baptist policy as "a majority of the brethren present shall perform the business and the sisters are consulted only to avoid grieving them immeasurably." A partial admission of special deference to women is imbedded in this statement, but neither were the Presbyterians immune to such charges. The Baptist rebuttal to the attack on Martha Howell threw Carnahan's charges back on his own congregation: "What is the propriety of your complaining of us, for admitting her into Christian pulpits, to relate the dealing of God with her, as above mentioned; when but a few months ago, a woman, a professed teacher of divinity, was admitted into your meeting houses, for the express purpose of fulfilling her mission."[20] Carnahan's rejoinder was merely to say that this anonymous woman spoke from the body of the church rather than the pulpit, a technicality that did not impress the Baptists. Still, both sects wished to dispel the impression that they in any way condoned female usurpation of male religious authority.

Closer examination of the exhortation of Deborah Pierce reveals the limits of her subversion, as well. She addressed herself to the male heads of households in an assertive but deferential manner, arguing that the blanket prohibition of female preaching would only lead to the weakening of male authority. On the other hand, Pierce advised the local ministry, "if you would follow the Lord yourself, and charge your family to follow you as you follow Christ, and fear God more than man, you would be more united in serving God, and the woman would more willingly obey, love, and fear you; and you would live together as the heirs of the grace of life."[21] In the promise of wifely obedience, of fear as well as love for the head of the household, Deborah Pierce subscribed to the sexual hierarchy of a little commonwealth. In the hope of "living together as heirs of grace" she endorsed the spiritual equivalent of a generational and corporate family. Once again the Baptists hesitated to translate their religious radicalism into familial and social terms. The Methodists also kept within the bounds of the patriarchal household: Their publications consistently downplayed and apologized for the heritage of assertive women that could be found in the English Wesleyan tradition and in the history of the sect in America.[22]

Nonetheless, cracks in the foundation of religious patriarchy were clearly visible and particularly alarming to the Presbyterian church fathers. Accordingly, some elaboration or modification of the pastoral position on the relations of the sexes was in order. Hence, a few minor adjustments in the doctrine of patriarchy were recognized in a pamphlet issued by the Utica Tract Society (largely a Presbyterian operation) in 1823. Entitled "Female Influence," this tract articulated what would become a central ideological tenet of nineteenth-century womanhood. Although the author fortified the public sphere against the intrusion of females and denied women the right even to "lead the devotions of the church," he at the same time invited the second sex to play an expansive social role. "That females are capable of exerting great and happy influences in the world cannot be doubted by any. And all who have a favorable view of the sex must see that influence preserved from diminution, and directed in its proper channels." The language here was precise and apt. Female influence operated not in a circumscribed sphere but as a network of "channels" through the local community. Woman's domain was not exclusively her own fireside but extended to all "familiar conversation" and along the many informal social avenues that lined the borders of the public sphere. A woman had the right to "unrestrained intercourse with Christian friends in both circles," that is, in both the household and the church community. At the same time she was permitted to teach her children and domestics, instruct her own sex in private, and collect alms in the wider private circles. To lead prayer in promiscuous circles outside her own home was, however, still strictly forbidden a female member of the Presbyterian Church.[23]

In itself, this codification of woman's place was not particularly novel. Rather, it was the heightened degree of influence attributed to women within it that is significant. As long as they acted through persuasion rather than authority, women were promised extensive power, particularly over children, and even over patriarchs. "And who can so successfully wield the instrument of influence than women. By force of persuasion, how often has woman prevailed, especially when accompanied by submission and entreaty, where strength and courage and boldness would have accomplished nothing . . . A sensible woman who keeps her proper place, and knows how to avail herself of her own powers, may exert, in her own sphere, almost any degree of influence that she pleases."[24] The Presbyterian faction had been moved to recognize some legitimate expansion of women's power but only outside the public sphere and even then in an almost covert and wily fashion. This prescient statement of the concept of female influence, like the interest in the Christian education of children, was the subject of essays in the press of each major Protestant denomination, Presbyterian, Methodist, and Baptist alike.

When these sects finally made their peace, however, it would be on a battleground strewn with such doctrinal casualties as the Abrahamic covenant, will-breaking, and patriarchal authority. The mild concessions to Christian education and female influence would not be sufficient to calm the troubled churches and households of Oneida County. The theological controversies of the second and third decades of the nineteenth century derived their special virulence from the social and familial dislocations that accompanied the closing of the frontier and the encroachment of market capitalism. It would take major ideological changes and a full-scale social movement to resolve them. This societal transformation is written into the historical record as the Second Great Awakening.

The demography of the Second Great Awakening

A glance through the membership lists of the evangelical churches of Oneida County reveals that this epochal upsurge in religious conversions began in the winter of 1813–14. It was at about the same time that the Reverend John Frost toured the vicinity of Whitestown and Utica inquiring about the state of local souls. His report provides a graphic portrait, a kind of spiritual demography, of the popular concerns that gave rise to the Second Great Awakening. When Frost made his pastoral rounds between 1813 and 1816, Presbyterians maintained a religious plurality over large numbers of Baptists, a few Methodists, and an occasional Quaker, Universalist, or infidel. Most striking of all, however, was the number of lapsed Christians, baptized members of any denomination, who were not in the habit of either attending church or practicing religion at home. Almost half the households did not contain a single practicing member of a local church. Of the remainder, only 46% enrolled the entire family, husband and wife and children, in some local demonination. The bulk of the remainder, 47% of the families of church members, were headed by women, who joined the congregation and often baptized their children without the sponsorship of the male head of the household (Table C.1).[25]

The Reverend John Frost's census of souls also revealed that this conspicuous absence of men in the churches of Oneida County was more than a matter of absentmindedness. It was accompanied by some genuine disenchantment with religious doctrines. The men Frost queried repeatedly gave vent to serious doubts about religious subjects and evinced a notable lack of deference to the pastor. A Mr. Kent, for example, made it known that "I have not settled my mind on religious subjects, not even on the immortality of the soul." Theodore Still had the most difficulty with the doctrine of original sin, which he could not "reconcile with our most common ideas of justice." His neighbor Mr. William Tracy expressed doubt on the subject of "atonement and free agency." Then he had the temerity to tell the minister, "I do not think it my duty to perform family prayer." The Reverend Mr. Frost's transcription of such dilute religious beliefs introduces a new dimension of local culture, one that is conspicuously absent in the publications of the local religious press. It would indicate that the Enlightenment had intercepted the passage of the New England way into New York State. Rationality, skepticism, a secular perspective, all projected a mentality that would subvert the Christian corporate community. It certainly did not seem conducive to a religious awakening.

An analysis of the response of women to Frost's interrogation reveals a completely different picture, however, and another prognostication. Mr. Kent's wife hardly shared his skepticism. She, like the majority of women, responded to the pastoral inquiries with a contrite and humble account of the state of her own soul and her prospects for salvation. "I have entertained some hope of several years; but my doubts are distressing." Similarly, the wife of the heretical Theodore Sill expressed "much anxiety on the subject and at times am very unhappy." Mrs. Tracy put it this way, again in direct contrast to her husband's response: "I am a poor creature. I have an increasing sense of the excellence of God's character." The women in the vicinity of the Whitestown Presbyterian Society not only accepted the terms of Frost's questions, and showed respect for his office, but also took the state of their own souls painfully seriously. The combination of humility, seriousness, and anxiety was taken to its extreme by a Miss Fowler who lived with a married sister and her family. "I am dead to the world, I have a long time felt that it cannot give me happiness. I have no object in view on Earth. I do not pray, I am good by selfishness, and I know that my prayers are not heard. I cannot go to meeting because that it will increase my condemnation. I would do anything I could to obtain salvation." The timidity and self-deprecation of other women was transcribed by Frost as "vile sinner," "poor guilty sinner," "afraid to hope."

These same women often expressed a sense of social isolation, the counterpart and contrast to the absorption with worldly concerns noted by their mates. Four women acknowledged that they were unable to attend meetings because they had young children to care for. Others lacked the clothes, shoes, or transportation to get them to church. Mrs. Hunston's neglect of public worship was excused simply enough: "She has not clothes decent to wear. She has no bonnet." Other women felt chilling isolation in the private relations: One noted pathetically, "Nobody visits me here"; another, "Nobody talks to me at meeting." At other times the religious anxieties of Frost's female respondents festered in the most desolate privacy. Sally Edmond confessed, "I do not go to meeting. I try to worship God in secret," and Widow Slater humbly acknowledged,

"I entertain some hope. I cannot read. I am unworthy. I am most of the time in the cellar. I endeavor to bring my children for the Lord. My children read to me." In other cases this isolation and self-abasement was exacerbated by subjection to tyrannical patriarchs. Mrs. Rebecca Leach, a baptized Presbyterian who retained "some hope" of salvation, went infrequently to meeting. Her husband, she said, was "unwilling . . . I shall unite with a church. I maintain secret prayer."

It was these timid and isolated women who formed the fragile backbone of the Whitestown Presbyterian Society. Prior to 1814, 70% of those admitted to full communion in the society were females. Male ministers might sermonize about family prayer and the Abrahamic covenant; male elders might sit at the church trials in stern judgment over family abuses; and male printers and publishers might address their pamphlets and magazines to patriarchs; but it was women who flocked into the local churches. It was women, furthermore, who most often forged the feeble generational links in the church corporation. According to Frost's church census, twenty solitary women, as opposed to only one man unaccompanied by his wife, brought their children before the church for baptism. In sum, on the eve of the revival cycle in Whitestown, it was women who were most receptive to the admonitions of the evangelical clergy, who were most eagerly awaiting salvation, and who were most concerned with the Christian education of their young offspring.

Contemporary observers of the revivals all concurred in the estimation that women and youth, and not household heads, constituted the majority of converts. There was considerable debate, however, over the nature, relationship, and legitimacy of their awakening to grace. Young men or women could enter a revival church as the grateful beneficiaries of the Abrahamic covenant, humbly taking up the religious standard bequeathed to them by their fathers, or they could be entering the church in audacious willfulness, inspired with a pious superiority to their own parents. Women, for their part, could be either obeisant and submissive recipients of Almighty grace or inspired to the aggressive religiosity of a Deborah Pierce. Children could rebel against patriarchy or succumb to women's influence, obey their fathers or desert their mothers, all in the same act of conversion. They could mount the anxious bench independently of family ties entirely. Every one of these interpretations found adherents among Oneida County observers.

The Presbyterian Church, the center of the Oneida County revivals for all denominations, was itself divided on the question, particularly after Finney's appearance. In 1826 the Reverend John Frost co-authored "A Narrative of the Revival of Religion in the County of Oneida," which put the most sanguine construction on the sex and age characteristics of the converts. According to Frost's calculations, Utica and Whitestown converts included a goodly sum of household heads, but the majority of the subjects were "among the younger class of society." In Frost's estimation these young converts behaved in an orderly and submissive manner. He observed that many had been the beneficiaries of baptism in their youth and that the parents of others had renewed their vows to catechize children and exercise family prayer. Frost also acknowledged some shift in the pattern of relations by age and sex during the course of the revival, namely, the formation of segregated circles of youth and women for the purpose of private prayer and education. These bodies were, in Frost's opinion, entirely decorous and legitimate. He even sponsored a resolution before the Oneida Presbytery allowing women to speak their conversion in public meetings.[26]

Other segments of the community were not as hospitable to these new methods. A pastoral letter was issued in 1827 by the Oneida Association, a group of Presbyterian ministers vehemently hostile to revivals and fearful of their familial consequences. Where Frost saw an orderly increment in the church membership, these ministers observed "disregard of the distinctions of age or station." They were appalled by the practice of "allowing anybody and everybody to speak and pray in promiscuous meetings as they felt disposed." The Oneida Association assembled evidence for each charge. They found "such language as this in the mouths of young men and boys, 'you old grey headed sinner, you deserved to have been in hell long ago,' – 'This old hypocrite' – 'That old apostate' – 'that grey headed sinner, who is leading souls to hell' – 'That old veteran servant of the devil' – and the like." Apparently adult female converts were not quite so impudent in their language, but after all women were not expected to utter a word in church and had to be reminded that "God has not made it their duty to lead, but to be in silence." Criticism like this came from the more conservative members of Baptist, Presbyterian, and Methodist churches.[27]

The revivals were also the object of criticism in more liberal quarters. Utica supported a small Universalist congregation, which boasted its own periodical published by one Dolphus Skinner. Skinner issued his first publication, *Utica Magazine*, in 1827 in direct response to Finney's tour of Oneida County. This publication and its immediate successor, the *Evangelical Magazine and Gospel Advocate*, conducted a systematic campaign to expose the Presbyterian faction, condemn revivalism, and propagate the opposing principles of "Free Inquiry, Religious Liberty and Intelligence." Skinner's accounts of the revivals were also laden with references to the age and sex of the converts. He described an "animal excitement" that engaged "some men but many more women and children." A few years later Skinner reviled the converts in the awakening at the Reverend Mr. Lansing's Presbyterian Church as "a few weakminded and ignorant females." He characterized the Methodist Camp Meeting of 1831 in a similar fashion. Although he did not observe a single adult male in the throes of a conversion, he noted that the females often approached the anxious seat with their children in tow. This procession followed upon the evangelist's exhortation: "Here comes mother; children your mother has come to seek religion. Now is the time to come along with your mother." According to the *Evangelical Magazine and Gospel Advocate*, the revivalists were manipulating ignorant women and children for sectarian purposes. Skinner had introduced a new interpretation of the lineage of conversions: Rather than destroying family ties, revivals wielded them in a novel and wily fashion, trapping large numbers of converts in a net of associations between women and children.[28]

In order to judge the accuracy of any one of these conflicting interpretations of the revivals, one needs to identify the actual membership of evangelical churches. Four church registries, three Presbyterian and one Baptist, survive to provide bits and pieces of empirical evidence about the convert population of Utica and Whitestown. All four concur, first of all, in charting an extended chronology of revivalism. New admissions to all the churches clustered in a similar lengthy pattern, which peaked in the years 1814, 1819, 1830–32, and 1838. Revivalism should be examined, then, not as the spontaneous outburst associated with Finney's arrival in the mid-1820s but as part of this undulating wave of evangelical fervor.[29]

A cursory analysis of these church records confirms the observation that revivalism was particularly popular among women. The distribution of Christian names within this population indicates that women were the simple majority during each revival and at every church. The proportion of female converts ranged from a low of approximately 52% in the Whitestown Baptist revival of 1814 to a high of almost 72% in that church's Awakening of 1838. Although the proportion of females in the revivals was in excess of their presence in the population of the township, it was slightly lower than their proportion of overall church membership. The preponderance of women also varied slightly over time, tending to decline in the middle of the revival cycle. Slowly, and at a rather minuscule rate, the sequence of revivals actually increased the representation of men in the church (Table C.2).

The male converts were rarely, however, heads of households. Although household heads and employed men above the age of seventeen were listed in the *Utica City Directory*, less than one-quarter of the male converts could be located in volumes of the directory issued within two years of each revival. Those converts who could be identified, furthermore, seldom headed their own households. Boarders constituted 65% of the male converts who could be located in the directory at all. The title "boarder" suggests youth, singleness, and deracination from the parental family. The majority of female converts probably resembled the males in age and marital status. Of the female converts at the Utica Presbyterian Church, 60% appeared in neither the marriage records nor as parents of newly baptized children. A substantial proportion of the converts of both sexes were young and mobile as well, according to the church records. Of the new church members, 30% requested official letters of dismissal within five years of their conversion. Countless others must have left the church more hastily and without this formality. Many of those who exuberantly confessed their faith during the revivals probably left for parts unknown even before their names could be inscribed on church ledgers. Women registered their intention of leaving the church less frequently than men, yet one-quarter of the female converts also requested letters of dismissal within five years. It is safe to make this single conclusion about the silent majority of converts: They were largely young and, in the short term at least, a peripatetic lot with fragile roots in church and community (Table C.3). This far it would seem that the Second Great Awakening expressed the waxing religious enthusiasm of a second generation, recently uprooted from their frontier families.

This is not to say, however, that these young, mobile converts acted alone and independently of parents and kin. Common surnames are, in fact, laced throughout the records of Oneida County revivals. Depending on which church or which revival year is considered, from 17% to 54% of the converts apparently professed their faith in the company of relatives (Table C.4). There is also reason to believe that females played a leading role in the kinship organization of revivals. The records of the Whitestown Presbyterian Society, for example, reveal that almost 30% of all converts had been preceded into the church by relatives, most of whom were females. Of these converts, 61% were preceded into the church by a solitary woman, 24% by relatives of both sexes, and only 15% by solitary men (Table C.5). In sum, the disproportionate tendency of men to enter the church accompanied, or preceded, by females might mean that Dolphus Skinner was onto something: That women cajoled, manipulated, or simply led their children into the evangelical sects.

Only precise evidence of kinship, confirmed by vital records, can provide a valid test of this hypothesis. Such records are very hard to find in Whitestown and Utica. The only religious body that recorded demographic events in sufficient detail and completeness was the First Presbyterian Church of Utica. Yet even here, within one of the most stable institutions of the community, only a minority of church members ever registered a birth, marriage, or death. Only 1 in 3 revival converts left any vital records, and these most often document a single event in the life cycle, a lone marriage, a baptism, or a child's christening. These records provide only a faint, suggestive track through the history of family and religion. Nonetheless, this documented minority commands attention, both as the historian's last resort and because of its more durable ties to the church and consequent capacity to affect the course of evangelism itself.

This narrower, but more detailed and accurate, analysis of the kin ties that surrounded conversion reveals a pattern not unlike the stages of the individual family cycle. The revival of 1813, for example, coincided with Sophia Clarke's entry into Utica's newly founded First Presbyterian Church. At the end of the revival cycle in 1838 her youngest child, then approaching adulthood, joined the same religious community. During the same period Sophia Clarke saw the village of Utica and the benevolent organizations she founded grow ever more dense and complicated as they expanded to occupy a whole regional marketplace. The minute examination of evangelism within Sophia Clarke's congregation exposes the structures of family, economy, and society that intersected at this religious nucleus of the region and gave a multifaceted meaning to the Second Great Awakening.

The revival cycle began in Utica with the conversion of the parents of young children. Although less than half of those men and women who professed their faith during the 1814 revival left any trace in the vital records, 65% of these (or 43% of all converts) were married. Almost 1 in 4 of them baptized an infant child within a year of their conversion. In addition, more than a dozen older children were promptly brought forward to be christened by a newly converted parent (Table C.6). The revival of 1814 offered direct testimony to a strong commitment to the Abrahamic convenant on the part of Utica's first generation. Coinciding with the highest birth and marriage rates in the history of the First Presbyterian Church, it planted the religious roots of many young families along the banks of the Mohawk.

The first revival also exhibited a relatively high degree of patriarchal sanction. Twelve of the sixty-four converts were accompanied into the state of grace by their spouses. The ministers were proud of pointing to the relatively large number of male household heads who assumed full church membership during this revival. The names of at least nine married men were inscribed on the church records in that revival season. Some of them represented the pinnacle of the societal as well as the familial hierarchy. Almost half the converts who could be identified in the *City Directory* were members of elite commercial families. The first revival witnessed the wholesale conversion of the Van Rensselaer family, scions of the colonial New York aristocracy. The prominent export merchants James and Jeremiah Van Rensselaer entered the church in 1814 along with their wives, Susan and Adeline, and sister Cornelia. Phoebe Stocking, the wife of a wealthy hat merchant and manufacturer, joined the church at the same time, as did Harriet Dana, consort of another substantial Genesee Street merchant. Lawyers and their wives and daughters were also conspicuously present in the front ranks of the revival cycle, constituting 16% of the converts and including members of prominent Federalist families, the Breeses, Ostrums, and Walkers. The publishing arm of the Presbyterian faction also pledged allegiance to evangelism in 1814. Horace Camp and Asahel Seward experienced saving grace at that time, and the Merrill family was represented among the converts by Bildad, Jr., and his mother, Nancy Camp Merrill. A fourth Presbyterian printer, Charles Hastings, would be converted in the revival of 1819.

It was in the later revival that the less prestigious and wealthy, but nonetheless respectable, families were gathered into the evangelical fold. In that year Utica's sturdy artisans and smaller shopkeepers advanced to salvation en masse. Only a handful of common laborers, however, are known to have joined the ranks of the converts in either revival season (Table C.7). The lower orders might have been more likely to join the Methodist and Baptist denominations. Yet these sects were not notably active during the early stages of the revival cycle. In sum, the revivals of the 1810s, the first decade in the history of Utica's Presbyterian Church, were conducted in conformity with the hierarchical social and family order; they enrolled the best families, often in corporate kin groups and accompanied by the head of the household. The only disappointment an old-light divine might have with these early revivals was the still meager, but growing, participation of male heads of households.

It was more often mothers than patriarchs who took the initiative in planting familial roots in the frontier church. Women certainly played a uniquely maternal role in the first revival: 12% of them were pregnant when they professed their faith. Mothers unaccompanied by their mates also accounted for the majority of the baptisms that followed in the wake of revivals in 1814 and 1819. A woman named Nancy Lynde exemplified this maternal fervor. Within two years of her own conversion in the 1814 revival, she had given six children to the Lord in baptism. The church records referred to the children's father, who was not a member of the congregation, by the truncated title Mr. Lynde. No family by that name appeared in the village directory of 1817. Yet in some later revival, perhaps somewhere to the west, the children whom Nancy Lynde baptized in Utica's first awakening may have fulfilled the Abrahamic covenant and entered another evangelical church.

The women behind the revival

The role of women in the inauguration of the revival cycle was actually more extensive than the roster of church members, contemporary observers, or historians have acknowledged. It was in the midst of the first revival that the Whitestown Female Charitable Society changed its name to the Oneida Female Missionary Society and began to sponsor the frontier ministry. More than half the female converts of 1814 would ultimately be found on the membership lists of this earliest evangelical organization. Another thirteen members converted five years later (Table C.8). These women were something more than passive converts, emissaries of their pastors, or private guardians of the Abrahamic covenant. They had created the organizational underpinning of the revivals that would follow. By 1817 they reported a success in the expansion of the frontier missions that "exceeds the highest expectations." By 1824 their reach extended beyond Oneida County. Renamed again as the Female Missionary Society of the Western District, they spawned seventy auxiliaries and contributed more than $1,000 annually to support dozens of missionaries.[30] These women orchestrated the revival and devised a sphere for women that had not been anticipated, either by the partisans of female influence or the castigators of female preaching.

The organizational and financial sophistication of this women's group invites comparison with the trading networks and political parties of Utica's merchant capitalists. Throughout their history the members of the Female Missionary Society elected presidents, vice-presidents, and trustees, met in formal annual meetings, and kept meticulous accounts, much in the manner of astute and conservative businessmen. The ties between Female Missionary Society members and male merchants were actually far more substantial than mere analogies between their modes of organizing. In fact, 31% of the members were married to substantial merchants like the Van Rensselaers, the Stockings, the Danas, and the Doolittles, who conducted a regionwide trade in agricultural commodities. The officers of the society had mates in the city corporation, on the boards of directors of banks and cotton factories, and at the helm of the Federalist party. Attorneys' wives made up 33% of the membership of the Female Missionary Society, and the perennial officers drawn from their ranks, Ann Breese and Sophia Clarke, continued their reigns long into widowhood. By contrast, smaller numbers of the wives of petty artisans and shopkeepers, majority occupations in Utica at that time, enrolled in the Female Missionary Society (Table C.9). It would appear that involvement in the organization of the missionary enterprise was characteristic of the sexual division of labor within Utica's more prominent merchant and professional families. By joining the Female Missionary Society women of the upper class publicly assumed the moral and religious responsibilities of their mercantile households and a major role in social reproduction. By efficiently and successfully fulfilling such social obligations, these women undoubtedly enhanced the elite status of their mates and added cultural and religious reinforcement to the male links in the local trade networks.

At the same time, these women's groups engineered a considerable expansion of woman's social role in a sphere that was organizationally independent of the male head of the household. Although not within the established centers of public power, their self-cre-

ated societies and offices commanded considerable notice in the
press and the community. Their formative contributions to revivalism and their innovative participation in the reorganization of sex
roles raises some perplexing historical questions.

One social characteristic of these women, in addition to their position in the Utica class structure, offers an especially important
clue to the social-historical origins of their activities. Analysis of the
City Directory reveals that almost 80% of the identifiable members
of the Female Missionary Society were married to men who maintained a business address that was detached from their place of residence. The comparable figure was 69% for merchants in general
and only 13% for the population at large. In other words, the members of the Female Missionary Society had been physically removed
from the corporate family economy well in advance of the mass of
the local population. These women were relieved from assisting in
the farming, artisan production, or sales that once took place within
the household workplace. Many of them were wealthy enough to
purchase household supplies in the shops on Genesee Street and to
employ servants to meet the domestic needs of husbands and children. It would follow that involvement in the benevolent activities
filled a vacuum recently opened in the everyday lives of urban upper-class women as the work of men was removed to the shops,
stores, and offices of Genesee Street. Or, to put it another way,
missionary societies might constitute one mode of exercising that
modicum of freedom that fell to women upon the disintegration of
the patriarchal home economy. The relative openness of the newly
settled community enhanced these opportunities to experiment
with such new roles, free from the scrutiny of entrenched authorities and without competition from long-established institutions.

The alternative roles that members of the Female Missionary Society designed for themselves were more social than domestic. The
primary interest was the financial and institutional support of missionaries; collecting and dispensing money, organizing auxiliaries,
issuing pamphlets, electing officers, were their forte. They set out
on an evangelical mission throughout the Western District and
through Utica's social ranks, not just within their own families.
This relatively impersonal approach to benevolence was typical of
the class, the period, the first stage of the revival cycle. The revival
of 1814 also gave birth to the first Sunday schools founded by the
teen-age daughters of the same mercantile and professional elite.
This junior partner of the Female Missionary Society also set out to
educate the children of the poor and the outcasts, rather than their

own brothers and sisters. Another recent convert, Eunice Camp, founded a school for the lowest rank of Uticans, black children. The founder of another school for the poor, Sophia Williams, incubated her benevolent enterprise in actual violation of maternal and domestic precepts. She came upon the humble objects of her charity while visiting a village outside Utica where she had placed her own infant with a wet-nurse.[31] All these by-products of the first revival tended to subordinate such personal interests to wider-ranging goals and a more highly rationalized and hierarchical mode of social organization.

The Female Missionary Society was at the same time very much atuned to the domestic concerns of the women of the Western District. When they petitioned for support in 1819 they used this rhetorical device as an entrée into the homes of Oneida County members: "Let us imagine a pious mother surrounded with a numerous family – none of them give evidence of possessing an interest in Christ. Without a public place of worship, and surrounded by vain amusements and unholy neighbors, the rural mother despairs of saving the souls of her children. When the itinerant minister is introduced into this sad picture by the Female Missionary Society, the mother's joy is too big for utterance; she manifests it by her tears. This is no picture of fancy. Our missionaries often witness such affecting scenes." The circulars of the Female Missionary society maintained regular communication with women in the more isolated frontier settlements. They were forever appealing to maternal anxiety about the salvation of children. The 1816 circular addressed the predicament of the pious frontier mother this way: "And when they sleep in dust, shall their children, who might become pillars in the temple of God, be abandoned to all the vices of the new settlement and *entail their examples to unborn generations*" (emphasis mine).[32] Such an oratorical ploy was calculated to strike a sensitive chord in the hearts of rural parents. It combined the ever-effective image of a dead mother with metaphorical allusions to generational ties and the process of land inheritance, hardly innocuous themes in the 1810s and 1820s.

Mothers enrolled in the auxiliaries of the Female Missionary Society sent back heartfelt messages of gratitude to the women of Utica: "We mutually look up to you as our parent society, both for information and direction." All along the network of the Female Missionary Society came "heartfelt communications, of hope, joy, and gratitude," always addressed to "beloved sisters." The society cherished the fact that a web of "mutual dependency exists be-

tween the units full force." This highly emotional interchange between the leadership of the Female Missionary Society and their
auxiliary members called forth a novel sequence of female responses and anxieties. It played upon a sense of religious intensity,
maternal concern, and social isolation among rural women, a state
of mind such as John Frost found on his tour of Whitestown's more
isolated households. The Female Missionary Society harnessed
these concerns and this energy to an evangelical purpose and
plowed a route of societies, churches, and conversions throughout
the Western District. Hundreds of women banded together in what
they considered "the greatest work in whch mortals are permitted
to engage, the salvation of immortal souls."[33]
From this and other sources came veiled instructions on how
these women might use their private powers to stir up saving
graces in the souls of kinsmen. These covert instructions are found
in the memoirs of the pious, which were a regular feature in the
evangelical magazines published in Utica. In this religious sphere
women outnumbered laymen and challenged clergymen for numerical domination. One plot line recurs over and over again in these
memoirs, almost as if the lives of women complied with a sentimental formula. The subject's heedless and happy youth was curtailed by a wrenching conversion experience, the premonition of
death, and a swift decline in health. Yet the young woman's influence grew apace with her final illness. Her deathbed became the
center of community and family attention, a kind of makeshift pulpit. One of the earliest examples of this literature was published by
Seward and Williams in 1814. The subject was Miss Huldah Baldwin,
an Episcopalian. At the time of her confirmation early in her teens
Huldah Baldwin forsook the secular delights of her youthful social
circle for the contemplation of the state of her soul. Her illness and
death followed quickly, almost as if it were a willful act of repen-
tence. At every turn in her frail health she gathered family and
friends to her bedside and ministered to their souls. The coup de
grace came on her deathbed with the following speech: "Oh beloved parent, my tender brothers, my affectionate sisters, my dear
friends, do you know how rending the thought that I may be separated from you through all eternity! O live not to the world but to
God. O live, O live for him that we may meet hereafter and enjoy a
blessed eternity together. If you have loved me; if you have loved
my company and still love it, live that you may enjoy it in
Heaven."[34]
Soon every denomination was publishing memoirs of this sort,

written either by a relative or the pastor of a pious young woman and often containing a few words or letter fragments from the deceased herself. *The Methodist Magazine* reached back into English history for the pious example of Mrs. Ursula Millward, whose deathbed oratory was prefaced by an invitation to "all the people in the town" to "come and see how a Christian can die." As the townspeople crowded around her bedside she admonished, "I fear you are on the way to destruction; you cannot be offended with me now, for I am dying." From closer to Utica, in the town of Norwich, comes the account of Eliza M. Hyde, who, being too feeble to attend church, gathered the "people of God to meet at her father's house" where, at age nineteen, she delivered similar caveats to endangered Christians. Other young women acquired a ghostly deathbed right to preach in the church itself by composing their own funeral sermons. Such death was no stranger to fiction: Emily Chubbuck drew on a stock of such personal experiences both during her conversion and in the course of her literary career. Her own sister Lavinia died according to the religious-sentimental formula to which Emily Chubbuck added one particularly maudlin garnish: She portrayed the dying Lavinia pathetically sewing funeral clothes for her young sisters. By 1825 the religious press was beginning to articulate the moral of these stories and to recommend it as a device to foster conversion. In that year the *Western Recorder* gratuitously reported the case of a mother whose saintly death led to the salvation of seven children.[35] This extraordinary measure would hardly become a popular conversion technique; few women chose to die in order to convert their kinsmen and neighbors. These deathbed scenes were, however, hyperbolic symbols of a new species of woman's influence, the right to hold forth on religious subjects from a position of apparent weakness and to wield the emotional persuasiveness that accompanied these pathetic scenes.

Early in the 1820s all these variations on the relationships between women and youth, mothers and children, began to percolate very close to the surface of religious history. They began to assume an organized, pseudopublic form. The session records of the Presbyterian Church for 1822 reported that meetings were under way among "pious females for prayer and religious conversation" and young men met "for religious conference and exercise and improvement." A few weeks later they noted: "An awakening is evidently going on among the female members of our church." In 1824 the Female Missionary Society observed that "it is true that no very general and extensive revivals are stated to have taken place . . . , but the still, small voice has gone forth, and in the ears of many, in different places we have reasons to hope, been heard and regarded." As Finney's tour was imminent, the Presbyterian pastor reported: "Christian mothers meet accompanied by their little children that they might in united prayer commend them to God and implore for their regenerating grace."[36] This last instance of evangelical organization was not as vague and casual as the pastoral observer implied. The minister of Utica's First Presbyterian Church was referring to tightly organized bodies of women who called themselves maternal associations and met bimonthly in compliance with the dictates of a formal constitution. Maternal associations, founded at the First Presbyterian Church in Utica in 1824 and in the Baptist congregation shortly thereafter, were the final fruition of a decade of cogitation about the religious bonds between mothers and children.

Again this organization had its New England precursor. The first maternal association, established in Portland, Maine, in 1815, was, however, almost stillborn on the New England frontier. When the Utica organizations were formed they were the first outside New England and arose almost simultaneously with the inaugural associations of Massachusetts and Connecticut. The constitution of the Presbyterian Maternal Association, adopted on June 30, 1824, had the following prologue: "Deeply impressed with the great importance of bringing up our children in the nurture and admonition of the Lord, we the subscribers agree to associate for the purpose of devising and adopting such measures as may seem best calculated to assist us in the right performance of these duties." From this premise the assembled women undertook an intensive campaign to save the souls of their children. The articles of the Maternal Association's constitution pledged each member to perform an elaborate set of religious and parental duties. These included: praying for each child daily, attending meetings semimonthly, renewing each child's baptismal covenant regularly, reading systematically through the literature on the Christian education of children, setting a pious example to children at all times, and spending each child's birthday in prayer and fasting. These women, unlike the Female Missionary Society, assiduously focused on the salvation of their own progeny. Their annual reports featured an exact accounting of the number of conversions among the children of members.[37]

The tenor of organization within the Maternal Association contrasted decidedly with that of the Female Missionary Society. Rather than a complicated system of officers and a wide network of

influence, the assembled mothers practiced the cooperative interchange espoused in article six of the association's charter. It simply
stipulated that each mother should "suggest to her sister members
such hints as her own experience may furnish, or circumstances
seem to render necessary." The personal bonds among members
were a prime concern, a major solace. The Maternal Association
reports tearfully announced deaths among the members or jubi-
lantly exclaimed that their loving band remained intact for another
year. They pledged themselves to rear the children of any deceased
sister. In sum, the Maternal Association was a neighborly grouping
of peers, which operated snugly within women's private but social
channels. It resembled a frontier anxiliary of the Female Missionary
Society more than the parent organization located in Utica.

These two organizations, the Female Missionary Society and the
Maternal Association, recruited members from two distinct populations of women. Only six women belonged to both groups and thus
spanned the two short generations of women's religious benevolence. These six were all representatives of the pioneer generation
in Utica, converted before 1820, and members of lawyer families. At
their center was the ubiquitous Sophia Clarke. Professional families were, however, poorly represented in the general membership
of the association. In fact, they were outnumbered more than two to
one by the wives of artisans, who assumed the dominant position
maintained by merchants' wives in the Missionary Society. The
class composition of the Maternal Associaiton better reflected the
actual social structure of Utica as of 1825, when more small manufacturers and shopkeepers joined the large wholesale merchants
who had originally settled along the commercial artery of Genesee
Street. It was in the Maternal Association, furthermore, that the
wives of the artisan aristocrats, the printer-publishers, congregated. The Presbyterian Maternal Association was full of printers'
wives. The Mmes. Thomas and Charles Hastings were founders.
No less than four Merrills as well as Martha Seward were also found
in the ranks of the organization. Wives of clockmakers, shoemakers, bakers, and blacksmiths joined the congregation of
mothers, making it an institutional expression of the old middle
class. Most of these skilled mechanics operated their own small
units of production and exchange, which employed only a few apprentices and kinsmen (Table C.9).

The family tensions endemic to this class have already been illustrated in the case of the Merrills. Julia Merrill, but not her quarrel-
some mother-in-law, was a member of the Maternal Association.

Julia had found that the difficulties of maintaining a three-generation artisan household could interfere with the Christian care of her
progeny. During the church trial of her mother-in-law, Julia Merrill
lamented that "my little children have often asked why Gramma
talks to me so and asked why mama cried so."[38] Such a difficult
atmosphere was not the recommended environment for the Christian education of children. It might, however, have been quite commonplace among the mistresses of artisan households, so many of
whom lived in or near their husbands' workshops. The members of
the Maternal Association were far more likely to be conducting
their household tasks in the company of workingmen, husbands,
sons, apprentices, than were the members of the Female Missionary Society. Only 35% of them (as opposed to 80% of the members
of the earlier women's organization) had husbands who listed a
separate business address. Their maternal roles were still performed amid the bustle, crowding, and din of the home economy.
These were not the best conditions in which to maintain vigilant,
undistracted watch over a child's soul. The literature of the Maternal Association repeatedly lamented the difficulty of fulfilling maternal duties along with all the "arduous responsibilities" of ordering the household. Understandably, the busy mistresses of artisan
households craved the more cooperative, mutually helpful style of
organization that was the Maternal Association. They had little
time to promote the salvation of souls in the remote regions of the
Western District.

Despite such obstacles, however, it was largely these women of
the middling sort who converted the relationships between
mothers and children into the building blocks of evangelism. It was
these women who knit together the sermons of the Abrahamic covenant, the essays on Christian education, and the suggestions of
female memoirs into a practical regimen for converting children.
Their collective construction of this bridge between the history of
women, the family, and religion was accomplished under the extraordinary conditions of Utica, New York, in the 1820s. The Maternal Association was founded just as the construction of the Erie
Canal was completed in Utica and continued on to Rochester, doubling the city's population and proliferating grog shops, boardinghouses, and brothels in the process. The cracks in the family
economy and fissures in the lineage of grace were particularly
threatening to those artisans and small shopkeepers who still attempted to practice the techniques of a generationally extended
family amid all the individualizing forces of a rowdy commercial

city. The steady influx of youth and the appearance of boarding as a prevalent style of residence must have generated special anxiety about adolescent sons and daughters. The wills of the period evidenced the shaky prospects of providing for the second generation of artisans. Artisan printers were capable of expressing these concerns through their presses. Their wives turned to the only power base they commanded: the personal and moral surveillance of their children during the early years of life before they were surrendered to their father's shop, the boardinghouse, or the new frontier. From their position as mothers they attempted valiantly to shore up the Abrahamic covenant and coincidentally set the stage for Charles Finney's arrival in Oneida County.

Financed by the Female Missionary Society, Finney had been generating modest revivals in the northern regions of Oneida County when he traveled on to Utica in the winter of 1825–26. His initial stop was the First Presbyterian Church where he inquired about the local religious atmosphere. The Reverend Samuel Aiken, the shepherd of a flock that included the Merrills, Clarkes, and the Hastings, recounted this telling incident to Finney: "One of his principal women had been so deeply exercised in her soul about the state of the church and of the ungodly in that city that she had prayed for two days and nights almost incessantly . . . when her strength was exhausted she could not endure the burden of her mind unless somebody was engaged in prayer with her, upon whose prayer she could lean." Finney put it aptly in his memoirs: "The work had already begun in her heart." From this inspired act of woman's influence, the revival took hold and proceeded to capture the heart of the commercial town. It proceeded out of the church and onto Genesee Street. Finney told of men who stopped for the night and stayed to be sanctified. Visitors to the city complained that one "could not go into a store but religion was intruded upon him and he could do no business." Even Bagg's Hotel, the center of the regional commercial network, was infested with religion, which enveloped the most stonehearted travelers and tradesmen.[39]

When Finney moved on to Whitestown, the birthplace of his wife, of the Female Missionary Society, and of the Presbyterian establishment of Oneida County, he catalyzed a revival of the industrial hub of the village. Again, it was a woman who lighted the first sparks. "As he entered the factory [Finney] looked solemnly at her and quite overcome she sunk down in tears. The impression caught on almost like powder, and in a few moments nearly all in the room were in tears. This feeling spread through the factory." When the Methodist evangelist the Reverend Mr. Giles arrived at New York Mills he met a similar reception. "Some of the younger class [were] grouped together in small companies, conversing and weeping in great distress of mind, being too much excited to perform their regular work." Benjamin Walcott stopped the machines to allow the revival to proceed among his young workers,[40] most of whom were female.

If these accounts are taken singly, it would seem that the outbreak of revivalism in 1825 occurred among the young of both sexes and was characterized by a sudden and intense emotional outburst to which women were particularly susceptible. The prior history of religion in Utica and Whitestown would suggest, however, that the contagion was not so spontaneous, that young converts were not as alone and deracinated as they seemed at first glance. It is just as reasonable to hypothesize that these young converts were the offspring of the first generation of church members, especially of mothers who had professed their own faith earlier in the revival cycle. Other converts might be sons or daughters of the rural members of the Female Missionary Society, recently displaced from the home economy by the waning of the frontier, who had migrated to the city or the mill town in search of employment. This uprooting and the uncertainty of a new environment might well foster the excited responses to Finney's exhortations. Nonetheless, the prayers, affections, and Christian rearing of evangelical mothers might well have accompanied many young men and women into the revival churches.

Unfortunately, the maternal links in the revival chain are rarely recorded in the fragmentary and far-flung records of the Second Great Awakening. But for Utica's First Presbyterian Church, at least, there is convincing evidence of a relationship between the family cycle and the revival seasons. Despite an increase in the proportion of mobile and migratory converts during and after the revival of 1825, more than 20% of the new communicants can be identified as the children of church members. Some of these very children had been presented for baptism in the full flush of their parents' conversions in 1814 or 1819. The revival of the 1820s and 1830s can be attributed, in part, to the echo effect of the high birth and baptism rates of the early nineteenth century. The children of the prolific first generation had come of age, grown in grace, and professed their faith in the church of their parents. To some extent, then, the family pattern of revivals was a reflection of the demographic history of the First Presbyterian Church (Table C.6).

Still, the family cycle is not a *sufficient* explanation for either revivalism or the conversion of the second generation. A long history of pastoral reminders of parental responsibility had preceded the entrance of the second generation into the church. These clerical directives were addressed specifically to male heads of households, however, and seem to have been unheeded. More than 68% of the converts affirmed the faith of their mothers but not their fathers. The later revivals brought some of Utica's mothers a pious sense of achievement when, after years of prayer and instruction, their children pledged their souls to Christ. Harriet Dana must have felt this satisfaction when her son John joined the ranks of the saved in 1826 and again in 1838 with the belated conversion of her son James Dwight (the famed natural scientist of Yale University). Mrs. Dana's own conversion had occurred in July 1814, at the zenith of Utica's first revival. She was most likely pregnant at the time; her son James was baptized the following September, his brother John two years thereafter. The religious biographies of eight more of Harriet Dana's children lie outside the purview of Utica's church records and beyond the time span of the revival cycle.

Another episode in the private revival of Harriet Dana, however, is worthy of note. In 1826 James Dana, Sr., officially joined the church of which his wife had been a member for a dozen years. This conjugal rendition of the kinship of conversion was not unusual. In the revival occasioned by Finney's appearance in Utica, for example, seven husbands took up full church membership several years after the conversion of their wives. This trend continued in the revivals that followed, much to the delight of the local ministry, ever eager to snare a head of household. One church history, written forty years after the event, recalled with special pride the conversion in 1838 of John H. Ostrom, lawyer, bank officer, and prominent Utica politician. The author failed to mention that Ostrom's wife, then the young Mary Walker and later "a principal woman" of the church and community, had converted in a revival that occurred almost a quarter of a century earlier.

Another example will illustrate the matrilineage that runs through the entire history of revivalism in the Utica Presbyterian Church. This story of domestic evangelism begins in 1814 with the conversion of Mrs. Sophia Bagg, who professed her faith on July 7, 1814, and helped to found the Oneida Female Missionary Society in the same year. Her daughter Emma was baptized the following September; the baptismal convenant was recited for her son Michael fourteen months later, and two more sons were christened before 1820. When Finney arrived in Utica, Sophia's daughter Emma, who was at least eleven years old, promptly entered the church. A Mary Ann Bagg who was examined for admission to the church at about the same time, whose baptism had not been recorded in the church records, may have been another of Sophia's daughters. At any rate, the family of Sophia Bagg figured prominently in the revival of 1826, for it was in that year that Moses Bagg, the hotelkeeper, a wealthy and respected son of one of Utica's very first entrepreneurs, joined his wife and children in full church membership. Moses Bagg was one of those "gentlemen of property and standing" who helped to organize Utica's anti-abolitionist riot in 1835. Even amid the uproar of the 1830s, however, the Bagg family continued quietly to play out the family cycle of revivals. Moses, Jr., ranked among the converts of 1831, and his brother Egbert enrolled in the church in 1838. The family of Sophia Bagg may be atypical only in social stability, public prominence, and consequent wealth of historical documentation. Perhaps countless anonymous women left a similar legacy of conversions across the frontier or in the poorly documented evangelical denominations, the Baptist and the Methodist.

Neither do the church records reveal the more extended kinship ties that underpinned the revival. Utica supplies one anecdote that illustrates this wider network of revivalism and at the same time suggests the modes of evangelism peculiar to women. The central female character in this religious homily generally appears in nineteenth-century church history under the name of "Aunt C." During the revival of 1825 and 1826 "Mrs. C." was visited by a nephew, a student at nearby Hamilton College. The nephew in question came from conservative Calvinist stock and looked with disdain upon the vulgar evangelist Charles Finney, a friend and temporary neighbor of his aunt. Thus "Mrs. C." resorted to a pious deception to entice her young kinsman to a revival meeting at the Utica Presbyterian Church. She convinced him to attend a morning service on the pretense that Finney would not be preaching until later in the day. Once in the church and in the presence of the despised preacher, the young man realized that he had been caught in a female trap. He recalled it this way: "When we came to the pew door [Aunt 'C.'] motioned me to go in and followed with several ladies and shut me in." When he attempted a second escape, the pious but wily aunt whispered in his ear, "You'll break my heart if you go!" Woman's role in the conversion that ensued would have remained forever unrecorded were it not that the convert in question was none other than Theodore Dwight Weld. The famed abolitionist's aunt turns out to be Sophia Clarke, whose many unheralded accomplishments included a founding membership in both the Female Missionary Society and the Maternal Association and the enrollment of at least three children among the revival converts.[41]

Women's role in the revivals was not confined to private, individual efforts like these. Rather, it was often conducted openly, in the quasi-public forums of the Female Missionary society and the Maternal Association. Despite the fragmentary records of these institutions, fully one-third of the converts, or their mothers, can be traced to one or the other organization. Harriet Dana, Mary Walker Ostrom, and Sophia Clarke, for example, were all members of the Female Missionary Society. Although the early awakenings enrolled the actual members of these organizations, the later stages of the revival cycle brought their children into the church. Eighteen of the converts of 1826 can be identified as children of the members of the Female Missionary Society and account for 15% of the conversions. That same revival brought saving grace to sixteen children (13% of all converts) whose mothers belonged to the newly formed Maternal Association. In the subsequent revivals, 1830 and 1838, the imprint of the older organization disappeared but the Maternal Association continued to exercise power behind the pulpit. All in all, known members of the Maternal Association brought at least fifty-five children into the revival ranks. Within these organizations, women consciously wove the social and familial ties that laced through the revival cycle (Table C.8).

In the aftermath of Finney's tour, Utica's male elite took greater interest in revivalism, now clearly a cause to be reckoned with. They quickly established several missionary societies of their own. The membership list of the Western Domestic Missionary Society, founded in 1826, reiterated the same surnames that stocked the earlier female organization: Bagg, Hastings, Stocking, Doolittle, and Van Rensselaer, to name a few. From the date of its founding, the Western Domestic Missionary Society courted the cooperation of women and within a year invited the female organization to become a formal auxiliary. The Utica-based leadership of the Female Missionary Society of the Western District voted to accept this invitation. Soon they were absorbed into the male association and women's identity as an independent force for revivalism was erased from the public ledgers. The names of these women no longer appeared in addresses, circulars, and religious periodicals; they were reincorporated into the household order of the male elite.[42] Women ultimately proved to be poor competitors for public stature, at least among the elite of the commercial town.

Off in the rural areas, however, the female organization of evangelism died a slower death and, in fact, experienced a brief renascence. The auxiliaries regarded the decision to consolidate with the Domestic Missionary Society as only tentative, and in 1829 they came back into operation. Even if the evangelical goals could be achieved without the Female Missionary Society, these women argued, "we should ourselves at any rate loose an important benefit. That pleasing interchange of views and feelings on the grand objects of our association – those heartfelt communications of hope, joy and gratitude, to which our connection gives rise, would nearly, if not entirely be lost. The deep interest produced by the work would give way to lassitude, and the living animation which they inspire be succeeded, we have reason to fear, by a chilling indifference." Significantly, neither Utica nor Whitestown appointed trustees to the revised association. In the absence of their sponsorship, the society collected only $365, sponsored one missionary, and disappeared within two years.[43] With the disappearance of the Female Missionary Society, the more expansive and broadly social wave of women's evangelism subsided.

It had served its purpose, however, and created a powerful successor in the Maternal Association. At the conclusion of the revival cycle, members of the Maternal Association accounted for more than one-third of the converts in the First Presbyterian Church. By this date, furthermore, the Maternal Association had acquired its own machinery for reaching out to women dispersed in their isolated homes. In 1833 the First Presbyterian Society commissioned one of its own members to edit a periodical on the subject of their mutual interest. *Mother's Magazine* was followed in but a few years by a Baptist equivalent, *Mother's Monthly Journal*. Other female organizations also continued to share in the exercise of women's converting power. The Sunday schools founded in 1815 flourished, expanded, and enrolled a broader spectrum of the population in the later stages of the revival cycle. The Sunday-school journal published by Merrill and Colwell regularly reported that scores of their students were converted during each revival season. Female academies were yet another organizational setting for revivals. A revival at the Select Female School of New Hartford, a Utica suburb, was engineered almost single-handedly by a female teacher in 1831.[44]

The domestication of religion

Such feminine methods of evangelism had become institutionalized and were almost routine by the close of the revival cycle. In the end it seemed that the women of Oneida County could do without the assistance of Charles Finney or any other minister. The accounts in the mother's magazines seldom recognized ministerial interference in the conversion of children. In 1833 the editor of *Mother's Magazine* put it directly: "The church has had her seasons of refreshing and her turn of decay; but here in the circle of mothers, it is felt that the Holy Spirit condescends to *dwell*. It seems his blessed rest."[45] Indeed, the last revivals were very domesticated operations. In 1838, 42% of all converts at Utica's First Presbyterian Church could be identified as children of church members (Table C.6).

The soberer nature of the later revivals was also attributable to their class composition. Merchant families recaptured the prominent position they had held in the first revivals. They were joined, however, by growing numbers of professionals and clerks. No laborers appeared in the ranks of the converts, and artisan families occupied only 6.3% of the places among the saved. If only the male converts are considered, the class nature of the 1838 revival seems even more homogeneous. The majority of the male converts of 1838 could be located in the *City Director* where, in almost equal proportions, they could be identified as merchants, professionals, and clerks. The converts who joined the revivals of the First Presbyterian Church in the 1830s were largely white-collar workers whose social status conforms to contemporary notions of the middle and upper-middle class. The high incident of clerks is particularly interesting. More than 15% of the converts had entered the most rapidly growing occupational sector within the commercial city. Thus the revival cycle ended on a quietly portentous note, with suggestions that the waves of evangelical enthusiasm may have had a transforming effect on class as well as family structure (Table C.7).

After 1838 church enrollments in Utica and Whitestown occurred at a slow and even pace. In the quiet after the evangelical fire storm, the men and women of the Burned-Over District took stock of a transformed religious and social landscape. They lost little time, first of all, in confirming a fundamental alteration in the relationship between age, parentage, and salvation. At the end of the revival cycle, the doctrine of infant depravity, long maligned by the Universalists, was dealt its final blow. The bluntest assault came from the Reverend Beriah Green, the controversial pastor of Whitestown's Congregational Church.

Writing in 1836, Green was prepared to be more explicit about the "moral agency" of childhood than were theologians a generation earlier. It was the peculiar dependency and vulnerability of infants and children, in Green's opinion, that made them susceptible to Christian education and open to the reception of grace. "Unembarrassed by any pretension to self-sufficiency [children] readily and affectionately receive from a supervisor whatever necessities may require. Their sense of dependence is as natural as their breath."[46] Whoever provided those necessities, it would follow, could wield considerable power over the formation of the child's character. Thus, in the privacy of the home, parents formed the cradle of both conversion and character formation. According to Green, the young home-bound child was nestled "amid circumstances and relations which naturally lead to such exercises of mind and of heart, as give his parents high advantages for instructing and impressing him respecting his relations, duties, and prospects, as a creature of God. Now is the time to conduct him to the bosom of the saviour." Green had traversed considerable theological and psychological territory in this brief essay. His depiction of a youth's route to salvation disarmed the concept of infant depravity, revised the theory of infant nature, and proposed a new method of rearing children to Christian standards of behavior.[47]

His typology also reordered the timing and changed the administration of childhood socialization. Brutal will-breaking at age two gave way to a more tender and gradual procedure. The brief and definitive interference of the patriarchal authority was supplanted by constant, monitory, and affectionate parental guidance from infancy through childhood. Both the touted affections of mothers and their superintendence of infancy and early childhood recommended them for this task. To the hallowed role of bringing souls to Christ, wrote, Green, "none have higher claims than mothers." Green reserved his fondest praise for the mother who administered Christian instruction along with the tender and faithful care of her baby. "Wise and happy mother! A better method to raise the hearts of her little one to heaven she could not have adopted."[48] The entire transformation of the process of conversion is compactly compressed into the Reverend Mr. Green's accolade: Children had become innocent "little ones," whose "hearts" (not minds or wills) would be led to God by the care of the mother (not the authority and responsibility of the father). This renovation of the relationship between children and the Calvinist church was articulated in Oneida County, New York, more than a decade before its usual dating, the publication of Horace Bushnell's *On Christian Nurture* in 1848.

In point of fact, the transformation was under way even before Green's tract appeared. Perhaps the first institution to employ this affectionate, maternal, and gradual method of courting children's souls was the Presbyterian Sunday School founded by five young women in 1815. In an address to the Utica Sunday School Union in 1824 a local pastor exclaimed, "Behold our beloved teachers – whose care for us is like a mother's for her infant child – whose kind instructions drop like honey from her lips." The pages of the *Sabbath School Visitant* supplied teachers with parabolic instructions for employing this technique. The successful practice was illustrated by this speech to two unruly boys: "I forgive you both," began the teacher, "and if you are sorry, and do so no more, may God forgive you, and your mother and I will be so happy." Gentle nurture reigned triumphant: "The children burst into tears. It was a triumph of kind and temperate discipline." The Sunday-school teacher was the first to be exempted from the suspicion of excessive affection heretofore negatively associated with doting and indulgent mothers.[49]

Maternal associations had been moving cautiously but surely toward this new method of child treatment since the early 1820s. The first pronouncements of the Utica Maternal Association conveyed a sense of urgency based on the traditional timing of the mother's role. "The time for your exertion is very short. Soon your children will arrive at the period of life when a mother's influence will be very feebly felt unless it is early exerted." Even before the children passed into the sterner jurisdiction of patriarchs and employers, however, these mothers aimed to keep parental affections under tight rein. A circular of the original Portland Maine Association, reprinted in Oneida County, included the admonition to avoid "that false tenderness and those ruinous indulgences, which, by forfeiting appetites and passions of your children, prepare them for a useless, wretched life, a still more miserable death, and a despairing eternity." Utica's Baptist Maternal Association chimed in: "The young passions and propensities of depraved nature gain strength by indulgence, and become inveterate by the force of habit." The members of the Maternal Association came to their responsibilities from a uniquely female, but nonetheless traditional, perspective: They were painfully aware of the brief tenure of their parental role and at the same time suspicious of emotionally intense bonds between parents and children. This state of mind was symbolized in the popular image of the pious woman who prayed that she might not "nurse a child for the devil."[50]

Maternal associations had, however, put in motion the forces that would lead almost inevitably to the new childrearing. As mothers, the members had assumed responsibility not only for the physical care of infants but also their salvation and the formation of character. They set out to investigate the implement the best methods to achieve that end at a time when patriarchs had become preoccupied with secular and economic concerns outside the household and in the marketplace. It is tempting to assert that all along women had been orchestrating changes in the theology of childhood from behind the scenes. After all, many printers' wives were deeply involved in the Utica Maternal Association, and when Beriah Green wrote his treatise on childhood he had an overwhelmingly female flock. The more likely process, however, was a transfer of functions from male to female as mothers' concern for child care expanded into a vacuum left by the indifference of fathers. This is illustrated by the history of the religious press. Most evangelical periodicals suspended publication after the 1830s, at which time the mother's magazines quickly took over the function of translating the morphology of conversion into a method of childhood socialization.

Mother's Magazine, nominally a Presbyterian publication, assumed from the first that children were sweet innocents, susceptible to affectionate rearing. The editors of the Baptists' *Journal* spoke out definitively in 1837 when they opined that God in his justice wouldn't do such a nasty thing as send a little child to Hell. The mother's magazines were also quite explicit about the change in sex roles their publication protended. In 1836 *Mother's Monthly Journal* put it this way. "Not that I would derogate from the prerogative of the father, or depreciate the influence which he is capable of exerting upon the character of his family; but the mother's appropriate sphere and pursuits give her a decided advantage in the great work of laying the foundation of future character; inculcating those principles and sentiments [which] are to control the destiny of her children in all future time."[51] The means to this ponderous maternal goal – "to control the destiny of her children in all future time" –

would be worked out in detail in the pages of the mother's magazines. They would pose a resolution to the problem first articulated as the fragility of the Abrahamic covenant. They were designed to bring the generations together on new terms, terms appropriate to a new age.

The revival cycle ended as it had begun, at a knarry juncture between family, society, and religion. Under its auspices, the relations of the ages and sexes had undergone a complex sequence of changes, which can be summarized only with difficulty and oversimplification. The transition from patriarchal authority to maternal affection as the focal point of childhood socialization was the linchpin of this transformation. But the historical process was far more convoluted and hesitant than a direct transfer of sex roles and a simple shift in childrearing techniques. This transformation passed through a period of particular flux and uncertainty in the 1820s. The most frenetic stage of revivalism centered around Finney's 1825 tour of Utica and Whitestown and coincided with the stagnation of population growth on the agrarian frontier and the completion of the Erie Canal. These economic changes entailed the migration of young men and women to the factories of Whitestown and the commercial shops of Utica. All along this regional economic network young men and women responded to the novelty and uncertainty of their positions with anxious, enthusiastic, and intense religious experiences. They seemed to announce their entrance into the busy commercial world of the canal era with an exuberant and independent mode of religiosity.

Yet the process of history and the lives of families are far more continuous than this, changing and stabilizing, breaking down and building anew, in one seamless process. The continuous and conservative element in the history of revivals was woven around the family cycle. A large minority of the young converts, particularly after 1825, could be definitely linked to parents who had long been members of the church. It cannot be denied, however, that their ties to the religion of their parents were forged in the fires of the Burned-Over District and in a new and ebullient fashion. The greatest innovations in the methods of conversion, furthermore, came from an unprecedented source, from women organized at the borders of the public sphere. Women's role in revivalism took two forms, diverging according to class and time. First, the wives of merchants founded a network of societies that built the infrastructure and financed the operations of the revival ministry. The less affluent, largely rural women of the 1820s seemed particularly responsive to the Female Missionary Society and acutely concerned about the salvation of their own children. Meanwhile, the middling ranks of the urban social structure, in particular the wives of Utica's artisans, were expressing their own anxieties about the souls of their progeny. It was out of this charged atmosphere that the maternal methods of conversion and child care emerged. The second mode of women's organization, the maternal association, contained conversion within the relationship of mothers and children and, in the process, did much to tame the righteous furor of the Second Great Awakening.

The revivals occasioned some fundamental shifts in the relations of class as well as gender. At first glance it may seem, as historians such as Paul Johnson and Anthony Wallace have argued, that evangelism was a weapon of class domination employed by local elites to bring their workers into compliance with the exigencies of capitalist development. Certainly the merchant leaders of Utica, many of whom sat on the boards of directors of local banks and nearby factories, played a prominent role in such revival organizations as the Domestic Missionary Society of the Western District. Their wives furthermore had played the key role in organizing the first revivals. The regional economy of Oneida County during the canal era did not, however, pit capitalists against proletarians. Rather, it linked large merchants to small producers, both farmers and artisans. The Female Missionary Society, accordingly, extended its influence horizontally as well as vertically, out through the agricultural hinterland and down through the middle ranks of the urban population. Both these directions led through the essential links of the regional marketplace where the husbands of female missionaries made their fortunes.

The fact that the top of the social structure exerted a powerful influence on religious and social change does not overrule the possibility that other ranks of society maneuvered successfully for their own measure of power. In Utica, New York, in the 1820s, at any rate, some robust and creative social influences percolated up from the middle ranks of the population. While the elite women of Utica were working out new religious relationships with members of other social strata, the wives of artisans, professionals, and shopkeepers devised major alterations in the internal family order. It was the Maternal Association with its strong constituency of artisan wives that did most to recast the lineage of grace in the prescient form of gentle motherly nurture. Finally, these families of the middling sort and the voluntary associations they formed seemed to serve as crucibles of further social changes. When the evangelical mothers brought their progeny into the church in the 1830s, a significant number of their sons had also secured clerical occupations and were on the path to white-collar careers. The suggestions of a relationship between the association of evangelical women and the development of the new middle class will be examined in subsequent chapters. For the time being, suffice it to say that during the Second Great Awakening the lines of gender and class crisscrossed one another in multiple and dialectical ways, giving play to creative social change among large segments of Oneida County's diverse and volatile population.

Finally, a moment's glance back over the history of revivals in Oneida County will spotlight a new pattern in the whole fabric of society. At the close of the Second Great Awakening, Oneida County could no longer be characterized as a community whose central constituting element was the patriarchal household. The most obvious alteration of the old New England way was the splintering of the Christian community into an assortment of religious sects whose members were recruited on the basis not of inheritance but of voluntary association. At the same time, the authority of those churches had been challenged by the aggressive involvement of families and voluntary associations in the religious socialization of the next generation. Within families, furthermore, it was mothers rather than patriarchs who exerted increasing control over the religious allegiances of the young. In other words, a more decidedly privatized and feminized form of religious and social reproduction was beginning to take shape around the relationship between evangelical mothers and converted children. This was perhaps the most significant social change that germinated on the charred landscape of the Burned-Over District.

3 The era of association: between family and society, 1825–1845

An evangelical publication of the late 1820s introduced a "Dialogue between a Little Girl and Her Mother" with this childish query: "Mother there are so many societies! . . . I longed for you this afternoon when I came home from school, and they told me you were gone to the Maternal Society: You go very often. Mother what is a Maternal Society?"[1] This fragment of fictional conversation is full of meaning for the history of family and society. Of particular moment in Utica during the canal era are two cryptic messages. The first is the intimation that even a child would be impressed by the sheer volume of "societies." When this dialogue was written in the late 1820s the town of Utica and the surrounding villages were in fact overrun with societies, or associations, as they were alternatively called. The village directory for 1828 listed twenty-one religious or charitable societies, three reform societies, five benefit associations, six fraternal orders, and six self-improvement associations. The number of such organizations listed in the *City Directory* peaked in 1832 when twenty-six religious and charitable societies combined with six reform groups to comprise the bulk of Utica's associations. The associational fervor began to subside around the mid-1840s. Until then, however, much of community life seemed organized around these associations, which garnered far more space in the directory than did public institutions or offices.

Second, this piece of juvenile dialogue harbors a more qualitative and startling clue about American social history. From it, even out of the mouth of a babe, it would seem, comes quiet approval of the mothers who left home for this larger world of "societies." Mothers joined fathers, sons, and daughters in the heavy traffic streaming out from the homes of Oneida County and into voluntary associations. The traffic was so voluminous and so diverse as to age, sex, and class background that the old boundaries between household, church, and society seemed blurred by a flurry of associations. The associations of the 1830s and 1840s first of all rerouted the concerns of evangelicals past the revival congregations and into more secular reform and benevolent societies, thereby detracting somewhat from the ideological hegemony of the church. Second, the reform associations assumed a role in social functions like childrearing that were traditionally assigned to the family. Maternal associations, temperance societies, and moral reform groups seemed to vie with the family as the agents of socialization. Third, associations seemed to remove the different age groups, sexes, and statuses from the household only to reassemble them in voluntary peer groups. Of the twenty-six religious and charitable associations listed in the *Utica City Directory for 1832*, for example, more than 1 in 3 was exclusively for females. Finally, the associations of the era seemed to wreak havoc with the orderly gradations of the social hierarchy, as the lofty and the lowly alternately mingled and fought with one another under the broad mantle of reform.

As this chapter goes on to recount the remarkable variety and vivacity of voluntary associations in the 1830s and 1840s, it may seem that these secondary social units had seduced the men, women, and children of Oneida County away from their families and absorbed the functions of the household. Actually, it would be better to take heed of the fictional child quoted above and conclude that the family and the association coexisted quite equanimously in the thirties and forties. In fact, it will be argued that the voluntary associations actually served as the crucibles of new domestic values and new relationships between the ages, sexes, and classes that would in the end heighten the importance of the conjugal family. The mothers of Oneida would, in the end, return from "society" to the home, bringing with them out of the associations more intense bonds with their children.

This distinctive mode of social organization took form under the demographic conditions specific to Oneida County in the canal era. The population of Utica, the regional vortex of association, remained less than fifteen thousand through most of the period. The town was large enough to sustain a variety of secondary social institutions and yet small enough to foster the causal familiarity and intermingling on which they throve. This community ambience is illustrated in a lithograph dated 1838 that portrays an intersection in the heart of town between Washington and Genesee streets.[2] In the artist's perception the city's associated activities were given equal play with its commerce. Merchants' Hall and the Presbyterian Church were featured just as prominently amid the shops and houses, and in between there was ample room for informal, neighborly interchanges. Men and women stopped beside a crude farm wagon to chat. Workers and businessmen paused in the street for leisurely conversation. Children used the same streets as their play-

Intersection of Washington and Genesee streets, Utica, 1838. Lithograph by
E. N. Clark (1872–1942) after W. H. Bartlett, 1838. Munson-Williams-Proctor Institute, Utica, N.Y.

ground. Voluntary associations were nurtured by, and entangled with,
this active street life of Utica in the age of commercial capitalism.

At the same time many of the occupants of these cozy social
spaces felt a dearth of formal institutions to meet their everyday
needs. Neither the public sector nor the church was equipped to
serve a population that more than doubled in the 1820s and grew by
more than 50% in the next decade. It was left to voluntary associations to provide such fundamental services as fire and police protection and the care of the poor. Much of the local population also
felt the lack of the basic emotional sustenance usually found in families. The city was inundated with young men and women, mostly
recent arrivals who had traveled to Utica without an entourage of
relatives. In the 1830s more than 1 in 4 Uticans was between the
ages of twenty and thirty and 1 in 3 adult males was listed in the
directory as a boarder rather than as head of a household (Table
A.3). Association was also called into play to provide psychological
services and supportive everyday human contacts to this deracinated population.

The social as well as the demographic structure of the canal era
was conducive to the development of voluntary associations. An

instant city like Utica was too volatile to support an invincible and cohesive ruling class. The merchant elite, which accounted for so large a proportion of the village's population in the 1810s, saw its ranks depleted relative to the muscular growth of the middle levels of the occupational structure. During the 1820s and 1830s Utica was particularly hospitable to artisans, who constituted the single largest occupational sector. Skilled workers who operated small shops employing only a handful of workers were the backbone of the social structure (Table B.3). The local shoemakers were typical of these small producers. The ranks of cordwainers increased sixfold between 1817 and 1840, and the majority of those who bothered to remain in the city into the next decade had become small proprietors, listed in the directory as owners of shoe stores or other retail establishments. Although the ranks of the shoemakers stopped growing in the 1840s, the local economy still accommodated a considerable number of small shoe manufacturers, typically employing five or six workers and investing $500 to $1,000 dollars in capital.[3] Utica's artisans, especially its shoemakers, found opportunities for creative self-expression in the ranks of reform associations. A second occupational grouping played a major and often controversial role in the associated life of the 1830s and 1840s. The ranks of salaried retail and office workers, known by the generic title "clerks," increased by a phenomenal 7,500% between 1817 and 1850. These young, often ambitious white-collar workers brought an element of novelty and modernity into the middle range of Utica's social structure and the mainstream of association (Table B.4).

Evangelism, abolitionism, and riot

The heyday of association would come in the thirties and forties when voluntary societies congealed around a variety of issues and generated considerable social controversy. The era of association would have a brilliant last burst of enthusiasm around temperance reform in the early 1840s. Voluntary association in itself, however, was not a novel creation of the canal era. It had many precedents, in eighteenth-century New England, in the large cities of the Northeast, and in the frontier Oneida County. Utica had its voluntary fire department as early as 1805; the Female Charitable Society formed a year later; and a number of mutual benefit associations emerged in the next decade. Beginning in the 1820s, however, these modes of association were dwarfed by what the *City Directory* labeled "Benevolent and Charitable Institutions." These societies were mostly

the by-products of the revivals and the promulgators of evangelical
education. They included the Oneida Bible Society, the Western
Sunday School Union, the Utica Tract Society, and, of course, the
Female Missionary Society. All shared a distinctive modus
operandi.

First of all, these early benevolent associations shared a conde-
scending attitude to the population they served. The Bible Society,
for example, was established "to carry divine instructions to the
poor – to send the precious Bible to those who are destitute."[4] The
Sunday-school scholar in the 1810s and 1820s was most often perceived not as the child of an upstanding church member but as
some poor urchin rescued from ignorance. The *Sabbath School Visitant* put its mission this way in 1825: "The children of the better
parents are taught at home, at the day school and at the sanctuary.
But the class of which we are speaking receive scarcely the least
moral instruction from any source. They are growing up in entire
ignorance of a future state, ripening for death." The Sunday-school
teachers were praised for going directly into the streets of the villages and recruiting stray waifs as the objects of their benevolence.[5]
The Infant School, founded by two Presbyterian women in 1824,
had the welfare of poor mothers as well as children in mind. Its
design was "to relieve indigent mothers, in populous towns from
the care of their younger children, that they might apply their undi-
vided attention to their daily toil." Thus these associations of private individuals could under cover of benevolence, penetrate deep
into the social structure and inside the conjugal family. The poor
children in the Infant School were as young as eighteen months of
age.[6]

These societies were also remarkably thorough and systematic in
their methods of social diffusion. No public institutions of the canal
era could rival benevolent societies in efficiency. The Oneida Bible
Society distributed more than one thousand Bibles across the
county in a single year. The Utica Tract Society had carved up the
city into thirty-one districts and sent some sixty voluntary agents
peddling their wares to every family they could find. They placed
an order for no less than eight thousand copies of the *Christian Almanac* in 1830.[7] Associations such as the Bible Society employed
paid agents who were instructed to collect subscription fees, with
interest. Associations like these paralleled the organization of the
regional economy. They were organized like corporations, complete with boards of directors and trustees. The board of directors
was usually composed of ministers from throughout the county.

The top officers of the board of trustees were Utica's premier merchants; below them were their counterparts in rural hamlets. The leadership of the Western Education Society, for example, included the familiar Presbyterian cabal, the Clarkes, Stockings, Doolittles, Baggs, and also enrolled such Episcopalian aristocrats as Abram Varick, successful land speculator, and Henry Semour, Sr., banker, canal commissioner, and state senator. These gentlemen were not bashful about their social eminence. They appended the title "Esquire" to their names in the lists of association officers.[8]

Behind this venerable leadership of ministers and merchants there assembled an army of women workers. It was left largely to women to distribute the Bibles and tracts and to teach Sunday school. Women were also responsible for much of the income of the early benevolent associations, which they collected in cash or kind, either a few dollars or a few yards of cloth. These women were rewarded with chivalrous homages. The Western Education Society asked the female auxiliary to provide the funds to purchase a full-time directorship for their ministers. "Very much depends on the aid which they afford, as to the perpetuity and permanence of our charitable institutions."[9] These kinds of appeals testified the solidity of the traditional sexual hierarchy, which regarded women as silent working partners in male associations as well as in male-headed households. It completes the organizational structure of the first benevolent and religious institutions of Oneida County: The line of authority and power ran from ministers and the male civic elite, through volunteer women workers, on to the passive objects of their beneficence, needy and ignorant families.

In sum, the societies of religious benevolence, the dominant form of association in the 1820s, combined a fervent evangelical purpose, with frequent intrusions into the family sphere, and a steep organizational hierarchy. This combination of characteristics became an easy target of suspicion and antagonism in the age of Jackson. When combined with evangelical and often sectarian purposes it became a prescription for opposition from the more liberal sectors of an increasingly diversified and cosmopolitan city. The Universalists and Dolphus Skinner led this opposition, mounting an assiduous attack on each and every benevolent enterprise they could associate with the Presbyterian faction. The opponents of evangelism had added cause for concern when these benevolent societies took a new turn beginning in the mid-1820s, which culminated in the reform movements of the 1830s: abolitionism, female moral reform, and temperance. First of all, they began to propound new standards of morality and attempted to alter everyday secular behavior in the community at large. Second, they resorted increasingly to inviting the young, the female, and the lower social ranks into their associations. As a consequence, evangelical reforms created major social conflicts and spawned opposing associations that split the community into competing interest groups.

The evangelical campaign to dictate secular morality and to reform everyday life opened in 1824 with the formation of the Oneida Society for the Promotion of Temperance. Although intruding itself into the new field of moral reform, the society was otherwise conservative. It perceived itself as a congregation of the upper sort determined to control drunkenness among the lower classes. The members of the society were fond of pointing out that they were oppressed taxpayers forced to play host to a mob of drunken parasites who filled the nation's poorhouses, prisons, and asylums. Their reform propaganda was addressed to responsible heads of households. Each member pledged to abstain from ardent spirits himself and to forbid alcohol within his patriarchal jurisdiction, that is, to "members of his household, or any of his friends and visitors" as well as to his "laborers or customers." The Society for the Promotion of Temperance went on to elect its president, vice-president, and other lofty officers and to set the date of its next annual meeting. It did not attract hosts of members.[10]

In 1828 the evangelical faction began a similar abortive campaign to restrict secular activities on the Sabbath. An attempt to prohibit business-as-usual on Sunday was opposed by a phalanx of Utica's merchants and clerks who unabashedly defended their own self-interest along with the "principle of private morality." The suspension of mail delivery on the Sabbath, they argued, was "repugnant to the rights of private property and irreconcilable with the free exercise of civil liberty."[11] Some of the Sabbatarians tried to found their own purified commercial system, exemplified by the Pioneer Line, a fleet of canal boats that did not operate on Sunday. The venture was an abysmal failure and took down with it such illustrious representatives of the old artisan economy as Bildad Merrill. An effort to provide Christian corporate living arrangements for the youth of the city sparked similar controversy. The editor of the *Evangelical Magazine and Gospel Advocate* became agitated once again in 1831, this time by the activities of the Young Men's Association, another associational arm of the Presbyterian Church. The Universalist periodical described their nefarious activities as follows: "Committees are appointed to ascertain the families, boarding houses, etc., where family prayer and obedience to the Christian party is kept up, and where they are disregarded. Young men are then warned, and prevailed upon not to enter such families as companions or boarders, where these duties are neglected." The Universalists accounted such a boycott "the subversion of character and the ruin of business."[12]

When the evangelicals took on the divisive political issue of slavery in the 1830s these conflicts reached the boiling point. Abolitionism was introduced into Oneida County by the circular of the Whitestown and Oneida Institute Anti-Slavery Society. It exhorted the reader as follows: "What then do we invite you to attempt? We invite you to form associations, male and female, as a medium through which you may communicate your views, and express your feelings and expand your resources in the sacred cause of universal emancipation. Thus, combined, you may, in a thousand ways, which we need not specify, receive and exert a powerful and benign influence. Thus you may help to reach the understanding, conscience, heart of the nation." The positive response came quickly. It would, however, reflect the realignment of the relations of age and sex that had occurred during the revivals. Soon Whitestown could list not only a male but also a female and a juvenile anti-slavery society. In Utica, five societies corresponding to the same age and sex categories had appeared by 1835. Nearby in the town of Clinton a chapter of the American Anti-Slavery Society was established at the Female Domestic Seminary.[13]

As was typical of the associations of the 1830s, the Anti-Slavery Society placed great stock in the moral power of its female and juvenile supporters. Beriah Green put it most forcefully in a speech delivered just before the Utica riot. "The plain truth is, that every man, woman and child, on finding himself involved in evil-doing is bound by obligation as high and sacred as the authority of God, immediately to break off his sin by righteousness." The same moral obligation enjoined each "man, woman, and child" to "do what he can to bring others to also harmonize with his views, feelings and actions." As Green spoke on, he cast the net of association ever wider and deeper. The "ever-widening circle of influence," he observed, should extend to "the obscurist child in the community, and ultimately reach the bravest philosopher or statesman or divine." In the end, Beriah Green reached to the lowest level of society for his moral influence, observing that "the most important reformations have begun with the sewing-maid in the kitchen." Indeed, most anyone was welcome in the ranks of Utica abolition-

ists. Green reported with delight and approval the abolitionist activities of one local girl. A mere tot, she greeted every visitor to her
father's home with a picture of an abused slave and an appeal for
contributions.[14]

Such tactics certainly were cause for raised eyebrows among con-
temporaries and are to be accounted among the more daring innovations of antebellum reformers. Some of Utica's principal citizens
had cause to resent the abolitionists' invitations to women. Beriah
Green revealed the extent of his subversion in a letter to James Birney. "Mrs. Kirkland, the very intelligent and excellent wife of the
Mayor of Utica – in opposition to her time-serving husband – is a
warm and active abolitionist."[15] Only two months earlier Mayor
Kirkland had been, in fact, a silent accomplice to a mob assault
upon the reform associates of his wife. Kirkland and his supporters
among the Utica businessmen also looked askance at local abolitionists from their liberal position in Utica's free market of ideas
and commerce. A major anti-slavery meeting planned to take place
in their city might put a damper on Utica's market season and dam-
age its reputation within national political parties, which were anxious to assuage the fears of the sensitive southerners. As the state
anti-slavery society prepared to meet in Utica in October 1835,
Kirkland and his cronies felt they had no choice but to convene a
meeting of the town council to prevent such harm to the civic good.
The city council reluctantly resolved to admit the abolitionists to the
city, if not to their public buildings. The simple majority vote of 7 to
4 did not, however, legitimate the convention to the angry anti-abolitionist faction.[16]

Neither the forces of the corporate community, nor the order of
associations, nor the rights of individuals reigned on the streets of
Utica on October 17, 1835. The mayor and civic elite stood passively
by and the Presbyterian women cowered in a prayer circle as the
Bleeker Street Church and the homes of Spencer Kellogg and Francis Wright were surrounded by an angry and arson-minded mob.
The three hundred to four hundred delegates to the New York State
Anti-slavery Society convention retreated to the rural outpost of Pe-
terboro, and the streets of Utica became the turf of the rowdy
crowd. The term for those who ruled the streets that night suggests
the antithesis of the male household head. Rioters of all ages were
scorned with the epithet "vicious boys." The contradictions of the
era of associations exploded into the streets of Utica in 1835.[17]

The composition of the opposing sides in the Utica riot of 1835
has been described in detail by Leonard Richards. Richards's anal-

ysis suggests that the anti-abolitionist faction was composed large-ly of the merchants of Genesee Street. Richards placed the members of anti-slavery associations a notch above their rivals on the social ladder. Many of them were full-scale manufacturers and thus repre-sentatives of the more modern economic and social organization.[18] Closer scrutiny of the community of Utica itself and of the ideol-ogical crosscurrents that ripped through its amorphous social structure in the 1830s prompts a slight revision of this interpreta-tion.

Merchants, first of all, were not necessarily less modern than manufacturers. In fact, a case can be made for the reverse classifica-tion. Anti-abolitionists like Moses Bagg, David Wagar, and Joseph Kirkland inhabited the commercial center of the Oneida County economic network. The febrile market conditions that were the life-blood of these men nurtured the highly individualized interests and fluid social relationships often used to identify the modern mentality. Manufacturers who supported abolition, on the other hand, often held more traditional attitudes. The major example of this species of entrepreneur is Benjamin Walcott, who created a manufacturing center in New York Mills, a quiet, orderly village that was much in the image of the old New England community, an epoch away from dense and busy Utica. Similarly, noted abolition-ists like Spencer Kellogg, Samuel Stocking, and Francis Wright were engaged in manufacturing but clothed in traditional Presbyte-rian social and cultural trappings. It must also be remembered that women and ministers provided the major organizational support for local abolitionism. Few would argue that either represented the vanguard of modernity in the economic sense commonly implied by the term. The class system was far too volatile in the 1830s, fur-thermore, to justify too fine a distinction between merchant and manufacturer. Samuel Stocking, for example, began as simply a hatter and as he enlarged his retail and production enterprises rose to the status of a "hat merchant and manufacturer."

The ferocity of the anti-slavery controversy was fed by the very fluidity of Utica's social structure in 1835. The moral and evangeli-cal fervor of the associations of the 1830s was spark to a powder keg of diverse and competing interests. It was clear that no voluntary association of individuals could long presume to speak for the het-erogeneous population of this busy entrepôt of commercial capital-ism. The memories of corporate communal morality, however, in-spired both the inflated ambitions of reformers and the exorbitant fears of conspiracy among their opponents. The debacle of the anti-slavery riot, the undercurrent of tension fed by Sabbatarianism, and a panoply of other reform associations demonstrated the dangers and limitations of associations that brandished strong notions about public morality and converted public issues like slavery into associational vendettas against sinners.

Even the citadel of evangelism, the First Presbyterian Church of Utica, was divided within itself in the 1830s. In December 1834 the session heard a complaint against one of the church's most illustrious members, A. B. Johnson, banker, writer, and in-law of the Adams family lineage, which included two American presidents. The church elders, in the company of the Reverend Samuel Aiken, instigated the usual "kind and brotherly measure." They called on Mr. Johnson "at the bank" and began the customary interrogations "without regard to wealth, rank, or other factitious distinctions among Brethren." Johnson then heard the accusation that his recent publication endorsing the transport of the mails on Sunday had "dishonored religion and truth." After a short and polite deliberation, the representatives of the church recanted, agreeing that the Sabbath mail was not a doctrinal issue and that Johnson was entitled to hold and express his own opinion.[19]

A. B. Johnson, the ambitious and opinionated son of Utica's pioneer cash merchant, was not about to submit to even this mild reproof with Christian humility. He mounted an irreverent countercharge against the church. The accusation against him, Johnson maintained, was politically motivated, launched by his Whig opponents with a woman parishioner acting as a major accomplice. In a letter to the session meeting, Johnson testified that a "distinguished female member of the Church" had "censured him on his political opinions."[20]

Things had come to pretty pass when the partisan politics, indeed, even the political opinions of women, could intrude into the citadel of Christian love and justice, the church trial. At this point the session lodged official charges against A. B. Johnson: He had committed "treasons upon all rules and Christian propriety, [which] justify a member in introducing disorder and misrule into the Church of God, which ought ever to be distinguished for harmony and fraternal confidence." Johnson did not disrupt the Christian community for very long. He simply failed to appear for his church trial and left the fold for a more liberal congregation. (Ultimately, Johnson joined the elite church of Utica, Grace Episcopal.) In the process, however, Johnson dealt a major blow to the system of church hegemony over individual opinions and private morals.

After that date church trials all but disappeared. During the remainder of the antebellum period an occasional member was queried about his neglect of public worship, but only two cases scrutinized the personal morality of believers: A charge of "unchristian behavior" was raised in 1849; a case of intemperance was noted in 1854. Either the First Presbyterian church was a congregation of cherubs or its leaders had all but suspended the practice of supervising the everyday behavior of the brethren.[21] The latter interpretation is given further credence by events in the founding institution of the New England way, the Whitestown Presbyterian Society. Here the issue was abolition, the troublemaker was Beriah Green, and the result was the same: a divisive, politically charged church trial followed by the curtailment of congregational surveillance of private morality. It would seem that evangelism had backfired and that the Presbyterian fathers could no longer presume to prescribe behavior for even their own parishioners.[22]

Female moral reform

At the same time, it seemed from the perspective of the deposed ministers that Utica and Whitestown had become open breeding ground for every sort of vice. To the imagination of Samuel Aiken, writing in 1834, the busy, crowded streets of the commercial town were playing host to "a whole tribe of libertines." A month later a visiting minister rose before the Bleecker Street congregation to warn against a "loathesome monster – licentiousness – [which] crawls, tracking the earth with his fetid slime and poisoning the atmosphere with his syphilitic breath." The sin might be intemperance, fornication, gambling, or Sabbath breaking, but the imagery of the sinners and seducers was always the same. In the imagination of the ministers, Utica was beset with reptiles (the frogs of Egypt being a favorite simile) lying in wait to ensnare and defile the sons and daughters of Christians. Certainly some new and stringent measures were necessary to preserve public morality in the face of this horrific attack and given the proven ineffectiveness of both the old communal methods and the novel evangelical ploys.

The first line of counterattack against the perpetrators of vice was simple publicity and exposure. Aiken recommended the collection of statistics on local sexual offenses, the menacing dimensions of which would "move public opinion" and, like "mounted pieces of artillery, pour upon the lines of licentiousness a stream of fire, spreading terror and dismay through the camp." Aiken's sermon on "moral reform" and a second on the subject of "lewdness' were published along with a letter of endorsement from some of the city's foremost citizens: Spencer Kellogg, J. W. Doolittle, Samuel Stocking, Thomas Walker, and even A. B. Johnson.[23] The clergy of Utica were long aware of the efficacy of the local printer in propagating their ideas. They also embarked on a second avenue to moral reform, public legislation. The vigilant citizens convinced the city council to tighten up the liquor-licensing law and to enact a statute against prostitution. From all accounts, however, this attempt to legislate morality was a failure. A fine of $25 for soliciting or harboring prostitutes was not the potent deterrent that the Reverend Mr. Aiken's stirring rhetoric called forth.[24] Neither public opinion nor the local police supplanted the church trial as the custodian of a straitlaced moral code.

It was yet another form of association that would fill this social and cultural vacuum. The first example of this new species of association peculiar to the canal era went by the generic title "moral reform," was organized by females, and set as its goal the promulgation and enforcement of a stringent code of sexual ethics. The Female Moral Reform Society, like other associations concerned with the public advocacy of personal ethics, flourished throughout Oneida County. Like the Maternal Association, it too drew its membership from a broader population than had the benevolent societies of the earlier period. The Utica chapter, for example, did not confine itself to one class but enrolled the wives and daughters of merchants, artisans, and professionals, as well as an occasional seamstress. The married, single and widowed of all ages joined the cause of sexual reform. The operations of the Female Moral Reform Society illustrate the creative blend of past and present, private and public, that so enlivened Oneida County in the 1830s and carried association, family, and society to a new level of mutual adjustment.[25]

In 1837 a notice appeared in the *Advocate of Moral Reform* (the New York City publication of the American Female Moral Reform Society) that a chapter had formed in the city of Utica. Utica actually trailed behind the outlying rural communities in this reform activity. Whitesborough already had a female moral reform society of some 40 members by 1835. The chapters in the small Oneida County towns of Clinton and Westmoreland boasted 84 and 181 members respectively by the time the Utica society, with approximately 100 members, was first established. Bands of reforming women seemed to grow up wherever the "lines of licentiousness" formed. And these were apparently omnipresent. The little town of Clinton, the location of Hamilton College, was reportedly "deeply tainted with the crying sin." The pioneer leader of moral reformers, New York's John MacDowall, had visited Whitestown in 1835, where he uncovered "alarming statistics" of lewdness and obscenity. His estimation that "thousands" had been corrupted by the vice was a measure of the very imprecise science of statistics as employed by antebellum reformers. Finally, a student at the Oneida Institute in Whitestown chimed in that licentiousness was not a problem for cities alone, for even farmers' sons were afficted with the contagion that seemed to have overrun Oneida County in the 1830s.[26] Female associations formed for the purpose of fostering public morality provided the line of moral defense that Samuel Aiken had called for in Utica in 1834. Tossing off their female timidity with allusions to their feeble instrumentality, their "talent though small," the women of Utica and the surrounding towns mounted a righteous, indeed a militant, crusade against the seducers of their sex, the predators of the bodies and souls of their sons and daughters.[27]

The members of the Female Moral Reform Society began by adapting traditional family and social forms to their reform purposes. They often worked within the home economy and the private social circle. Mrs. Whittelsey, who endorsed female moral reform from the editor's desk of the *Mother's Magazine*, depicted one such tactic in 1833:

> Such has been my sympathy for my sex, I cheerily testify, that for many years, no young woman has come to my dwelling, seeking temporary employment, or a permanent situation, toward whom I have not endeavored to reach forth the hand of compassion. When I could, I have either written a note or sent with them a messenger, to such of my friends as might be able either to employ them themselves, or direct them to others. Were this course or some other equivalent oftener pursued, (I speak from experience) many of the unfortunate victims of vice and wretchedness, which at present claim the attentions and charity of enlightened benevolence, would be greatly diminished. Yes, it is for mothers in Israel to say how many of the unfortuante "Magdalenes," the present year,shall be found clothed with Savior's righteousness, washing his feet with their tears, and wiping them with the hairs of their head.[28]

Mrs. Whittelsey had performed one favored function of female reform, the protection of young women from seduction and prostitution, without stepping outside the boundaries of woman's customary role. By placing vulnerable young women as servants within the households of her friends, she activated a women's network as a kind of informal employment agency and working girls' protective association.

The adaptability of the women's network for reform purposes was recognized by correspondents to *MacDowall's Journal*. A male representative of Utica's publishing industry, Charles Hastings, wrote to MacDowall in July 1833 to report that the work of promoting moral reform was already under way in Utica. Hastings pleaded preoccupation with other business but was pleased to report that "a female in my family says she will go around among the families and see if she can't get something for your support." Support for *MacDowall's Journal* and female moral reform in general was collected in this piecemeal process of female solicitation. Contributions came in small sums of cash or poignant donations like that from "a lady in Utica" dated February 1836 – "two rings and a breast pin." This distinctive method of association was described in the language of the Female Missionary Society and the Maternal Association as a communication between "Dear Sisters," as a "labor of love." At least in one case the sisterly connections between these associations were direct and enduring. The longtime president of the Utica Female Moral Society, Fanny Skinner, had been present at the founding of the Female Charitable Society of Whitestown in 1806.[29]

As time went on, and the magnitude of licentiousness loomed even larger in the imagination of its members, the Female Moral Reform Society resorted to increasingly radical tactics. At first the most belligerent method of the reformer was ostracism, a method described by the Clinton society as "discountenancing all men reputed to be licentious, in excluding them from our society and by every other laudable means in our power." These women were in effect using a strategy similar to the church elders' sanction of excommunication. The tactics of the Utica society were significantly escalated in 1838 after a meeting with the representatives of the parent society. Utica's reformers were reawakened to the "vital importance of the cause" and the growing magnitude of the evil. "Even our small children are infested by it. Who among us have not had our hearts pained by the obscenity of little children; who among us does not tremble lest some who are dear to us should be led away by the thousand snares of the destroyer. Who among us can tell that our sisters and daughters are safe while the seducer is unhesitatingly received into our society and treated with that attention which virtue alone can claim."[30] The suppression of lewdness now bore the stamp of a woman's reform; it focused on the defense of females from the dishonorable intentions and inordinate lusts of men and aimed to relieve mothers of the heartache of a child's moral degeneration.

At this point the female reformers began to entertain the notion that a good offense was the best defense. Timidly, the Utica society began to tread out into the world of the seducer. A visiting committee was formed in 1841 and ventured out into the streets of Utica with something less than high hopes and bold spirits: "For should we meet opposition we felt that we should balk in our weakness and leave the ground for the enemy." The expectations of this anonymous little band were quickly raised by the warm response of the city's mothers. One widow tearfully accepted a tract (entitled "Mother Will You Read It?") saying, "I need assistance to train up my fatherless boys in purity." At another home the visiting committee heard the story of a son who had become a hopeless drunkard and of a daughter "lost to iniquity." The distraught mother's problems were compounded by the callousness of her husband, who "was not willing she should go anywhere [not even to church]; they keep boarders who on Sunday expect something extra for dinner." The Reverend John Frost had encountered similar examples of tyrannical and irreligious household heads in 1813, but now they reached a sympathetic female ear and received a supportive if impotent response: "Poor woman! She should have remembered the injunction of Paul, 'Be not unequally yoked together with unbelievers.'"[31] The report of the visiting committee told another sorry tale of a sick wife whose husband took her nurse to bed each night. On this occasion the female reformers rose boldly in defense of their sex. This remark, which clearly identified the offending male to local readers, was appended to the report: "This man has the charge of a paper the object of which is to criticize public morals. May we not ask how long shall men like these occupy responsible stations, and be tolerated among a Christian people?"[32]

Still other informants offered the Female Moral Reform Society models of militant opposition to immorality. In July 1842 the visiting committee submitted a full report to the *Advocate of Moral Reform* on the trials of another widowed mother. Her son, only recently converted during a revival, had been absenting himself from home night after night while his mother occupied the time "sometimes walking the room and weeping, sometimes trying to find some consolation in prayer." Finally, she could endure the waiting no longer. She marched straight to the nearby brothel and forced her way inside. "I seized a candle and found my way to the chamber. Finding it locked, I called to him, told him to come that I had sent for his father and a constable." The brothelkeeper hurled this pious woman down a flight of stairs. Still, she returned home to find a repentant son.[33]

Buoyed up by tales like these, the reformers themselves became more energetic and audacious. In 1841 a committee of eight women secured between two thousand and three thousand signatures on a petition to the state legislature calling for criminal sanctions against seducers and prostitutes. Another woman visited twenty-two families "mostly among the poor and laboring classes" in a one-month period. Slowly, the visiting committee began to approach men as well as women. The pious ladies called upon the city fathers to demand statistics about the extent of lewdness in Utica. They also accosted licentious men in the streets and entered taverns to interrogate bartenders. On one occasion they even took their case into the public court. A young girl had come to a member of the society and confided to her the "revolting behavior" of the man to whom she was bound in service. The society felt it their "imperious duty to visit her without delay and offer so far as practical to act for her in the place of parents." They exposed the culprit, one John West, and brought him to trial. They provided his victim with legal counsel, personal care, and a new job in a respectable home.[34] In actual function the Female Moral Reform Society was to reinstitute the methods of moral surveillance similar to those long practiced by the corporate institutions of church and state. They scrutinized private behavior, brought offenders to trial by public humiliation, and sheltered victims in the good graces of Christian homes. The performance of these functions by women, within their own self-created association, however, constituted a remarkable transmutation in the relationship of family and society.

The Female Moral Reform Society also worked to transform previous notions of sexual propriety. All the church trials in Utica and Whitestown involved cases of adultery, that is, implicated at least one partner in extramarital sexual intercourse. The accusations of the Female Moral Reform Society, on the contrary, revealed no special concern about licentiousness among married men and women. They were, in fact, most alert to the sexual transgressions of the young and the single. The novelty of this code of sexual morality was openly acknowledged. One young man of Oneida put it this way: "From my boyhood to this time, the subject of marriage or the intention to marry through necessity has been treated with the utmost lightness and frivolity, and the boy who was not afraid to trifle with the most forward of girls was esteemed above his years and almost a man, thus by the countenance of even our dear parents and friends and public opinion making it honorable for one to be first in the pathway to hell, going down to the chambers of death." This same informant, identified only by the initials S. H., also told of current debauches at Hamilton College where more than a score of young women were "seduced and trained in the school of vice, almost every night witnessing to their debaucheries. This fact I have from the mouth of a young man who was himself brought to the verge of the grave by his excessive sexual indulgence with those females."[35] The Female Moral Reform Society made such young men and women cognizant of a standard of premarital celibacy that applied to both sexes and that was now deemed essential to personal health as well as to social order.

There is no hard evidence to support the claim of moral reformers that sexual license was mushrooming in Utica after 1830. A survey conducted by the Female Moral Reform Society uncovered only two arrests for prostitution and nine cases of illegitimacy in the criminal files of 1841. Even given gross underreporting, this rate of misbehavior is hardly sufficient to indict a city of almost thirteen thousand persons as a modern-day Sodom. A more relevant statistic is found in the shifting age structure of Utica during these years. During the 1830s the centers of female moral reform were invaded by young, single men and women, marking a sudden and dramatic increase in the population of unprotected sons and daughters for whom female moral reformers expressed particular concern. In Utica it was young clerks, seamstresses, and domestic servants who swelled the ranks of potential victims and perpetrators of licentiousness. In Clinton it was the students at Hamilton College who caused particular worry. Societies grew up around the factories and boardinghouses of Whitestown, in Oriskany Falls and New York Mills. The secretary of the society of New York Mills explained this circumstance as follows: "The state of society in this place is peculiar to manufacturing villages. Multitudes of youth are here collected, who need light and instruction on this subject, and our population is constantly changing, so that with suitable exertion much may be done here to promote the cause of purity and virtue."[36] Wherever the young and mobile congregated, their pious mothers had cause for anxiety. The old mechanisms of the patriarchal household order were no longer available to regulate and supervise the sexual habits of the young. Neither the church nor the patriarchal family was there to ensure a marriage, for example, should errant youngsters conceive a child out of wedlock. The Female Moral Reform Society had devised a means of preventing such sexual offenses and social problems. By propagating refined notions of chastity, they strove to plant the force of sexual repression within the individual character of a mobile youth.[37]

Under cover of privacy, without benefit of official encouragment, in association with one another, women exerted real social power and engineered major social change. This was especially true of the groups like the Female Moral Reform Society and the Maternal Association that arose during the 1830s in the wake of revivalism. The social consequence of these women's associations is nowhere more convincingly evidenced than in the fearful reactions of the Universalists. In 1827 the *Evangelical Magazine and Gospel Advocate* was almost jocular in its attack on women reformers. They were simply comical village do-gooders. By 1835 the editor had changed his tune considerably. Female associations now appeared as dangerous weapons of religious conservatives. Even the daughters of Universalists were being seduced into attending gatherings arranged by benevolent evangelical women. Once within the viselike grasp of the Presbyterian faction, these young women lured their sisters, brothers, beaux, and even parents in the same direction. Such, according to the alarmist Universalists, was the nefarious web of the women's reform network: "The circle spreads and enlarges till it embosoms a large proportion of the youth – not because they are opposed to liberal principles but because they love society and prefer going with the multitudes." Women's associations, in the estimation of the editors of the *Evangelical Magazine and Gospel Advocate*, were responsible for the "overwhelming balance of numbers" maintained by conservative churches: "The secret is contained in the well-directed energies of some half-dozen active and zealous females." The Universalists had quite correctly gauged the power of these voluntary, affectionate, and private networks of women. In the face of this formidable opposition, the male leaders of Utica Universalism asked every mother to "put the question seriously and concisely to themselves – whether they had rather devote a few hours once or twice a month to social and religious purposes or consign their daughters to the proselytism and service as well as the creed of some more zealous sect." This concession on the part of the editors of the *Evangelical Magazine and Gospel Advocate* is forceful testimony to the strength and creativity of the women's associations.[38]

The sources of this power deserve more historical attention than a single community study can provide. The bits of biographical information about the three major leaders of Utica's women's groups do, however, offer some important clues.[39] All three leaders were married, but none of them were burdened with the full set of duties of the mistress of a large household. Neither Fanny Skinner nor Paulina Wright bore any children. Sophia Clarke was a mother of three, but an independently wealthy widow. More important, all three women must have gained support from one another, for they were part of the same circle of active Presbyterian women that had roots back as far as 1806. All of them built their local associational empires in the well-trod paths of the evangelical church. Each of them had a personal network of kin and neighbors to cultivate as well. Sophia Clarke worked through family contacts that extended back to Connecticut, and then carried her influence on to a second generation in the activities of her children Erastus and Susan, as well as her nephews Edward Vernon and, of course, Theodore Weld. Sophia Clarke also lived conveniently next door to the First Presbyterian Church and parsonage. Fanny Skinner parlayed her connections as a boardinghouse keeper into the major support group for moral reform. Fanny Skinner's resourcefulness was forged amid family necessity. Her husband, as the local histories tell it, was once a promising young lawyer who quickly fell upon bad times and was largely supported by his wife. Fanny Skinner, interestingly enough, proselytized quite effectively for moral reform among the young law students who boarded with her.

The third major leader of women's association in Utica, Paulina Wright, came to the cause almost a generation later than Clarke and Skinner. She arrived in Utica to begin her reforming career buoyed up by the reform beliefs and merchant wealth of her husband, Francis Wright. She immediately familiarized herself with the women's network that had been built up by her sisters in the Presbyterian Church. Paulina Wright pumped that network for every reforming supporter she could find. She went the familiar women's route from door to door, promoting moral reform, distributing temperance tracts, promulgating abolitionism, and in 1837 she circulated a petition in support of the Married Women's Property Act.[40] The women's network of Oneida County could, in the end, even lead to the borders of conscious feminism. Fanny Skinner also approached Wright's position when, in 1838, she invited Angelina Grimké Weld to speak before her friends in the anti-slavery movement.[41] The emergence and growth of women's associated power, in sum, was nurtured in an intricate and reinforcing set of personal ties between the reform-minded women of Oneida County.

The Female Moral Reform Society was not, however, received by the local population with any greater unanimity than were Sabbatarians and abolitionists. In this case, it was the junior partners of the merchant elite, the clerks of the city, who resisted the reformers' blandishments most obdurately. A direct confrontation between the clerks and the Female Moral Reform Society occurred in the winter of 1836 and 1837. The attack was opened by the Reverend Mr. Dodge, whose public lecture on the issue of moral reform included an indictment of clerks of Utica as notorious violators of the seventh commandment. The Female Moral Reform Society was so well pleased with Dodge's discourse that they published a resolution in his support, in the next issue of the *Oneida Whig*, above the bold-faced signatures of Fanny Skinner, President, and Marietta S. Savage, Secretary. The clerks responded with public meetings and resolutions in their own defense, again printed in the *Oneida Whig*. Another group of men, also purporting to be clerks, joined the fray in support of Dodge and his female allies. Each side to the controversy secured the signatures of more than one hundred men who endorsed their position.[42] It is a testimony to the success of evangelical women that the clerks did not question the exacting standards of sexual purity to which the Female Moral Reform Society subscribed. Their objections revolved around the reputation of the city's clerks and the techniques the reformers used to obtain their worthwhile goals. The outraged clerks rose in their own self-defense by charging Dodge with the gross exaggeration typical of the reformers of the age, who, whether they were calculating the number of inebriates, papists, or libertines, could seldom conceive of a number system that began below six figures. The group's spokesman, a young attorney named Ward Hunt, maintained that the Reverend Mr. Dodge had committed character assassination upon a class of upright young men. "We esteem good moral character, based on the integrity and virtue, as our most valuable capital, and regard those as our best friends and kindest benefactors who caution us against temptation, warn us of our danger, and thus labor to secure our highest interest." In other words, the protesting clerks welcomed the more private and persuasive advances of female moral reform but rejected the public techniques of exposure and shaming that could ruin the reputation of the innocent.

It is impossible to overlook the rhetoric in which the clerks protested against this zealous crusade. They spoke in defense of their "valuable capital," "the highest interest," and "compensation." These references to individual self-interest within the capitalist market found their moral equivalent in the veneration of private opinions and personal ethics above some communal code of ethics. As Ward Hunt put it, "One of the first lessons to be learned by young men is to carry the guide of their lives, and the regulator of this conduct in their own bosoms." The proper safeguard of purity should be, in the estimation of the clerk faction,[43] a matter of individual character, not community regulation. The groups of men who rose in support of Dodge and the moral reformers and to concur in their indictment of the city's clerks subscribed to another sociology of morals. They proposed this remedy to lewdness: "That such a change should be reached in the form of contract between the employer and the young man, that the latter may be more effectively shielded from temptations to dishonesty and dissipation." This faction invoked a corporate rather than an individualistic moral system. The clerks' employers, like the head of a Christian household economy, should be bound to provide for the moral well-being as well as the financial remuneration of their workers.[44]

An analysis of the living arrangements and occupations of the parties to this controversy identifies the social and material base from which these disparate perspectives emerged. One of the three instigators of the endorsement of Dodge's remarks boarded in the home of the president of the Female Moral Reform Society, Fanny Skinner. The two others also resided in facsimiles of Christian corporate households: They were Presbyterians who still lived with their parents. All in all, the signatories to the defense of the Reverend Mr. Dodge were a more settled, home-based group. Only 20% of these men were listed as boarders, and even one-fifth of these lodged with either their kin or their employers. The majority of those who attacked moral reform, on the other hand, boarded in private households, unattended by either parents or employers. A full 78.4% of those signing the protest against Dodge fit into this category. Many of these young men, furthermore, resided in the largest, most impersonal boarding places, for example, the National Hotel and the Bleeker Street House. The positions of the two groups on privacy and morality reflected their own living arrangements and degree of independence from the family and the household economy (Table D.1).

The household economy was linked to moral reform through the occupation as well as the residence of the protagonists. Most of the supporters of the associational method of moral surveillance were

not clerks, as they tried to pretend. The bulk of support for moral
reform actually came from the ranks of craftsmen. Two-fifths of the
total represented those classes most likely to retain productive
property within the family unit: artisans, craftsmen, and mechanics. Three farmers even emerged from the urban milieu to lend
their support to the older family order, as enforced by the Female
Moral Reform Society. The society's critics, on the other hand, were
largely clerks (72% of those identified), followed by small numbers
of artisans and professionals (Table D.2). At one point the opponents of moral reform called upon their employers to testify to their
good names. Still, these merchants were clearly identified as a separate, distinct, and detached class of men. Economically, domesti-
cally, and morally, these clerks proclaimed their independence. In
sum, the controversy over female moral reform in 1837 pitted two
diverging family patterns against one another: The partisans of private morality who lived independently of their families squared off
against the representatives of a communal ethic who more often
resided within a household economy.

Although female moral reform seemed to hark back to an older
household order and garner strength from within the ranks of the
old middle class, it also gave birth to some inventive social and
familial forms. Most important, these associated women enhanced
the power of their sex and devised novel methods of sexual control,
to be lodged not in legal and religious institutions but in the man-
date of public opinion and the character of individuals. Even the
opponents of moral reform, including the clerks, endorsed this latter proposition.

Age, occupation, and the proliferation of associations

For all their social influence, however, female moral reformers
helped to produce further cracks in community. In particular, they
acted as catalysts in the creation of a self-conscious interest group
out of a very select element of Utica's social structure, the clerks.
The youthful age group that the clerks represented had actually
demonstrated a strong penchant for associating some time before.
The sheer numerical superiority of the young in the burgeoning
commercial city was bound to give rise to at least informal groupings among men and women of this age. As early as 1814, for example, it was to "young men" that the call for planning the Fourth of
July celebration was addressed. A year later, it was young women
who founded the first Sunday schools and young males and females

who would meet regularly to plan and discuss this special mission of youthful evangelicals. It was also an appeal to young men to attack the "monied powers" that had launched the Jacksonian political organization in Utica.[45] Youth became an explicit basis of formal association in the 1830s. Ward Hunt, the spokesman against the associational methods of moral reform, was himself a member of two of these groups, the Young Men's Association, founded in 1834, and the Literary Club, founded two years earlier.

The official requirements for membership in youth organizations were minimal and simple, merely a matter of biological age. The Young Men's Association was the only such organization to specify this criterion of membership, and it was defined very loosely as being between the ages of fifteen and thirty-five. Older men, furthermore, could retain membership if they paid a slightly higher annual fee.[46] The unofficial defining feature of the membership of these organizations, however, was more specialized. Examination of the *City Directory* reveals that members of the Young Men's Association and the Young Men's Literary Club conformed to a common pattern of residence. In the 1830s, 90% of the members of these associations were boarders. Most of them appeared to reside with individuals to whom they were unrelated, and large numbers hung their hats in the big, impersonal hotels and boardinghouses of the city (Table D.3).

The young men's associations of Utica also recruited their members from a select segment of the local occupational structure. Their membership lists by no means represented a cross section of the town's population. Only 14% were artisans and even fewer were merchants or shopkeepers. More than 50% of those who allied with these organizations were professionals, predominantly lawyers and law students. The city's clerks were the second major presence in young men's associations; they constituted 21% of the members whose occupations could be identified, about three times their proportion among the adult males of the city (Table D.4).

In terms of age, residence, and occupation, then, this mode of association emerged out of the most fluid elements of the population. It appealed to young migrants to the city who resided with fellow transients while they embarked on their careers within the new, white-collar middle class, especially as fledgling lawyers or clerks. The latter group was in special need of the services of associations. With the increasing scale of merchandising, the large stores and offices of Genesee Street required more retail clerks and bookkeepers than could be boarded in the households of the merchants.

Whereas 30% of the city's clerks had resided with their employers and were part of a traditional mercantile apprenticeship in 1828, that figure had declined to only 10% by 1840. Only a minority of the remainder lived in private households or with their relatives. Consequently, a full 44% of the clerks had nowhere to go but to the homes of relative strangers or the narrow chambers and crowded lobbies of the multistoried hotels and boardinghouses that clustered around Bagg's Square in the heart of the commercial district (Table B.5).

Many of these clerks joined a young men's association in the hope of encountering the warm human intercourse and mutual support lacking in their boarding places. The Literary Club, for example, met first in the residence of one of the few home-owning members and later adjourned to a room of their own in the Washington Hotel. The association became a kind of makeshift home in the hours after work. The members acted as keepers of a common hearth, resolving in November 1831: "That the members of this society in alphabetical rotation sweep this room and make the fires and put the room in order preparatory to the meeting of the society."[47] The Young Men's Association ultimately created a cozy surrogate home for the boarders of Utica; they purchased an old family residence and stocked it with a library of several hundred volumes.

Young men's associations, in other words, assumed some of the emotional and personal nuances of everyday family life. Some former members of the Young Men's Association, all recently moved to New York City, recalled this function in a letter to their "young friends at *home*." They spoke nostalgically: "While memory holds her seat, your interest and your fortunes will live in our remembrance." The feelings of the departed youth for the former haven of the Young Men's Association can only be described as ardent, for they sent a timepiece and prayed that "the vibration of the pendulum may be as true as the pulsation of the hearts, which present this tribute of respect, and affection."[48] The youth associations operated like a family of brothers, resembling the sisterly reform networks of their era more than the hierarchical benevolent societies of their parents. In the process of associating, young men in the 1830s were forming a new kind of social bond, one based on common interest, age, and status and nourishing warm, democratic, mutually supportive emotional ties.

The clerks and lawyers who composed this association craved more than emotional support: They also came to the city in search of employment and ambitious for advancement. Members of the

Literary Club described their impetus to association this way: "It is deemed expedient to form a society of young men for the purpose of debate and general improvement."[49] The weekly debates held by the club were particularly useful to young lawyers who jumped at a chance to perfect their skills as public speakers. The debates, lectures, and libraries, in addition to the informal business contacts, and practice in the social graces offered by young men's associations were serviceable to ambitious clerks as well as lawyers. Young men's associations actually functioned as collective forums for *self*-improvement. The benefits of association accrued to individuals in the form of better career prospects. For this reason and because young men inevitably aged and became disqualified for membership, this mode of association had a particularly transitory character.

The composition of the young men's associations also illustrates the rather unstable class distinctions that were entangled with the bonds of association. The clerks did emerge briefly from under the cover of young men's groups in the year 1841. They rose, moreover, in awareness of their distinct economic position and in protest against their employers. Their demand was meager enough, simply that the local retail stores where the clerks were employed close their doors at eight rather than nine o'clock each evening. The tone was certainly respectful. The clerks presented themselves as "duly sensible of the many acts of kindness which have been extended to them by their employers."[50] Even this degree of cohesion as an occupational group and the directness of this confrontation with employers was nearly unprecedented in the history of Utica. The solidarity of the clerks, as presented in a public meeting and in resolutions printed in the local press, was undoubtedly cradled in their earlier associational history. It reached this relatively high level of articulation, further, in a social space for removed from the family economy. All the leaders of the clerks' protest were boarders; only one shared a residence with a relative; only one resided with his employer.[51] No permanent organization of any sort seems, however, to have emerged from this brief crystallization of an occupational interest group.

Solidarity and organization were also visible but primitive among other economic groupings. Artisans and laborers, printers, cordwainers, and cartmen customarily paraded as corporate associations on the Fourth of July but apparently did not engage in collective action of economic matters. The impulse of class consciousness made a fleeting public appearance in the 1830s under the banner of the Oneida Workingmen's Association. This group, founded in 1832, was open to "the producing classes – the farmers, mechanics and other working men," the broad spectrum of occupations typical of such organizations in the 1830s. The purpose of the organization, furthermore, "the general improvement" of the producing classes through the sharing of "useful and practical knowledge," was more associational than economic.[52] The Workingmen's Association was foreshadowed five years earlier by a similar voluntary society for the purpose of mutual improvement and benevolence. A group of artisans met at John King's tavern in 1827 to found the Mechanics Association whose membership was to be confined to "practical mechanics." Within a few years, however, the Mechanics Association had become merely a handsome public auditorium where the middle and upper classes gathered to hear scientific lectures or view exhibits of technological wonders.[53]

There was only one occasion on which laboring men organized exclusively in their own self-interest. This occurred in 1834 when an ad hoc Mechanics Convention met in Utica to protest the state prisons' use of convict labor. In protesting competition from prison labor, the mechanics delineated their own class position in the usual broad and imprecise terms. They associated their interests with those of farmers, merchants, and professionals. In a move bound to frustrate an American historian in search of working-class consciousness, they disparaged prison-trained artisans as "men destitute of capital." The principals in the Mechanics Convention included the likes of Alfred Munson, maker of burrstones, who within a decade would become the wealthiest single individual in Utica.[54] It is not that these mechanics were bereft of class consciousness, for they accurately articulated their place in Utica's mode of production. They were small manufacturers in a pre-industrial city, whose independent skills and property put them in positions analogous to farmers and shopkeepers and even in reach of the local haute bourgeoisie.

This plastic notion of class became most apparent when the mechanics commented on family matters. The assembled small producers expressed particular concern for the prospects of their sons. Their broadsides contained several arguments to this effect: "Suppose a respectable farmer or other citizen should send his son to some mechanic to learn a trade; and on finding him at his workshop would find him seated by the side of a discharged convict; might he not complain . . . who would have approved the presence of his son in such company." The mechanics let it be known that they anticipated geographical and social mobility for their progeny and some novel ambitions for their sons. For example, they expressed their alarm at price competition from the products of convict labor as follows: "The mechanic with his family . . . has the honest right not only to a livelihood for himself and them, but to save from his earnings the means of education for his children; and comfort for himself in old age."[55] In making such an argument, Utica's mechanics exiled to the past the ideal of corporate household, which progressed through the family cycle in slow and predictable stages. Rather, these mechanics seemed, first, to anticipate the purchase of a child's vocational training outside the artisan household and, second, to contemplate spending their old age without the filial protection of a son's household. "Improvement" and the projection of such mobility for the sons of artisans and farmers were endemic to the fluid class structure of the 1830s and contributed to the vivacious but unstable nature of associations.

By the close of the 1830s the process of association seemed to have reached an impasse. It had engendered open and virulent conflict and splintered the community into myriad interest groups. No single association could any longer presume to speak to or for the general public or to define the common good on moral, political, or economic matters. Should an association issue its exhortations in too shrill a voice, it might expect a riot in response. Even an evening of mutual improvement at the Young Men's Literary Club, among age and class peers, could end in bitter quarrels over national poltiics. In such a community context, associations could serve only more limited purposes. They could offer mutual support on some circumscribed terms and for a very homogeneous group. An association could, for example, still pay death benefits for Welsh immigrants. The potential of associations to assume major societal functions or to reform a whole community, however, would seem to have been exhausted.

Temperance: the apotheosis of associations

Nonetheless, observers of the Thanksgiving Day parade in the year 1840 would find that the ranks of association had been replenished once again in support of a widely popular reform. The marching units for that year included the Utica Total Abstinence Society, the Catholic Total Abstinence Society, the Youth Abstinence Society, and the Utica City Total Abstinence Association. When it came to the issue of temperance, and indeed even its most extreme doctrine, total abstinence, a wide spectrum of the community endorsed and participated in association. A collection of temperance songs, published in Utica and called the *Washingtonian Pocket Companion*, voiced the new wave of associationism in the following dulcet tones:

> Hark! hark the sweet music that sounds o'er the land,
> And thrills in the ears of us all;
> As louder and more loud does each cold water band
> Respond to the temperance call;
> While thousands spring up from each valley and hill,
> And seizing the spirited strain,
> Send back the glad challenge with hearty good will,
> From hilltop to valley again.

The Washingtonian movement, founded in 1840 by some apprentices in Baltimore, Maryland, was particularly popular in Utica and throughout the hills and valleys that the market town served. One chapter of Washingtonians met nearly every weekday evening in Utica in the 1840s, when it was estimated that eight thousand citizens had signed the Washingtonian pledge to abstain from the use of all intoxicating beverages. Another chapter in New York Mills enlisted more than 350 members at its first meeting in 1842.[56]

Temperance men and women, assembled in their various divisions, perhaps marked off by occupational, neighborhood, ethnic, or religious affiliations, together constituted one large cold-water army. Cognizant of the pitfalls of association in the age of evangelism and Jacksonianism, the Washingtonian association pledged "carefully to avoid any course of conduct which shall give countenance to one particular religion or political sect of men in preference to another."[57] The benign yet ennobling nature of the cause legitimized the participation of everyone regardless of age or sex. Children could, and did, form juvenile temperance associations without challenging adult authority. Sunday-school pupils joined the cold-water army, following in the age ranks that included the Sons, and the Cadets, of Temperance. Women were welcomed into the Daughters of Temperance and the Martha Washington Union. The potential for ethnic or class conflict was defused by the pluralism of temperance associations. Irishmen formed their Hibernian associations, and a group of self-conscious members of the producing classes formed the Workingmen's Temperance Union. There was even a contingent of black women in Utica's cold-water army. The separate associations respected one another's boundaries and were tolerant of outsiders and even of inebriates. The Hibernian

Total Abstinence Society, for example, patiently held a cold-water celebration every St. Patrick's Day in the shadow of the major celebration, which featured the convivial drunkenness produced by a score of toasts and was sanguinely tabulated the following morning by bleary-eyed newspaper editors.

The membership of the temperance associations of the 1840s was characteristically presented as a group of young men, as "sons of temperance," not as patriarchal heads of households. The commonest symbol of their solidarity was the metaphor of fraternity. The literature of the Sons of Temperance painted brotherhood in the warmest colors: "It is love that prompts us to open the hand of kindness to a brother's want – to watch by his couch in sickness – to wipe from his brow the dew of death at last to bear his remains to the solemn place." The last allusion refers to the funeral benefits that temperance lodges often administered. More often, the fraternal relations of the temperance members were presented in unadulterated emotional terms, as effusive evocations of the sentiments of love. The Washingtonians sang it repeatedly:

> Love is the strongest tie
> That can our hearts unite;
> Love brings to life and liberty
> The drunkard chained in night.[58]

Such gushes of sentiment seemed to transcend class differences. On the one hand, the movement had the endorsement of the community elite. The Walcott family enrolled in the New York Mills Washingtonian Association and Benjamin served as its first president.[59] Utica's city fathers also smiled on temperance and welcomed each association to the line of march in the Fourth of July parade (hardly a reception that abolitionists or female moral reformers could expect). The rank and file of the temperance movement, however, came from a different social background. The temperance press, which included a long run of weekly newspapers, was particularly deferential to the "producing classes," to farmers, artisans, and workingmen. Conversely, the editors were known to cast a disdainful glance upon the city's "upper ten." They systematically courted the support of Irish immigrants and even had good words to say about factory girls. When one local pundit defined a reformer as "a hatter, a tailor or a shoemaker," he might well have been speaking of the temperance movement. The ranks of artisans were well represented in the scattered lists of officers for the various temperance unions. (The Merrill family, by the way, sent two sons, Bradford and George, into the Cadets of Temperance.) In the absence of a precise accounting of the overall membership of Utica and Whitestown temperance societies, it can only be said that a wide range of occupations and statuses were represented, within a movement whose literary productions rang with the praises of the sober middling sort of the pre-industrial city.[60]

Class and occupation could at the same time also take on a chameleonlike quality in the perspective of temperance advocates. Intemperance, on the one hand, was conceived of as the classic precipitant of downward mobility; abstinence, on the other, was the highway to wealth. One temperance newspaper supplied its readers with advice on "How to Rise in Business" and assured them that under the discipline of temperate habits "nothing can hinder you from accumulating."[61] Temperance was advanced as a kind of class characteristic in its own right, a sure guarantee of respectability, reliability, and general moral and economic worth. According to no less an authority than A. B. Johnson, sobriety was a basic component of sound business practice. The good old days when business could be blended with the brew, and when adolescent drinking was a sign of manliness, had long passed. In the risky market conditions of the canal era, a shrewd businessman would not place his stock in the hands of an intemperate clerk of lawyer.[62] In other words, temperance was advertised as a kind of solvent of whatever class differences were developing within the commercial city. All occupations would benefit from its practice and each rank might find in it the avenue to upward mobility.

The hierarchy of sex and age seemed equally vulnerable to the leveling tendency of temperance association. It is quite likely that, contrary to all the rhetoric about brotherhood, women dominated the temperance ranks. In the New York Mills Washingtonian Society, for example (the only Oneida County temperance group to leave an extensive roster), 61% of all members were female. Furthermore, contrary to the sex segregation of most associations, this society enrolled males and females in one common organization. The leveling of age distinctions was also officially sanctioned by the temperance movement. In 1850 the *Utica Teetotaler* found it archaic to presume that "young men are fit neither for generals nor statesmen, and that they must be kept in the background until their physical strength is impaired by age, and their intellectual faculties become blunted by the weight of years."[63] In the estimation of the editors, men in their twenties and thirties were fit to exercise civic power and responsibility. The status of youth seemed, like that of women, to rise wherever the forces of association gathered strength.

The last remnants of the old household order seemed to be dissolving in the fraternal draughts of Oneida County teetotalers. The very walls of the homes of Utica appeared to break open as all ages, both genders, and a range of occupations streamed out into the reformers halls. The temperance meeting was in itself a kind of ersatz and sentimental home. The *Utica Teetotaler* printed a poetic rendition of this theory of association in 1850.

> I was far from my home not a relative near
> To sooth all my sorrows or quell the deep sigh;
> Not a friend could I see, or a voice could I hear
> To cheer me in hope that could brighten my eye . . .
> Then she lifted her banner high o'er my head
> Whose folds are all cherished on land and on sea
> When the trumpet of wisdom awoke from the dead
> My soul when I found a mother to me.[64]

The metaphor of a maternal embrace, like that of fraternity, affirmed affection as the primary bond between members of both associations and families. In the 1840s in Oneida County, however, this hallmark of the cult of domesticity found its most enthusiastic expression not in the family itself but in the temperance association.

The alliance of family and association

It would be erroneous, nonetheless, to regard family and association as arch competitiors for the loyalties of the men, women, and children of Oneida County. The history of reform, particularly in its more evangelical and democratic phase of the 1830s and 1840s, is interlaced with alliances between the family and association. In fact, many men, women, and children made their way into the ranks of reformers as kin groups. The membership lists of the New York Mills Temperance Society, for example, read like a rhythmic litany of common surnames. Of the signers of the Washingtonian pledge, 90% were accompanied by kin. They entered the lists against drunkenness, furthermore, in tightly ordered family ranks. For example, the names of two males of the Loomis family appear together on one page and on another are two females by the same name. Benjamin Chapman and Benjamin Chapman, Jr., are listed at one point in the ledger, and Mrs. Chapman and two other women by the same name appear together farther down the page. The pattern is endlessly repeated and accounts for the vast bulk of the Washingtonian's membership.

A glance at the few membership lists of other associations elucidates the same relationship. The Maternal Association, it will be
recalled, harbored four women named Merrill. Also numbered
among the association's seventy members were two Butlers, three
Clarkes, two Doolittles, two Manchesters, two Parsons, and an unknown number of blood sisters who did not share a surname. Kin
ties abounded even within the association, which attracted the
most mobile and deracinated population, the clerks who organized
to oppose female moral reform. Slightly more than one-fourth of the
young men who signed the protest against the Reverend Mr. Dodge
had the support of a relative, usually a fellow clerk, who boarded in
a separate household. The proponents of Female Moral Reform had
essentially the same rate of kin associations. In this group are found
the old Presbyterian families that huddled together throughout the
history of revivals and reform: the Merrills, the Vernons, the Kel-
loggs, the Hastings, the Ostroms, the Doolittles.

These tangled links between families and reformers were, however, voluntary, diffuse, detached from the workplace, and thus essentially versatile and portable as well. Those brother-pairs of
clerks most likely left home together and traveled to Utica in search
of employment. The records of the Mercantile Agency reveal a similar pattern. The capital for numerous local businesses was drained
away to support brothers and sisters in Detroit and Chicago, to
name two favored destinations of Utica émigrés. The dual ties of
kin and reform association were just as transportable. The *Utica
Teetotaler* frequently reported on the whereabouts and fidelity of
departed members. They were happy to announce, for example,
that one of their departed brethren and a son of the local temperance leader, Jacob Vanderhyden, had joined the gold rush to California and remained temperate all the way. Other departed sons
would write back to their parents assuring them that they had
found a surrogate home within a local chapter of the Washingtonians.[65] The corporate household may have been dissolving in the
frenetic conditions of commercial capitalism, yet family and kinship endured and exercised their social influence in this more diffuse and voluntary manner. Many of the family's characteristic
functions, however, were shared with a purely voluntaristic social
unit, the association.

Family and associations were not only allies in such causes as
temperance and sexual reform; they had come to resemble each
other in internal organization as well. The economic bonds between kinsmen themselves were not entirely unlike the links be-

tween members of voluntary associations. The credit records of the 1840s reveal a very high level of family cooperation in business matters. As measured by the Mercantile Agency records, 60% of all enterprises resorted to partnership, ad hoc and temporary but nevertheless legalized association, at some point in their usually speckled careers. The kin network was a major recruiting ground for such business partners. Three of the nineteen partnerships listed in the 1817 village directory involved consanguinal kin, and an equal number are known to have united in-laws.[66] The records of the Mercantile Agency allow a more precise account of the pattern of family partnerships in the 1840s. Of all partnerships, 36%, or 20% of the total businesses, united family members in this dissolvable and contracted economic association. Blood was much more important than marriage in forming these business units; although fathers and sons were the principal parties to partnerships, more than one-fifth of all family businesses were managed by brothers (Table B.6).

Formalized partnerships were only one of the voluntary family associations favored by Utica businessmen. Almost 1 in 5 of the investigations of the Mercantile agent led to the identification of the family as a source of credit and capital. These financial ties did not necessarily descend in the old patriarchal fashion: In 20% of the cases, wives, sons, brothers, or in-laws, not fathers, were the source of needed capital. Similarly, Utica's businesses were passed on to a variety of relatives, usually by purchase rather than by inheritance. Businesses were transferred to fathers, wives, and mothers, as well as inherited by sons. Relatives also exercised the freedom of association in the negative. The Mercantile Agency reported on more than one occasion that a wealthy relative, and even a wife, refused to extend credit to a needy kinsman. All these statistics point to more diffuse and voluntary relations among relatives; the family economy had become a sort of mutual benefit society for kinsmen (Table B.7).

The wills and credit records speak to the experience of only a small group of property holders and businessmen. There is also evidence, however, that the less affluent families were forming qualitatively different economic bonds. The work ledgers of the New York Mills Company offer concrete testimony to these reformulations of the relationship between work and family.[67] The records available for the 1840s show that workers were no longer congregated in family units, with fathers at their financial head. Another form of kin association held strong in the absence of the former

patriarchal and corporate arrangements. Two-thirds of all the
workers were accompanied to the factory by persons of the same
surname. Most of them worked in the actual presence of one another in the very same sections of the mills, be they spooling rooms,
warping rooms, or weaving rooms. Most of the kinsmen who
worked together in New York Mills were of the same sex and similar age, probably young brothers and sisters. As such they were
bonded together by common interest and experience, without the
supervision of the household head and in opposition to an often
alien work situation. Such conditions were the makings of a real
sisterhood and brotherhood of workers, not just the fictive kinship
of benevolent and reform associations.

It was actually the reform association that best articulated the
more affectionate and voluntaristic ambience of the family. The
Washingtonians sang hymns to this new domesticity to the tune of
"Home Sweet Home." The ideal of family life can be read between
the lines of a typical maudlin tableau:

> Oh sad was the heart of his grief-stricken wife,
> Whom he vow'd at the altar to cherish for life.
> His children once fondled, now trembled with fear,
> As the sound of his footsteps fell sad on their ear."[68]

This favorite image of the temperance writers assumed that the
good and sober family had an affectionate infrastructure, where
wives were "cherished" and children "fondled." At the same time,
this temperance literature prescribed a distinctive division of roles
and differentiation of personality within the ideal home. The refrain of the poem quoted above put the responsibility for domestic
disaster squarely on the shoulders of the husband and father: "He
felt all the world, but himself was to "Blame. Blame. Blame." Hymn
number 26 in the *Washingtonian Pocket Companion* rendered the
same message in an even more incisive manner. "The Song of the
Drunkard's Child" began this way:

> Oh, pity me lady, I am hungry and cold;
> Should I all my sorrows to you unfold,
> I'm sure your kind breast with compassion would flame,
> My father's a drunkard – But I'm not to blame.[69]

It was the temperance movement that most actively and emphati-
cally enjoined men to practice the prudence and self-control incumbent upon them as husbands, fathers, and breadwinners.

At the time of the Washingtonian movement, the fathers of Utica
were particularly hard pressed to execute their economic roles.
Countless small businesses, the livelihoods of the middling sort

who flocked into the temperance associations, were destroyed in the Panic of 1837. Even when the local economy revived in the 1840s (at a time when credit records are available for the city of Utica), small businesses were still precarious operations. One firm in four was declared a failure, and the average business endured only six years or less. Utica's shoemakers, those incorrigible reformers by local accounts, were particularly hard hit in the 1840s. The city sustained a dwindling proportion of cordwainers after 1840, and thus it became increasingly difficult for shoemakers to employ their sons in the beleaguered family business. At the same time, the chances of moving slowly upward from the shoemaker's bench to becoming the owner of a small business were dramatically curtailed. The incidence of such advancement to independent proprietorship was cut in half between the 1830s and the 1850s (Table B.4). Both paternal anxiety and temperance reform were logical, if not inevitable, by-products of these economic conditions. Temperance expressed and symbolized all the ways in which the men of the commercial city were required to toe a straight line through these risky economic circumstances.

Simultaneously, the temperance movement projected revisions in the familial roles of women. The grieving wives and bountiful ladies honored in the Washingtonian hymnal seemed exempted from the economic burdens of husbands and fathers. Their specialty was pure, altruistic moral service to their families. One writer put women's role this way: "with gentle weapons of filial, maternal and conjugal persuasion [to] accomplish more than men even if clad in a panoply of steel."[70] The details of this gentle ministry had been worked out not in the temperance movement but in the women's organizations that predated it, especially the maternal associations and female moral reform societies. These two associations devised methods of cultivating temperate habits and restraining sexual drives, as well as appetites for liquor, in their husbands and children. The remodeled female role of maternal socialization, as well as the image of the Victorian wife setting a pure standard for her more passionate husband, were first enunciated by associated women in the 1820s and 1830s and were put to the service of the temperance cause in the 1840s.

These gender stereotypes of males as responsible, self-controlled breadwinners and of females as gentle nurturing mothers were flanked in the temperance literature by yet another central familial image – that of the young man about to depart from home for a new walk in life. Although such young men found opportunities to exercise some independence and establish autonomous associations among their peers in the city by the canal, they were also being pulled back into familial relationships that were deemed particularly supportive of moral reform. Some fathers made their son's inheritance contingent on keeping the Washingtonian pledge. The will of Ebenezer Ames, probated in 1854, illustrated this explicit connection between temperance and economic well-being. Ames granted his son's inheritance on the condition that he remain "free from all vicious habits and doesn't drink spirits or use tobacco in any form from boyhood to his twenty-first year." One Joseph Seaton resorted to a similar strategy for the reform of his son John, whose legacy was not to be awarded until he had "established a character for temperance and sobriety for the period of one year."[71] Mothers, for their part, resorted to emotional rather than monetary pressure, as learned in maternal associations or the temperance or moral reform movements, to similarly tighten the bonds with their children. In either case the new kind of family persuasion had replaced the patriarchal sanctions of the household economy. If not a farm, a set of artisan tools, or the wherewithal to open a shop, the mothers and the fathers of the canal era could offer their young sons who were about to leave home some moral capital in the form of training in temperance, purity, and prudence.

Out of the reform associations, in other words, had come a new kind of bond between the generations, one that had been anticipated by the family organizations of the Second Great Awakening. Whereas revivals had cultivated grace in the souls of sons and daughters, reform associations trafficked in sound character-traits. The reformers' objective for their children was not salvation but a good reputation. This new family collateral was honored not just in heaven but in the commercial marketplace of Utica as well. The credit records of the 1840s were replete with references to young men with "small capital, good character."

The agent of the Mercantile Agency, forerunner of Dun and Bradstreet, considered the virtue of temperance among the criteria for a good credit rating. Utica's agent was known to shatter the hopes of an enterprising young businessman with such epithets as "intemperate habits," "likes to drink too much," or "leads a sporting life." The Mercantile Agency might have been in collusion with the Female Moral Reform Society as well as the Washingtonians. The economic epitaph of F. W. Marchisi was written in the credit records as follows: "Got mixed up with a bad woman." In another report, that for "J. H. Read and Sons, grocers," two generations were banished from the rolls of sound creditors with this single indictment: "Only of fair character and run after the women." Wills and credit records – loving parents and calculating businessmen alike – agreed that the cost of intemperance and sexual licence was measured in money, not just in the tears of mothers, wives, and children.[72] In this instance, then, the temperance and moral reform associations performed a function that would later be assumed by the family, the socialization of children and young adults to the traits of character necessary to secure a comfortable social and economic niche, one that must be achieved, not ascribed nor contingent on the caprice of the family cycle. Associations, in sum, were working changes in class and economics as well as age, gender, and familial roles.

In the end the reform associations of the thirties and forties seemed the means to a larger end, that of adjusting individuals to the new economic and social order. It was becoming increasingly clear moreover that the family and not the association would assume this key role in the system of social reproduction. As early as the 1840s the raucous aspects of revivalism and reform produced some appeals for retreat into familial and private spaces. The Universalists eschewed public and even family prayer in favor of "moments of privacy and meditation." The relish for privacy came even from evangelical quarters by the close of the 1830s. The Reverend Raymond Weeks attacked the protracted meetings of his church for distracting Christians from "the duties of the family and the duties of the closet."[73] Similar arguments also rose up from within the reform movements themselves. *Mother's Magazine* had, by the late 1830s, lost interest in the associated activities of female reformers and advised that it was woman's fate to "pass her life in domestic privacy."[74] Little more was heard of maternal associations in the 1840s, and the Female Moral Reform Society collapsed in 1845. At the same time the male reformers were turning away from moral persuasion into more political channels. The anti-slavery societies turned away from the local community network to form the Liberty Party and devote their energies to national politics. The temperance movement turned toward the larger political arena a few years later, with its focus on the legislative prohibiton of the sale of alcohol. The decline of the associational brotherhood was tellingly recorded by the Sons of Temperance in the 1840s when they dispensed with collecting sick benefits for one another and contracted instead with an insurance company.[75]

The associated mode of community organization could not maintain its preeminence much beyond 1845, when Utica's population would begin to rise again and diversify with the advances of large-scale industrial production. For close to two decades, however, Utica and some of the surrounding communities had maintained a unique form of social organization. Much of the region's social life was conducted in association and thereby infused with a sense of voluntarism, equality, and ingenuity that would thrill the heart of a Fourth of July orator in the age of Jackson.

The association had become the fulcrum of public opinion and influence within a specific set of social circumstances, circumstances that existed in Oneida County in the 1830s and 1840s. The social relations of a pre-industrial, but aggressively commercial, regional economy opened up copious opportunities for association in social spaces once absorbed by the trilogy of household, town, and church. Groups of individuals and circles of women were freed from the home economy and hierarchy of the church to construct their own ways of supplying social services, promoting favorite causes, and finding human companionship, all on a voluntary basis. At the same time that association thrived on the maturation of commercial agriculture, it required strict limitations on urban growth and diversification. Only in a relatively small and homogeneous town could association provide a major and expansive component of social organization. The men and women of Utica were in easy reach of one another in 1840 when the entire city was only ten blocks square. Only then could individuals rely on informal, face-to-face contacts as the mechanism for providing extrafamilial social services, education, and entertainment. Associations could divide up the community on the basis of differences in sex, age, religion, and adjacent ranks in a predominantly property-holding population, without risking complete social disintegration. The openness and fluidity, as well as the relative smallness and familiarity, of Utica in the canal era were the breeding ground of associations.

For a brief but critical moment in the 1830s and 1840s, family history was suspended between the patriarchal household and the middle-class home. In that moment the men and women of Oneida County stepped outside their households and into associations where they collectively devised novel modes of social support and security as a counterpoise to the frenzy of a rapidly growing market town. In the decades to follow, as Utica's economy thrust onward toward industrial capitalism, the popularity of associations would subside and the ideological and social functions of moral reform societies would become the stock-in-trade of private conjugal families. This retreat into the private family was propelled in part by the same forces that gave rise to associations, the social and psychic discomfort of an increasingly mobile, segmented, and impersonal social order. Yet the associations themselves had designed or anticipated much of the specific content, character, and inner workings of these newly constructed middle-class homes. The chapters to follow describe the legacy and culmination of the era of association: the coalescence of the volatile gender, age, and class relations that characterized Utica before 1850 into the family strategies that reproduced the American middle class.

4 Privacy and the making of the self-made man: family strategies of the middle class at midcentury

Voluntary association did not suddenly fade from the American scene after 1845. In commemoration of the Union victory on July 4, 1865, the spirit of association paraded down the streets of Utica in full regalia. Fifteen lodges, at least one temperance society, and five fire companies joined the patriotic procession. The typographical union, the carmen, and the cabinetmakers filed into the streets just as in decades past. They were joined by some newer contingents as well. Five associations composed of immigrants and Roman Catholics entered the line of march to give a more cosmopolitan tone to the celebration of the nation's birthday. Even the growing proletariat was welcomed into this parade of associations. The Utica press reported that the "operatives of the Cotton and Woolen factories" marched in a body. It would seem that at least in the jubilant spirit of the Fourth of July the distinctive fragments of an increasingly complicated urban society, with its ethnic complexity and industrial sector, could still come together to form a pastiche community.[1]

A closer look at some of the marching units in 1865, however, reveals some important nuances in this ritual of community solidarity. Those fire companies, for example, were no longer voluntary associations but rather an assemblage of paid public servants. Behind them in the parade came another curious innovation, a wagon carrying thirty-six young women, chosen, we are told, for their fair faces and fine proportions, each one carrying the insignia of a state in the Union. These harbingers of municipal bureaucracies and beauty pageants suggest a subtle but important shift in the organization of urban society. Once the whole town was knit casually together by face-to-face bonds and alliances; now new sorts of social glue were required: first, an expansion of the formal public sector as illustrated by the city fire department and, second, a recourse to symbolic modes of social cohesion such as a carload of local beauties who represented some abstract notion of national unity.

Further evidence of a quiet transformation in Utica's social order can be spied *between the lines* of the Fourth of July procession – in the segments of the population that were conspicuously absent

145

from the patriotic procession. No Protestant association or reform
group made a public appearance. Neither did the growing ranks of
the new middle class; neither professionals nor clerks formed themselves into a marching unit. The absence of these groups, which
had played such a prominent role in the associated life of the canal
era, would seem to be deliberate and self-conscious. Six years earlier the minister of the Utica Presbyterian Church made this observation about the participants in the Thanksgiving Day parade, a
town festival originally instituted to commemorate the traditions of
New England Protestants. "There were the working and laboring
classes of our city who had little time for enjoyment and the time of
most of them was for this world. If they knew the joys and pleasures
that flowed from pure religion how sweet would be their rest at
night – when the tasks of the day are done."

In this pastor's opinion, parades were an amusement of the lower
classes and manual workers and an illegitimate one at that. Respectable people celebrated Thanksgiving in the church and at home, not
in the public streets. A few years later a parishioner of the same
church, Lavinia Johnson, observed the Thanksgiving Day parade
from the quiet of her parlor. To Mrs. Johnson, such rituals served
only "to draw the rabble of the city." She was particularly shocked
to find females participating in this unseemly public activity. "Why
can't women stay at home," she asked. "Poor women, and try to
make home comfortable and take care of their children?"[2] Just a few
decades earlier, the women of Lavinia Johnson's congregation had
taken to the streets on a variety of evangelical missions and won the
reputation of noisy, prying, obtrusive busybodies. Now they withdrew into their private homes and shunned public rituals, including
such Yankee traditions as Thanksgiving Day and the Fourth of July.

Varieties of social retreat:
domesticity, privacy, and the self-made man

This apparent retreat into a private world was endorsed by a voluminous body of popular literature that historians have labeled the
"cult of domesticity."[3] The literate middle-class population of Utica
had subscribed to the ideology of domestic privacy for some time.
In 1837 a local publication entitled the *Young Ladies' Miscellany*
enunciated the most central proposition of the cult of domesticity
when it prescribed that "woman lives best, and most powerfully in
the private role, where the historian yet seldom penetrates – in the
causes of events, which he seldom deeply investigates and in the

modes of action which he seldom finds."[4] By midcentury the middle-class man as well as his wife was being enticed into the same darkened corner of history. The popular literature of the 1850s courted men away from their male associations – from taverns, political clubs, lodges – into the feminine world of the home. *A Voice to the Married,* published locally, told the husband to regard his home as "an elysium to which he can flee and find rest from the stormy strife of a selfish world."[5]

This privatizing trend was articulated not only in the feminine ideology of the cult of domesticity but in a more masculine mode as well, the doctrine of the "self-made man." *A Voice to the Married* did not advise young men to form themselves into associations, neither unions nor mutual benefit associations. The author postulated instead that "a good character must be formed, it must be *made* – it must be built *by our individual exertions*" (emphasis mine). Popular literature at midcentury directed a responsible breadwinner, no less than a loving mother, into a narrowing social universe, one even more solitary than privacy – the domain of the self, the individual, of "manly independence."[6]

Both the cult of domesticity and the mythology of the self-made man were built on the assumption that the household was no longer the place of production, the locus of breadwinning. For most native-born Uticans with middle-range occupations and above, this assumption was correct. According to the listings in the *City Directory,* professionals, white-collar workers, and even prosperous artisans and shopkeepers left home each day for an office, store, or workshop that was detached from their place of residence. Some writers and domestic architects would like to deepen and widen the moat between home and the workplace by relocating middle-class families in bucolic settings on the outskirts of the city itself. At least some of Utica's husbands and fathers had begun this diurnal shuttle before the Civil War. Lavinia Johnson described such a practice in this account of her daughter's living arrangement one summer: "Will will come in the stage every morning to his business and Mary will meet him every night at the carriage in New Hartford to take him to their abode."[7] Such families seemed so determined to secure domestic privacy and isolation that they would fend off both society and history by retreating along the back roads of American economic development into quiet rural villages like New Hartford.

This reverence for quiet, seclusion, and privacy was usually portrayed in popular literature as a reflexive reaction to repellent developments outside the household. *Mother's Magazine* repeatedly warned women to protect their children from the "contamination of the streets." The newspapermen of Utica hardly encouraged their readers to regard the public thoroughfares as a safe and comfortable habitat. By the 1850s calls for "law and order" were front-page news. The *Morning Herald*, for example, ran a regular column entitled "Crimes and Casualties," which, with perverse exuberance, enumerated railroad, steamboat, and industrial accidents, as well as bloodcurdling acts of personal violence – murder, arson, infanticide, and rape. The scene of such atrocities was usually a hostile city street. In 1861 the *Herald* reported the fate of a woman who asked a passerby for directions to the railroad station: attempted rape by four men. In this incident and countless other grisly crime reports, the newspapers of Utica seemed to advertise the streets of their city as alien and threatening social spaces.[8]

But certainly this is something of a libel against the city at mid-century and, conversely, an exaggeration of the quiet and harmony of the American home. The local press also recounts copious examples of convivial social life outside the household. This was the era of Sunday-school picnics, ice-cream socials, and civic baseball games, as well as Fourth of July celebrations. With a population under twenty-five thousand in 1865, Utica's streets were not yet open territory for rapacious criminals. That case of attempted rape, for example, ended with protective interference by observant neighbors. Furthermore, the newly appointed law enforcement officers found more cases of violence within the city's domestic spaces than on the streets. Then, as now, wife beating was the most common violent crime.[9]

When middle-class writers or women like Lavinia Johnson vacated the streets and retreated into the private home, they were responding to more subtle changes in urban social life, to the transformation, rather than the breakdown, of the social order. First of all, the native-born Protestant was reacting to the increasing heterogeneity of the local population. Lavinia Johnson returned bewildered from the nearby railroad station: "Such a crowd of people together and most all strangers to each other, so many strangers."[10] Strangers to Lavinia Johnson were often members of diverse, but internally cohesive, new groups within the local population. Uticans gathered together, for example, in twenty-eight different churches in 1855. What disturbed the likes of Mrs. Johnson was not social and religious anonymity but the fact that the largest such institution brought together Roman Catholics, not her fellow Protestants. The inundation of Utica by Catholics was a result of in-

creasingly massive immigration beginning in the late 1840s and
coming more often from Ireland and Germany than from England or
Canada. By 1845, 40% of the city's residents and a full 60% of the
local heads of household were foreign-born. It was a stream of alien
ways and foreign tongues (not criminals) into the streets of Utica
that caused the native-born middle class such apprehension.

The streets of the city at midcentury were no longer bordered by a
smooth line of small shops and houses. The urban horizon was now
broken by more massive commercial and industrial enterprises.
The steam textile factories founded in the late 1840s were joined by
three large garment works in the next decade, each employing four
hundred workers or more. The 1860s witnessed the sudden growth
and industrialization of the local shoe industry. The largest such
factory contained some eighty sewing machines and could produce
150,000 pairs of boots annually.[11] Even Genesee Street was invaded
by these relatively gargantuan enterprises. William Stacy's Dry
Goods Store at number 104 was enlarged to stock a prodigious array
of goods, including, for example, the forty-two different items of
personal and home furnishings advertised in a single newspaper
notice. Gaffney's Cheap Irish Stores, The China Emporium, and the
warehouses of Lord and Taylor and G. W. Muir of New York City
flooded Genesee Street with commodities and transformed retailing
into such a bustling and impersonal process that shoplifting became a serious local problem. The mass of goods, hum of machinery, and hordes of workers, often of foreign birth, could not but
impress older residents of Utica with the qualitative and disquiet-
ing changes that were occurring in their community.

The larger scale and greater complexity of urban life was apparent
in Utica's political structure as well. A diverse population of more
than twenty thousand people could hardly settle their differences
and make public policy on a face-to-face basis. Only the small villages of Oneida County, such as Whitesborough and New Hartford, held town meetings after 1850. Utica had long since resorted
to an elected town council and employed an increasing number of
salaried, appointed officials – city engineers, policemen, and over-
seers of the poor. Nothing better demonstrated the impersonal
quality of public life than this charge to police officers written into
the city charter of 1862. "Each policeman shall acquire such knowledge of the inhabitants within his beat as to enable him at once to
recognize them. He shall also strictly watch the conduct of all persons of known bad character." Utica's citizenry had abjured their
responsibility to know and assist their neighbors and had foisted it

off on a paid public official who operated within a bureau of the municipal government.[12] In other respects, the people of Utica saw political authority pass entirely out of local jurisdiction. After all, Utica was linked only by the impersonal threads of representative government and party politics to the decisions made in Washington and at Fort Sumter that held the power of life or death over the young men of the town in the 1860s. The preoccupation with privacy had developed in tandem with the enlargement, remoteness, and increasing formality of this public sphere.

All these permutations in urban social life were etched into an engraving of Utica dated 1850.[13] A local artisan named Lewis Bradley portrayed Bagg's Square as the hub of a busy urban scene, placed just to the rear of the primary symbols of the city's commercial and now industrial growth: the Erie Canal and the Utica and Syracuse Railroad. The urban space that radiated out from Bagg's Square was punctuated eleven times by bellowing smokestacks, which dwarfed the fewer, more diminutive church spires. In the far western corner of the panorama, not far from the textile factories, stood the grandiose columns of the New York State Lunatic Asylum, its massive granite a fitting symbol of the power and remoteness of the public sphere. Around these icons of industrial production and public life, Bradley assembled, almost as an afterthought, a largely undifferentiated sea of private dwellings. Most appeared to be two-story one- or two-family houses, except for larger barracks-like residences near the factories. Bradley bothered to depict only two central streets, which cut through this maze of buildings like narrow shaded caverns. The human figures who occupied these streets, furthermore, were either formally attired and were on public display or appeared to be passing briskly through commercial arteries toward some more important destination. Gone were the casual poses, rustic costumes, and leisurely postures favored by the artists who set their easels in Bagg's Square during the canal era. The urban ambience had been transformed into a more massive and formally organized social space, one that arranged social life into private and public sectors.

Lewis Bradley sketched a cool, massive alabaster urban scene. It did not, however, suggest a threatening urban jungle. Neither this sketch nor the social reality of Utica at midcentury justifies the sometimes hysterical urgency with which popular writers advised retreat into a private and individualized world. The reasons for this nervous stance toward the city must be located within the immediate experience of middle-class, native-born Protestants. The decade before

Utica, 1850. Lithograph by D. W. Moody, I. N. Phelps Stokes Collection, Print Collection, New York Public Library, Astor, Lenox and Tilden Foundations.

the Civil War was especially difficult for the old middle class of Utica, the small producers and retailers who once waxed in the abundant opportunities of the canal era. This sector of the occupational structure employed a shrinking proportion of the local population after 1845. Between 1845 and 1856 the relative ranks of both the shopkeepers and the craftsmen were reduced almost by half (Table B.3).

The history of shoemaking during this period illustrates the predicament of the old middle class. Cordwainers in Utica, as in cities throughout the Northeast, saw the value of their skills and business steadily decline as shoemaking became a fully mechanized factory operation. As late as 1860 the Utica economy accommodated considerable numbers of master shoemakers with capital investments in the four figures and a handful of skilled workers in their service. By 1870, however, the solid middling ground of the shoemaking craft had eroded and in its stead stood, on the one hand, massive factories with capital investments of up to $130,000, and, on the other, the small shops and idle benches of shoe-repair men. A worker in Reynolds Shoe Factory might well earn a wage that was comparable to, or even higher than, that of the artisan shoemaker, yet he had clearly surrendered the cherished privileges of the old middle class: title to his own productive property, his own tools, and his own control of the pace and conditions of work.[14] Simultaneously, the journeyman or apprentice shoemaker saw his prospects of becoming an independent artisan diminish apace. Half the cordwainers of 1828 eventually opened small businesses of their own; less than 5% were so fortunate in the 1860s. With the establishment of large garment factories in Utica, the city's hatters and tailors could contemplate the same unhappy fate (Table B.4).

Utica's retailers felt a similar pressure at midcentury, exerted by competition from larger local department stores and the aggressive merchandising of New York wholesalers. Many of the city's shopkeepers were dealt a fatal blow by the Panic of 1857. The records of the Mercantile Agency reported twenty-six outright failures that year and double that number by 1860, complete with sheriff's sales and bankruptcy proceedings; countless other firms quietly "closed up" or "went out of business." The dimensions of the crisis were indicated by the report for the firm of Murdock and Andrews: "Only jewelers in Utica that did not fail during the panic." All these falling fortunes were clearly implicated in the machinations of a complex market system that reached far beyond Utica. The nationwide scope of the panic as well as more intimate business experiences made this patently clear. For example, when Utica's prominent Presbyterian businessman Spencer Kellogg closed his store in 1857, the Mercantile Agency attributed his failure to unsound investments in New York City. The critical link in the disastrous downturn in the national business cycle was Kellogg's own son, of Bliss and Kellogg, New York.[15]

The telescope of family and generational history magnifies the predicament of the old middle class at midcentury. Small-business men who were struggling to keep their own firms solvent were particularly hardpressed to put their progeny on a sound economic footing within the middling sort. Of all the wills processed in Utica after 1850 a mere five witnessed the transfer of a store or workshop to a second generation. The records of the Mercantile Agency also contain paltry testimony to the family networks of small-business men. Between the 1840s and the 1860s the proportion of family partnerships was reduced to one-fourth its former size. Of the 331 businesses reported on between 1860 and 1865, only 10 noted that a son had followed in his father's footsteps. Most of the sons of the old middle class who would come of age in Utica at midcentury could expect to be unceremoniously catapulted into the status of a self-made man (Table B.6).

Just what these young men would make of themselves remained, however, an open and anxious question. A self-made man was by no means assured of being a rich man, for the ranks of large merchants, financiers, and manufacturers accommodated less than 3% of Utica's adult males. Meanwhile, a place within the old middle class, among artisans and shopkeepers, was becoming harder to find and less comfortable to inhabit. The positions in the factories, although they often paid relatively good wages, were insecure and did not attract many native-born youths. Certainly the ranks of day laborers were without allure and, like factory jobs, were given over largely to the foreign-born or their children. More seductive and accessible than any of these occupational niches were posts within the new middle class, chiefly the professions or white-collar jobs. Although white-collar employment was one of the most rapidly growing sectors of the local job market, it could hardly be called booming. In fact, the increase in such positions did not quite keep up with the growth of the population. Clearly, midcentury was a sober time for middle-class families, a time of special anxiety about the economic prospects of the rising generation and a time, perhaps, to withdraw into the private home to assay the prospects ahead.

However, a middle-class family crisis does not translate automatically into a process of privatization. Something more was at work than an instinct to withdraw from an uncertain and threatening world into some familiar space full of loving kin. A more complete explanation of the impulse for privacy must be sought, first of all, within the increasingly individualized nature of middle-class occupations themselves. The corporate, collective aspects of the household economy and the master artisan's retinue of journeymen and apprentices had by the 1850s become overwhelmed by the imperatives of maximizing individual gain in a competitive market. A producer or retailer turned inward to his personal resources, his ability to manage labor, manipulate credit, and set prices in such a way as to outdo his competitors. The newer components of the middle class were more severely cut off from any economic collectivity. A professional or white-collar worker relied increasingly on his own skills, be they as lawyer or bookkeeper, with which to barter for his livelihood. In the more impersonal economic networks of the growing and industrializing city, furthermore, it was incumbent upon members of both the old and the new middle class to demonstrate their own finely tuned aptitudes for business, to display, if not the financial wizardry of an entrepreneur, at least the prudence, honesty, and good sense of a reputable small merchant. Not even inherited wealth could exempt a modern-day businessman from these requirements. Consider the case of James Stocking who, despite all the riches and reputation of his father, Samuel, was dismissed by the Mercantile Agency as "a rich man's son who has been a pretty wild chap. He never was educated to economy."[16] In sum, a kind of geological shift gently quaked beneath the formerly more solid ground of the middling sort, casting asunder the old associational and collective forms and elevating more highly individuated, more private, concerns and imperatives.

Although the processes of individuation and privatization both turn in the same inward direction, away from more expansive social relationships, they are by no means one and the same thing. The doctrine of privacy venerated not the isolated individual but rather a set of intense and intimate social relations, essentially those of the conjugal family. Privacy was a social construction, in other words, and, as a consequence, a product of concrete historical actions. As the previous chapters have recounted, an unusually exuberant history went into the definition of the private sphere. In the crucible of revivals and reform associations, the men and women of Utica had elaborated an array of new social relationships and services and then earmarked them as the responsibility of families. The reforms favored by the old middle classes during the canal era were particularly innovative and productive, contributing to the private sphere such social functions as a new method of childrearing, new standards of self-control, new bourgeois virtues such as temperance and sexual restraint. In short, privacy had been sketched out in sufficient detail before midcentury so as to constitute a palpable set of social relations and functions. Accordingly, it was more than the last refuge of beleaguered individuals fleeing a hostile environment. It exerted its own positive social pull and had many concrete advantages to present to confused men and women. In fact, the associations of the thirties and forties had adumbrated a sequence of private activities that might guide the middle classes out of their predicament at midcentury.

Midcentury Utica, in sum, was at an intricate confluence of social and historical changes: Steady advances in the scale and capitalization of industrial production, shifts in the middle ranges of the occupational structure, and alterations in the social and political arrangement of the city converged with the associational legacy of innovative family forms. The consequences of these commingled forces can be sorted out in several ways: as the divergence of private and public life, as the separation of male and female spheres, as the emergence of a cult of domesticity and the parallel masculine ideal of the self-made man. I have chosen to draw out one salient strand in this complex historical fabric, the process whereby the native-born Protestant members of the middle class learned to work within the private sphere to maintain their own positions in the social structure and to provide similar comforts for their progeny. What follows should not be construed as a systematic, causal analysis of class formation. It does, however, identify a sequence of family practices typical of the native-born Protestants who would, in a period of major economic changes, maintain middle-range positions in the local social structure. The rest of this chapter, then, will describe some strategies whereby the American middle class reproduced itself in an industrializing society.

The birth and rearing of Victorian children

These strategies began with biological reproduction itself. A look at the completed family size of mothers in their fifties in the year 1865 (and hence whose fertility cycle began in the 1830s) indicates that native-born parents had begun to rationalize the process of reproduction at an early date. This generation of women would bear on the average only 3.6 children as opposed to a mean score of 5.8 for those twenty years older and 5.08 for those only ten years their seniors. In other words, an abrupt drop in the fertility of the native-born women of Utica occurred during the heyday of the canal era. The parents of these smaller families had already forestalled and reduced the problems of reproducing the middle class. At least they would have to worry about placing only one or two sons on the ladder to comfort and respectability.

It is not entirely fallacious to impute such conscious fertility control to the native-born men and women who began their families in the thirties and forties. The determination of native-born couples to intervene in the natural rate of procreation is underscored by the contrasting fertility rate for foreign-born females, who on the average bore two more children than did the natives and continued to bear children until later in life (a difference of two to three years by one inexact measure of the mother's age at last birth). More telling perhaps is the fact that native-born women of every age group mothered fewer children than their foreign-born counterparts. Women in their twenties reported a mean number of births of .612, compared with 1.04 for immigrant mothers. Native-born women in their thirties and forties also maintained fertility rates substantially lower than foreigners, having given birth on the average to 2.3 and 3.2 children, respectively. The determination of native-born women to control births throughout their fertility cycle is further evidenced by the longer intervals between the ages of their resident children. An average interval of 5.1 years for native-born women as opposed to 3.5 for the Irish and 3.5 for women born in Germany is suggestive of deliberate methods of prolonging the period between conceptions (Table E.1).

These prudent procreators had at their disposal a variety of methods of limiting births – withdrawal, abstinence, sundry folk potions and patent medicines, and abortion. James Mohr has argued convincingly that before it was thoroughly outlawed late in the nineteenth century large numbers of middle-class women resorted to abortion for this purpose. An advertisement in the *Utica Observer* dated 1833 explicitly recommended one patent medicine as an abortifacient. In 1834, however, the Oneida County Medical Society expelled a physician for performing an abortion and New York State legally restricted this method of fertility control soon thereafter.[17] Still, advice on abortion was hidden away in the fine print of the local advertising pages at midcentury. Advertisements for female pills often contained less than cryptic messages about abortion, warnings, for example, that certain potions should be shunned by pregnant women as they invariably caused miscarriage. A testimonial for Golden Female Pills dated 1856 claimed to be a miracle drug indeed, guaranteed to "prevent pregnancy."[18] Although female pills were ineffective methods of contraception, their existence, like all the references to abortion, testified to the fact that large numbers of women were painfully anxious to control their reproduction but were, as yet, without any reliable prophylactics.

The evangelical and reformist tradition of Utica had, however, recommended one very reliable, if Draconian, method of reducing family size: sexual control to the point of abstinence. Historians such as Daniel Scott Smith and Linda Gordon have argued that sexual abstinence, as enforced by pure womanhood, was one not insignificant means of curtailing births within the Protestant middle class.[19] Certainly one would expect that this method had its partisans and practitioners in Utica. The members of the Female Moral Reform Society had installed refined standards of female purity at the center of local culture by the late 1830s and supplied an elaborate rationale for sexual abstinence. It is also very likely that this ideology influenced the private relations and reproductive strategies of the middle class. At any rate, the standard of female purity was generally accepted by Utica's Protestant middle class at mid-century when native-born fertility had been put securely in check. Sexual matters had been relegated beyond the pale of polite conversation. Sometimes even family intimates were reticent about such topics. For example, Lavinia Johnson and her daughter did not broach the delicate issue of pregnancy until labor pains had begun. When an occasional church trial raised such unseemly issues, the details were veiled in feminine delicacy. One Elizabeth Dudley managed only to blushingly confess to the Whitestown session meeting that she had "allowed herself to be seduced." The *Oneida Whig*, meanwhile, let it be known that any attempt to educate women on these subjects, as proposed by the veteran moral reformer Paulina Wright, was an affront to femininity.[20]

Although Victorian purity may have been a code word and rationale for sexual control within marriage, it is unlikely that this was the sole method of limiting family size or that contraception was the unilateral practice and concern of females. There is direct evidence that men took an interest in birth control and had their own devices whereby to achieve it. Male culture, in fact, was the receptacle of some of the most explicit injunctions to keep families small. A businessman could even have been denied a loan on the grounds that he had sired an exorbitantly large family. The crudest expression of this norm was issued by the Mercantile Agency, along with an ethnic slur. The agency's records predicted the business failure of one German shoemaker with the report that "there are too many little Dutchmen around to make ends meet." A native-born man who failed to conform to this notion of the ideal family size could also see his credit denied on the grounds that he had a "large and expensive family."[21] Suitably prudent artisans and shopkeepers could resort to one ancient method of staving off such criticism, one that required considerable self-control but not utter self-denial, that is, coitus interruptus. Whether achieved by abortion, ordained by female purity, or controlled by masculine rationality, and more likely by some combination of the three, the curtailment of fertility involved an exacting, tense, and deeply internalized family strategy. It resided awkwardly at the most intimate connection of men and women.

Once birth had occurred, however, the process of social reproduction was increasingly delegated to females. Well before midcentury it was clear that the mother's control over the socialization of infants and children had been expanded and extended. Writings on childhood education during the 1820s were still a bit confused about the gender of the primary agent of socialization. Both Methodists and Presbyterians used male adjectives even when they described a mother's responsibilities, employing such curious phrases as "paternal love" or "paternal instructions." By 1833, however, *Mother's Magazine* regarded the transfer of parental obligations from male to female as a fait accompli: "The character of the man or woman is substantially laid as early as that period when the father is engaged in the bustling affairs of life." Through the remainder of childhood and until male children had entered that bustling world in their own right, mothers were placed in charge of shaping the character of the next generation. In this aspect of social reproduction, women were even admonished to dispense with that hackneyed but flaccid method of invoking paternal discipline, the warning "wait until your father comes home."[22]

With this change in the gender of the primary parent came a wholesale transformation in the preferred method of infant socialization, one recognized once again by *Mother's Magazine* as early as the 1830s. *Mother's Magazine* introduced its readers to this new method with a fictional rendition of an outdated and ineffective method of discipline employed by a woman called Mrs. F. "When they are little," said Mrs. F. of her children, "I suffer them to take their own way, so I think it is useless to attempt to control a child much before the age of six." As her son William grew more "passionate" with the approach of that fearful date in the old chronology of childhood, Mrs. F. awaited the right moment to begin a course of discipline in earnest. She swung into action when William violently attacked his sister. "After this Mrs. F. undertook to conquer her little son. A whip was placed on the chimney in the sitting room; and this, with the dark closet where he was told ugly creatures would catch him, frightened William into decent behavior while in the presence of his mother." In her absence, however, he was willful, disobedient, and, as any reader of *Mother's Magazine* could surmise, doomed for a tragic and wicked youth. The editor of *Mother's Magazine* categorized the mother who employed this childrearing method as follows: "An interesting woman, a kind neighbor and active in her religious profession. She was in society what many women are, useful and respectable." As a mother of the new era, however, she failed utterly, for she neglected her foremost maternal duty, "cultivating a knowledge of her own Heart." With this cool indictment of what might well have been one of the "principal women" of the socially active evangelical church, the *Mother's Magazine* banished the old methods of will-breaking from the modern and respectable home.[23]

A few years later the editors of *Mother's Monthly Journal* offered a detailed example of a more reliable method of dealing with stubborn and willful three-year-olds. After observing the child's birthday with prayer and fasting, the mother explained to the little girl, "in the simplest language, the sacrifices she was making in her child's behalf," all the while "caressing her affectionately." The clincher came when the mother told her daughter that she had abstained from eating for a full day in order to save her child from that "evil disposition that was destroying her happiness." At this the child reformed immediately, saying, "Well, ma, if you will go down and take something to eat, I will henceforth be a good girl." Another model mother had demonstrated the same foolproof method in the pages of *Mother's Magazine* five years before. This mother described to her little son the course of action she preferred to take in cases of disobedience. Eschewing corporal punishment or material reward, she greeted misbehavior with emotional withdrawal. "I would not smile upon you, I should not receive your flowers, but should have to separate you from my company." The fictional son responded appropriately: "Mother I should rather have your sweet kisses, and your pleasant smiles than ten rolls of gingerbread. I could not be happy if you did not love me." The practice of love withdrawal and the device of maternal martyrdom were two sides of the same coin, a method of socialization that used a child's close emotional ties to the mother as a pawn in a game of conformity and passivity. An anonymous mother writing to the *Mother's Magazine* described her strategy this way: "Why does an infant love its mother better than any other friend? Because her voice is gentlest, her eye beams with fondest affection; she soothes his little sorrows, and bears with his irritability with the tenderest and untiring patience. These silken threads are harder to burst than the iron chains of authority."[24] Put simply, love had vanquished force and authority, the female had replaced the male, in the social relations of childrearing.

To be effective, however, this method of discipline would require more than a sudden act of will-breaking at some specified age. It necessitated routine and intense maternal vigilance. One correspondent of *Mother's Magazine* illustrated this imperative of material socialization by recounting exacting episodes of maternal discipline that recurred at age four months, six months, seven months, twelve months, fifteen months, eighteen months, twenty-seven months, and, supposedly, ad infinitum. A local poet put the matter more simply when he enjoined the model mother "to mark [her child's] growth from day to day." Soon the temporal bounds of motherhood reached their absolute limit: "Every day and every hour the mother is with her child." Something of the rigor of the maternal role was indicated by the "Maxims for Mothers" issued by the Utica Maternal Association. Some fifty in number, they included such bland injunctions as "teach each child to cultivate kind feelings and to do good" and "endeavor to make your child punctual at all appointments." Other maxims were introduced by the conjunction "if" and called for a finer sense of maternal strategy: "If a child asks a favor examine the propriety for granting or denying the request before you decide, and abide by the answer you first give unless there is an obvious reason for altering it." In the end, almost every aspect of the child's behavior should be monitored by the ever-attentive mother. Even the most routine physical care of infants and children, their feedings, diet, and attire, was now invested with moral as well as material meaning.[25]

Just what all this maternal supervision was designed to accomplish was seldom stated in any detail. At times the goal of maternal care seemed merely to keep order in the house, to make for polite, quiet, obedient children underfoot. Yet assumptions about the long-term socialization of children and the process of social reproduction clearly underlay this regimen. Nineteenth-century theories of childrearing identified the enduring consequences of maternal care by a moral rather than a sociological term, the awesome word *conscience*. One of the first appearances of the term *conscience* in Utica occurred in the *Evangelical Recorder and Gospel Advocate*, which defined the novel expression this way: "God has implanted a monitor within called conscience which warns against all sinful indulgence. Though he does but whisper, his language is clear and strong. He makes the bosom flutter and beat high with anxiety when the mind is directed to deeds of daring iniquity." One need not look very far to find more mundane sources of the pangs of conscience. The very same issue of this Universalist magazine contained an essay entitled "Early Impressions and Habits Formed in Infancy and Youth," a standard euphemism for the mechanisms of maternal socialization.[26]

Countless essays in both the religious and secular press advocated the same loving methods of installing parental values deep in the child's personality, at some psychological space called conscience. *Mother's Magazine* exposed the parental origins of conscience in such titles as, "The Necessity of Cultivating the Conscience in Early Life." The Maternal Association of Utica put the point of conscience directly to children in this maxim: "Always act as if your parents were invisibly present." All the gentle admonitions and sly manipulations of maternal socialization conspired to equip children with sensitive consciences. This faculty would operate as a kind of portable parent that could stay with the child long after he left his mother's side and journeyed beyond the private sphere out onto the streets and into the public world. The values that this elaborate system was designed to implant in the child's personality are almost too mundane and obvious to recount: the usual array of petit bourgeois traits – honesty, industry, frugality, temperance, and, preeminently, self-control. Already in the 1830s, during the infancy of the young adults of the Civil War era, the literate native-born Protestants of Utica had worked out a set of strategies for the reproduction of a middle-class personality. In the process they defined the upper as well as the lower boundaries of the middle class, for the model child was infused not with the spirit of a daring, aggressive entrepreneur but with, rather, that of a cautious, prudent small-business man.

The mother's method of socialization was not, however, capable of training the progeny of native-born Protestants for specific occupational roles. The members of the Maternal Association might inculcate the virtue of frugality, but they were ill-prepared to teach bookkeeping, marketing, or shoemaking. In an increasingly privatized home, denuded of productive tasks, middle-class mothers could, at best, merely simulate the activities of adult breadwinners. In 1837 the members of the Baptist Maternal Association explored this strategy by asking, "Is it proper to supply our children with toys? If so, what kind of toys should they have?" To the first question the editors of *Mothers' Monthly Journal* gave an emphatic yes, and in the following issues they offered more detailed instructions about the use of toys in inculcating good work habits. For boys, they recommended "hammers and hatchets"; for girls, there were such occupations as "dressing dolls" and "mimicry of housekeeping." This, of course, was only make-believe work, designed to have "a semblance of the sober activities of business." The *Mother's Monthly Journal* also advised, however, that a little bit of actual labor would not be amiss. A few exercises in sewing "might be instructed with pleasure and profit to both sexes."[27] Clearly, the profit was collected in moral rather than monetary currency. Whatever work had occurred in this idealized childhood contributed to building character in individual sons and daughters, not to the material support of the family.

The extended moratorium on productive labor was most troublesome for male children. Females, after all, could continue to act as assistant housekeepers or were, at least, in a position to observe the performance of their mothers in the role of adult female. Boy children, however, were increasingly distanced from the roles of their fathers. Their remoteness may account for the fact that boys were often described as restless inhabitants of the private domain. In a story appearing in the *Mother's Monthly Journal* in 1838 a little boy voiced his discontent: "Oh, how I wish I were grown-up! If I were as tall as father I would be happy." Another article dated 1842 and entitled "Boys!" exposed an alarming breach between mothers and boys. "'Who can love boys!' says one mother – 'They are awkward, ugly things, always in the way and always in mischief! they are neither companions nor pets.'" Boys themselves, according to this account, heartily reciprocated these sentiments: "They are ungrateful to their mothers and indifferent to their sisters."[28]

Clearly, something had to be done to help families navigate more smoothly through this awkward later stage of male childhood, that problematical period called boyhood. The tactic of the mother's magazines of simply drawing the bonds of love ever closer as the child grew older could not solve the problem of vocational training. A sounder strategy might be to construct some intermediary world between the home and the labor force, one that could more adequately prepare boys for entry into economic adulthood. In other words, boys needed schools.

In the fourth decade of the nineteenth century a movement was already under way in Utica to establish the school as a social base for boyhood. Before that decade a few dame schools offered an erratic education to those who could pay for it, and public schools operated briefly on the Lancaster plan, which attempted to instruct more than two hundred pupils at a time. In 1830 some prominent Utica citizens, including Stephen Van Rensselaer, Fortuce C. White, and Hiram Denio, attended a meeting of the Friends of Education, convened in Utica to publicize the wretched conditions of the New York State schools: the impossibly large class size, the untrained teachers, poor facilities, and sporadic sessions. It was reported that some of the state's schools closed their doors arbitrarily for as long as nine months a year. The same meeting resolved to investigate the number of children between the ages of three and fifteen who were enrolled in common schools throughout the state, inquiring at the same time whether or not the beginning of schooling should not be postponed by a few years. The concerned fathers called for a common school system that would "keep pace with the age in its improvements" and prepare youngsters to "calculate their own profits in the world, and promote the limited views of their own individual interest." By 1830 Utica's city fathers had pointed to the need for the systematic preparation of young children for adult life in their commercial habitat. Concomitantly, they appealed for the systematic, long-term placement of children within educational institutions. They had begun, in sum, to rationalize the social life of children between the ages of five and sixteen – to convert it into the world of the schoolboy.[29]

By midcentury these goals had to a large extent been met. According to the New York State Census for 1845, the majority of children between the ages of five and sixteen were enrolled in schools. The figure stood at almost 80% in Whitestown and at 69% in Utica. More than 90% of Whitestown's schoolchildren were enrolled in public institutions. The comparable figure for Utica, which by this time had a number of parochial schools as well, was 52%. Utica's public schools were now more than purely custodial institutions. They were an increasingly efficient and bureaucratized educational system under the supervision of the city school commissioners. In 1842 the annual visiting committee found the local schools in exceptionally good order. The progress within the fourth school, once "virtually the prison of the disorderly ruffians" of the poorest ward of the city, particularly pleased the commissioners.[30] "Now the well-trained teacher ran the school with 'commendable emulation' which inspires the youth to orderly behavior, and stimulates them to the work of improvement." The city's private schools were also becoming a more highly structured social universe for children. The Whitestown Seminary included a "juvenille department" for children between the exact ages of six and ten. Whether private or public, the schools of the mid-1840s and beyond imposed a systematic order on the daily activities of youngsters, measuring off their young lives by classes, semesters, and the hours of a school day. Even this habitat of childhood was supervised by women, however. As of 1855, all twenty-six of Utica's public-school teachers were females. At the margins of academic life, meanwhile, mothers stood guard, having been advised to be at home when their offspring returned from school.

Some lacunae inevitably emerged between the diurnal and seasonal jurisdictions of the school and the home. It was in between these two social spaces that the more raucous activities of boyhood transpired. The term *boy* was often synonymous with prankster in the pages of the Utica press. The notable exploits of Utica boys included digging holes in the unpaved streets to trip passersby and stocking the butcher's sausage machine with exorbitant proportions of garlic. These idle youths could also pass the time in more structured play. Organized sports had become the essence of "Fun for the Boys" in the 1850s, when one's carefree youth could be relieved forever on the sandlot. In the summer of 1860 the *Utica Evening Telegraph* reported that "everybody of the masculine gender, young, middle-aged, and old is seized with the fever of playing base-ball and cricket."

For the "boys" under the age of sixteen, this playtime often mimicked adult roles and responsibilities. The 1840s saw boyish equivalents of many adult social groupings. The Cadets of Temperance, for example, were junior even to the "Sons" in the ranks of that reform group. The next decade brought the formation of poltiical groups that were even junior to the young men's parties of the Jacksonian era. Boys as young as fourteen could affiliate with the Democrats as members of the Little Giants and face off against their miniature Republican opponents, the Wide Awakes. These juvenile parties were hardly serious political institutions. Their chief function seems to have been to march through the streets around election time carrying the banners and shouting the praises of the candidates selected by their elders in the party.[31] At about the same time, another curious expression of boys' culture emerged on the Utica scene. The early 1850s had seen the proliferation of the "boys' press," a variety of newspapers edited, published, and printed by children between the ages of twelve and fifteen.[32] In every way, from their logotypes to their subscription rates, these postage-stamp newspapers tried to imitate their adult models. They even engaged in juvenile parodies of misogynist humor and ethnic slurs.

The tiny pages of the boys' press also offered abundant testimony to the puerility of this youth culture. The papers bore such names as the *Star*, the *Sun*, the *Diamond*, the *Eagle*. The serious reporting and adult prose of the editors were frequently interrupted by an observation such as: "Horse chestnuts are fine things to pelt girls with." The boyishness of these publications becomes more starkly apparent when they are placed alongside the serious products of an apprentice printer only a generation before. In this contrast lies the distinct character of boyhood; rather than participating in productive activities even at the level of the apprentice, the youngsters of the 1840s and 1850s were practicing for adulthood in a make-believe world all their own. The editors of the boys' press were quite aware of the transitory and playful nature of their activities. They observed knowingly that their peers were under the delusion that a three-cent cigar could make a boy a man. They even concocted their own designation of the temporal parameters of boyhood: "Boys should remember that they will soon be men and that it is between the ages of 12 and 18 that character is finally formed for good or for ill."

Boys into breadwinners

At some time during this period of the life cycle, the male children of Utica would have to take a giant step beyond boyhood and onto the lowest rungs of economic manhood by earning some portion of their support. Under the age of fifteen, according to the 1855 census, less than 4% of the males of Utica listed an occupation. Those who had entered the labor force at this early age, furthermore, were rarely apprentices embarking on serious and specific training for their life's work. Only two-tenths of 1% of the employed males of the city claimed apprentice as their occupational title. The juvenile worker by midcentury was more likely to hold a very marginal economic position, such as that described in this advertisement dated 1839: "Situation wanted – young lad eleven years old who would be willing to do almost anything for his board and clothing – would be good for doing errands, etc."[33] Soon after the age of fifteen, however, young men became a significant component of Utica's occupational structure. The public schools closed their doors to most youth around this age, and the *City Directory* listed all males aged seventeen and over among the "employed persons and household heads" of the city. At this point the ability of native-born parents to reproduce the middle class would be put to its crucial test: Now their sons would pass the midpoint of their teens and seek an occupation outside the private world of the home and beyond the cloistered space of the school.

The ever-garrulous local informant Emily Chubbuck chose the age of seventeen to designate the threshold of economic adulthood. In a story entitled *Allen Lucas*, Chubbuck encapsuled the timing and tension of youth in this image:

> "Seventeen years old today!" said Allen Lucas as he seated himself on a large stone, half embedded in the thick golden moss and the other half descending into the water – and in seventeen more

> I shall be a man, my character formed, my habits fixed, my destiny in the world decided, – a busy man in this busy world, independent of control, of guidance, doing whatever I like and answerable for everything. Thirty four years! The very meridian of life."[34]

Poor Allen Lucas contemplated straddling the world of childhood and manhood for a full seventeen years. Yet he had his ultimate goal squarely in view. He had his task set out for him by the popular ideology of his age. He was, as Chubbuck's subtitle proclaimed it, on the path of the "Self-Made Man, or Life As It Is." Emily Chubbuck was hardly alone in celebrating this notion of the self-reliant American youth. The Oneida County press held it as one of its most cherished clichés. One of Utica's booteries, for example, advertised its wares especially to those trusty lads who wished to stand on their own two feet rather than step into their father's shoes. The newspaper editors of Utica customarily added a titillating fillip to the doctrine of the self-made man, the prospect of rising from rags to riches. In the midst of the Panic of 1857, the *Utica Evening Telegraph* cited the happy case of Thomas Maynard who had arrived in the city twenty years before with a half dollar in his pocket and had become one of the city's wealthiest merchants.[35]

For a young man to "make himself," be the final product rich or poor, was simply making a virtue of necessity in the world where Emily Chubbuck grew up and where she situated the story of *Allen Lucas*. Allen was the third son of Reuben Lucas, "a small and honest simple farmer who being always watchful and industrious contrived at the end of the year to balance accounts without saving a penny." Allen was not in line to inherit the family farm, nor could he expect his father to pay his way through school, college, or professional training. The education of a second character, the fiercely ambitious Robert May, was financed by his family but at an exorbitant domestic cost. Robert's father mortgaged his farm, his mother lost her health, his sisters forfeited their prospects of marriage, all to put him through college and law school. Robert was a selfishly made man but still a relatively autonomous one. No less than Allen Lucas, he achieved an occupational status that was all his own, completely distinct and separate from that of his father.[36]

For all the contrasts in their character and worth, Allen Lucas and Robert May followed similar paths out of farm families and away from the old middle class. Both began to give earnest consideration to their life's work in their mid-teens, but neither arrived at his occupational destination until after age thirty. Both ultimately found themselves within the professional sector of the new middle class, Robert as a lawyer and Allen as an architect. Both gave their single-minded attention for upwards of a decade to building what could be loosely called a career, proceeding slowly upward through the ranks of a single carefully chosen occupation. Finally, both Allen Lucas and Robert May deferred the social and sexual gratification of marriage until their career goals were well within sight. "Allen Lucas remained a bachelor until he was more than thirty years of age and, by industry and economy, he had amassed a little fortune." Robert May also postponed marriage, and even then subordinated his personal preferences to his career goals, choosing as his wife the daughter of a politician whose influence he coveted. As Chubbuck portrayed it, a large portion of the male life cycle, approximately from the ages of fifteen to thirty, would be devoted to pursuit of a comfortable economic status and would transpire in a vast domestic lacuna, remote from the parental home and antecedent to matrimony.[37]

In some features this fictional account of the making of the new-middle-class man is remarkably similar to the outlines of the male life cycle extrapolated from the manuscript census schedules for 1855 (which will be detailed as this chapter proceeds; see Tables E.2, E.3, E.4). First of all, the native-born youth of Utica began to file into the labor force roughly according to Chubbuck's timetable. Three out of five males between the ages of fifteen and twenty had secured some kind of job. Second, many of these young workers were, according to one interpretation of local mythology, "self-made." Like Allen Lucas and Robert May and endless Horatio Alger characters, a significant proportion of the young men who came of age at midcentury obtained positions in the social structure that differed from their father's generation. For example, whereas only about 6% of Utica's middle-aged household heads filled white-collar posts in 1855, 16% of the city's young men had secured such positions. At the same time, the proportion of young men within artisan occupations was more than 15% below that of their elders. Chubbuck seemed clairvoyant in yet another respect. The majority of native-born men, like Chubbuck's characters, were tardy about marrying, with large numbers of them waiting until their thirties to begin families of their own.

On another score, however, Chubbuck was considerably wide of the statistical mark. Although unmarried, the young men of the 1850s were rarely homeless. Forty percent of the native-born males between the ages of fifteen and thirty and the majority of those who had secured white-collar or professional occupations were living with their parents. By 1865 a full 60% of the native-born youths were living under the parental roof. Simultaneously, the practice of boarding became increasingly uncommon. Only 29.7% of the native-born youths were boarders in 1855 and a mere 11.1% in 1865 (Table E.5). Even the once restless and roving clerks had become more domesticated by midcentury. As of 1860 almost 40% of them, double the ratio of a decade earlier, were living with kinsmen, usually their fathers or mothers (Table B.5). Young native-born shopkeepers and artisans were becoming equally attached to their parental homes: 25% to 35% remained there into their twenties. Extended residence under the parental roof was the favorite strategy of native-born youth and the middle class in particular, for the vast majority of immigrants (88%) and of unskilled workers (90%) lived apart from their parents by the time they reached their twenties. Continuing residence with parents tarnished the luster of a young man's self-made image. It suggests that parents still could exercise considerable care and authority over adult children and, accordingly, that obtaining middle-class status was not just a matter of self-creation: It was also the culmination of a parental strategy.

Prolonged residence in the family of origin could influence the occupational status of native-born youth in a variety of ways. It was associated, first of all, with delayed entry into the labor force. As of 1855, 43.5% of all native-born youth between the ages of fifteen and twenty had not yet secured an occupation. This contrasts markedly with the figure of 28.4% for the foreign-born (Table E.2). Native-born fathers of the new middle classes were the most likely of all to forestall the employment of their sons. Of the professional and white-collar fathers with adult children living at home, 80% kept their progeny out of the labor force. Although only about half of Utica's artisan and shopkeeping fathers followed suit, they, too, were more likely than the foreign-born and unskilled fathers to harbor children above the age of fifteen (Table E.6). Some of these home-bound youths were simply basking in the salubrious home influences recommended by childrearing theorists who would prohibit children "from encountering prematurely the seductive wiles that the wicked world will be sure to throw around them." Others were pursuing some form of education preparatory to their ultimate entrance into the world of work.[38]

In the absence of any precise information about school attendance in Utica, it is impossible to determine the relationship between delayed employment and extended education. Abundant impressionistic evidence exists, however, to indicate that native-born parents, particularly those on the margins of the new middle class, were well aware of the advantages of prolonged formal schooling. A fair proportion of the wills probated in Oneida County at midcentury made explicit provisions for the continuing education of their sons. The stipulations of some of these wills suggest that parents perceived education as a substitute for the family property whereby fathers of the past settled an economic status directly on their progeny. Charles A. Mann, a wealthy merchant and prominent financier, left his estate in trust until each of his children had reached the vintage age of twenty-five. His rationale was as follows: "I wish my children to be well educated and to be brought up to some useful profession or business with true habits of industry and economy which I consider more valuable than all the wealth I can give." Utica's ever-sagacious Sophia Clarke also wrote this family strategy into her last will and testament, leaving to her son Erastus, "the benefits of a liberal education and of acquiring a profession by means of which, with use, industry and economy, he can support himself and his family comfortably." To Sophia Clarke, the makings of middle-class status (such as the legal careers of both her husband and her son) consisted not in a stock of cash, tools, goods, or real estate but in training acquired at secondary schools or colleges.[39]

The groundwork for such a family strategy had been laid in the 1830s. Erastus Clarke, Jr., for example, would complete his secondary education at the Utica Free Academy, an institution that his father had helped to found during the canal era. The educational innovations of that era had been multiform and ingenious. In addition to public primary schools and academies, the 1830s gave birth to some less conventional educational experiments. Prime among these was the Oneida Institute, "a manual labor school," which operated in Whitestown during the canal era. Here was truly a school for self-made men. Students at the Oneida Institute, usually the sons of farmers and mechanics, many of them considerably older than the typical college or high-school student, labored in fields and workshops maintained by the school in order to support themselves. The Oneida Institute, yet another example of the more volatile youth associations of the canal era, spawned its own reformist fervor, which was led by such illustrious alumni as Theodore Dwight Weld.[40]

By midcentury, however, the Oneida Institute had sold out to a more conventional boarding school called the Whitestown Seminary. This secondary school was a way station for youth, neatly tucked under the extended eaves of the parental roof. Parents, not students, most often arranged and financed secondary education at midcentury. The staff of the Whitestown Seminary instructed mothers and fathers to "state very frankly and fully your wishes in reference to the studies, the intellectual and moral training of children, so that the teachers may feel at liberty to give you all that information which an intelligent and considerate parent desires when entrusting a son or daughter to the authority of strangers." The school, in turn, obligingly assumed the role of surrogate parent. Its official policy stated that if students failed to "govern themselves in accordance with precepts of sound morality," "energetic and decided measures" would be taken. In addition, the catalogue of Whitestown Seminary assured parents that every residential building would contain a supervising teacher to act in loco parentis. Whether a young man attended a boarding school like Whitestown Seminary or a public high school such as the Utica Free Academy, he did not escape adult surveillance nor assume total self-direction. In the 1850s even the Democratic press, once the outspoken champion of dauntless independent youth, advised that children who remained at home and were supported by their parents, regardless of age, were obliged to respect, honor, and obey their mothers and fathers.[41]

The secondary schools of the 1850s did not open up a very direct route toward economic independence. The academies and seminars were designed primarily for college preparation. The classical programs at Whitestown Seminary and the Utica Free Academy provided little vocational education per se, and aspiring professionals were obliged to go on to college and postgraduate training in law, medicine, or the ministry. The teacher training programs instituted by Oneida County secondary schools in the fifties and sixties proved most attractive to females. A commercial program developed by Whitestown Seminary in 1865 might have been more appealing to young men in search of white-collar jobs. Still, only a minority of even the sons of the native-born middle class could count on formal secondary education as an entree into professional or white-collar careers. It is unlikely that secondary education was much more prevalent at midcentury than it was in 1845, when in all of Utica there were only 140 high-school students and 33 collegians.[42]

Vocational training for the middle class was largely an informal, on-the-job, and catch-as-catch-can process. Aspirant clerks and bookkeepers could, for example, make use of a growing body of self-help literature. Until the late 1820s they were dependent upon *Daboll's Schoolmaster's Assistant* and its primitive set of instructions in merchandising, including demonstrations of barter and rudimentary commercial concepts. For example, Daboll defined "loss and gain" as follows: "A rule by which merchants and traders discover their profits and losses in buying and selling their goods; it instructs them how to rise or fall the price of their goods so as to gain or lose so much percent." Daboll's homespun economics was superseded in 1829 by the first Utica printing of *Preston's Manual on Book-Keeping*, which contained directions for calculating interest on sums that went into six figures and advised ambitious youths to consider such modern business issues as "what is meant by the term Capital Stock?"[43] By the 1860s the young men of Utica could also enhance their business credentials by taking a short course at one of the city's commercial and bookkeeping schools.

Acquiring training for white-collar, professional, and mercantile careers was expensive in both time and money, and much of this cost was born by middle-aged parents. Many parents were unwilling or unable to make these sacrifices at a difficult stage in the family cycle. The families of the old middle class, both shopkeepers and artisans, clung quite tenaciously to the old expedients of the household economy by accumulating the earnings of young adult children in a common pool. According to the 1855 census, for example, the majority of households headed by craftsmen still counted on their children over fifteen to be gainfully employed (Table E.6). They included families like that of Daniel Harrington, a machinist, fifty years of age. Harrington had at least nine children, aged five to twenty. Four of them were in the labor force, all in manual jobs, as weavers, spinners, and tailors.

Other families more often those headed by professional and white-collar workers but occasionally those headed by members of the old middle class as well, organized the labor of their adult children in such a way as to foster better prospects for their sons. Take the case of Warren Armes, a native of Rhode Island, who was also a machinist of fifty years of age. The Armes household was more typical of the middle class at midcentury: It contained only four children, neatly spaced in age, between seven and twenty-one years. The oldest male child, Henry Armes, was seventeen and already on his way to the new middle class, having secured a job as a clerk. At the same time, Henry's elder sister, Harriet, was working as a tai-loress and his mother made a sizable contribution to the family in-come by taking in two boarders. This consolidated income allowed the Armes family to purchase a house valued at $1,000 and might have contributed to the educational advantages that went into Henry's qualification for the job of clerk. This collective and com-fortable income boded well for the younger Armes children, who were likely to enjoy the leisure, the family resources, and the educa-tion that went into middle-class careers.

The occupational pattern of the Armes family was routine within the households of the native-born new middle class. Children of white-collar and professional fathers were the latest to enter the work force, the longest to remain with their parents, probably the most highly educated, and hence the most expensive to rear. The relatively ample income[44] of professional and white-collar fathers no doubt eased these families through the difficult stage of the life cycle, but still the making of a middle-class son entailed effort, planning, and sacrifice. It was often women, moreover, who as-sumed a major portion of such labor and responsibility. Contrary to common assumptions, the native-born middle-class women of the Victorian Era were not entirely disdainful of paid employment. Al-though only a small minority ever listed an occupation with the census taker, native-born middle-class wives were more likely than the spouses of immigrants to enter the paid labor force (Table E.7). In 1865 the proportion of native-born working wives had grown appreciably, and the wives of white-collar workers reported occu-pations in considerable strength of numbers. In fact, about 1 in 7 of the latter held a job.

Neither were the daughters of the native-born middle class all that shy of employment outside the home. In fact, the employment of females, be they mothers or daughters, was relatively common among the native-born. Female workers were found in 14% of the households headed by natives, as opposed to a figure of 13% for the households of immigrants. Craftsmen were the least reluctant to employ women outside the home: 1 in 5 of the households of na-tive-born skilled workers contained a gainfully employed female. Yet even the nonmanual middle class endorsed women's paid labor with some enthusiasm, for 15.4% of the households of professional men sent a kinswoman into the labor force. Finally, it was the na-tive-born middle-class household that was most likely to take in boarders, yet another source of household income. One in four na-tive-born households resorted to this female mode of enhancing the family's economic well-being. Although conscious motivation cannot be imputed to heads of these complex household economies, it is very tempting to see a kind of trade-off at work here. On a small scale, middle-class native-born families seemed to be substituting the labor of wives and sisters for the employment of sons, who could therefore prepare at their leisure for higher-status jobs. Regardless of the motivation of individuals, however, the native-born middle-class households typically organized the labor of their members in such a way as to allow for the prolonged support and assistance of young adult males.

By remaining at home through the earlier years of their economic adulthood, the sons of the native-born middle class reaped social and psychological as well as material rewards. The family of origin was there to assist a young man in both securing a job and parlaying it into a secure, perhaps lucrative, career. This combination of parental influences is evidenced in the correspondenc of a Utica physician named Horatio Dryer. Dryer invested considerable thought and energy in the career prospects of his son. "I am disposed to let Bob try for business," he wrote. "It will stimulate him to do something for himself. I have very little encouragement of getting a place here for him in a hardware store with a very fine man and one of the best businessmen I have ever met."[45] Paternal measures such as Dryer's (exposed only by a rare collection of letters) might have been a common way of securing a job in the mid-nineteenth century. At the same time, Horatio Dryer's plans for his son were more intricate than simply finding a place of employment. Dryer strived to "stimulate" his son's self-sufficiency and scrutinized the business skills as well as the payroll of his prospective employer. In other words, middle-class parents like Dryer were acutely conscious of the intangible aspects of career success and gave considerable thought to the best way to provide their sons with a legacy of skills and aptitudes as well as capital.

Another prominent father of Oneida County carried this parental awareness and its attendant anxiety to its extreme. The letters that passed between Hugh White, Jr., and his son William, that is, between the second and third generation of Whitestown's founding family, reveal the paternal vigilance demanded in a new era. At the time this correspondence began, the founder's grandson was not situated on a farm adjacent to his father's. Rather, William White was away at college, preparing to assume some undetermined economic role commensurate with the illustrious history of his family. Hugh White, Jr., did not, however, launch the third generation off into the world alone. He wrote his son long letters every week or oftener and demanded the same in return: "If you will sit down in the evening and write not only what has been done during the day, but give a statement of things in general, it will be very acceptable to me and make no innovation upon your scholarly pursuits." In Hugh White's mind, the parent's role in the socialization of children did not end when a young man left for college. He continued to oversee his son's conscience, stating, for example, that "it is exceedingly gratifying and adds largely to my peace and comfort to feel sure in the personal morals of my sons." His paternal jurisdiction extended to cultivating orderly habits and self-discipline as he presented William with an ascetic, indeed compulsive, work schedule.[46]

Hugh White's most assiduous campaign was to prepare his son for the world he would enter after graduation, the dangerous habitat of the businessman. And here the confidence of Whitestown's patriarchal lineage seemed to falter. Father and son encountered particularly sticky ethical questions when it came to business matters. On the one hand, proper business morality was simple. Hugh White assured his son that "the direct, straight-forward, manly course; open, frank candid, is the only one which will give either you or me any real satisfaction." At the same time, the world-weary father alerted William to the absence of such virtues among many of his business colleagues. He warned that every man must be "an expert in the observation of men, which ever quality of the soul it may be, always awake to note the good and evil around you." The cause of Hugh White's cynicism had been revealed in a few earlier letters when he described the caliber of men he caballed with in the railroad industry: "Cunning and unscrupulous men resort to all and any means and expedience for success. Open, honest, and manly proceedings would not serve them . . . rather, intrigue, treachery and corruption."[47]

Just how much benefit young William White derived from these parental admonitions is open to question. The tenor of Hugh White's letters often conveyed anxiety and trepidation rather than confidence. He kept his son posted on a seemingly endless sequence of "pecuniary troubles" and a wide array of accompanying physical maladies. One business setback, the senior White confided, "affected my stomach to such a degree that now all such trouble seems to center there deranging my digestive organ." Hugh White was plagued in his stomach, his back, and his head, which ached "almost to madness." He gave the impression that all these pains were the routine occupational hazards of the adult world his son was soon to enter. Armed with all this knowledge of the insidious machinations of capitalism's higher circles, young William White went back to the old family farm upon graduation from college. Not even the management of an agricultural enterprise, however, was left to the young man's discretion. Hugh White continued to send his son regular instructions on everything from planting potatoes to hiring a cook. The case of the White family proves that neither physical distance nor intergenerational occupational mobility need sever the cord of support and advice between father and son.[48]

This same family correspondence described very weak bonds between a young man and his mother. Mrs. White occasionally appended a note like this to her husband's letter to their son: "I would just like to say that you are thought of continually by your affectionate mother." On other occasions her husband might report "your mother says she can't think of nothing, ain't that rich?" The White family was probably the exception rather than the rule in this regard. The packets of letters sent to parents by Civil War soldiers, for example, were more often addressed to mothers than to fathers. Sons' correspondence with their mothers was full of the more prosaic details of everyday life and particularly replete with requests for victuals, socks, and medicines. At the same time, mothers' epistles were steeped in concern for the character and morality of the young men. Mrs. Mary Perry wrote to her son this homiletic note: "My very dear boy, take good care of yourself, keep out of temptation, avoid bad company, try and do good. My dear Win, once more be a good boy, don't forget your Mother who thinks of you when the rest of the folks are asleep. Much love and kisses to yourself." Young Perry reciprocated with regular letters to his "dear homely mother," "Dear Ma," "Dear Mammy." The rare correspondence between fathers and sons was typically more stilted and instrumental. When asked to dictate a last epistle to his father, one dying boy reputedly lisped, "Tell him to send me money."[49]

At the same time, the homey warmth of maternal influence was not entirely unrelated to financial matters. Maternal sympathy might provide more reassurance to a young businessman than did the nervous twitches of Hugh White. Maternal admonitions to live soberly and prudently could also prove effective financial advice for aspirants to more routine middle-class jobs in the 1850s and 1860s. The influence of early maternal education often retained its efficacy after sons had entered the male world of business. In 1837, for example, the Utica Maternal Association had discussed "How are we to teach our children to be prudent and economical?" One member of the association, Mrs. Julia Merrill, left the mark of such rearing in the ledger of the Mercantile Agency a decade later when her son was described as "Honest, Industrious, Small Means."[50]

The citation of the virtues inculcated by maternal associations within the credit records was not mere coincidence: It represented the real matrilineal ties that were woven throughout the male life cycle. The importance of maternal influence was given further expression in the wills of Oneida County. The majority of wills probated between 1845 and 1865 transferred the whole of the father's estate directly to the wife and mother. This stipulation testified, first of all, to the ability of women to dispense the smaller estates that consisted of consumable rather than productive property, that is, cash and household furnishings rather than farms and workshops. Second, it was based on the increasing importance of maternal socialization rather than on property or vocational training in determining the economic status of children. The will of Lewis Bailey made this reasoning explicit: Bailey granted his full estate to his wife, "praying that she may have wisdom from on high given her to train up her children in the fear of the Lord which will be better for them than all the wealth of the Indies."[51] This expanding maternal role opened yet another avenue through which the family of procreation continued to exert its influence until quite late in the life cycle of its male offspring.

The family was not the sole source of emotional and moral support for young men of the industrial era. Associations of young men continued to assume an important role in Utica life in the 1850s and 1860s. The youth associations of this era, however, came more and more to resemble surrogate homes. The Young Men's Association had disbanded in the mid-1840s. Its successor, the Young Men's Christian Association, founded in 1859, was designed as a kind of halfway home for young men recently uprooted from the parental family. The association appealed to "kind friends, these fathers and sisters and mothers," for funds. Its library was touted as a refuge for "many half-homeless wanderers in these streets." The once-bold banner of independent youth faded into an image of pitiful waifs: "Many a young man in this city of yours," went one appeal from the YMCA, "spends his days at work, perhaps in some mechanics shop, or mill, or office, or in your stores, [and] when night comes has nowhere else to go, for at the best the little room he calls his own is no *Home* to him."[52]

The YMCA was not the only men's association that identified itself in these domestic terms. The Order of Oddfellows, which flourished in the 1850s, also cloaked itself in the rhetoric of an ersatz home and constructed benign and cozy lodges where controversial reform associations once stood. "Odd" fellows were simply domestic anomalies, solitary men, whom "business, pleasure, or necessity call far away from the homes of their youth, and the society of their heart – unknowing whither they are going, or what may befall them in a land of strangers."[53] The literary associations, as well as the lodges, of the 1850s and 1860s aimed to provide emotional support for these uprooted men and boys. The Phoenix Society, composed of students at Whitestown Seminary, met to "promote kindly feeling," dispense "good cheer," and, incidentally, to exercise talents for public debate. The young members eschewed subjects that might provoke partisan rivalry and debated instead rather innocuous issues, such as the merits and the methods of the self-made man. Favored topics of the Phoenix Society debates included "Does education make a man more independent than wealth?" "Is corporal punishment in the schools to be tolerated?" and "Does success in life depend more upon a man's own exertion than upon the circumstances attending to his life?" These young men did not seem particularly restless under the limitations and constraints of their student status. Rather, they stepped gingerly toward their public and adult roles. Within the protective fellowship of the debating society, for example, a young man could advance cautiously from the "first embarrassing and stammering speech" toward the "ease, grace, and self-possession" required of an adult man. The members of the Phoenix Society, like Oddfellows and members of the YMCA, were not as eager as the youth of the canal era to assert their manliness in social, economic, and political life. One member captured the trepidation of youth at midcentury in this description of graduation from secondary school: "stepping from the routine of schoolboys, to mingle in life's sterner scenes, on the stage of action."[54] In sum, the sons who came of age in Utica during the decade before the Civil War seemed more conservative, more patient, and more attached to domesticity, be it in their parents' homes or the YMCA.

All this parental assistance, both material and psychological, seemed to be paying off at midcentury. In 1855 and 1865, according to the census, the majority of the native-born workers of Utica maintained positions within the old or the new middle class, either as artisans, shopkeepers, professionals, or white-collar workers. Only 12% of the city's native sons were found among unskilled or factory laborers, where immigrants abounded and where more than one-fourth of all adult males found employment (Table E.8). The younger generation of the native-born, furthermore, had become particularly well situated, advancing steadily into the newer sectors of the middle class. Only a small and probably insignificant proportion of the young native-born workers had, in the face of the encroaching obsolescence of some artisan occupations, moved into factory jobs. A far larger number became white-collar workers or professionals. A comparison of the occupational status of the two different age cohorts, young men between fifteen and thirty and household heads with children fifteen and over, demonstrates a definite generational shift in the pattern of middle-class employment. Of the younger men, 21% were employed in the skilled manual trades, as opposed to 37.5% of their elders. Within the white-collar and professional sector, on the other hand, the relationship was reversed, as young men outranked the old by more than 2 to 1 (Table E.3).

Comparing the occupational achievement of young workers who were still residing at home with that of household heads presents a similar contrast. Home-bound youth were especially apt to shun artisan and shopkeeping jobs as well as the new working-class positions opening up in the city's factories. The occupational magnet of the new middle class was especially powerful to these young men. More than 40% of the young men who resided with parents, as opposed to 28% of the native-born heads of household, had found employment in high level, nonmanual jobs, chiefly professionals or white-collar workers (Table E.8). The class background of the clerks who appeared in the *City Directory* of 1860 illustrates the pattern of generational occupational change. Of those clerks who resided with their kinsmen in 1860, 16% maintained the same white-collar status as the household head. The bulk of the remainder, however, came from the households of the old middle class: 37.7% made their home with relatives who were shopkeepers and 29.5% with artisans. Of those remaining, 11.5% boarded with kinsmen who were unskilled laborers. This suggests that there was considerable motion within the middle ranges of the occupational structure of Utica. The movement was particularly strong in a horizontal and intergenerational direction, as the sons of artisan and shopkeeper fathers shifted to professional and white-collar stations within the American middle class. Sons who continued to reside with their fathers as they embarked on economic adulthood had especially good chances of making the lateral movement from the old to the new middle class. Through the extended residence of young sons and a variety of attendant parental services, the family helped to ensure the reproduction of the middle class, even if it required horizontal movement from skilled manual to white-collar jobs.

Domestic dénouement

It would be foolish to attribute a young man's occupational accomplishments entirely to the efforts of his parents. Although hardly a pure incarnation of self-reliance, the native-born youth assumed some self-direction and invested abundant self-control in his career. By staying prudently and frugally under the parental roof, for example, a young man denied himself the social gratification of marriage and heading his own household. Native-born males were especially slow to embark on wedded life. Only 18% were married in the age group twenty to twenty-four; a bare majority, 50.4%, were married in the age group twenty-five to twenty-nine. (The comparable figures for immigrants in the respective age groups were 34.1% and 66.3%.) The new middle class was most obdurate about delaying matrimony. Only 35.3% of the white-collar workers in the age group twenty-five to twenty-nine were married; among professionals, the parallel figure was a paltry 26.7% (Table E.4). If maternal socialization and Utica's history of sex reform had left any imprint on the character of these young men, singleness would ordain celibacy as well. By postponing marriage and passing by Utica's infamous "nymphs du pave," a native-born youth enacted his own heroic strategy of achieving middle-class status.

By so doing, he also acted on the advice of domestic writers. According to *A Voice to Youth*, the prudent and responsible young man would not marry until he was capable of supporting a family "in circumstances of comfort," predictably at age twenty-four or twenty-five at the earliest or as late as age thirty. The quintessential circumstance of comfort, a single-family dwelling to which the youthful household head held the title, was seldom obtained before the age of thirty. In the meantime, a young man was expected to maintain a delicate imbalance between his sexual needs and his career objectives, postponing gratifications of the former to enhance the latter. Something of the tortuous quality of this regimen was expressed in the correspondence between Hiram Denio, a prominent Utica attorney, and his wife-to-be, Ann Pitkin of Connecticut. The timing of this courtship, although it transpired in the

1830s, corresponds with that of the professional men of the 1850s. Denio was already twenty-eight years old when he proposed to Ann Pitkin; by their wedding day, he was almost thirty. He had been a practicing lawyer and boarder of long standing when he finally set off on a trip through Connecticut in search of a wife. Over the course of months, Denio gingerly approached his favorite, proceeding from a chilly formality to the most ardent romance. On the eve of his engagement, Denio wrote to Ann Pitkin: "My heart beats audibly and I can hardly hold my pen." Once he had won the hand of his favorite, however, Denio's thoughts turned more somber. After seeking out a commodious home in which he and his bride could board, he had second thoughts. Convinced of the value of domestic privacy, Denio decided to purchase a modest home of his own. From then on he fretted and grumbled about the expense of setting up housekeeping and burdened his bride-to-be with complaints that he was "depressed" about professional matters.[55]

Meanwhile, Ann Pitkin was not exactly devil-may-care about the approach of matrimony. She took pains to interrogate her suitor about the soundness and sobriety of his character. She asked pointedly in one of her first epistles just how much liquor Denio had consumed during his social rounds on New Year's Day.[56] Women like Ann Pitkin, in keeping with the caveats of popular writers, proceeded toward the altar in a cautious and calculating manner, aware that their own middle-class comfort would hinge on the temperate character and business habits of their mates. The prospective bride was not, however, completely helpless in this regard. She was repeatedly advised that she could use her allure as a marital and sexual partner to lead young men along the path to morality and middle-class competence. As one Utica publication put it: "That hope which aims at a beloved partner – a family – a fireside – will lead its possessor to activity in all his conduct. It will elicit his talents, and urge him to his full energy and probably call in the aid of economy."[57] Again the cult of domesticity and the arbiters of the local economy recommended similar family strategies. In 1855, for example, one report of the Mercantile Agency based its optimistic forecast for a young businessman on the following observation: "has been pretty wild but has recently married and will probably be more steady now."[58] Ideally, then, marriage transferred this salubrious female influence over male passions from mothers unto wives.

The formation of the second-generation, middle-class household lies largely outside the temporal boundaries of this study. There is considerable suggestive evidence, however, that many of the young men of the 1850s would find a secure footing in the middle class. The census taken immediately after the Civil War indicates that males aged thirty to thirty-nine held occupational titles that were quite similar to those obtained by men in their twenties ten years earlier. A slight increase in the number of unskilled workers was balanced by an expansion of the elite. The distribution of occupations in later age groups retained a similar resilient, middle-class shape (Table E.9). The records of the Mercantile Agency took note of a handful of "industrious young men, formerly clerks," who rose to considerable wealth. Andrew Ketchum who appeared as a clerk in the *City Directory for 1850* illustrates a more modest middle-class mobility. By 1870 he was self-employed as a music dealer. Ketchum was not, however, typical of his cohort, less than 30% of whom rose from clerks to proprietors of their own business. Other clerks of 1850, like A. A. Bogue and B. F. French and 1 in 5 of their peers, still retained the same occupation in 1870. More than one-third of the clerks of 1850 claimed loftier occupational titles twenty years later, like bookkeeper, accountant, cashier, or salesman. They remained, however, hired nonmanual employees, that is, white-collar workers. One Joshua Church, for example, advanced from clerk to secretary in 1870, and William Coffin had become the treasurer of the woolen factory. Their peer and fellow clerk, George Knapp, advanced to the position of a bookkeeper by 1870 but by a more circuitous route, having in the interim tried his hand as a combmaker (Table B.4). Regardless of the erratic and variable pace of their careers, these tenacious white-collar workers, a majority of the clerks who began their careers at midcentury, testify to the slow emergence of a quasi-permanent new middle class; being a clerk was no longer the monopoly of young men but an occupation that could endure through a large portion of the male life cycle.

With occupational stability came entrenched domesticity for the native-born middle class. After a few years of boarding, be it with parents or strangers, most clerks listed a private home address in the *City Directory.* By the time they reached middle age, the majority of Utica's native-born household heads owned thier own dwelling houses. The modest but comfortable homes of the middle classes were concentrated in the fourth ward of the city, just to the east of the commercial hub and across town from the major factories and their immigrant workers. Typically, the artisans and shopkeepers of the fourth ward could boast of owning a home worth somewhere between $1,000 and $2,000. An advanced white-collar worker, such as P. W. Rogers, bank cashier, had real estate worth $4,000. These single-family dwellings, perhaps ornamented with the gingerbread trim popularized by such domestic architects as Andrew Jackson Downing and stuffed with the bulky mahogany furniture and rococo iron stoves hawked by local merchants, gave a material expression and sense of permanence to the middle-class status of their owners. In turn, such evidence of domestic sobriety continued to serve as moral collateral in the marketplace. The mercantile agent smiled at a "man of family" of any age. Domestic impropriety could still bring his frown and withdraw his credit. The Mercantile Agency gave Urial H. Kellogg a bitter lesson in home economics in 1852. Kellogg, formerly a clerk with good family connections, had been described as a "careful small businessman." After about five or six years of modest and wholesome living, Kellogg bought a dwelling house for his growing family. This expense, according to the Mercantile Agency, "detracted from his capital in business" and led to a prediction of bankruptcy. Sure enough, one year later Urial Kellogg went out of business.[59] Other businessmen incurred the disapproval of the Mercantile Agency for being too extravagant in spawning children. A large family, for a modest businessman, was considered a profligate waste of resources. Once again, the middle class was reminded to exercise self-control and continue even into middle age the exacting regimen necessary to the maintenance of their class position.

In the meantime, the parents who had supervised the first stage in the cycle of reproducing the middle class were reaching old age. This epoch in the middle-class family cycle was not clearly demarcated in social or biological time. There was no mass retirement at some specified age like sixty-five. The rate of unemployment began to rise as men entered their fifties, but still more than 90% of all the men in this age group remained on the job. Of the men over sixty, 80% still listed an occupation with the census taker (Table E.2). Neither do the records of the Mercantile Agency leave any perceptible evidence of a uniform age of retirement. On the one hand, a man like Jason Davis, age unspecified, ran a business from 1859 to 1871, at which time he was described simply as "used up." On the other hand, there was the career of John Tunbridge who had, over the years, built his painting and blazing business into a modest fortune worth $10,000. At age seventy-one, the Mercantile agent found him "still good and active." The work and retirement of Edward B. Paine tells yet another story. At age sixty-four he had been in business twelve years, still remained at the status of journeyman, and was reputed to be living "from hand to mouth." Two years later he was declared "too old to work."[60] The work history of middle-class men at midcentury was not neatly ordered into the advancing ranks of a clearly measured and predictable career. It ended as it had begun with ambiguous timing and a firm but never certain, not quite self-assured, foothold in the middle class.

Most of the native-born men of Utica could rely, however, on domestic security through the remainder of their life cycles. Three out of four of them headed their own households even as they passed the age of sixty. Four out of five could count on having a wife by their side as they passed into old age. The minority of elderly men who were widowed and no longer headed their households, furthermore, was taken in by their adult children. More than 30% of native-born women in their sixties (who were far more likely than their mates to be widowed in old age) took up residence with their children (Table E.10). Not until after the Civil War, when the Sisters of Charity and later some benevolent Protestant women established homes for the aged, did the city of Utica provide any institution exclusively for the care of older citizens. Many indigent immigrant elders would, of course, be carted off to the poorhouse, but few native-born residents ever met this fate. Most of them spent their declining years nestled in private homes, in the company of kin and insulated from the public sphere. A few privileged elders of the community ended their lives in quiet contemplation. One founding father of the town, Judge Ezekiel Bacon, devoted his old age to writing verses. In a volume entitled *Vacant Hours*, Bacon bid this adieu to life:

> Shed no tears
> Have not a groan
> But pass on quickly
> And leave me alone.[61]

The men who completed their lives in Utica and Whitestown in the 1850s and 1860s had lived through one of the most unsettling eras in the nation's history. Most had traveled afield of the homes of their own boyhood and had watched an industrial city grow up where there once had been a few scattered farms, shops, and churches. The sons who survived them and remained in Oneida County lived out a quieter and smoother life cycle. These young men of the 1850s and 1860s spent large portions of their life searching for an economic anchor and awaiting entry into conjugal homes of their own. For the native-born middle class, careful nurture in infancy, as well as the accompanying moral education, could be extended through boyhood and even into young adulthood when large numbers returned from their first jobs to the comfort and warmth of their paternal and maternal homes. When native-born youth of the fifties and sixties finally left the parental nest, after perhaps a short interlude of boarding, they would be restored to domestic protection. They would be insulated again by womanly solace and nurture, now dispensed by a wife rather than a mother. Most would live out their lives with their spouses as the head of their own households. Thus the mid-nineteenth century may have cut the family off from economy and workplace, but it hardly set workingmen adrift in an anomic and friendless world. The bread-winners of Utica were always sustained by a network of familial relations. In this lies the essential irony of nineteenth-century individualism. The vaunted autonomy and egotism of the nineteenth-century male was not a monument to self-reliance. Quite the contrary, it was conceived, cultivated, pampered, and protected within a revitalized American home.

In retrospect, it seems that the native-born residents of Utica, New York, had carried through an elaborate and largely successful strategy for reproducing the middle class. Their story is not a dramatic case of upward mobility but rather a sustained battle to maintain middle-range occupations for themselves and their children. As Utica began to industrialize, the native born evaded the clutches of the factories, avoided unskilled day labor, kept skilled trades and small shops afloat, and in significant numbers entered the ranks of professionals and white-collar employees. The sequence of tactics that they employed to this end can be summarized as follows. Prescient native-born couples began in the 1830s to limit their family size, thereby concentrating scarce financial and emotional resources on the care and education of fewer children. Second, as indicated by the popular childrearing literature circulated through Utica beginning in the 1830s, native-born Protestant parents initiated methods of socialization designed to inculcate values and traits of character deemed essential to middle-class achievement and respectability. Next, native-born parents tended to keep their children within the households of their birth for extended periods, often until their sons were well over twenty years of age. By this strategy, mothers and fathers prolonged their moral surveillance and material support of the second generation even as it advanced out of the home into the labor force. At the same time, the parental generation had created the educational institutions and financed the schooling that qualified their children for more skilled and lucrative occupations. As a result of these parental strategies, the native-born youth of the 1850s not only secured middle-class jobs but also circumvented the declining segments of the old middle class and won a foothold in white-collar occupations. It was quite late in the family cycle, then, that the leadership of the household passed on to the second generation. The young men of the 1850s married late, steered a relatively steady course through the labor force, and partially repaid their parents at the end of their lives by taking widowed mothers and a few stray widowers into their homes. Clearly, neither the ties between the generations nor the links between the household and the labor force had been severed by the advances of industrialization in Utica, New York.

They did, however, take a radically different form. The members of the household were no longer meshed together by common productive property and shared work experience. In the urban middle-class setting, at least, family bonds were woven of deliberate strategies – decisions, for example, to finance an education or take in a boarder at a critical time in the family cycle. The ties between the generations were knit of more intangible materials of affection, self-sacrifice, guilt, and all the mysterious machinations of conscience. Moreover, the generational balance of family relations had shifted on its axis somewhat. Where the son of a farmer, artisan, or shopkeeper had once been a major source of household labor, he was now often a drain on family resources, especially if he had designs on the occupations of the new middle class, which required high investment in training and accrued highly individualized rewards of professional and white-collar careers. Finally, it should be noted that much of private labor, intelligence, and energy that reproduced and re-created the middle class at midcentury was expended by women, especially the mothers who cared for infants, socialized children, bestowed moral influence upon breadwinners, took in boarders, and even entered the labor force in their own right – all helping to maintain or advance the status of the men in their families. Such women have appeared in this chapter largely as the nurturers of male careers, the selfless supporters of self-made men. Their role in the home and the social order is far more complex than this and far more integral to both society and economics. The sphere of the middle-class woman requires a chapter unto itself.

5   A sphere is not a home: woman's larger place in the city at midcentury

On September 11, 1859, the Reverend Philemon Fowler, pastor of the First Presbyterian Church, delivered a eulogy for one of his most venerable parishioners. The subject of Fowler's sermon, Mary Walker Ostrom, had a more prolonged and formative influence on the church than did its current minister. Mary E. Walker's prominence in the First Presbyterian Church went back at least forty-three years, when at the age of fifteen she and four of her peers founded the first Sabbath school in Utica. Her religious status and involvement grew with the crescendo of the revivals that followed. Of the 1826 Awakening, Fowler said, "Probably no actor in the memorable scenes was more powerfully exercised than was Mary Ostrom. Fowler likened Mrs. Ostrom's evangelical zeal to a "living fountain" whose "streams were poured about *abroad* and at home, at home and *abroad*." Mary Ostrom's benevolence paraded abroad in secular as well as religious circles. Her name appeared regularly in the local press below the reports of the Orphan Asylum, which she had also helped to found. She was a personal and familiar sight to large numbers of Utica's residents as "month after month, for a long series of years, she passed around an appointed circuit in the distribution of tracts." At her death on the eve of the Civil War, Mary Walker Ostrom was still fired with evangelical fervor. Reputedly her parting words were: "Don't be afraid, not afraid, fight Satan; stand up for Christ; don't be afraid." Even on her deathbed she sent her religious testimony aggressively "abroad" into the local circles of her influence.[1]

Mary Ostrom represents a whole generation of women who wove a web of influence around revivals, associations, and benevolence. The Reverend Mr. Fowler invoked the names of many of these women in Ostrom's obituary sermon. They included the esteemed founders of the Female Missionary Society and Maternal Association, the Mmes. Clarkes, Merrills, Doolittles. All these women disappeared from Utica's public life in the 1850s, when the completion of their collective life cycle was marked by the small public ceremony of a funeral sermon. This remarkable generation in the women's history of Utica was also memorialized in secular circles.

186

The deaths of Mrs. Ostrom and of Sophia Bagg occurred within a few months of one another and each was noted by a large black-bordered obituary in the local press. A generation of women who had begun their adult lives under injunctions of silence ended them with at least this public testament to their important place in founding and shaping the city of Utica.

Mary Ostrom's death also occasioned some pastoral pronouncements on the subject of woman's place. Her eulogy was printed and distributed locally under the title "Women's Sphere of Influence." By choosing Mary Ostrom as a model of womanhood, the Reverend Mr. Fowler endorsed a relatively wide range of legitimate activities for females. Indeed, the life of Mary Walker Ostrom admonished women to undertake an expansive program of social action. "She calls on you not to be content with what you can do in the family"; "she feels aspirations beyond which none must dare to repress, and she possesses capacities for service beyond which none must dare to restrain." Propelled by religious enthusiasm and fortified by association, women like Mary Ostrom had opened up a considerable number of local avenues for female activity outside the home. The Sunday school and the Missionary Society were only the beginning. "Penitentiaries and hospitals and asylums likewise give free ingress to women, and she is received there with the right to inspect and improve the management of the offices as well as to commiserate and alleviate the condition of the inmates."[2] The generation of women that followed in the footsteps of Mary Ostrom could enter these wider spheres without a struggle, without provoking even a raised eyebrow.

The place that the Reverend Philemon Fowler proffered to the women of the 1860s would, however, soon become the ideological terrain on which new struggles for women's autonomy would be fought. In the very act of recognizing the advances of the pioneer generation, Fowler also set constricting limits on the women who survived them. Fowler had, after all, employed that troublesome term *women's sphere*, a phrase that conjures up images of clear, precisely drawn social boundaries around the lives of females. His whole sermon was premised on the rejection of any movement to "crowd the sexes into a single, indistinguishable sphere, to associate them, not only in the pursuits of literature, science and art, but also in the markets of trade, the scenes of politics and popular agitation, the courts of justice and the halls of legislation." Fowler had chosen his model for future womanhood very carefully. He did not present Fanny Skinner, Paulina Wright, or even Sophia Clarke as his archetype of the true femininity. Each of them had let evangelical and reform enthusiasm override meek, retiring, and feminine qualities. Mary Ostrom, however, had never joined the ranks of female moral reformers, abolitionists, or that most recent crop of reformers in the Burned-Over District, the advocates of women's rights. Mary Ostrom maintained the standard of true womanhood despite "all the danger to which she was exposed, of passing beyond her legitimate sphere; . . . passing through seasons of religious excitement, when a transcending of her province might have been approved in her, if not demanded of her; who in this congregation – who in this community – ever saw or heard of aught in her which the most fastidious would consider incompatible with her sex?" Fowler's female parishioners, who now far outnumbered males, were warned not to wander beyond the social network that Mary Ostrom had traversed. They must never trespass beyond the feminine boundaries of the home, church, and charity, into the world of "rough and rugged labor, the publicity of the platform and pulpit, the conflict of the hustings, the senate-house, and the forum." Indeed, women must be "fastidious" in maintaining these bounds of womanhood.[3]

Women's sphere as defined by Philemon Fowler was fastidious in yet another sense. He enjoined females to adopt very prim manners and comportment. Wherever a woman trod, she was to go lightly, quietly, purely. Even her excursions "abroad," along the path of benevolence, were to be conducted in this unobtrusive manner. "With the spirit of a true Sister of Charity, she may glide through the walls of hospitals and steal into the hovel of penury, and minister at the beds of sickness and pain." A woman's sphere was coterminous with her temperament, as defined by Philemon Fowler. "Constitutionally compassionate and kind, susceptible of spiritual truth, 'last at the cross and first at the sepulchre'; glowing with the ardor of her affectionate love for the Saviour, and clinging to him with the indissolvableness of her sacrifices, she becomes a Christian, humanly speaking, more easily than man; and she is more earnest in feeling and zealous in service, and the soul's wants and woes meet a readier and better response from her. What she can do she is more sure to do well." Fowler had effectively divided up human mind and character as well as behavior into two spheres defined by sex. His obeisance to the superior Christianity of females did not camouflage the basic restriction and condescension of this tenet of the doctrine. After all, it was only "what she *can* do" that woman accomplished so generously and sublimely.[4]

Finally, Reverend Mr. Fowler took this occasion to inform women of their primary responsibility. Mary Ostrom never set out on her altruistic rounds, he reminded his listeners, until she had fulfilled all her household duties. As Mrs. Ostrom was childless, the mothers of the parish probably recognized that they themselves would have fewer opportunities to travel abroad. For all practical purposes, most of women's life cycle would still be enclosed by the family. "Home is her peculiar sphere, and the members of her family her peculiar care. Household duties must be discharged, and well discharged."[5] Although it might be consistent with tradition to consign women to household tasks, Fowler was drawing a novel social boundary around women. As he wrote in 1859, the homes of his parishioners were far narrower than when Mary Ostrom arrived in Whitestown in 1803. The advances of the marketplace, followed by the growth of local factories, had progressively denuded urban households of economically productive activities. As such functions as providing public welfare, education, and religious instruction were transferred from the household to municipal institutions, the social breadth of the home was constricted even further. The pastor of the First Presbyterian Church had, in fact, given a lesson in the geography of gender, which simultaneously sharpened the boundaries between male and female and narrowed woman's social space.

The Reverend Mr. Fowler's homily on the subject of gender was merely a local expression of a notion of woman's place, which was installed at the center of American popular culture. In fact, by midcentury Utica residents took lessons in masculinity, femininity, and domesticity from strangers, writers like Lydia Sigourney, William Alcott, Mrs. E. D. E. N. Southworth, Catharine Beecher, and Harriet Beecher Stowe, whose pronouncements on thse matters were distributed nationwide by powerful publishing companies based in large northeastern cities. The content of this literature is well known and can be neatly (perhaps too neatly) capsulized in the phrase "cult of true womanhood."[6] The few publications that still bore a Utica imprint at midcentury were sterile parodies of that cult, without even the local historical sense of Philemon Fowler. They need be described only briefly.

The cult of true womanhood was first of all a gilded pedestal for a sexual division of labor and social roles. It ordained that the male "go into the world and engage in business or laborious occupation for the maintenance of the family" while his spouse waited at home to "advise and counsel her husband in his doubts and perplexities, and by her presence, her affection, and her smiles to make home an elysium to which he can flee and find rest from the storm and strife of the selfish world." Whether ministering to her husband or her children, the ideal woman adopted a set of personal characteristics appropriate to her domestic roles. The female of the species was "created by the great giver of all good as a helpmate of man – formed in a superior though more fragile and delicate mold, endowed with purer and better feelings, stronger and more exalted affection, to play a distinct character in the great drama of the created world." Popular writers hastily translated this sexual differentiation of roles and temperaments into an allocation of social space, "the doctrine of the spheres." "Each has a distinct sphere of duty – the husband to go out into the world – the wife to superintend the domestic affairs of the household." "Man profits by connection with the world – but woman never; their constitutents of mind are different. The one is raised and exalted by mingled association. The purity of the other is maintained in silence and seclusion." This was a brazenly unbalanced division of territory, allotting no less than "the world" to men, whereas it banished women to the domestic circle.[7]

This imbalance was disguised by another central tenet of the cult of true womanhood, the doctrine of women's influence. "So long as a fireside and a home exist, so long must woman exercise a boundless power over the destiny of man." Women's power, so the theory went, never assumed a public and official dimension but worked through intimate social relations and spoke in the meekest tones. "She has but one general course of procedure to obtain an influence over those with whom she is connected, or in whose welfare she is interested and that is by persuasion, by kindness, by gentleness and affection, by the continued exhibition of sweet temper, and of a soothing and forgiving spirit." Women, in other words, influenced society at large only indirectly, vicariously, through their husbands and children. By the same token, women's influence was aggregate but not collective. It was the sum of all the private domestic activities of millions of American women who presumably never associated with one another in any concrete manner. Women's influence derived from "ten thousand little republics," to use the modest scale of Utica rhetoricians, but was "not less great because unseen and silent." In sum, the very location of the individual in society, as well as the roles, temperaments, and spaces assigned males and females, was implicated in the doctrine of the spheres, a notion that was as grandiose as it was vague. A whole theory of being had been constructed around gender differences, a veritable ontology of sex.[8]

For all its pomposity, this doctrine was not a product of the stratosphere. Any cultural construct that achieved such popularity bore some resemblance to social reality. This much at least is true. At midcentury, middle-class urban males and females were more starkly separated than in times past. Women's roles had indeed become more domestic than social, more privatized, less communal. At the same time, women did exert considerable social power from their private stations. This is, in fact, the import of the preceding chapter, which demonstrated that private family strategies, often assumed or directed by women, could have a defining effect on urban class structure. As women historians have argued and the first segment of this chapter will describe, significant sex segregation cut an especially deep rift through American life in the nineteenth century, dividing culture, society, and even human emotions into male and female domains. The doctrine of the spheres takes its cultural power from this real historical change.

At the same time, the doctrine of the spheres, like most cultural abstractions, disguised a multitude of variations, complexities, and contradictions within the actual experience of women. This chapter will go on to elaborate four such distortions as it details the larger, extrafamilial social and economic implications of woman's place in Utica at midcentury. First of all, it will adumbrate the multiple and powerful effects of women's home labors on the local economy. Second, it will identify the very active participation of women, including middle-class native-born females, in gainful employment outside the home. The third deviation from doctrine of the spheres consists in the female contribution to social reproduction outside the home and among nonrelatives, especially through church and charitable institutions. Finally, a full depiction of women's sphere at midcentury must account for the many females who for some portion of their life cycles lived outside the essential unit of domesticity, the marriage relation. Through all their journeys "abroad," however, the middle-class women of Utica remained shackled by the limitations and contradictions of the doctrine of the spheres.

The bonds of domesticity

If the only concern is to contrast the experience of males and females, then it can certainly be argued, relatively speaking, that woman's place was in the home. Native-born females resided with their kin longer and more continuously than did their brothers. In the teen years, for example, when almost half the native-born males of Utica had departed from the parental home, only 3 in 10 females had left the nest. If a female vacated the family of origin, furthermore, it was seldom for very distant climes. In the age group twenty to twenty-nine almost 70% of all females resided with either parents or spouses. The remainder were more likely than males to reside with extended kin or as servants in other households. In sort, very few women ever found a place of residence apart from kinsmen and away from the supervision of fathers or husbands (Table E.11). The major social transition for these women, then, was simply from the homes of fathers to those of husbands. Most women of native birth, furthermore, put off this domestic passage until quite late in life. The majority of native-born females remained single until twenty-five, and 45% were still unmarried between the ages of twenty-five and twenty-nine (Table E.12). After marriage, native-born women were quite securely ensconced in their conjugal homes. Even after the age of sixty, when half of all native-born females were widowed, more than 90% of them continued to reside with their families, the majority as heads of household and more than 30% with their adult children. The mother-child bond was particularly durable at midcentury, when 2 of every 3 women still dwelt with their offspring even after the age of sixty.

The home, furthermore, was an especially comfortable space for a female. After all, it was the turf of her own sex. A female infant might feel a particularly warm welcome into a world defined more by mothers than fathers. This is the import of these stanzas written by a local poet named Eliza Coxe. Her ode to childbirth began:

> God has brought me a daughter
> Oh the music of that word
> Sweeter than the flow of fountain
> Sweeter than the song of bird.

Coxe's delight in the sex of her newborn child waxed more profound, if not more poetical, with each line. She maintained this feeling right through the obligatory final stanza, which, according to the sentimental convention of the era, invoked an image of death:

> Then may the daughter God has given
> Beam latest on thy sight
> And be it thine to welcome her
> Up to the gates of light.

In both poetry and prose, Oneida County's writers pictured an enduring cycle of mother-daughter ties. Infant daughters inspired a special contentment and ease, whereas tense and conflicting maternal sentiments were reserved for the boy child.[9]

A mother's bond with her daughter was drawn tighter and endured longer than the attachment to her son. Young females did not pass through a stage in the life cycle comparable to boyhood, when the male child chafed under maternal bondage. There were no reports in the prescriptive literature that girls were particularly restless at their mothers' sides, which after all were facsimiles of the social space in which they were destined to spend much of their life cycle, the home. Accordingly, females were in no great haste to enter the world outside the household where boys found male companionship, work opportunities, and a glimmer of their adult sexual identity. Quite the contrary, female children encountered the vocational training and workplace and role models appropriate to their sex simply by staying at home. One of the first issues of *Mother's Magazine* even enlisted little girls in the regimen of moral education. "When your daughter is old enough to be your companion and friend allow her to participate in your cares and duties. It is the affectionate daughter and kind sister who will make the self-denying wife, and devoted mother."[10] Local literature portrayed mothers and their adolescent daughters as genteel companions, lolling in placid domesticity. A "Sketch for Misses in their Teens," for example, presented a circle of females who "seated themselves with countenances strongly expressive of that eager desire for entertainment so common with the young." The object of their enthusiasm was a table full of "books, drawings and shells for their amusement." This almost eerie calm of woman's world was also chronicled in the diary of young Rachel Williams, whose life in the 1850s was insulated in feminine company and avocations. She attended the Utica Female Academy but only irregularly, preferring the company of her "babies" to writing compositions. She also enjoyed playing the piano, being read to by her mother, and occasionally such exertions as skiing or sleighing. Rachel Munson Williams, the daughter of a wealthy businessman and politician, shared only one activity with the industrious farm girls of the past, frequent church attendance. At the same time in life when Hannah Gilbert had been busily employed in all the productive activities of the farm household of the 1810s, Rachel Williams congratulated herself and her sister on this record of industry: "This day we have been better than usual we hardly played a bit, but worked considerable. I worked on something for papa and Maria did too, but she mostly sewed on a little calico apron for some poor child." "Work" to young women of Rachel's class consisted of little more than the ornamental sewing that adorned parlors or filled charity boxes. For a daughter of affluence, adolescence was a smooth, easy training in domestic womanhood.[11]

Without doubt, the placidity of the domestic environment left some imprint on the development of female personality. In fact, the home life of the Utica middle class at midcentury conforms very closely to the set of social relations in which Nancy Chodorow has situated the psychodynamics of the "reproduction of mothering."[12] As in Chodorow's typology, the Victorian daughter enjoyed a privileged position in a feminine universe where, with relatively little trauma and at an easy pace, she learned her adult gender role from her mother, the source of her first and most enduring emotional connection. Because she was embedded in this satisfying emotional environment, the female child might not develop the striving, rational edge to her personality that a boy acquired in the course of his struggle to identify with a more distant and impersonal role model. It is also likely, to continue Chodorow's analysis, that this comfortable female work worked against the formation of unambiguous and exclusive emotional and sexual attachments to males. Again, the local poets provide evidence of such tenacious bonding between members of the same sex. This was the theme that the poet laureate of the *Utica Observer*, R. Barber, chose as his, or her, hymeneal motif in 1833. In the first verse a mother bid her daughter a reluctant good-bye: "Go, go and in a husband's love you'll find / A fair exchange for all the friends behind." The wisdom of this bargain or, more precisely, the relative value of a husband's love was left open to question. The poet resorted to the conditional tense when he/she placed these words in a mother's mouth: "A husband's love *may* equal yet mine own" (emphasis mine). Still, this mother stoically sent her daughter on to the next uncertain stage of her life: "Ah shudder not to pass upon the stream / But venture all the hopes and cares on him."[13]

Although the pivotal passage in the life cycles of such a woman proceeded merely from one home to another, it entailed a difficult disengagement of female bonds and required a shift of emotional focus from one sex to another. It is not entirely extravagant to propose that middle-class women experienced something akin to an Oedipal crisis in their late twenties when the majority married. This psychic crisis was not always successfully resolved, if another

local poet is to be believed. This anonymous writer addressed a
lament to her mother under the title "The Bride's Return."

> I left thee! – like the dove of old
> I left thy parent breast, –
> But on life's waste of waters cold
> My soul hath found no rest!
> And, back the weary bird is come,
> Its woes – its wandering o'er;
> Ne'er from the holy ark to roam –
> Yet this is home no more. [14]

Women who inhabited sex-segregated networks outside the home
also experienced a similar premarital crisis. At the time of her marriage, Emily Chubbuck broke painfully with her "heart home"
among the teachers and students of the Utica Female Academy. In
fact, she defined her heterosexual attachment in opposition to these
intense female bonds. Chubbuck wrote somewhat unconvincingly
to her sisters in Utica that her love for her groom was strong enough
"to break all the ties which were twined with tenfold strength about
my heart." [15]

The strength of the female bonds formed before marriage undoubtedly lingered on and affected the quality of the marital relation itself. In at least one case, that of J. S. May and his young wife,
Desire Babcock May, the strain reached the breaking point. From a
few fragments of correspondence it would appear that Desire Babcock inhabited a dense and emotionally sustaining female network.
Her cousin sent letters, for example, replete with news about children and female friends and full of happy recollections of visits
with her kinswomen. "It seems like a dream," she wrote Desire
May. "I think of your and Delia's visit here. You cannot imagine
how much I missed you. I was very lonesome. I think much about
you." At about the same time Desire May received missives of ardent affection, perhaps too ardent for her female taste, from her
husband who stood accused of a familiar triptych of male sins, of
being a "drinking, gambling and licentious husband." For these
crimes, Desire had left her mate never to return, despite his earnest
pleading. [16] The only diary of married life extant in Utica from this
period tells of a marriage that survived such differences but only as
a bitter mode of coexistence. Mrs. Lavinia Johnson gave little attention to her mate, and when Mr. Johnson's name appeared in the
diary it was accompanied with references to his incorrigible drunkenness and draped with such epithets as "stupid" and "a trouble
and a disgrace." This marriage hardly constituted a satisfying he-

terosocial bond. Lavinia Johnson reacted to dining alone one evening with the admission, "I had rather be alone than have Mr. Johnson."[17]

It would be a mistake to indict the marriages of the nineteenth-century middle class on this limited and extreme evidence. Most couples remained together and forged a complementary relationship between two spheres, exchanging male support for female influence. Yet these examples illustrate the potential for marital tension that was built into the structure of gender at midcentury. The more separate the spheres, and the more distinct the temperaments of men and women, the smaller the chances of conjugal empathy. The imperative of sexual control for the middle class further distanced husband from wife. The model of female influence with its injunction that wives coyly persuade and slyly manipulate husbands could introduce suspicion into a marriage as well. Conversely, the commonality of values, the shared experience, and the long, close bonds that linked females might deflect emotional currents away from husbands and fathers.

At any rate, it is clear that female bonds laced through the everyday life of the middle class and formed a denser social and emotional network than ties between the sexes.[18] The fullest diurnal account of the private world of females is Lavinia Johnson's diary, written in a small hand, filling more than eight hundred pages, and detailing less than two years in the life of a middle-class woman. During that period in the late 1850s Mrs. Johnson rarely even mentioned members of the opposite sex. She seemed to have totally discarded the possibility of communicating with her husband and seldom referred to her son James, who had migrated to New York City. Her son-in-law William appeared in the diary quite frequently but only as the stock figure who married her daughter. Likewise, her pastor played a minor role in the pages of Johnson's diary: His was a slightly awkward presence in the midst of a feminine church circle. The daily life of Lavinia Johnson transpired in an almost perfectly segregated female culture.

Mrs. Johnson's daily round of activities rarely took her out of female circles. The center of her life was the home of her married daughter Mary Taylor, whom she visited nearly every day and for whose children she cared, sewed, and shopped. At church it was the ladies' circle as much as the Sunday sermons that commanded her attention. She was a member of the Ladies' Benevolent Society and taught Sabbath school in the company of members of her own sex. She also maintained contact with the members of the Young

Ladies' Sewing Circle, to which another daughter, Jane, belonged. When Mrs. Johnson ventured off to the Mechanics' Institute for the annual fair, it was the "ladies' fancy work" that captured her interest. Even the diary itself is a testament to the intensity of female bonding. Mrs. Johnson's diary originated as a diurnal report to her daughter Jane, then a missionary in Asia.

Lavinia Johnson's female network was not a terribly expansive territory. Hardly a single female friend was mentioned by name or paid a personal visit in the two-year history that the diary recorded. Even the female church circle had lost much of its intensity by the late 1850s. The pastor of the Presbyterian Church had to call a special church meeting so that his flock "might become acquainted with one another." Mrs. Johnson's female network was largely a kin association, which did not extend much beyond her own daughters. The narrowness of women's society was described by Lavinia Johnson herself. "What a wilderness would this world be without my children, I should have none to love, nor anybody to take care of me. Father is a trouble to himself as he is to me." Mrs. Johnson could not see past her immediate family relations as a source of support, either emotional or material. It was within the female lineage, furthermore, that she found her occupation in old age. Upon the birth of a child to her daughter Mary, she wrote: "And now my dear I have another one to love and if he lives, will in all probability take much of my time and care. May my Father in heaven fit me for all my duties. I have looked forward to this time with a good deal of anxiety."[19] At this last stage of her life cycle, Lavinia Johnson still regarded motherhood as her vocation. At the same time, her fondest hope was that her daughter Jane, age twenty-five, would return from the Far East to live with her mother.

To women like Mrs. Johnson, women's sphere enclosed the life cycle and provided its own consolation in the loving bonds between mother and daughter. She had no sympathy for those who would break free of these bonds of womanhood. She scorned the female reformer as one who "aping mannish manners . . . wears absurd and barbarous attire, who talks of her wrongs in harsh tone, who struts and strides, and thinks that she proves herself superior to the rest of her sex." Mrs. Johnson was even skeptical of her daughter's pious journey to the benevolent borders of women's sphere. Of Jane Johnson's missionary activities she said, "I gave my consent, because I thought if she felt it her duty to go I would give her up cheerfully, if I could. I did try. My Father has been very kind to me and given me grace to bow in submission to his will."[20]

Thus, Mrs. Johnson would be quite happy to install a second generation in the cycle of domesticity.

A world of work

The bonds between women were woven of the shared experience and common concerns of the sphere they cohabited. The community of womanhood was composed not just of rarefied feminine values but also of the mundane details of women's work. Lavinia Johnson could rely on her daughters to take a personal interest in an array of activities that her husband and son would probably find alien and trivial. "I washed my parlor windows, the blinds, cleaned the shades, my kitchen window the large window in the chamber, wiped, dusted, and cleaned and was home all day." Two days later Mrs. Johnson reported a mundane retinue of female chores, washing, ironing, and shopping. The last activity provoked some perennial woman's complaints as well, about the cost of living. In exchange for kerosene, meat, apples, milk, and butter, she was charged the exorbitant sum of fifty cents. The rhythms of her work shifted with the seasons. In the fall she tackled the local harvest, pickling and preserving cucumbers, blackberries, peaches, and plums in massive quantities. In the evenings and at odd hours she picked up her sewing basket, and then her diary, recording all the intricacies of style and fabric that went into her latest creation.[21] In all this arcana of women's world Lavinia Johnson had actually described a major change in the system of reproduction, the emergence of what every woman would recognize as "housework."

Housework was identified as a specialized field of labor as early as the 1840s when a Domestic Seminary in Clinton set up a course of instruction organized around four simple categories "cooking, clothing, cleaning and dishes." In the middle-class homes of the 1850s these forms of domestic labor took on a patina of artistry that suggests qualitative changes in the process of household labor. The universal function of cooking, for example, had become something more than simply preparing food for human consumption. Even publications addressed to farm women contained increasingly elaborate recipes for cakes and cookies and desserts, all recommended as symbols of domesticity as well as for their nutritional value. In diaries like Mrs. Johnson's, in endless treatises on domestic economy, in kitchens, parlors, and county fairs throughout America, women hummed with the special knowledge and esoteric secrets of their private world of work and expertise.

Outside this sphere and in the minds of males, the cult of house-keeping was perceived with diffidence or dismissed with ridicule. Even the boys' press of Utica participated in this male bonding in opposition to housework. The juvenile editor of the *Eagle* observed the rite of spring cleaning with masculine condescension: "Such a general upturning in the domestic department, 'housecleaning'; furniture moving, painting and whitewashing. These later per-formances we hate with all our hearts. If we ever get to be a man and have a wife, the first thing we shall make her promise is that she will dispense with this household nuisance. She shall keep neat and clean all the time." To the compiler of *A Book for the Millions*, such general disparagement of woman's home work warranted a chivalrous chapter on "The dignity of the housekeeper." The argu-ment proceeded from the presupposition of women's influence. The housewife, said the author, was not "ministering to the wants of a few bodies, considered merely as bodies, but through these bodies to the wants of immortal souls." An earlier local publication admitted to some more material functions of women's home labors, describing the economic roles of male and female as follows: "It is the husband's duty to bring into the house and it is the duty of the wife to see that nothing goes wrongly out of it." This roughly trans-lates into a definition of the male as breadwinner, the woman as wise and frugal consumer.[22]

Twentieth-century economists are more aware of the vast impli-cations of women's work in the home. Neoclassical writers, calling themselves practitioners of the "new home economics," have iden-tified the household as the site of cost accounting, as families and women organize their labor time in such a way as to maximize household income. At the same time, Marxists are beginning to pay greater attention to the reproduction of labor power, which encom-passes all the unwaged domestic labor of women to maintain and replenish the work force. American households at midcentury, even those comfortable homes of the middle class nestled behind the scrim of domesticity, were replete with such vital economic ac-tivities.[23]

The urban household was, first of all, vitally connected with the advances of both the marketplace and the factories. As economic historians have argued and any glance at the advertising pages of the Utica press quickly substantiates, the home at midcentury was the targeted destination for a voluminous flow of consumer goods. The largest advertisements and the most prominent spaces in the local papers hawked articles for middle-class consumption. Notices "to the ladies" informed readers of styles that changed with the seasons or even monthly. For all its "conspicuous" characteristics, such consumption was vital to the local industries specializing in hats, cloaks, skirts, and ladies' shoes. Heavy industries located outside Utica were also heavily invested in producing for a middle-class domestic market. At midcentury the back pages of the local newspapers were pasted with etchings of bake ovens, plate stoves, flatirons, parlor furnaces, washing machines, sewing machines, and numerous smaller home implements – all the "new inventions and improvements" distributed by the growing metal and machinery industry. Combined with abundant ads for home remedies, parlor furnishings and bathroom fixtures, these lists of commodities identify the home as a major and essential market for the advances of industrialization at midcentury.

They also adumbrate another major object of women's time, effort, and decision making: her role as consumer. A student at the Utica Female Academy chose shopping as the subject of one of her compositions: "For indeed it should be considered a hard day's work as it is not an easy matter to walk from one end of the city to another in the hope of finding something to suit our needs."[24] Mid-nineteenth-century America had not, however, seen the dawn of an age of consumer extravagance. In fact, the ideal performance of woman as shopper was enacted with great reserve and frugality. One "Aunt Lizzy," the product of another young lady's literary imagination, struck the right posture. The avuncular Lizzy gave the same advice to the working girl who coveted a new dress and to the young wife who eyed a new sofa or comely hat: Think carefully about the validity of your needs. Aunt Lizzy put it this way, "A good motto is that, 'I can do without it,' and one of great practical importance in every department of life. It is the very cornerstone of economy, and the grand recipe for hard times; its observance could fill the public treasury and larder and preclude the necessity of the bankrupt law." The female manager of the middle-class home, in other words, was expected to mediate between the family and the marketplace in a parsimonious but active manner, to consume enough to accommodate a growing commodity production and yet to save enough for the continuing accumulation of capital during this early period of industrialization. In both respects, as implied by Aunt Lizzy's references to the public treasury and the bankruptcy law, shopping was vitally connected to the larger economy. The *Utica Evening Telegraph*, in the person of a male editor, used the same financial rhetoric to describe the ideal home economist: "A

saving wife at the head of family is the very best savings bank yet
established – one that receives daily and hourly with no costly machinery to manage it." Indeed, the *Evening Telegraph* had captured
the essence of the frugal housewife's value. She operated "costly
machinery" without payment in the form of a wage.[25] Only a small
minority of Utica's households made cash expenditures for domestic labor. Among the native-born at midcentury fewer than 1 in 5
housewives had the assistance of a hired servant.

The Utica housewife contributed to the family economy in a more
traditional way as well, by the actual production of goods within
the household. A large fraction of the family's groceries, even in a
city of more than twenty thousand inhabitants and paved streets,
was still produced in the family garden. The spacious, manicured
lawn of the Munson Williams mansion served as more than an ornamental display. Mrs. Helen Munson Williams sent her servants
there to care for domestic livestock and to retrieve a daily supply of
vegetables. As late as 1845 the agricultural census counted about
three thousand swine and an equal number of chickens and cows
within the city limits, ample testimony to the continuation of the
traditional chores of the farmer's wife. Most of this production, like
the tiny remaining produce of family spinning wheels and looms,
was only for domestic consumption and had about it a slightly out-
moded and undervalued quality in the age of capital and commerce. The "ladies department" at the mechanics and agricultural
fairs classified women's products as "old-fashioned" and "home-
made goods." But the fact remains that women's home production
was at least a savings to the families of the city. A casual look
through a nineteenth-century recipe book reveals countless other
ways women minimized cash expenditures, by concocting medicines, varnishes, cleansers, dyes, almost every household potion
imaginable.

Without leaving her home the middle-class wife contributed am-
ply to her family's well-being, not only by economizing but also by
earning money in her own right. In 1855 and again in 1865, 1 in 5
housewives earned money by selling housekeeping skills to
boarders. By this expedient, women converted their domestic services – cleaning, cooking, washing, and mending – into a source of
income. From the perspective of the organization of economic and
social services, women were managing the equivalent of hotels,
restaurants, and laundries; they incorporated into the home many
of the lucrative activities that are now assigned to the service sector
of the paid labor force. Women were also indirectly responsible for

a second major source of family income, the earnings of the employed children found in 1 in 4 homes. By physically and culturally reproducing these potential wage earners, women added yet another contribution to the home economics of the nineteenth-century city. The multiplication of family income through the reproduction of children and the keeping of boarders was not a trivial matter, for a full 40% of Utica's households contained more than one worker (Table E.14). Women were also instrumental in collecting these dispersed sources of income into a common pool. We have at least one example of this function in Utica. When young Daniel Perry went off to the Civil War, he paused in battle to send the major portion of his paycheck back to his mother and father in Utica. With a remittance of $22 in July 1861 he sent the request that the contribution to family income not be disclosed to his neighbor, Mrs. Kimball, whose son Jim had accompanied Daniel Perry off to war. "It might make her feel kind of bad," Perry observed, "that he did not send as much as I did."[26] In this instance and in doubtless many other cases as well, the moral influence of a mother was seen as a major pressure to deposit earnings in the family coffers. Women, in other words, worked to consoldiate as well as generate family income.

It should be clear that women's work in the home was more than a small vestige of household labor that remained after production fled to factories. Women's domestic workshops were also geared up and transformed in the era of early industrialization. Like the factory, the home had its own form of capital investment that enhanced efficiency and productivity. The housewives of Utica were kept informed of the "latest advantages and improvements" available for adoption in the home. In 1860 the *Utica Herald* gave up space on the editorial page to endorse "Rogers improved washing machine" or the "patent-washer-woman." "Ten-twelve minutes sufficed for work that other wise would require an hour," observed the awe-struck editor. He went on gleefully measuring the value of this laborsaving device: "Washing for a family of ten or twelve, usually so burdensome, becomes not a difficult task for a single person." The *Herald* was not alone in its enthusiasm for the mechanization of the household. The editor of the *Evening Telegraph* sang the praises of all kinds of home technology: sewing machines, stoves, flatirons, and heaters. He recommended each as a means of performing household labor in a "more expeditious, more convenient, or less laborious manner." Homes equipped with all this machinery might appear more modern than the typical artisan's shop.[27] Certainly the well-equipped kitchens of Utica were closer to the mechanized industrial work process than those offices where male members of the new middle class laboriously wielded their quill pens.

The home was infused with some semblance of the "time and work-discipline" venerated by large-scale manufacturers. *A Voice to the Married* resorted to a highly rational expression to describe good home management, delegating to women the responsibility to "regulate the expenses of the households." The timing of family life was also calibrated by the exigencies of urban work patterns. The *Utica Daily Gazette* recommended innovations in the scheduling of meals in 1856. The hectic pace of the workday, the editor observed, no longer allowed for a major meal at midday. Rather, a small lunch at noontime would suffice, to be followed by a full family dinner in the evening. The editor admonished the working men of Utica that "when they returned home it is to dine, to leave off work, to enjoy their meal as Christians ought to enjoy it, with their families and friends around them." There was an opaque quality to women's household labor as seen in this idealized family dining. Its consequences were displayed at the margins of a male workday, dispensed at a gracious, leisurely pace and invested with expressive, rather than instrumental, meaning. Yet the family dinner was the culmination of a full day's work, the product of discipline, management, and exertion.[28]

Although women's work went on in the shadow of the more public and lucrative labor of males, it was vital to family and economy. The connections women forged between the household and economics were hydralike, shooting out in multiple directions, via shopping to the marketplace, through home production to family subsistence, from keeping boarders to assembling household income, by way of frugality to the capital in local savings banks. Even the labor spent dusting knickknacks, polishing silver, and pruning rosebushes defined important economic and social functions; at one and the same time, they provided a market for domestic goods and gave some public display and social confirmation to the otherwise privatized middle class. Those shining windowpanes and whitewashed gates, no less than starched white collars, gave a material expression to the formation of the American middle class.

Women's domestic work, despite all its variety and importance, hardly exhausted the economic contribution of women to their families and to the economy of Utica. Women also entered the paid public labor force in remarkable numbers. Thirty percent of the city's women were gainfully employed in 1855, and they were not merely beleaguered immigrants from broken families: About 28% of all native-born adult females had also secured jobs in that year. As demonstrated in the preceding chapter, women workers brought income into about 1 in 7 households of the native-born. From the standpoint of the local economy, women's work was even more significant. In both 1855 and 1865 women constituted more than one-fifth of the local labor force. The especially high proportion of women in the native-born population meant that they contributed an even larger share to the wage-earning population of their ethnic group. In the peak year for female employment, 1855, an impressive 30% of the native-born labor force was female. This would come as rather startling news to those who celebrated women's place in the home, for the middle-class native-born females also secured 3 in 10 of the positions in the paid labor force. Even this figure fails to account for seasonal work, such as that suggested by newspaper accounts of mass pilgrimages of women, some three thousand strong, to pick hops during harvest season (Table E.13).[29]

When women went to work outside the home in such large numbers, they encountered yet another women's sphere, a sex-segregated labor force perhaps even more rigidly bounded than today's job market. The female labor force was a truncated version of the male occupational structure. Insignificant numbers of women were found among entrepreneurs, shopkeepers, and white-collar workers. They concentrated in two fields, skilled crafts and personal service, which together accounted for more than 86% of all female workers. Above them were a few professionals, who topped the dwarfed occupational pyramid for women (Table E.13).

In 1855 the crafts were the single largest employers of native-born women. A few skilled female workers could be found working among men or at traditionally male tasks, at bakeries, cigar factories, and metalworks. The majority of skilled female workers, however, were employed in Utica's growing garment industry, making hats, cloaks, mantillas, skirts, and shirts. The clothing trades were the largest, most variegated sphere of work for women and one with a long local history. During the canal era the advertising pages of Utica newspapers had been stocked with invitations to seamstresses. At one time the want ads recruited twenty women to braid straw bonnets and offered tempting wages to an unspecified number of females willing to fashion fur hats. In April 1844 a job seeker would find this encouraging notice: "A few girls wanted to learn dressmaking business. Apply to No. 10 Blandina St., Mary Whiffen."[30] The occupation of dressmaker, like the thriving millinery business, could offer women a source of apprenticeship, not just casual and low-paid employment. It could, in addition, lead to relatively high-status positions, perhaps even the independent proprietorship that Mary Whiffen had secured. Dressmaking and millinery were, in fact, the chief avenues of entrepreneurship open to local women. In the canal era, women proudly advertised themselves as expert manufacturers of frocks and bonnets. It was almost entirely through these occupations that women entered the world of the small independent producers and retailers. Women milliners accounted for no less than 11% of all the Mercantile Agency's records for the 1850s.

The Mercantile Agency recommended the loan of only small sums of credit to these female proprietors. Some milliners, like Mrs. A. Pullam, had very brief careers. Her economic adventure ended in a sheriff's sale within two years of its founding. The agent of the Mercantile Agency scrutinized the marital history of businesswomen with special care. Miss R. B. Lumbard, Milliner, was described as an "old maid worth only a small amount." The sole female shopkeeper found in the Mercantile Agency records was treated with suspicion. A "Mrs." King who operated a fancy-goods store caused the credit agent particular worry, for he "could not find out if she was married or not." In Mrs. Eli Maynard, the agent had more confidence: "Widow of former editor of the *Observer* . . . depends on industry, a very good character!" Mrs. Maynard remained in business more than twenty years. Businesswomen with less lofty reputations also turned out to be quite reliable small proprietors. Miss Lumbard carried on a business for at least fourteen years despite the handicap of being an "old maid." Miss E. Meyers, another spinster, who arrived in Utica with little collateral in 1847, soon acquired some $300 to $500 and was "doing very well" by 1869. As for Mrs. King, she worked steadily on, purchased her store, invested in real estate, and bequeathed the thriving business to her daughter. Thus, the young women of Utica had their own models of rags to respectability. They would find them not in the ladies' books but in the shops on Genesee Street.[31]

With the passage of time and the advances of industrialization in Utica, however, such modest female ambitions were blighted somewhat. The midcentury census of manufacturers showed small garment shops headed by women becoming eclipsed and driven out of business by large factories headed by male capitalists. Only four female milliners, each with $2,000 or less in capital and only a handful of co-workers, survived into the more industrialized era. They could hardly compete with large mechanized companies such as Yates Clothing was $93,000 invested in sewing machines, whose four hundred workers received higher wages than did the employees of small women's workshops. At the same time, the factories began to substitute machines operated by boys and men for the nimble fingers of the female sex. The garment firm of Palmer and Kellogg, and the textile factories as well, had a majority of male workers in 1860. Although this trend was reversed in 1870, it was clear that women's opportunities for skilled work were not dependable.[32]

At the same time, one segment of the labor force remained a female stronghold: In 1865 domestic service was the largest employer of native- as well as foreign-born women. Domestic service employed 1 in 4 females in the age group twenty to twenty-nine. Women willing to become servants were seldom thwarted by a glutted job market. Advertisements for maids, cooks, housekeepers, and nurses peppered the local newspapers, even in those hard times when men faced the specter of unemployment. The Orphan Asylum, for example, was beseiged with job offers for its female wards, even when it was hard pressed to find work for its male charges. Domestic service was a readily available and basically undifferentiated mode of female employment. The qualifications for the job seemed to inhere in gender rather than in specific training or skills. A typical notice of domestic employment went like this: "young woman to do the usual business of small family." Occasionally an ad would detail a more elaborate division of household labor, calling for one woman for child care, cooking, and sewing and another to devote her time to washing clothes. In 1865 a domestic employer was arrogant as well as vague in this address to servants: "Anyone wanting a good home and willing to make herself useful, can come recommended." This mode of work, which simply carried the female employee from one home into another, was notably lacking in the accouterments of a modern job, specified training and qualifications.[33]

If one Utica woman had her way, some order and system would be brought into this mode of women's work. The mistress of Utica's most elegant household, Helen Munson Williams of Fountain Elms, interrupted her fashionable lassitude long enough to pen a set of instructions for her servants. Her blueprint for domestic labor resembled a time-motion study in its precision and fragmentation of tasks. Mrs. Williams's maid was told to begin the workday as follows: "Lay down bedclothes. Open window, come into the front part of the house. Open window in hall room. Take down tray." All in all, her morning labor was dissected into more than forty small tasks. Mrs. Williams also considered it within her purview to regulate the personal lives of her servants. The morning began with this order: "Rise at half past five o'clock, wash, brush hair and dress neatly." She even advised her maid on questions of intimate apparel. "All underclothing is to be made in the simplest manner by the girl herself and possibly all her working clothes." Servants were also forbidden to receive visitors at the Munson Williams house and barred from leaving their posts without the permission of the mistress of the household.[34]

In many respects Mrs. Williams seemed to have come up with a rationalization of the domestic work process that rivaled the engineering of her industrialist father. Yet she was completely ignorant of one fundamental tenet of capitalism, the importance of the wage. Her program for household efficiency was part of what she called "home missionary work," aimed at introducing servant girls to the principles of true womanhood. She had the temerity, or the naïveté, to suggest that young women perform the exhausting labors she prescribed without any recompense save their own education and edification. Her scheme to deny domestic workers a wage was not particularly eccentric. Several reports of similar practices appeared in the public record of Utica. The *Evangelical Recorder and Gospel Advocate* described such an incident in the 1830s. A woman on Broad Street, one of the pious and benevolent ladies of the Presbyterian circle, the Universalist editor allowed, had been paying her servant with old clothes and firewood from the stock of her favorite charity, a rather deflated rate of compensation. Two decades later the *Evening Telegraph* reported on what appeared to be a prevalent custom within wealthy households. "The fashion for taking old worn-out dresses of the mistress for wages, at about double the price they could be obtained for anywhere else, is becoming much the style with the upper class, as the mistress says 'take them or you get nothing' and the servant can't afford to go to law about it." Even women, it would seem, subscribed to the mystique of domestic labor, regarding it as a mode of work that existed beyond the world of the wage and could be rewarded only in use values. Emily Chubbuck recounted a similar problem in a story called "The

Bank Note," whose plot revolved around a servant's temptation to steal from a mistress who was tardy and absentminded about paying her domestic employees.[35]

This is only one of the reasons that domestic service, despite its prevalence, was not a favorite work experience among women. One native poet spent more than a score of stanzas describing the frustrating conditions of this form of woman's work. The anonymous author sent these lines to the *Evening Telegraph* in 1860.

> Oh what a weary life we lead,
> Twixt work and scorn!
> We toil in constant slavery
> Night, noon, and morn.

The author ended her long account of the tedium of service with a plea for understanding and consideration from the mistresses of Utica households.

> Be just! And you'll have far less cause
> To call us rude.
> We are in nature like yourself
> One sisterhood.[36]

Such awkward rhyming bespeaks the contradictions of domestic service. Although the employer and the servant were of the same sex and shared a common residence, they did not live together in a sisterly women's sphere. In fact, they experienced the conflicts inherent in a wage relationship planted right in the middle of at least 1 in 10 of Utica's households.

In sum, the majority of Utica's large army of women workers were performing traditional female tasks in households, factories or shops, under conditions that failed to rival those of their brothers who were moving, however haltingly and cautiously, into the individualized occupations of the new middle class. The major entry point into middle-class careers, that of clerking, was jealously guarded from females, despite the fact that shopkeepers' wives and daughters customarily assisted in the family business. In the domesticated era such female work was repellent to the city fathers. One local editor discharged the full arsenal of his journalistic rage when he heard that a female had been employed as a clerk in a local dry-goods store. He regarded this offense against female delicacy as more odious than the most backbreaking physical labor. A position in a retail store at midcentury was deemed a transgression against feminine "privacy."[37]

Although a woman hardly ever called herself a clerk, about 3% of the adult female population and close to 10% of the city's women

workers secured a place in the professions. A few women even entered the male professional citadel of medicine. One Caroline
Brown, for example, practiced medicine in the 1850s and won a
public endorsement from the press when she took another woman
doctor named Mary Stowell into her office.[38] Most female professionals, however, had entered yet another women's sphere, that of
teaching. By midcentury females monopolized the lowest ranks of
this profession, teaching at the elementary level in the public
schools. Their ranks thinned out in the higher grades and positions, yet significant numbers of them could still be found in secondary academies and among school principals. Several women
built the career of schoolteaching into a prestigious status in the
community. The successive principals of the Utica Female Academy, Urania Sheldon and Jane Kelley, were women of stature in
Utica and beneficiaries of frequent, deferential notice in the press.
Schoolteaching, furthermore, was an occupation that women held
onto more tenaciously in later life; in the over fifty age group it
accounted for 15% of all workingwomen.

The school and the women's network that wove through the
Utica Female Academy also served as the incubator of another female profession. Emily Chubbuck stayed on at the Utica Female
Academy to become its composition teacher. It was there, with the
friendly encouragement of Urania Sheldon, that she began to submit light fiction to local periodicals like *Mother's Magazine*. With
this small start she soon became one of the more popular American
authors of the 1850s. Writing under the pen name Fanny Forrester
and posing as the homely chronicler of village life, Chubbuck created something of a literary career for herself. Countless other
women made an avocation of writing stories or verse, for little monetary reward or public acclaim. When, in 1893, the women of western New York prepared a list of local female authors for the Colom-
bia Exposition, Oneida County could boast of more than 140
notable and increasingly self-supporting literary women.[39] Like
Chubbuck, most got their start in a women's sphere – in schools or
female magazines – and wrote on domestic themes – childrearing,
domestic fiction, or sentimental poetry. By the 1860s Utica had
spawned a second generation of women writers, the most notable
of whom was Mary Clemner Ames. Ames began to write essays for
the *Utica Herald* at age sixteen in order to help support a large family of seven children, sired by an impecunious father. By 1860 she
was a full-time and affluent authoress, writing newspaper columns
and best-selling novels. She had worked her way through women's

world to a highly individuated professional status and wrote under her own name, rather than some timid feminine pseudonym favored by women writers a generation earlier. Her novels boldly championed women workers. One of her heroines recited this daring oration: "The accident of sex, the fact of being a woman did not make me less determined nor less aspiring."[40]

The careers of women like Urania Sheldon, Caroline Brown, and Mary Clemner Ames all expose cracks in the fortifications around women's sphere that allowed a few females to go in search of something of the independent, individuated status claimed as a birthright by middle-class males. They were, of course, a tiny minority, yet their successes are a significant, if marginal, component of the gender system at midcentury. They demonstrate, first of all, that the ideological boundaries between male and female were not so airtight that females never inhaled the heady vapors of the ethic of individualism. These women, like men, participated in the spirit of independence released with the fragmentation of the patriarchal household economy. In order to make a "self," however, women relied on support not from families but from female peers. Their ambitions were cradled in female institutions, like the female academies and women's periodicals. They found solace and encouragement in other women, Chubbuck with Urania Sheldon, Dr. Caroline Brown with Dr. Mary Stowell, Ames with sister authors like Abby Carey. Even female individualism and achievement, in other words, was testimony to the strength of women's sphere.

Providing for the public welfare

The annals of Utica at midcentury included another notable female, Louisa Shepherd, who in 1865 secured the professional title of city missionary of the Presbyterian Church. With the handsome female salary of $500 a year, Mrs. Shepherd built women's religious sphere into an arena of public prominence. Her post as city missionary was described in a set of professional responsibilities: "She will devote her whole time to the work, prayer meetings and meetings of public worship."[41] Mrs. Shepherd had come to her lofty status through a familiar female route. Her name first appeared in the local records of a small revival, which occurred at Westminster Presbyterian Church in 1863. That awakening operated through a familiar women's lineage. By then, women outnumbered men in the church by 4 to 1: 65% of the converts were female; 40% shared a surname; 56% were preceded into the church by relatives, and an additional third of the converts were either the boarders or neighbors of church members. Most of the converts were young: The median age for males was eighteen, and more than half of all female converts were under fourteen. By this time the institutions of evangelical womanhood had closed in on a narrow class base. Almost all the new church members came from white-collar or professional families; a rare artisan was the closest thing to a member of the working class to participate in the revival of 1863.[42]

The pious women of the 1860s did not, however, confine their religious work within the boundaries of their own place of worship nor within family networks. Mrs. Shepherd went directly from conversion into the East Utica mission in the heart of the working-class district. She journeyed out of her sphere in the company of the Presbyterian Benevolent Society and its many female volunteers. Having located themselves in the slum neighborhoods of Utica, furthermore, these women of midcentury took on a far more tough-minded demeanor than the ladies of the past. The city missionary and the Presbyterian Benevolent Association operated a complex organizational structure, which included four major committees, two composed of both men and women, one of local ministers, and another all-male finance committee. This staff administered a panoply of subsidiary services: the missionary chapel, an industrial school, a night school, a library, and Sunday schools. The benevolent machine extended its bureaucratic arms deep into the working-class district, as groups of men and women, called family visiting committees, looked everywhere in search of souls. The course of evangelism ran more like a threshing machine than a brush fire in the 1860s. The constitution of the Benevolent Association described the new modus operandi tersely and adamantly: "A systematic visitation of families will be maintained."[43] The city missionary and the family visitors were also increasingly concerned with the secular well-being of the poor. The Benevolent Association set these priorities in dealing with the city's paupers: "The principal work is their religious and eternal salvation, but subordinate and tributary to this and highly important is the improvement of their present conditions." To this end the association provided training in dressmaking for the daughters of the poor, night schools in English for immigrants and illiterate workers, and instructions designed to "add to the comfortableness and attractiveness of the homes" in the slums. The family visitors also adopted something of the suspicious frame of mind we have come to associate with welfare agencies: "Be sure that no deception has been practiced on you before alms are procured." Mrs. Shepherd's ministry and the Benevolent Association represent a real metamorphosis in the relationship between the sexes and the sects and another expansion and transformation of women's sphere. Women had made their way outside the home and outside their own class into professional tasks, social welfare functions, and the social problems of industrial society. They had taken up an extra-domestic role in social reproduction, acting to help maintain, socialize, and replenish the work force for industrial society.[44]

Mrs. Shepherd and her co-workers were neither alone nor the vanguard of this progression of womanhood. The first and, by 1865, most venerable example of women's welfare had been established in 1830 within the Female Society of Industry, a simple sewing circle that met at the social hub of the canal era, Sophia Bagg's parlor in the landmark hotel that bore her husband's name. With the income accumulated from sewing and inheritances, these women purchased a modest house, hired a needy widow as matron, and installed three orphans under her care. Such was the unpretentious beginning of the Utica Orphan Asylum. By 1850 the Orphan Asylum harbored some 50 children in a fine old mansion and could boast of having supervised 730 charges over the previous thirty years. Their budget had grown from the contents of Mrs. Bagg's sewing basket to upwards of $2,000 a year. They served not only orphans and half orphans, but any child whom parents surrendered to their care for fifty cents a week. As the children aged, the ladies served as employment agents, securing jobs for servants, skilled workers, and clerks. The managers of the Orphan Asylum represented a range of religious denominations and acted independently of church elders and town fathers. They had become the caretakers of stray children and the founders of a new institution, intermediary between the family and society.[45]

By midcentury the Orphan Asylum and the Benevolent Association were only two examples of a maze of female agencies of social service. Both Catholic and Episcopalian women had also founded orphan asylums. The Sisters of Charity opened the first hospital in Utica at a time when the city fathers and public sector refused to set up such an expensive institution. In 1849 the local press applauded the "private work" under way to extend hospital care: "A number of benevolent persons, among whom of course, a large portion were ladies, had taken up the cause."[46] By this time the female welfare system was known under the generic title of "ladies' relief" and expressed itself whenever ad hoc committees of females got together to collect firewood and blankets during severe winters, to found "ragged schools" for poor children, and to run charitable fairs to raise money for needy families. By the 1860s ladies' relief had pretensions to become a national welfare system. In May 1861 the women of Utica met, as so many had before in the First Presbyterian Church, and founded the Soldiers Aid Association. Rechristened the Ladies' Soldiers Relief Association, it linked up with the national network of the Sanitary Commission and sent tons of supplies to the Union troops fighting in the South.[47] One of the association's most active leaders was Mrs. Louisa Shepherd. She proposed that such effective benevolence be continued after the Civil War as a citywide welfare administration, to be called the Ladies Christian Commission.[48] In 1865 it seemed that women were poised to make an assault on the male sphere and were determined to take direct control of municipal social services.

The virtual absorption of public welfare functions by females did not go unnoticed by the leaders of Utica. At first the city fathers were somewhat suspicious of such female activism. Incorporated female charities like the Orphan Asylum carefully wrote clauses into their constitutions that exempted the husbands of the benevolent ladies from financial liability. During the same period a few niggardly newspapermen complained that the generosity of Utica ladies was luring indigents into the city in hopes of an easy dole. Slowly, however, local leaders began to spy some financial benefits of female charity. Early in the 1840s and again in the 1850s, the problems of public welfare and the assets of women's charity were debated in the local press. On April 6, 1841, the *Oneida Whig* gave special notice to the annual report of the Utica Ladies' Society for the Relief of the Poor. These benevolent women, who remained unnamed, had proven themselves particularly ingenious at generating public charity. They operated an industrial school where poor children were set to work procuring their own means of support. The boys, for example, chopped wood for their needy families and thereby eliminated one of the major expenses of the Poor Commission during the winter months. "The girls are taught to work, and in payment receive the garments necessary." The surplus produce of these young seamstresses, which included "90 pounds of carpet rag made into blankets," was sold to help cover the school's expenses. The Ladies' Relief Society was still flourishing a year and a half later when the editor of the *Oneida Whig* published its economical principles of benevolence. "It proposes to relieve poverty by promoting industry. It attempts to take away the curse of idleness by furnishing the means of employment. It gives nothing without some equivalent in labor, except the helplessness arising from sickness, old age, tender years, or other causes beyond the control of the sufferer." In addition to their many other forms of public service, the ladies demonstrated the work ethic to the progeny of the poor.[49]

The editors of the *Utica Daily Gazette* felt indebted to the ladies in far more tangible ways than this. They felt the value of women's charity in their pockets as well as in their principles. The *Gazette* was most impressed with the frugality of the Ladies' Relief Society:

> A few benevolent women in so short a time with so little noise and pretension, without previous experience, and with such limited means have been able to alleviate so much suffering. With a few hundred dollars they have bestowed a much larger measure of relief, and considering its moral influence, have done incalculably greater good than the thousands of dollars which in the years past were raised and distributed by the "Fathers of the city" through the medium of ward committees.

The Ladies' Relief Society was not the only case of such masterful charitable engineering. In 1843 the *Whig* offered long overdue recognition to Mrs. Emma Crowley, who founded an infant school in the days of the revivals and continued to operate it for some fifteen years. Again, the editors were intrigued and impressed by her financial methods: "The whole annual expense managed with the admirable female economy costing about $320 including the payment of the instructors, firewood, repairs, books, etc."[50]

In the following decade the *Utica Daily Gazette* again led the applause for women's charitable prowess. Its editors singled out the Young Ladies' Relief Society for special praise. There was, said the *Gazette*, "no better and almost no other institution or association to care for the poor." This society had adopted sophisticated methods of relief, much like those of the Presbyterian Benevolent Association. "It has been the practice of the young ladies of the society for several winters to visit every poor family in the city in which there was sickness or evident want." The young ladies had been particularly intrepid during the severe winter. "They frequently traversed every portion of the city in which destitution was to be found, exposed not only to the wear of the weather, but oft times to the contagion of disease." "Surely," said the editors of the *Daily Gazette*, "men should at least be willing to do something to encourage and support wives and daughters in such missions of love and charity." In 1851 the men of Utica were asked to contribute directly to the

Relief Society rather than through the usual intermediary of a ladies' fair, whose "expense and labor" the society had decided to eliminate. Still, the ladies of Utica had performed Herculean labors and garnered substantial savings for the city. "And it may well be to say that the money before passing through the hands of the society acquires a double value, as a result of the industry of the members – the fund being expended mostly in the purchase of material for clothing and other necessities which are economically made up before distribution." In the next year the exchange rate for women's charity had risen even higher: The *Gazette* maintained that the Young Ladies' Relief Society could convert a $100 contribution into $1,000 in value.[51]

Hyperbole and chivalry aside, the newspaper editors of Utica had accurately assessed the social saving implicit in women's charitable activities. The women's welfare system was just as effective as a municipal savings bank, as was the frugal housewife. The combined services of sundry orphan asylums, hospitals, sewing circles, and relief associations surely surpassed the annual city appropriation for the poor, some $3,000. The proceeds of two female charities alone, the Utica Orphan Asylum and the Ladies' Fair at St. Patrick's Church, exceeded this amount. The men of Utica were never delivered a formal bill or tax assessment for all this public service. Ladies seemed to create provisions for the poor out of nothing. Their welfare work had a kind of magical quality about it and was draped in myths of female altruism. In 1860 the *Utica Herald* obliquely recognized the nexus between sex and charity when the editor suggested that "the ladies who are forever getting up fairs" generate welfare funds by dispensing kisses at a fair price. More often, women's welfare work was rewarded in another form of sex-typed currency, the characterization of female social services as a "labor of love," not money.[52]

Women's welfare work and the generation of social savings by females were more complex and systematic than this. The labor was voluntary and unpaid but nonetheless expensive and neatly integrated into the class sytem. The leadership of local charities was drawn from the elite families of the city. In 1860, 9 out of 10 officers of the Orphan Asylum were wives of merchants or lawyers with property valued at between $15,000 and $125,000.[53] Twelve of the fourteen officers who could be identified had servants, six of them two or more. The ladies of the Presbyterian Benevolent Association were slightly less well off and included many wives of white-collar workers. Still, most of their mates had estates worth more than

$10,000 and employed servants.[54] The male elite at least paid some indirect private costs for wives' social services, purchasing the domestic labor of servants and thereby freeing their wives to engage in charitable activities. Still, charity in itself depended almost completely on voluntary female labor and was even less costly than employing a skilled seamstress or washerwoman. This was the first economic secret of the women's welfare system, its ability to get away with a minimum of expenditures for labor, not only from the elite but also from the armies of volunteers who baked and sewed, collected door to door, taught in industrial schools, and organized bazaars. Almost every middle-class woman contributed at least some time and energy to these enterprises.

The institution of the ladies' fair illustrates women's acumen for converting their own unpaid labors into cash. Hardly a week passed without some coterie of women – from the Colored Ladies Relief Association to the Friends of St. Elizabeth's Hospital – getting up a bazaar or carnival in behalf of their favorite charity. Such events created money, without any overhead; the goods sold, as well as the labor, were provided by women free of charge. Women were extending their customary work, producing use values in the home, outside the market, but for a larger social purpose. In this case women sold their pastries, jellies, and needlework (if not kisses as the *Herald* advised) not for personal profit but for public charity or support of the church. The ladies' fair was an exhaustive and well-organized way of circumventing the cash nexus to provide for the public welfare. Other female charitable activities took another route around the capitalist sector. Institutions like the ragged schools, industrial societies, and hospitals worked to reproduce labor power without civic or capitalist expense. The training school prepared shoemakers and seamstresses for working in local industry, and hospitals and infant schools saw to it that mothers and fathers need not leave work to care for the sick. The services of ladies of mercy relieved families and employers from part of the cost of reproducing the working class. If the ladies could also, as they intended, inculcate the work ethic in the children of the poor, the value of their charity was redoubled.

Most women were only half aware of the social and economic implications of their altruism. Nonetheless, they were shrewd enough to know how to pry open the tightfisted hold of businessmen on their capital resources. The skill with which benevolent women stepped adroitly around the cash nexus in collecting charitable funds was described in a story written by Whitestown satirist

Miriam Berry. In the voice of her garrulous persona, the Widow Bedott, Berry described the skill with which a Mrs. Birsley wrenched some support for her sewing society from a miserly merchant. This shopkeeper begged off from making a donation, saying he needed all his cash on hand to pay for a shipment of goods that was about to arrive from New York. The quick-witted Mrs. Birsley swiftly picked up a bolt of cloth and said, "We know 'twould be more of a satisfaction to you to give us five dollars if it was convenient; but seeing it ain't we're perfectly willing to take this so please dew it up.' He hesitated a minute, and then and you believe it; he actually took the cloth and tied it up! – but I till ye I never see such an uncomfortable looking continance as his'n."[55] By such devious methods as this, through the charitable marketplace of the fair or by resorting to the parlor production of the sewing circle, the women welfare workers of the nineteenth-century city saved incalculable sums of tax money.

By midcentury women commanded through their charitable activities a vital post outside the home, one of crucial importance to the social order of the city. They had not, however, entered the formal public sphere nor the realm of capital. Their benevolence was still conducted under private auspices, not in an authoritative, legally sanctioned public arena. However much they saved capitalists, they never soiled their own hands with profits. In Utica it was largely women who "discovered the asylum," to use David Rothman's phraseology, and who provided public welfare in what Sam Bass Warner has called "the Private City." Consequently, women were centrally implicated in the limitations of nineteenth-century social organization that these historians have described.

First of all, the private female method of dispensing welfare was highly inefficient. Poor relief and social services were entrusted to dispersed, ad hoc associations that were seldom capable of responding systematically to community needs. The different private segments of the women's welfare system even competed for clients. The orphan asylums and hospitals run by different religious denominations, both Protestant and Catholic, strove to bring the city's poor under the jurisdiction of their own beliefs and culture, rather than to meet the material needs of a diverse population in a simple, straightforward manner. A second limitation inhered in this method of welfare. In the absence of any formal public accountability, female charities could impose their own ethnocentric values on a dependent population. Aggressively benevolent Protestant ladies propagated the work ethic, the King James Bible, and the cult of domesticity, as they distributed alms. The elite Protestant managers of the Utica Orphan Asylum, for example, were the guardians of immigrant children, often of Catholic background. These children were subjected to an annual inspection by some of the wealthiest matrons of Utica, who scrutinized "the situation as to neatness and economy . . . the progress of the orphans in their education . . . the general conduct of the family."[56]

For all its inefficiency and inequity, the city at midcentury was unwilling to part with the economical system of private female charity. When Louisa Sheldon attempted to bring some order into this system in 1865, the city fathers expeditiously escorted her back into woman's place. She convened a public meeting for the purpose of founding a citywide charitable organization, only to have Judge Bacon and a male leader of the Sanitary Commission take the podium and advise the assembled women against such an ambitious project. The group compliantly withdrew, back into the fragmented private arenas of their charities.[57]

The troubled borders of women's sphere

The women's welfare system was but one element in a complex and gerrymandered women's sphere, part of a whole social geography of gender that meshed with its male complement to ensure the production and reproduction of urban society. In its structure and operation this system seems like a clever piece of social machinery, with multiple, interconnected parts, regularly oiled with a supportive ideology (both the myth of the self-made man and the cult of true womanhood) and functioning smoothly to meet social needs and guarantee social order. But what functions for society is not always comfortable for human beings and never rests in a condition of perfect stasis. The gender system was full of tension, ever-changing, and even buffeted by some conscious protest movements. Both these tensions and this dynamic inhabited women's sphere itself.

Even a model, compliant, and nigh "true" woman like Lavinia Johnson experienced and expressed some of the contradictions of the gender system. Mrs. Johnson was nearly as fond of quoting from the local press as is this historian. In the process she put her personal seal of approval on the doctrine of the spheres. She excerpted the following admonition from the *Utica Herald* in 1859: "Be true to your own sex, thus be a true friend to the other. Blessed are the household women, God's noiseless workers who lay their calm hand upon the plastic brows of infancy, and so shape immortal destinies. When man and woman learn to treat each other reverently, each to honor the work of the other not as they mark it out – but as it is apportioned by the hand of the omnipotent, the millennium finally reigns." In thirty-one years of marriage, to a man who apparently did not live up to his responsibility in the sexual division of labor, Lavinia Johnson stayed noiselessly in her sphere.[58]

A stealthy and suspicious reader, however, can detect some subterranean discontent with women's lot. Johnson's favorite selections from local popular culture included this poem delivered at Mechanics' Hall in February 1860:

> There is a love far holier than the rest,
> The yearning love which fills a mother's breast,
> Burns with the babe whose little wailing moan
> Asks aid and pity in a world unknown.
> Still clinging closer as advancing years
> Enlarge her hopes and multiply her fears,
> Chidding the truant with beaming Joy
> That he who grieved her is her darling boy.
> In manhood flush, in fevers wasting flame,
> But most in grief, in sorrow, and in shame.
> In mother love her precious little child attends
> To human toil angelic lustre lends,
> Cheers the pale wanderer at his parting breath
> And pierces even beyond the gate of Death.[59]

Verse like this had been a staple of women's culture in Utica for nearly a half-century. Writers like Lydia Sigourney and R. Barber had stocked the local papers with these bittersweet paeans to mother love. The entire genre, furthermore, was characterized by a certain ambivalence about the sacred and poignant subject. Like the poem Johnson quoted, it was full of painful images: of "moans," "fears," "wasting," "grief," "sorrow," "shame," "sin," and "toil." Inevitably, such poems ended, like this quotation of Lavinia Johnson, on the theme of death. The literary staple of the middle-class women of Johnson's generation associated pain, loss, and death with the keystone of their sphere, the relationship between mother and child.

The nearly insatiable popular appetite for this kind of verse arose from the whole complex of contradictions in women's experience. First of all, such poetry expressed and indulged genuine grief at the loss, or anticipated loss, of a beloved child. After the demise of the New England way, neither Calvinist stoicism nor the rituals of community mourning could suppress such grief. After 1820, obituary sermons in Utica no longer enjoined survivors to accept the death of their children with a stony gratitude to God. Similarly, the first mother to testify in the evangelical literature to her special grief at the death of her infant was careful to express it only after the funeral, when the social constraint on individual grief had passed away, along with a multitude of friends, neighbors, and fellow Christians. As the bereaved correspondent of 1829 put it, "the kind officiousness of neighbors has kept me from a solitary indulgence of grief until now."[60] The more urban, secular, and privatized culture of the canal era gave free expression to the emotions associated with the death of intimate family members. This same culture, and the domestic arrangements that characterized it, may also have exacerbated the normal pangs of death in the family. The narrower social spaces of middle-class urban homes permitted women to concentrate more of their psychic energies on private relationships, particularly their ties to their fewer children. The whole purport of maternal nurture was to weave tight emotional bonds between women and children, which would, in turn, make an infant's death all the more painful. Thus, literary invocations of maternal mourning were an understandable by-product of changes in the nineteenth-century woman's vocation.

But why should these images become such an obsession among women readers? Certainly actual infant deaths did not occur with anything like the frequency of poetic infanticides. The symbol of a child's death could evoke, however, a variety of more commonplace and expectable events in the female life cycle. The most immediate of these is the inevitable departure of children when they come of age. Every mother knew, after all, that the infant in whom she was investing so much of her energy and identity would eventually leave home for school, a job, marriage, perhaps even to pursue goals of which she did not approve. In the case of sons, furthermore, a child became something of a stranger to his mother at an early age, for he was destined to inhabit a world quite foreign to women's sphere. The image of a bittersweet death could anticipate these emotional losses. There may have been some catharsis in the ubiquitous vision of a child's small grave; death in its finality cut short the tension inherent in the exhausting but "dead end" occupation of motherhood. Mary Clemner Ames articulated this inherent contradiction of mothering in one of her novels: "Here is the mother's loneliness which in this country must come to the parental heart with a keener pang than in any other. For it is not the inevitable separation only, which soon or later must come to most every parent and child, but it is separation in condition. Someday the father and the mother wake to the consciousness that the children to whom they have given birth belong to another race and time, and come back to them almost as strangers."[61] Such were the contradictions of the middle-class woman's occupation in the industrial city. It was her task to prepare children to embrace new conditions and to move away from her own domestic confines.

Authors such as Ames or Emily Chubbuck were in a position to mull over the plight of women and in the process bring the tensions of women's sphere to a higher level of consciousness than did Lavinia Johnson. At times a heightened consciousness brought special pain to these more individuated women living on the outreaches of the female sphere. Emily Chubbuck, catapulted to literary fame out of her village parochialism and obeisant evangelical Calvinism, experienced the contradictions of womanhood with special acuteness. Chubbuck projected her personal anguish onto a character named Dora in a short story of the same name. Dora was blessed with a brilliant singing voice and had within her grasp the fame of a Jenny Lind or perhaps a Fanny Forrester. Yet she returned to her home village from a concert tour only to collapse and die. Her last words were these: "Mother! Mother! – I have come home to you – I am sick, I am weary. Give me a place mother – a place to die." With individualistic accomplishment within easy reach of her heroine, Chubbuck pulled back from this variety of happy ending and turned instead to the maudlin conventions of graveyard verse. This twist in the plot registered her own ambivalence about professional success as well.[62]

Such destructive images infested Emily Chubbuck's autobiography as well as her fiction. Most of her heroines found their happy endings in marriage, a ritual that evaded Emily Chubbuck until she was almost thirty years of age, when she consented to marry the eminent Baptist missionary Adoniram Judson and followed him off to Burma. Her letters to her betrothed were filled with self-abrogating speeches, which were foreshadowed in her fiction. This woman, trying to patrol the border between a male career and women's sphere, was as ambivalent about matrimony as she was about literary success. She wrote to Judson: "Oh how entirely I must belong to you . . . there is something so sweet about this heart slavery. Take the hand I place upon your lips and lead your 'unuseful' one through life up to heaven." Again, Emily Chubbuck resorted to images out of her fiction. She headed off to Burma with her new spouse, convinced she would find both "her hearthstone and her grave" in a foreign mission.[63]

Fanny Forrester, but not Emily Chubbuck Judson, was buried in Burma. Chubbuck spent most of her time there in a state of physical collapse. After a difficult pregnancy, she left her bed only to work on a book that Judson had commissioned, a memoir of his two previous wives. In addition to this morbid project, Chubbuck clothed her own experiences in images of death. "My husband will lay me in the grave and return to the house, leaving me away in that cold place alone . . . my image will gradually fade from his mind, my children will look about for their mother and perhaps cry and then they will forget me." It was actually her husband who died shortly after these words were written. Chubbuck's own death did not occur until shortly after her return to western New York on the first day of June 1851. It was said that she had hoped to die in June, the month of her beloved sister's death and of her own marriage.[64] The last chapters of Emily Chubbuck Judson's life were as sentimental and eerie as her own early fiction. Both fact and fiction spoke half-consciously to the strains of inhabiting women's sphere.

A generation later Mary Clemner Ames embarked on a literary career with far greater confidence and self-assurance. Two of her heroines, the major characters in *Eirene* (1871) and *Victoire* (1864), walked off into the future with all the aplomb of self-made men. "Had genius a sex?" asked Victoire as she left her native France to make her fortune in America. Eirene announced her departure from a New England village with this speech: "I am going away to seek my fortune. Boys always do, you know."[65] Ames herself emulated these heroines. Even as a youth she demanded a full-scale salary as the New York correspondent for the *Utica Herald*. She soon moved to Washington, D.C., and supported herself with the proceeds of her writing. Her statements about womanhood rang with the spirit of independence and achievement. "It is not half a woman who talks about being 'only a woman' or makes a plea becasue you are one. No race can be strong until it is proud of itself." Yet even Mary Clemner Ames had some difficulty living up to her own standards of womanly strength and self-sufficiency. "It would be so much easier and better to die. I am sorry to find myself so utterly a woman. I wish that God had infused a little iron into my fibre."[66] Because gender lines cut deep into the temperaments ascribed to male and female and into the process of socialization as well, those women who, like Chubbuck and Ames, skirted the borders of their assigned sphere inevitably experienced some degree of self-doubt and confusion.

Such psychic pain and intellectual struggle was in part a luxury of education and individuation and was felt most intensely by only a minority of women. Yet the experience of Chubbuck and Ames resembles that of many more ordinary women who, like themselves, spent large portions of their life cycles outside the central relationship of women's sphere, the conjugal family. Ames and Chubbuck were denied the protection of strong, financially competent fathers and remained single through most of their adult lives. Countless other women shared this experience, one of the most widespread contradictions of the doctrine of women's sphere. At any given moment at least 1 in 4 of the adult women of Utica was either a spinster or a widow. The highest proportion of wives in the native-born population was in the age group thirty to thirty-nine, when only 77% of all women were married; more than 45% of the women in their late twenties were single; half of those over sixty were widows. The doctrine of the spheres must have rung a little hollow for thousands of women who made their living and built their lives on the fringes or amid the remnants of domesticity (Table E.12).

Most all of them found shelter among relatives if not with husbands. The majority of both spinsters and widows resided with a branch of their family, in exchange no doubt for the proverbial services of grandma or maiden aunt. Their surplus labor was also absorbed by female social services outside the home. Single women and widows were among Utica's most productive and celebrated public servants. Mrs. Louisa Shepherd was a widow as was Sophia Clarke, her peer in benevolent power during the canal era. Charlotte Derbyshire, the spinster sister of Sophia Bagg, lived in an all-female household and was the mainstay of the Orphan Asylum. Emma Crowley, another spinster, found many adopted children in her infant school. These women were among the 50% of all unmarried native-born females who were secure enough financially to be spared from entering the ill-paid female labor force.

The other half of the single population was not so fortunate. If a middle-class woman was widowed early in life, she was hard pressed to support herself and her young children. Almost half of those women widowed in their thirties worked outside the home. Even the widow of a prominent editor, Eli Maynard, became a supplicant before local employers. She applied for a rare job of paid social service, the position of matron at the New York State Lunatic Asylum. Mrs. Maynard was so intent on securing this position that she promised her prospective boss that she would give the care of her infant over to others and take up solitary residence at the asylum.[67] Some years later Mrs. Maynard had acquired enough funds to go into business for herself as a milliner, an ideal way to support herself and her children and keep shop and home together. Other young widows were less fortunate than Mrs. Maynard. Their plight was symbolized by an anonymous woman in black who captured the attention of the editor of the *Utica Morning Herald* in 1859. Each morning and evening this solemn figure walked down Genesee Street and back again, carrying a large bundle, probably a stock of shirts or cloaks that she had finished for some local garment manufacturer. The editor put an optimistic cast upon the scene. Soon after her widowhood, he surmised, this woman obtained work and wages. "By honest and cheerful labor she supports herself and family and no doubt is happy in the privilege. We hope that she may always do so and that health and strength may befriend her in time and we are quite sure that when the veil of the future shall be lifted to her gaze she will be marching up to the strain of angelic music."[68]

Utica's widows cannot be dismissed so easily, confident that they marched heavenward with no more than the "deep melancholy" that titillated the newspaper editor. Their wages did not come so easily nor in great abundance. Piecework probably paid far less than full-time factory employment, which is recorded in the manufacturing census. According to the 1850 and 1860 censuses, female wages were only a fraction of male paychecks. Most firms allotted women one-third to one-half of the average monthly wage for male workers. P. B. Rice's garment works set the most inequitable scale of remuneration, paying its seventy-five female workers $7.50 a month as opposed to $50 for his twenty male hands. Women were given a better deal at the textile mills, where they made $11.50 monthly in contrast to the $20 that male workers earned on the average.[69] The professions were no less gracious to females. In 1843, for example, female teachers were awarded $5 to $7 a week, males $12 to $14. Mrs. Shepherd's annual earnings of $500 as city missionary compare with the minister's salary of $1,200. Mrs. Shepherd had seven children to support, and she was hardly alone among women workers; in fact, 15% of Utica's households were headed by females. These women could not escape the contradictions of the gender system: They were caught between a male's responsibility for supporting a family and the female standard of low wages.

Young, single, childless women – the bulk of the labor force – faced the consequences of discriminatory wages in greater dependency on the support of their fathers and kin. Both spinsters and widows found women's sphere a hazardous one. The highly differentiated gender system at midcentury assumed that males and females would be joined through marriage in a complementary, symbiotic relationship. Yet the marriage market operated by the same unreliable laissez-faire principles as did the job market. In fact, the two systems of supply and demand sometimes worked at cross-purposes. Utica's job market offered more positions for young women than it did for their male peers. There were, in fact, 135 women for every 100 males within the native-born population between the ages of fifteen and thirty. Not all these women would find mates in Utica and many of them would be stranded in the social anomalousness and economic straits of prolonged or lifelong spinsterhood.

Intimations of feminism

It was the blatantly obvious, easily quantifiable, sexual inequality of wages that generated the most forceful and direct criticisms of the gender system. Even the local press found merit in the feminists' demand for equitable remuneration of woman's labor. Wage discrimination sparked one of Mary Clemner Ames's most sterling social protests. She prefaced one of her novels with this dedication: "May this faint reflex of the lives of three bring you rapport with thousands of orphaned and homeless girls, which in every city and town in the land are striving to live by the toil of their hands." In *Eirene* she pleaded the cause of a more seasoned and demanding workingwoman. At one point in her highly mobile career, the heroine worked as a bookkeeper and negotiated with her employer for equal pay for equal work. Eirene complained that "she did bear a man's responsibility without receiving his reward." Ames's novels sometimes read like the feminist tracts of the twentieth century.[70]

Indeed, Mary Clemner Ames clearly identified herself as a partisan of women's rights and was an acquaintance and admirer of Elizabeth Cady Stanton. Her novels were riddled with feminist exhortations. She forestalled the happy ending of *Eirene* to allow her heroine an opportunity to recite this speech to her husband. "Darling," she disarmingly began, "I never had an equal chance with you since I was born. As a woman I could not have had it if I had been born to the same condition in life. George William Curtis never spoke truer words than the other evening when he said, 'There is nothing so barbaric as for a human being to say to another that thus far shall he be developed and no further; and that there is no other subject on which so much intolerable nonsense is laid as upon the sphere of women.''' Mary Clemner Ames seemed determined to dismantle the whole doctrine of the spheres.

This impression was dispelled, however, in the very next sentence. "'Why Pierre,' said Eirene to her husband, 'how can any man or woman get very far out of their sphere. God and nature have set grounds on every individual which cannot be overpassed.'" Ames went on to place clear practical limitations on women's rights. "I suppose I have the natural right to many things which as a woman I may not ever wish to do. My personal obligations are more to me than my abstract rights. What I owe my husband and children is the first and deepest obligation of my life, but not my only one. If I had no husband or child, if I were a solitary force in the world, I deny the right of any man to set a limit to my advancement, as I deny mine to set one to his."[71] Ames carried women's rights only so far and then tripped over the boundary of women's sphere. She saw no justifiable limits on the rights of single women. Wives and mothers, however, were expected to adhere to self-imposed and God-ordained restrictions on their range of action.

The story of protest against the gender system of Oneida County does not end with the small and limp arguments of Mary Clemner Ames. It found an older and more radical expression in the person of Paulina Kellogg Wright Davis. The entire history of society and family in the Burned-Over District comes together in her life and work. From the special lucidity of her vantage point at the cutting edge of history and the boundary of public and private life come intimations of a broader vision.

Paulina Kellog was born of New England parents in Bloomfield, New York, in 1818 and bred in the rural heartland of the Second Great Awakening. Like so many of the women of her remarkable generation, young Paulina Kellogg experienced a Calvinist conversion and resolved to become a missionary. Her benevolent purpose was diverted, however, when she married a young merchant from Utica named Francis Wright. A devout Presbyterian himself and a fervent abolitionist, Wright assured his wife-to-be that "there were heathen enough in Utica to call out all the religious zeal she possessed." Certainly the controversies of the canal era demanded all the courage Paulina Wright could muster. During the anti-abolitionist riot of 1835 an angry mob surrounded her home with torches poised for burning. Paulina Wright survived the mob's furor. Childless and comfortably supported by a wealthy mate, she devoted her full energies to local reform. Her name appears in the reports of the Female Anti-slavery Society, the Female Moral Reform Society, and the Martha Washington Temperance Union. She was a seasoned veteran of women's networks, having trod the streets of Utica in search of signatures on one petition after another.[72]

The power available to women in the Burned-Over District during the canal era fostered Paulina Wright's first act of feminism. In 1836 she put her female network to work in behalf of one of the very first women's rights causes in American history. In the company of Ernestine Rose and Elizabeth Cady Stanton she circulated petitions in support of New York State married women's property act. Years later, in her brief account of the history of the American women's movement, Paulina Wright Davis traced the origins of feminism back even further, to controversies over women's speaking in church during the revivals of the Second Great Awakening. The first intimations of feminism, for Paulina Wright as for countless other early feminists, emerged from that social and historical moment when the New England way confronted first the New York frontier and then the commercial town.

Paulina Wright's critical consciousness did not mature, however, until she had acquired some historical and social distance from that tradition. She recalled in her reminiscences, recited to Elizabeth Cady Stanton, that "I was not a happy child nor a happy woman until in mature life, I outgrew my early religious faith and felt free to think and act on my own convictions." She left few clues as to when this point of "mature life" was reached. At the death of her husband in 1840, however, the course of Paulina Wright's life turned beyond the local networks of Oneida County. Fortified by her experience in the Female Moral Reform Society, she set out on her own to deliver lectures on female physiology, equipped with a *femme modèle*, which she had acquired on a trip to France. Perhaps it was in the course of her lecture tour that Paulina Wright parted with the self-effacing baggage of Calvinism.

Along the way she encountered women of more cosmopolitan backgrounds and beliefs, including Susan B. Anthony, Elizabeth Cady Stanton, and Margaret Fuller. Uprooted from the cozy networks of Utica evangelism, she could see the relations of the sexes in a new light. Exposure to the recurrence of female discontent in one locality after another permitted Paulina Wright to comprehend a general and abstract pattern of sexual inequality. A full articulation of feminist principles also required a clear formulation of the social prohibitions against women's freedom. The Victorian constraints were not rigidly enunicated until the doctrine of the spheres had achieved a mass circulation at midcentury. Here again, Utica probably had a shaping influence on Paulina Wright's feminism. The city's prime exponent of that doctrine, Philemon Fowler, was singled out for special condemnation in the first volume of *The History of Woman Suffrage*, which was compiled by Stanton, Anthony, and Matilda Gage.

In sum, Paulina Wright's consciousness grew with both Utica and the national culture of which the city was a part. The social ecology of Utica in the canal era allowed her to experience womanhood with the force and energy of associated reform activities. By the 1850s the more rigid social structure of urban industrial America and its accompanying domestic ideology threatened to eviscerate that local network and desiccate the former source of women's power and collective expression. At this point Paulina Wright's fate, like that of Utica itself, became tied to a wider national system. Her circuit through the parlors of the Northeast in the 1840s provided the cosmopolitan experience that made possible a conscious feminism.

The cross-fertilization of Wright's past and her present, her local roots and her national roamings, bred a radical feminism. By 1871, for example, her concerns as a female moral reformer had escalated to a feminist pronouncement. Women's right to "self-ownership," Wright now argued, emancipated her from the "deadly despotism" whereby husbands demanded sexual services and "compulsory maternity" from their wives. Wright was not expounding the nineteenth-century doctrine of the moral superiority of women. She attacked, on the contrary, the whole ontological dichotomy of male and female. In 1850 she wrote that "the harmony, unity and oneness of the race cannot be secured while there is a class legislation; while one half of humanity is cramped within a narrow sphere and governed by arbitrary power."[73] At least one Utica resident was capable of the intellectual and political daring that directly challenged the doctrine of the spheres.

Wright was radical in yet another sense: She recognized that the whole social order stood in opposition to the ideal of sexual equality. In 1870 she described the movement of which she was a part as one "intended from its inception to change the structure, the central organization of society." Unfortunately, Paulina Wright has not left historians a very full account of her arguments in support of this radical notion. She was from the first an activist rather than a writer or a theoretician, a woman whose ideas were always engaged with the history of her time and place. We can at least identify the social-historical vantage point from which this social criticism emerged – antebellum Utica, New York. Whether in the Female Moral Reform Society or sitting in Philemon Fowler's congregation, Paulina Wright could perceive myriad ways in which women contributed to the maintenance of society, usually without just reward, public authority, or a sense of individual achievement. As a wealthy, childless widow, unburdened by private responsibilities, free to travel the world and courageous enough to mount public podiums, she could not see why sex should deny half the human race the same autonomy and status she enjoyed. Somehow, Paulina Wright also sensed that women's sphere was at the interface of an elaborate system of production and reproduction and built into the very foundation of the social order. She sensed, however vaguely, that to achieve full women's rights was to "change the structure, the central organization of society."[74]

Paulina Wright was a rare critique of the doctrine of the spheres, in Utica and in America at large. To the mass of Uticans, the subject of women's rights was little more than an easy target for the sophomoric humor of the local press. Most women and men of Utica were too caught up in the everyday operation of that social system to achieve Paulina Wright's critical distance. The complex structure of urban society was held together in large part by the private resources and unsung labors of their families, which connected at multiple oblique angles with the public sphere, the world of work and the realms of capital, commerce, and industry. Perhaps the operation of family and gender in a mid-nineteenth-century city is better represented by Lavinia Johnson, with her anonymous and broken husband and her spunky missionary daughter. Or perhaps an ordinary anonymous family selected at random from the census listings bespeaks this system more realistically. Yet any social order creates its critics and its conflicts as well as "representative" or "typical" families. Thus in the end Paulina Wright stands as a fitting personification of the history of Whitestown and Utica, Oneida County, New York. Her vision, among all others, leads in a tortuous and long path toward the continuing feminist critique of the American family and American society.

Conclusion: family change and
social transformation

The pursuit of family history in Oneida County, New York, has proceeded along a serpentine path, through a variety of themes, sources, and methods of analysis. At times the reader may have felt waylaid in bogs of anecdotes of primarily local and antiquarian interest. A brief backward glance will reveal, nonetheless, that considerable historical territory has been covered, that by the middle of the nineteenth century the world of 1790 had been transformed. From the vantage point of 1865, illuminated by the hindsight of the present, it is possible to discern the broader contours of this historical transformation and identify a pattern that elucidates the structural relationship between the family and social change.

The extent of this transformation can be gleaned by drawing a simple and somewhat artificial contrast between two families, one dated 1800, the other 1865, each typical of the native-born middle ranks of Oneida County's population. On one score, continuity rather than change seemed to mark this episode in family history. The mean size of households in Oneida County varied by less than two members over the whole period. It did not decline appreciably until after 1860 and by that date smaller families characterized all sectors of the regional economy – the farm, the factory, and the commercial districts. Household structure was also quite uniform over time. The vast majority of Oneidans resided in nuclear households throughout this entire period of rapid social and economic change. Within the minority of more complex households, however, a subtler and more significant shift can be detected. When a farm family admitted an additional resident in the 1810s, it was usually an extended kinsman and often a third generation. In the urban industrial districts of the 1850s and 1860s a boarder was more often responsible for the extension of the household (Tables A.4 and A.5).

This seemingly minor variation in household structure provides a clue to more important changes in the organization and meaning of the family. Payment for room and board was but one element in the aggregation of household income, the mode of home economics that distinguished the urban industrial family from its agrarian predecessor. The farm and artisan families of the early nineteenth century operated corporate home economies, based on productive property, a domestic division of labor, and generational continuity. The industrial age, however, dispersed family members into a variety of different jobs, workplaces, and economic roles. The family's economic unity was now expressed primarily at the point of consumption rather than production. This separation of the place of work from the place of residence was of central historical importance. Still, the latter-day households were hardly stripped of economic functions. Rather, home economics now inhered in the strategic allocation of the labor of different family members. The typical family strategy was woven of decisions about the work of husbands, wives, children, and kin, in and outside the home, through paid labor and in residual domestic production. The housewife continued to command important material resources. By keeping boarders, frugally organizing consumption, and performing a variety of therapeutic functions for husband and children, she, in effect, staffed what we now call the tertiary sector of the work force, that very substantial slice of the economy that qualifies as neither agriculture nor industry.

These complex economic strategies of the industrial era had also transformed the internal dynamics of family life. The corporate farm economy bound its members seamlessly together in the process of working out their mutual subsistence. In the industrializing city, on the other hand, the labor of family members became divisible into the wages, salaries, and profits of individual workers, who consequently enjoyed independent access to the marketplace. In other words, participation in the family economy of the modern epoch entailed more personal volition – or at least gave more play to independent action than in families past. The extreme poles of this comparison might be drawn between the daughter who sat docilely at her spinning wheel awaiting a dowry and the mill girl who might squander her small wage on a new bonnet. Built into the updated family economy at any rate was a new measure of voluntarism, which could express itself either as cavalier individualism or in family loyalty of a more deliberate and conscious sort.

As a consequence, the internal order and experience of family life had been considerably altered. Within the ideology of Oneida County, this change was characterized as a shift from patriarchal authority to domestic affection. Even in the 1820s some local writers still championed a patriarchal family government; but by 1850 the father's authority had been dissolved in paeans to loving domesticity. In fact, the idea of fatherhood itself seemed almost to wither away as the bond between mother and child assumed central place in the constellation of family affection. This veneration of motherhood was more substantial than the waft of sentimentality that blew through nineteenth-century culture. It signaled a new and important family function. Most directly, mother love was the linchpin in a new method of socializing children. A mother's tender ministration was actually the substitute for patriarchal will-breaking and the modus operandi of childrearing in the new age. The mother's role was not to bludgeon obedience and conformity into her offspring but, through subtler and gentler means, to transfer parental values into the character of the child. This regimen was explicitly designed as a mode of socialization in the most vulgar sense, molding the child's personality to the specifications of adult society. A whole string of other family changes followed from the premise of maternal socialization. The infant child was exonerated from the charge of depravity and passion and became instead innocent, plastic, and fully receptive to the soft wiles of the moral mother. The establishment of this new mother-infant bond gave a new direction and pace to the course of the human life cycle. Sons, for example, were now slowly guided from the maternal cocoon into the wider, more masculine and grueling universe. The family, in this instance, had become more of a launching pad into the world than a microcosm of society. The relations between adults and children, by the same token, were characterized by emotional interchange rather than strict hierarchy.

As the meaning of age shifted, the division of labor and status by sex also shifted. The male household head retained preeminent economic power and political authority and must have carried much of the weight of this status into his domestic relationships. Still, the modern home left little space in which he could exercise his masculine power. A father in a Victorian parlor was something of a bull in a china shop, somewhat ill at ease with the gentle virtues enshrined there. The revered mother dominated the emotional space of the home. The injunctions to female silence and obedience that were regularly heard in frontier churches had given way to effusive praise for the queen of the household empire. In the narrowing home sphere, at least, women had undisputed title to psychological leadership. The absence of her husband from that domain for most of the working day removed the most immediate and direct experience of sexual subjugation and reduced the number of occasions for wifely obedience. As the women of the mid-nineteenth century sidestepped into an increasingly sex-segregated world, their secondary status took a somewhat less oppressive and grating form. The balance of sexual power had not been turned upside down, but it had shifted on its axis a few degrees.

Elevated status in the home does not, furthermore, automatically translate into enhanced power in society at large. On this score, as on many others, it is essential to identify the contrasting social contexts and shifting boundaries of the family in 1800 and in 1865. The two family types occupied starkly different places in the larger matrix of social relations. The families of the agrarian era repeatedly interwove and overlapped with church and town. Members of families, furthermore, mingled together in the larger network of face-to-face relations that formed the local community. In 1865, by contrast, the middle-class family stood out in bold relief within a more complex social order. In the popular mind at midcentury social space was often divided up between the "home" and the "streets," warm, personal, and stable ties as opposed to cold, brittle, and threatening encounters. In fact, the family no longer inhabited the center of the social order; society was no longer composed of interlocking families. In the city of Utica in 1865 economic production had deserted the home and with it went a great variety of social services, such as caring for the poor, the aged, and the orphaned. Consequently, the less subjugated status of children and women within the home combined with their increasing alienation from external sources of economic and social power.

These changes in the family can be arranged along another conceptual pole: the distinction between public and private life. These hypothetical spheres were not always well defined or antithetically posed in the minds of Oneida County residents. As of 1800 or even 1830 it was difficult to sort out private from public life. Distinctively, public activities could, on the one hand, be singled out from the casual relations of everyday life. The most notable public settings of Oneida County were the town meetings and church trials, where heads of household met to determine and enforce the common good. Life outside these public forums, on the other hand, could not be called private. Social relations were too various, overlapping, and expansive to be corralled into the enclosed space connoted by the term. Neighbors, church brethren, or the exuberant fraternity of the benefit association shared warmth and intimacy within a social, rather than a private, sphere. Conversely, the family was not the exclusive place of affectionate human contact. The family circle was not marked out as an especially secluded social space. In fact, church, town, and neighborhood, regularly and with impunity, violated the privacy of the home as they propagated the gospel, pursued social deviants, and foraged for gossip in the inner sanctums of Oneida families.

By the mid-nineteenth century the terms *public* and *private* had much more currency among the literate middle classes of Oneida County. The public sphere seemed to expand and become more awesome, austere, and remote. Public authority was more forcefully represented by the august halls of the nation's capital or the massive columns of the New York State Lunatic Asylum than by the familiar visages of the village officers or church deacons. The adjective *public* at the same time began to designate an unstructured and intimidating social space. To be in a public place was to be in a crowd of strangers, adrift in the anarchy of the streets. Middle-class urbanites would beat a hasty retreat from this alien public world; they would seek their refuge in a *private* home. The family residence had by midcentury acquired a special sanctity, a privileged position remote from public contention and impenetrable to prying outsiders. The ideal of privacy found material expression in the second half of the nineteenth century in the cottage architecture and picket fences that physically set the family off from public view. Once society was a congregation of families; now it was construed as some mysterious, impersonal web of forces existing beyond the cottage gate.

If not a composite of households, then, society could only be seen as a conglomeration of detached individuals. The citizen at the ballot box, the laborer in search of work, the pauper in need of relief, were deemed discrete and individuated human atoms. In actuality, almost every individual in Oneida County still carried heavy family baggage out into society and the economy. When middle-class sons and husbands went off to work they went forth laden with homegrown values, maternal guidance, wifely support and family resources. In other words, individuals should actually be seen always in transit from home through society and back again. The most rugged individual did not remain away from home for very long. Most of the native-born circumvented the family for only short intervals in the life cycle and even these brief episodes of independence were greeted with apprehension. Significantly, the major public institution to be expanded and systematized in the antebellum period, the school system, was designed to facilitate the passage of children out of the home and into society and the economy. As Utica's boys passed to adulthood they would spend their lives in diurnal passage from home to work and back again. The distance, if not the dichotomy, between home and society was built into the rhythm of their everyday lives. Women, however, tended more often to spend most of their life cycles and their lifetimes in domestic seclusion. Still, their home labors, be they as devoted molders of infant character or diligent laborers in kitchens and gardens, were essential to shaping and sustaining male "individualism." Thus the family and its female custodians may have stood somewhat behind the scenes at midcentury, but they were hardly irrelevant to the development of the economy or the keeping of social order.

These changes can also be classified as a reorganization of the process of social reproduction. During the frontier epoch, social reproduction in Oneida County was organized around the tripartite arrangement of church, town meeting, and household. Aping old New England and Puritan practices, the residents of the county granted the town and church considerable authority over both the cultural elements of reproduction, the maintenance of common values, and the supervision of personal behavior, as well as such societal dimensions of reproduction as caring for dependent members of the population, the poor, the widows, and the orphans. At the same time, the household was the central location in which these social tasks were performed. Farmhouses were regarded as places of worship, families were held responsible for the education of children; households took in orphans and widows. By midcentury many of these social functions had been redistributed along a jagged border between family and society. On the one hand, specialized public agencies – the schools, the police force, the poorhouse, the lunatic asylum – assumed responsibility for many aspects of social reproduction. On the other, the private middle-class family claimed more autonomy and privacy in the socialization and acculturation of its own members. Finally, a whole array of quasi-private, quasi-public, and primarily female groups – orphan asylums, ladies' relief societies, and industrial schools – provided for the physical and cultural reproduction of the lower classes. In sum, midcentury brought a more complicated geography of social reproduction and further gerrymandered the borders of private and public life, as well as the male and the female spheres.

It is quite easy to draw this contrast between the corporate household and the privatized home. Yet it only begs more difficult historical questions. Why did this change occur? When, by whom, and how was it accomplished? Can a sequence of causation be extracted from this wide array of shifting family and social forces? To simply invoke the structural transformation of the regional economy, which coincided with this family change – the swift passage from a relatively simple agarian economy to the beginnings of urban industrial capitalism – is to go a long way toward such an explanation. The shifting material conditions that these concepts identify clearly exerted a powerful influence on family change. It was a fundamental crisis in the organization of farmland and labor that set the sequence of changes in motion. The foundation of the corporate family collapsed when Oneida County no longer contained enough unimproved land to sustain a second generation of farmers. The ebullient freedom of the commercial market during the canal era drew children off the farm and also fostered experiments in more voluntaristic family strategies, as indicated by the centrality of kinship to the formation of business partnerships, the supply of capital, and the furnishing of collateral. In the next generation, shifts in the urban economy – the decline of artisan production, the rise of factories, the expansion of white-collar jobs – ordained that many family members scurry about in different directions in search of income and career advancement.

To point out these structural connections is not, however, to provide a satisfying *historical* explanation, that is, an account of how all these changes were accomplished in time and by people. This process of change unfolds through the whole seamless narrative of family history in Oneida County. It cannot be easily summarized. It is possible, however, to isolate one particularly important element in this cycle of transformation. The second quarter of the nineteenth century marked a particularly volatile episode in the history of family and community in Oneida County. At the peak of the Second Great Awakening and in the salad days of the Erie Canal, the family seemed held in suspension as the residents of the commercial town and mature farmlands experimented with a variety of new modes of social organization. This experimentation was nurtured by social and cultural as well as economic factors, particularly by the recent passage of the frontier, unstable demographic conditions, vivid memories of New England traditions, and the ebullience of artisan culture. At any rate, during the canal era the men and women of Utica stepped out of their traditional family roles to create some very novel social practices and organizations.

Most of these innovations took the form of an "association" or "society," a voluntary, democratic grouping of peers outside the home and independent of the official community. On the one hand, the association could act as a substitute for the family. The Young

Men's Association, for example, provided a common living room for the city's boarders. Other associations performed social functions formerly maintained by families acting in conjunction with church and town, for example, clothing the poor and educating the ignorant. Yet others, like the Maternal Association, were designed to assist individuals in the performance of their family responsibilities. Almost every association, however, in some way contradicted patriarchal notions of family order and honored a new set of social values. They celebrated vibrant affectionate bonds between peers rather than stern reverence to elders. The members of temperance associations, for example, eschewed father figures and banded together as brothers. One-third to one-half of all associations did away with fathers entirely, enrolling women or youth exclusively. Sons flexed their muscles in the young Republican club, and their mothers explored new avenues of social power in groups like the Female Moral Reform Society. The era of association, in sum, was a time rife with experiments in new ways of organizing society, ways that might challenge or undermine the power of the family.

Yet the members of Oneida's associations conceived their innovative schemes in an atmosphere of current crises, churned by memories of more comfortable times. The fervor of associated men, women, and youth was kindled amid doubts about the future of their own families, especially those of the middling sort – farmers, artisans, shopkeepers, and clerks. This was particularly true of the women's groups of the 1830s and 1840s that bonded together in order to defend their homes against the onslaught of an aggressively secular, fanatically mobile, and morally suspicious commercial culture. Evangelical women united in prayer circles and missionary societies to shore up the lineage of salvation for their children. The militant ladies of the Female Moral Reform Society girded themselves with righteous indignation and braved public stares in hopes of protecting daughters from seduction and sons from moral ruin. Other women saw the temperance association as a bulwark against the domestic disasters incurred by drunken husbands. Members of the maternal association concentrated their reforming zeal on their own children, hoping to devise techniques of socialization that would bind them to their mother's values no matter how far they might roam from the parental home.

It was in association, in other words, that the Oneidans of the 1830s and 1840s worked out their family problems. In the process they incubated a whole flock of new domestic values, practices, and functions. Such Victorian ideals as the pure, loving mother, the so-

ber, cautious breadwinner, the docile, passionless child, were first
heralded by reform associations. Yet the institution of the family
was destined to become the custodian of these values. In the end
the maintenance of religious conformity, sexual purity, and temperance would be superintended in the home and by women. All
these virtues would proliferate in the future, it was thought, if
women concentrated their moral efforts on the consciences of their
own children and the characters of their husbands. Thus the social
experiments of the canal era followed a convoluted, almost circular
path: Individuals left the confinement of the household to form
larger social groups wherein new ideals of personal virtue were for-
mulated and propagated. Yet all the while, members of these associations, and female reformers in particular, maintained an intense
focus on the members of their own families and especially on their
children. As the city of Utica grew larger, its streets became
crowded with a diverse population and overshadowed by a more
massive scale of enterprise, the narrow circle of relatives seemed
both more vulnerable and more inviting. In the end, the veterans of
the reform era and their progeny would withdraw into the conjugal
family, the better to nurture the values that had been cradled in
association. In other words, the association itself helped to usher in
the ultimate triumph of the privatized home. The men and women
of Utica's associations had worked out this new arrangement between family and society before the specter of "industrialization"
had advanced into the city limits.

By midcentury, five years after the erection of Utica's first steam-
powered factories, the most exuberant, creative, evangelical phase
of association had ended, and the responsibility for maintaining
purity, sobriety, and docility had been largely absorbed by the private family. The legacy of the moral reform associations was most
treasured in the households of the native-born middle class. Their
homes had become shrines to temperate living, moral fortresses
against the chaos of the streets, now inundated with a foreign population whose hallmarks from the middle-class perspective were
dirt and drink. Family practices learned in association might ensure
that the children of the middle class did not descend into the un-
wholesome world of the industrial lower classes. Sexual constraint,
temperate habits, maternal socialization, and extended education
were productive of small families, conservative business policies,
dogged work habits, and basic literary skills – that is, the attributes
required of the owners of small shops and stores and an increasing
number of white-collar workers. The complexities of this historical

pattern require further investigation, but its outline is clear: The making of the middle class in the industrial age was conditioned by family changes dating from the canal era. Thereafter, the family itself became the cradle of middle-class individuals.

A similar dialectic of class and family history wound through the history of the local elite. The wives of the leading merchants were perhaps the first group in Oneida County to experience a major change in family organization. By the second decade of the nineteenth century most of them saw the family's economic base transferred to the offices, countinghouses, and stores run by their husbands and their own household chores delegated to domestic servants. In the face of their dwindling household functions, the ladies of Utica sought out new roles outside the home. By the canal era the female elite had formed a handful of charitable organizations – the Orphan Asylum being the most impressive – in which to occupy their time and through which to assume social responsibilities. The institutions they founded and the services they performed acquired even greater social importance in the industrial age. By midcentury female benevolence led by elite women and sustained by scores of middle-class volunteers had matured into a full-scale welfare system, capable of caring for the indigents of Utica without detracting from the single-minded accumulation of capital. Upper-class women also organized and staffed a series of infant schools, industrial schools, and hospitals whose effect was to maximize the labor capacity of the city's lower class. Again, the relation of class and family had a gnarled and elongated history; in this case, a change in upper-class sex roles in the 1810s was felt by middle- and lower-class families a half century later.

The story of the formation of the working class in Oneida County, with links to the history of the family that extend even to kinsmen across the Atlantic, remains to be told in another volume. The connections between family, society, and economy can be drawn on ad infinitum, to the point at which they become obvious and tautological. The important conclusions here are more specific. First of all, fundamental changes in the family were under way before the industrial era proper. The conditions of commercial capitalism in the Oneida region (given a special vitality and fluidity by the frontier history and small size of Utica) opened up both the family and the community to the possibility of change. Second, the history of the family in Oneida County illustrates that men and women took advantage of these opportunities and in their collective action exerted an impressive degree of control over the course of family and social history. The case of Oneida County exposes the hesitant, unknowing, and haphazard ways in which men and women reshaped the institution of the family, and how families, in turn, made their mark on the progression to industrial society. Third, it was not just elites, but women, the young, and the middle ranks of the population who participated in this social change. In fact, the case of Oneida County suggests that, acting within the substantial sphere of human experience designed by the concept of social reproduction, women have exerted a degree of leadership, power, and creativity quite disproportionate to the humble role granted to them by historians. Ordinary men and women in Oneida County during the 1830s and 1840s found the reserves of power with which to influence the course of family history and social and economic development.

The middle-class families that were formed thereafter were scattered along the sidelines of public life but at the same time performed a multiplicity of social functions. In fact, the family of the nineteenth century is distinguishable from that of the twentieth by the Herculean social services performed within it. It served as dormitory boardinghouse, consumer market, insurance agency, hospital, psychiatric clinic, recreation center. One could go on and on, siphoning off much of what is now called the service sector of the economy into the household sphere. Those public services that were not absorbed by the family were often maintained by teams of volunteer women. It would not be long before a new breed of female reformers, organized into groups like the Woman's Christian Temperance Union, would hold males and society itself to their domestic standards of morality. The family and women formed, in sum, a bloated, if not an expansive, social sphere. The veil of privacy merely and imperfectly camouflaged these extensive and essential components of the social system.

The vital connections between family, society, and economy were further disguised by the scrim of ideology that venerated gender differences. Family and privacy were considered almost equivalent to, and coterminus with, women's sphere. The importance of this sexual segregation cannot be overemphasized. On the one hand, as historians of women have often pointed out, isolation in a single, common sphere could nurture a self-conscious female identity and foster strong loyalties among women. Such a heightened consciousness of sex was a precondition to the development of the women's rights movement. On the other hand, sex segregation tended to mire women in a world that was remote from the public spheres where men continued to wield power. The women of the nineteenth century, in other words, were caught in the contradictions of that problematic notion of "separate but equal." Through most of the nineteenth century the division of labor in the private sphere was seldom called into question, even by advocates of women's rights. It was assumed that women could obtain their full rights without tampering with such fundamental elements of the sociology of sex as maternal socialization. Even most feminists of the nineteenth century were taken in by the mystique of the spheres, their critical powers stymied at the border of privacy and family life.

Indeed, the association between womanhood and the private, domestic side of American society was not directly and boldly challenged until the feminist revival of the 1960s. This challenge was not posed until the family system, which dated from the early nineteenth century, was found to be in considerable disrepair. Many of the functions of the nineteenth-century family had been absorbed into the public sphere or the service sector of the economy. Young and old were increasingly in the care of the state, be it under the jurisdiction of public schools or the Social Security Administration. Even the care of infants could be provided by the marketplace in chains of day-care centers. Concomitantly, masses of women had assembled in the social and public labor force; by the mid-1970s the majority of adult females were wage earners. The skyrocketing divorce rate and the unprecedented popularity of the single-person household seemed to doom the staid middle-class family cycle to extinction, making it just as moribund in the 1970s as was the patriarchal farm household of the 1820s. The women of the era moved into this breach in the family system just as audaciously as had the women reformers of Oneida County's canal era. Their creativity had generated such new social forms and ideas as the consciousness-raising group, the politics of personal life, the call for genderless parenting, and a plethora of women's centers and self-help agencies.

In the late 1970s, the forces of family conservation also presented a well-organized and vocal political force, mobilized in opposition to abortion, the Equal Rights Amendment, and homosexual rights. In the United States a New Right has dug its trenches at the last line of defense for the old family system. It has many sympathizers. Even some feminists are reconsidering whether women can delegate child-care responsibilities to men without incurring exorbitant human cost. Most important, the critique of the family raised by the women's movement still strikes terror in the hearts of masses of

Americans, as well it might. For in twentieth-century America, as in nineteenth-century Oneida County, the family, for all its internal contradictions and sexual inequality, still operates, however imperfectly, as a chief means of survival, a last refuge of integral human support and mutual care.

The last quarter of the twentieth century may well witness fundamental family changes and another rearrangement of those basic elements in the the social system, the sexes, the ages, the private and public spheres. Much like the men and women of Oneida County in the mid-nineteenth century, this generation will make its way into the future tripping over the values of the past and hamstrung by the fears of the present. In the 1980s, at least, we will also have the benefit of considerably rethinking of the nature of the family and particularly its implications for the equality of the sexes. Such rethinking cannot be too intense nor too critical.

Appendixes

Most of the quantitative information in the first four appendixes (A through D) pertains to a small population that was analyzed in its entirety. Because no sampling was involved and all calculations were done by hand, these tables are straightforward and need no further elaboration. All the tables in Appendix E, however, are based on a large sample drawn from the manuscript schedules of the New York State Census for 1855 and 1865, which were analyzed by computer. The methods of organizing and interpreting this data require some further explanation.

Appendix E records the social and family characteristics of more than 15,000 individuals whose names appeared on the census tracts for Utica in 1855 and 1865. It represents a 1-in-3 sample of the total population in the region. Such a large sample ensured that a sufficient number of members of certain highly specialized segments of the population would be included in the population analyzed. For example, this wide a net captured only 75 Irish males between the ages of 21 and 26, a large enough number, however, to permit a statistically significant comparison with, for example, 82 natives of Oneida County of the same age and sex. These individuals were selected by means of a systematic, rather than a random, sample of the dwelling units, namely, information was recorded for all the individuals in every third house contacted by the census taker. This procedure has been found to be statistically reliable and the most efficient method of sampling the manuscript census.

All information relating to each of the individuals in the sample was converted to numerical codes by research assistants. In most cases the coders simply transcribed information directly from the manuscript census; they were not required to make independent interpretations of the document. For example, they simply translated the notation "cousin" in the column headed "relation to household head" into a numerical symbol. A random sample was drawn from this coded data to check for accuracy. The error rate for the variables used in the final study was less than 3%; in most cases it was less than 1%. By this process, 21 variables were created from the census of 1855; 23 for 1865. Most of the variables in the following tables are simply the answers given to the questions of the census marshal. In only a few cases was it necessary to reorganize the census data into new categories of analysis. The only complicated procedure of this sort involved the creation of a manageable number of occupational groups from the more than 270 jobs listed in the census itself. The occupational classifications that appear in the following appendixes combine many different job titles into a maximum of eight ranks. These categories, based on the occupational groupings employed by other historians of nineteenth-century cities (see Theodore Hershberg et al., "Occupation and Ethnicity in Five Nineteenth-Century Cities: A Collaborative Inquiry," *Historical Methods Newsletter* 7 [June 1974], 174–216), were expanded to include jobs unique to Oneida County. The following list details the entries in each of the eight major occupational groupings, which were in turn consolidated into larger categories; for example, categories, 6, 7, and 8 were often combined to constitute unskilled laborers.

Occupational categories

1. *Merchants, manufacturers, financiers:* Banker, lumber merchant, manufacturer, manufacturing, merchant, merchant and manufacturer, shoe merchant, woolen manufacturer.

2. *Professionals:* Artist, clergy, civil engineer, dentist, editor, engineer, foot doctor, law student, lawyer, missionary, music teacher, physician, officer, student, teacher.

3. *Shopkeepers and small commercial enterprises:* Boat captain, clothing dealer, coal dealer, contractor, druggist, dry-goods dealer, farmer, flour merchant, fruit dealer, grocer, hostler, hotelkeeper, innkeeper, jeweler, landlady, landlord, liquor dealer, livery keeper, livery stable, presides in saloon, restaurant, saloonkeeper, shoe dealer, shoe store, storekeeper, tavernkeeper, tobacconist, undertaker, victualer.

4. *White collar and public service:* Accountant, agent, attaché, bank clerk, bank teller, bookkeeper, broker, clerk, commission agent, conductor, dry-goods clerk, exchanger, fireman, floriculturalist, freight agent, insurance agent, librarian, patent agent, policeman, postmaster, post office clerk, railroad agent, railroad supervisor, sales agent, salesman, shoe agent, steamboat agent, telegrapher, traveling agent, traveling salesman.

5. *Craftsmen:* Apprentice, baker, barber, blacksmith, bleacher, boatbuilder, boilermaker, bookbinder, brass finisher, brewer,

bricklayer, brickmaker, brickmason, brushmaker, builder, butcher, cabinetmaker, cab maker, carpenter, carpet weaver, carriage maker, chandler, chemist, cigar maker, cloakmaker, confectioner, cooper, cordwainer, dressmaker, dyer, engraver, file cutter, finisher, furniture maker, furrier, gas fitter, glass blower, gunsmith, harness maker, hat finisher, hatter, joiner, locksmith, machinist, marble polisher, mason, master mechanic, mechanic, midwife, miller, milliner, millwright, molder, nail maker, organ builder, organ manufacturer, painter, paperhanger, papermaker, patternmaker, photographer, piano maker, plane maker, plasterer, plumber, printer, puddler, saddlemaker, ship carpenter, shipwright, shoebinder, silversmith, soap and candle maker, soda water manufacturer, stonecutter, stonemason, stove fitter, tailor, tailoress, tanner, telegraph instrument maker, tinsmith and coppersmith, tin worker, turner, typesetter, upholsterer, vestmaker, wagonmaker, watchmaker, weaver, wheelwright.

6. *Unskilled (commercial sector):* Assistant (female), baggageman, bartender, bill poster, boatman, brakeman, canal basin worker, canal worker, carman, carpenter, carter, cartman, drayman, errand boy, express carrier, express messenger, farm laborer, ferryman, fisherman, gardener, gatekeeper, general worker, peddler, porter, public works, quarryman, railroad laborer, railroad worker, sailor, works in saloon, seaman, teamster, track tender, waiter, watchman, yardman.

7. *Factory employment (semi- or unskilled):* Chair factory, cloth dresser, cotton factory, cotton spinner, cutter, factory, foreman, furnaceman, lab man, laborer, spinner, woolen factory, wool sorter.

8. *Personal service:* Chambermaid, cook, domestic, keeps boarding house, general housework, general helper, helper, housekeeper, housewife, housework, laundress, nurse, seamstress, servant, washer, washwoman.

A large portion of the tables, particularly those describing the male and female life cycles, are drawn directly from this sample of the individuals living in Oneida County. Others are based on a second file that arranged information about the co-residents of each household into a second unit of analysis. The process that created this household file was accomplished by a computer program devised by Michael Haines of the Philadelphia Social History Project. The major operation performed by this program was to consolidate information for all members of a household, for example, to list the age of each resident. It also created a few new variables by combining information about the different members of the household. For example, the space between births was estimated by subtracting the ages of different children one from another. The household file contained a total of about 50 variables.

The long string of numbers found in the following tables constitutes descriptive statistics. All were created by some simple arithmetic operation, chiefly calculating a percentage. Relationships between groups of variables are presented as cross-tabulations, chiefly comparisons of percentage distributions of certain family attributes within different age, sex, ethnic, and occupational groups. More elaborate mathematical scoring was not warranted by the data at hand, most of which was not numerical in form.

Most of the tables in Appendix E draw solely on the 1855 census. Statistics for 1865 are presented only when a given variable was not available a decade earlier or when significant changes occurred over time.

Appendix A   *Demography and family structure*

Table A.1. *Sex ratios – males per 100 females, 1790–1960*

	Whitestown	Utica
1790	156.4	—
1800	108.2	—
1820	101.4	105.6
1830	91.9	103.1
1840	89.6	96.9
1850	91.7	91.8
1860	88.8	86.9

Source: United States Census, 1st through 7th.

Table A.2. *Population growth*

	Whitestown	Utica
1790	1,891	
1800	4,212	
1810	4,912	
1820	5,219	2,972
1830	4,410	8,323
1840	5,156	12,782
1850	6,810	17,565
1860	4,367	22,529

Source: Census of the State of New York (Albany, N.Y.: Franklin B. Hough, 1867).

247

Table A.3. *Age structure, 1800–1865 (in percent)*

| | Persons aged | | | | | | |
	0–10	11–15	16–25	26–45		46+	
1800							
Whitestown	37.3	15.1	17.6	21.7		8.1	
1820							
Whitestown	27.8	17.5	22.9	17.8		13.7	
Utica	31.0	14.3	21.7	25.0		7.2	

	0–10	11–20	21–30	31–40	41–50	51–60	61+
1830							
Whitestown	26.5	25.1	21.8	10.6	7.3	4.5	3.9
Utica	27.8	22.0	26.1	13.1	6.2	3.2	1.9
1840							
Whitestown	24.4	24.5	21.9	11.3	8.3	4.8	4.7
Utica	25.1	24.5	22.2	12.6	8.6	4.3	2.6
1855							
Whitestown	24.3	23.9	17.2	13.5	10.2	5.3	5.6
Utica	26.2	21.8	21.6	13.8	8.5	5.0	3.1
1865							
Whitestown	24.8	20.4	16.1	12.6	10.4	7.5	8.2
Utica	26.3	20.4	17.7	13.4	11.2	6.5	3.9

Sources: United States Census, 2nd through 5th; New York State Census, 1855 and 1865.

Table A.4. *Mean household size, 1790–1860*

	Whitestown	Utica
1790	5.8	—
1800	6.2	—
1820	6.9	6.2
1830	6.9	6.5
1840	6.3	6.8
1850	6.4	6.1
1860	5.3	5.1

Note: Calculations are based on either published census data or hand-counting and are, therefore, subject to some inconsistency and error.

Table A.5. *Family structure – Whitestown and Utica (in percent)*

	1813–1816	1855	1865
Simple nuclear	71.8	65.1	72.4
Extended	11.8	6.9	5.9
Nuclear and servants, apprentices	3.2	8.47	7.3
Nuclear and boarders	7.7	10.7	9.4
Combination (servants, boarders, extended kin)	5.5	7.4	3.6

Source: John Frost, "Families Within the Boundaries of the United Society of Whitestown, April 1813–July 1816" (N = 211); Manuscript Schedules, New York State Census, 1855–1865.

Table A.6. *Fertility ratio – children ages 0–9 per 1,000 women 15–45*

	Whitestown	Oneida County	Utica
1800	2,091		—
1810		2,018	
1820	1,307		1,387
1830	942		1,021
1840	822		885
1850	809		870

Note: Calculations are based on published census data and thus vary according to the age aggregations used during different census years. From 1800 through 1820 the figures include women between the ages of 15 and 45; the ratios for 1830 and 1840 are based on women ages 15 to 49; for 1850 the age aggregation of women is 15 to 44.

Appendix B *Family and economic structure*

Table B.1. *Wives' inheritances*

	N	Cases with reference to wife	Entire estate to wife	Reference to dower	Restricted to widowhood or natural life
1798–1824					
Whitestown	36	20	8 (40.0)	11 (55.0)	8 (40.0)
Utica	12	7	2 (28.6)	1 (14.3)	2 (28.6)
Combined	48	27	10 (37.0)	12 (44.4)	10 (37.4)
1825–1844					
Whitestown	35	18	3 (16.6)	8 (44.4)	5 (14.0)
Utica	58	31	12 (38.7)	6 (19.4)	17 (29.0)
Combined	93	49	15 (32.0)	14 (28.5)	22 (23.0)
1845–1865					
Whitestown	52	28	13 (46.4)	5 (17.9)	7 (13.0)
Utica	185	93	55 (59.1)	12 (12.9)	35 (18.0)
Combined	237	121	68 (56.2)	17 (14.0)	42 (17.0)

Note: Figures in parentheses are percentages.
Source: Will books of Oneida County, Oneida County Court House, Utica.

Table B.2. Distribution of inheritance among children

	N	Cases with reference to children	Simple equality	Unequal by sex	Unequal by age and sex	Unequal-unclear arbitrary criterion
1798–1824						
Whitestown	36	29	3 (10.3)	6 (20.6)	4 (13.8)	16 (55.0)
Utica	12	11	5 (45.5)	3 (27.3)	1 (9.0)	2 (18.2)
Combined	48	40	8 (20.0)	9 (22.5)	5 (12.5)	18 (45.0)
1825–1844						
Whitestown	35	18	1 (5.6)	6 (33.3)	0	11 (61.0)
Utica	58	28	15 (53.5)	6 (21.4)	1 (3.5)	6 (21.4)
Combined	93	46	16 (34.7)	12 (26.0)	1 (2.2)	17 (36.9)
1845–1865						
Whitestown	52	23	8 (34.7)	2 (8.7)	4 (17.4)	9 (39.1)
Utica	185	84	48 (57.1)	8 (9.9)	4 (4.8)	24 (28.5)
Combined	237	107	56 (52.3)	10 (9.3)	8 (7.5)	33 (30.8)

Note: Figures in parentheses are percentages.
Source: Will books of Oneida County, Oneida County Court House, Utica.

Table B.3. *Occupational structure of Utica 1817–1865 (in percent)*

	Merchants and manufacturers	Professionals	White-collar workers	Shopkeepers	Crafts-men	Unskilled and factory laborers
1817	17.4	9.9	5.17	8.9	42.5	16.1
1828	11.1	8.0	4.8	12.5	46.1	15.1
1845	2.7	7.7	10.2	11.2	45.4	20.2
1855[a]	2.9	5.1	8.6	6.6	40.1	24.1
1865[a]	3.7	5.1	9.4	6.2	33.6	23.8

[a]These figures are based on the state census enumeration of the occupations for employed males over the age of 15 and thus are roughly comparable to those earlier figures drawn from the city directories.

Table B.4. Social mobility of shoemakers and clerks (in percent)

	N	Number remaining in Utica 10 years or more	Occupations 10 years later					
			Same occupation	Small business	Merchant or manufacturer	White-collar professional	Artisan skilled labor	Laborer
Shoemakers								
1817	18	7	42.9		14.3	14.3	14.3	
1828	76	24	29.2	50.0	8.3	4.2	4.2	
1840	109	41	44.0	36.6	2.4	9.8	4.9	2.4
1850	110	31	48.3	25.8	3.2		6.4	16.1
1860	116	54	75.9	3.7		5.5	5.5	9.3
Clerks								
1817	2		18.2	45.5		18.2		
1828	55	11		52.2		13.6	15.9	
1840	152	44	15.9			21.2	18.5	
1850	175	38	21.1	39.4		34.2	4.2	
1860	273	120	22.5	28.3			10.8	

Source: Utica City Directory for various years.

Table B.5. *Residence of clerks (in percent)*

	N	Own home	Board with private families	Board at hotel	Board with relatives	Board with employers
1828	55	41.8	20.0	3.6	3.6	30.1
1840	152	15.8	44.0	11.2	18.4	10.5
1850	175	10.9	32.0	37.7	13.7	5.7
1860	273	16.9	31.9	11.7	37.3	0.2

Source: Utica City Directory.

Table B.6. *Family partnerships*

	N	Total partnerships	Total family partnerships	Relationships of partners		
				Father and sons	Brothers	In-laws
1844–49	137	78 (56.9)	28 (20.4)	22 (78.0)	6 (22.0)	0
1850–59	245	80 (32.0)	41 (16.7)	22 (53.6)	6 (36.6)	4 (9.8)
1860–65	331	38 (11.0)	17 (5.0)	10 (58.8)	0	7 (41.2)

Note: Figures in parentheses are percentages of total business.
Source: Records of the Mercantile Agency, Baker Library, Harvard University.

Table B.7. *Family sources of capital*

	N	Family source of capital (% of all business)	Relatives who supplied capital (% of cases of family capital)		
			Father	Brother	Wives/In-laws
1844–49	137	33 (24.0)	27 (82.0)	1 (3.0)	5 (15.0)
1850–59	245	40 (16.3)	12 (30.0)	5 (12.5)	23 (57.5)
1860–65	331	22 (6.6)	14 (64.0)	0	8 (36.0)

Source: Records of the Mercantile Agency, Baker Library, Harvard University.

Appendix C *Family, religion, and revivals*

Table C.1. *Church membership by family status, 1813–16*

	Husband, wife and children	Husband only or husband and children	Wife only or wife and children	No church members
Number of families	40	6	41	124
Percent of all families	18.9	2.7	19.3	58.7
Percent of church families	45.9	6.8	47.8	

Source: John Frost, "Families Within the Boundaries of the United Society of Whitestown, April 1813–July 1816." $N = 211$.

Table C.2. *Females as percent of all converts*

Year of revival	Utica First Presbyterian	Whitesborough Presbyterian	Utica Second Presbyterian	Whitesborough Baptist
1814	69.2 (65)	69.6 (45)	—	52.3 (44)
1819	67.9 (90)	56.9 (65)	—	70.0 (70)
1826	59.3 (123)	67.1 (134)	71.6 (53)	63.2 (87)
1830	58.6 (121)	55.4 (110)	59.3 (236)	—
1838	56.1 (57)	—	69.7 (76)	71.9 (82)

Note: Figures in parentheses refer to the number of cases.

Table C.3. *Indexes of the mobility and age of converts, Utica First Presbyterian (in percent)*

Year of revival	N	Converts in church records	Converts dismissed within 5 years	Converts in directory	Male convert boarders
1814	65	48	8	14 (1817)	
1819	90	37	31	9 (1817)	—
1826	123	34	35	17 (1828)	—
1830	121	25	38	22 (1832)	28
1838	57	44	25	24 (1838)	44

Table C.4. *Percent all converts with shared surnames*

Year of revival	Utica First Presbyterian	Whitesborough Presbyterian	Utica Second Presbyterian	Whitesborough Baptist
1814	41.5 (65)	36.9 (45)	—	52.2 (44)
1819	27.7 (90)	54.5 (65)	—	44.2 (70)
1826	35.1 (123)	26.9 (134)	30.0 (53)	40.2 (87)
1830	29.7 (121)	44.8 (110)	31.0 (236)	—
1838	42.1 (57)	—	17.0 (76)	46.0 (82)

Note: Figures in parentheses refer to the number of cases.

Table C.5. *Family precedents of conversion, 1800–38 (in percent)*

	Utica First Presbyterian	Whitesborough Presbyterian	Whitesborough Baptist
N	456	354	201
Converts related to church members	29.7	29.3	30.0
Cases in which males are the first professors	20.7	15.3	29.5
Cases in which females are the first professors	48.3	61.2	43.1
Cases in which couples are the first professors	37.0	23.5	36.2

Table C.6. *Conversions and the family cycle, First Presbyterian Church*

Year of revival	N	Number of converts in vital records	Married converts	Infants baptized within year	Children of members
1814	65	31	28 (43.0)	15 (23.0)	0
1819	90	33	16 (17.0)	7 (8.0)	0
1826	123	41	6 (4.0)	1 (0.8)	25 (20.0)
1830	121	30	1 (0.8)	1 (0.8)	22 (18.0)
1838	57	25	0	0	24 (42.0)
Total	456	160	51 (11.0)	24 (5.0)	71 (16.0)

Note: Figures in parentheses are percentages. Percentages are of all converts. The ratios among identifiable converts are much higher.

Table C.7. Occupation and conversion

Revival year	N	Occupation[a]							
		Identified	Merchants	Professionals	Clerks	Shopkeepers	Artisans	Laborers	Widows/ working women
1814	65	36 (55.0)	17 (47.2)	6 (16.6)	0	0	11 (30.5)	0	2 (2.7)
1819	90	44 (48.8)	6 (13.6)	5 (11.3)	3 (6.8)	2 (3.7)	23 (52.2)	3 (6.8)	2 (3.6)
1826	123	68 (55.3)	16 (23.5)	10 (14.7)	2 (2.9)	15 (22.0)	19 (27.9)	3 (4.4)	3 (4.4)
1830	121	66 (54.5)	13 (19.6)	13 (19.6)	5 (7.5)	9 (14.3)	25 (37.9)	0	1 (1.5)
1838	57	32 (56.1)	9 (28.1)	11 (34.3)	5 (15.6)	1 (3.1)	2 (6.3)	0	4 (12.4)

Note: Figures in parentheses are percentages. The table is based on occupation of household head.
[a]The percentage of converts whose occupations have been determined.

Table C.8. *Links between revivals and women's organizations*

Year of revival	N	Number of female converts	Converts in Female Missionary Society[a]	Converts in Maternal Association[a]	Mothers of converts in Female Missionary Society	Mothers of converts in Maternal Association
1814	65	45	23 (51.0)	3 (6.6)	0	0
1819	90	57	13 (22.8)	4 (7.0)	0	
1826	123	73	1 (1.3)	4 (5.4)	18 (14.6)	16 (13.0)
1830	121	71	4 (5.6)	3 (4.2)	7 (5.7)	21 (17.3)
1838	47	32	0	1 (3.1)	6 (10.5)	18 (31.5)
Total	476	278	41 (14.7)	15 (5.3)	31 (6.5)	55 (11.5)

Note: Figures in parentheses are percentages.
[a] Percentages are of female converts only.

Table C.9. *Class affiliations of members of women's organizations (in percent)*

	Female Missionary Society (N = 55)	Maternal Association (N = 65)	Total directory listings	
			1817	1828
Merchants and merchant/ manufacturers	31	25	19	10
Professionals and white collar	33	18	14	12
Artisans	16	35	40	42
Shopkeepers and farmers	11	14	8	13
Laborers	—	—	15	14
Widows	7	5	4	6
Female occupations	2	3	2	3

Appendix D *Social characteristics of members of associations*

Table D.1. *Residences of participants in moral reform controversy*

	N	% of Total located	% of those located		
			Household head	Boards with relatives or employer	Boards alone
Supporters of moral reform	174	67.8 (118)	78.3 (92)	3.3 (4)	18.6 (22)
Opponents of moral reform	86	58.2 (51)	11.8 (6)	9.8 (5)	78.4 (40)

Note: Figures in parentheses refer to the number of cases. Percentages refer to those located in the directory only.

Table D.2. *Occupation of participants in moral reform controversy*

	N	% Located	Merchants/ manufacturers	Shopkeepers farmers	Artisans	Professionals/ managers	Clerks
Supporters of Moral Reform Society	174	67.8 (118)	22.9 (27)	13.6 (16)	36.4 (43)	17.8 (21)	9.3 (11)
Opponents of Moral Reform Society	86	58.2 (50)	2.0 (1)	4.0 (2)	10.0 (5)	12.0 (6)	72.0 (36)

Note: Figures in parentheses refer to the number of cases. Percentages apply to the 168 members whose occupations were listed in the *City Directory.*

Table D.3. *Residence of members of young men's associations (in percent)*

N	Household head	Board with relatives	Board with employers	Board alone	Total boarders
71	9.8 (7)	21.7 (15)	19.7 (14)	49.3 (35)	90.1 (64)

Note: Figures in parentheses refer to the number of cases.

Table D.4. *Occupations of members of young men's associations (in percent)*

N	Lawyers and law students	Other professionals	Clerks	Merchants/ manufacturers	Shopkeepers	Artisans
67	46.3 (31)	4.5 (3)	20.9 (14)	11.9 (8)	1.5 (1)	14.9 (10)

Note: Figures in parentheses refer to the number of cases. Percentages apply to the 67 (of 71) members whose occupations were listed in the *City Directory*.

Appendix E *Family cycles and family strategies, New York State Census*

Table E.1. *Mean number of children by age and nativity of mothers, 1865*

Women in their	20s	30s	40s	50s	60s and over
Native	.612	2.266	3.276	3.643	5.072
Foreign	1.046	3.688	5.192	5.222	6.536
Total	.777	3.026	4.406	4.512	5.837

Note: $N = 2,946$. These statistics are based on responses to the question "How many children have you ever borne," which was asked of all mothers by the 1865 New York State Census. It is a more complete and reliable measure of fertility than is usually available at this early date.

Table E.2. *No occupation, 1855 (in percent)*

	Males ($N = 2,116$)		Females ($N = 2,556$)	
Age	Native	Foreign-born	Native	Foreign-born
15–19	43.0	28.4	59.6	36.3
20–29	10.3	4.2	64.9	56.2
30–39	2.9	7.3	84.7	87.7
40–49	2.6	.5	81.3	90.0
50–59	9.3	3.7	90.4	94.7
60 or above	21.8	19.8	95.8	95.5

Table E.3. *Occupation by generation, native-born males, 1855 (in percent)*

Occupation	Young men 15–30 (N = 490)	Household heads with children 15 or over (N = 112)
Merchants/manufacturers	1.1	9.4
Professionals	7.1	10.9
Shopkeepers	8.1	15.6
White collar	16.1	6.3
Crafts	21.0	37.5
Factory/unskilled	15.9	11.6
Unemployed	29.5	12.5

Table E.4. *Percentage of males married by age, nativity, occupation, 1855*

Age	All foreign (N = 354)	All natives (N = 309)	Natives				
			Professionals	White collar	Shopkeepers	Craft	Unskilled
20–24	34.1	18.0	15.8	13.3	a	28.6	a
25–30	66.3	50.4	26.7	35.3	64.3	66.7	66.7

aToo few cases for a meaningful percentage.

Table E.5. *Residential patterns, young men 15–30 (in percent)*

	Heads of households	Children	Servants/apprentices	Other kin	Boarders
1855					
Total population	22.8	21.2	6.4	7.1	27.3
Native	17.1	40.8	3.3	9.1	29.7
Foreign	38.0	22.5	9.3	5.2	25.0
1865					
Total population	22.1	53.1	0.3	7.7	13.5
Native	17.3	61.7	0.2	7.8	11.1
Foreign	30.4	39.9	4.6	7.3	17.7

Table E.6. *Households with children (15 or over) in the labor force, 1855 (in percent)*

		Occupation of household head					
	Total	Merchants/ manufac- turers	Profes- sionals	White collar	Shop- keepers	Craft	Unskilled factory
Native (N = 476)	45.6	23.1	20.0	20.0	46.4	51.9	[a]
Foreign (N = 852)	60.3	[a]	[a]	[a]	[a]	53.5	72.9

Note: Calculated only for those households where children 15 and over were residing.
[a]Too few cases for significant percentages.

Table E.7. *Percentage of households with female contributions to income*

	Foreign total	Native total	Natives by occupation household head					
			Merchants/ manufacturers	Profes- sionals	White collar	Shop- keepers	Craft	Factory unskilled
1855								
Working females	13.0	14.0	7.1	15.4	6.3	11.1	20.0	11.6
Working wives	1.4	4.3	3.6	2.6	3.1	2.6	4.4	3.2
Keeping boarders	14.2	25.1	17.9	25.6	12.5	30.2	20.9	11.6
1865								
Working females	16.7	17.3	4.2	18.3	18.0	15.9	21.6	6.6
Working wives	3.8	6.0	2.1	4.3	13.3	3.0	7.8	7.3
Keeping boarders	8.9	16.4	12.5	14.3	13.7	13.6	14.0	14.7

Note: 1855: N = 854 (foreign total); N = 476 (native total). 1865: N = 914 (foreign total); N = 550 (native total).

Table E.8. *Comparative occupational structure foreign- and native-born household heads and native-born youth living at home, 1855 (in percent)*

	Foreign-born household heads (N = 1,124)	Native-born household heads (N = 773)	Native-born youth living at home (N = 623)
Upper class and white collar	6.7	27.6	41.1
Shopkeepers	4.9	15.0	7.1
Crafts	49.3	45.9	37.6
Unskilled	39.0	12.5	13.5

Table E.9. *Occupation native-born males by age and over time (in percent)*

	Age 20–29, 1855	Age 30–39, 1865	Age 40–49, 1865
Merchant/manufacturer	4.0	8.4	14.4
Professionals	11.3	7.3	11.5
White collar	21.0	18.4	13.7
Shopkeepers	6.7	7.3	5.8
Craft	36.0	34.6	31.7
Unskilled	10.3	14.9	15.1
Unemployed	10.7	9.5	7.2

Table E.10. *Family status age 60 or over, 1865 (in percent)*

	N	Widowed	Household head	Living with kin
Males				
Native	63	15.6	87.5	9.5
Foreign	135	25.4	75.6	5.5
Females				
Native	108	55.5	63.9	30.2
Foreign	114	63.2	61.6	30.4

Table E.11. *Residential patterns, native-born females by age, 1855 (in percent)*

Ages	Spouses or household heads	Children	Boarders	Servants	Grandparents	Other kin
15–19	3.3	68.0	13.4	8.9	—	6.3
20–29	33.0	34.3	20.1	4.6	—	8.6
30–39	78.4	5.3	12.1	3.2	—	5.3
40–49	75.9	6.9	6.9	2.3	1.7	5.2
50–59	76.8	—	10.1	1.0	7.1	6.1
60 +	45.8	—	7.0	—	36.1	9.8

Table E.12. *Marital status native-born females by age, 1855 (in percent)*

Age	N	Single	Married	Widowed
0–19	268	95.9	4.1	—
20–24	251	63.3	35.9	7.9
25–29	157	45.2	50.9	3.8
30–39	196	16.8	77.6	5.6
40–49	152	9.2	71.05	19.7
50–59	94	9.6	58.6	30.9
60 +	70	7.1	40.0	52.9

Table E.13. *Occupation females by age, 1855 (in percent)*

	Unemployed	Service	Professional	Crafts	Factory
15–19	59.6	14.2	3.1	20.1	2.8
20–29	64.9	5.4	3.4	24.1	1.7
30–39	84.7	4.6	2.0	8.7	—
40–49	81.3	7.5	1.3	9.4	—
50–59	90.4	3.2	—	3.0	—
60 +	95.8	1.4	—	2.8	—
All ages	72.7	7.3	2.6	16.1	1.2

Note: N = 1,225.

Table E.14. *Multiple sources of household income (in percent)*

	Native-born	Foreign-born
1855		
Households with boarders	22.5	14.2
Households with two workers	16.8	15.2
Households with three or more workers	10.7	6.4
1865		
Households with boarders	16.4	8.9
Households with two workers	17.0	12.3
Households with three or more workers	8.8	9.6

Notes

Introduction

1 Talcott Parsons and Robert F. Bales, *Family, Socialization and Interaction Process* (Glencoe, Ill., 1955); Peter Laslett and Richard Wall, *Household and Family in Past Time* (Cambridge, England, 1972); Michael Anderson, *Family Structure in Nineteenth-Century Lancashire* (Cambridge, England, 1971); Joan W. Scott and Louise A. Tilly, *Women, Work, and Family* (New York, 1978).

2 Philippe Ariès, *Centuries of Childhood: A Social History of Family Life* (New York, 1962); Lawrence J. Stone, *The Family, Sex and Marriage in England, 1500–1800* (London, 1977); David Levine, *Family Formation in an Age of Nascent Capitalism* (New York, 1977); Edward Shorter, *The Making of the Modern Family* (New York, 1977).

3 John Demos, *A Little Commonwealth: Family Life in Plymouth Colony* (New York, 1970); Philip J. Greven, *Four Generations: Population, Land and Family in Colonial Andover, Massachusetts* (Ithaca, N.Y., 1970); Michael Katz, *The People of Hamilton, Canada West* (Cambridge, Mass., 1975); Richard Sennett, *Families Against the City* (Cambridge, Mass., 1970); Daniel Scott Smith, "Population, Family, and Society in Hingham, Massachusetts, 1650–1880," doctoral dissertation (University of California at Berkeley, 1973); Bernard Farber, *Guardians of Virtue: Salem Families in 1800* (New York, 1972); Herbert Gutman, *The Black Family in Slavery and Freedom, 1750–1925* (New York, 1976); Tamara Hareven, "Modernization and Family History, Perspectives on Social Change," in *Signs: Journal of Women in Culture and Society 2* (Autumn 1976), 190–207.

4 Barbara Welter, "The Cult of True Womanhood 1820–1860," in *American Quarterly 18* (1966), 151–74; Daniel Scott Smith, "Family Limitation, Sexual Control, and Domestic Feminism in Victorian America," in *Feminist Studies 1*, No. 3-4 (1973), 40–57; Kathryn Kish Sklar, *Catharine Beecher* (New Haven, Conn., 1973); Patricia Branca, *Silent Sisterhood: Middle Class Women in the Victorian Home* (London, 1975); Nancy F. Cott, *The Bonds of Womanhood* (New Haven, Conn., 1977); Mary P. Ryan, "American Society and the Cult of Domesticity, 1830–1860," doctoral dissertation (University of California at Santa Barbara, 1971); Mary P. Ryan, *Womanhood in America from Colonial Times to the Present* (New York, 1975), Chap. 3 (this work significantly revises the author's earlier interpretation of the origins and implications of the cult of domesticity). Carroll Smith-Rosenberg, "The Female World of Love and Ritual: Relations between Women in Nineteenth-Century

America," in *Signs: Journal of Women in Culture and Society* 1 (Autumn 1975), 1–29.

5   Clyde Griffen and Sally Griffen, *Natives and Newcomers* (Cambridge, Mass., 1978); Stuart M. Blumin, *The Urban Threshold* (Chicago, 1976); Peter R. Decker, *Fortunes and Failures* (Cambridge, Mass., 1978).

6   Robert Frederick Berkhofer, Jr., "The Industrial History of Oneida County, New York, to 1850," master's thesis (Cornell University, 1955); Diane Lindstrom, *Economic Development in the Philadelphia Region 1810–1850* (New York, 1978); John Martin Roberts, "The Social Dimensions of Urban-Industrial Structure: Evangelical Religion, Reform and Economic Growth in Oneida County, New York," paper, n.d.

7   W. Freeman Galpin, *Central New York, An Inland Empire* (New York, 1941), 211–32.

8   English Staffordshire China, Exhibit: "Made in Utica," April–September 1976, Museum of Art, Munson-Williams-Proctor Institute, Utica.

9   *Utica City Directory*, 1828–45; *United States Census of Manufacturers*, Manuscript Schedules (Utica, 1850).

10 Berkhofer, "Industrial History," Chap. 3.

11 *Utica Daily Gazette*, May 15, 1845.

12 Bruce Laurie, Theodore Hershberg, George Alter, "Immigrants and Industry: The Philadelphia Experience 1850–1880," in *Journal of Social History*, Winter 1975, 219–67.

13 Whitney Cross, *The Burned-Over District: The Social and Intellectual History of Enthusiastic Religion in Western New York* (Ithaca, N.Y., 1950); Paul E. Johnson, *A Shopkeeper's Millennium: Society and Revivals in Rochester, New York, 1815–1837* (New York, 1978).

14 Johnson, *Shopkeeper's Millennium*; Anthony F. C. Wallace, *Rockdale: The Growth of an American Village in the Early Industrial Revolution* (New York, 1978).

15 Burton J. Bledstein, *The Culture of Professionalism: The Middle Class and the Development of Higher Education in America* (New York, 1976).

16 C. Wright Mills, *White Collar: The American Middle Classes* (New York, 1951), ix; David Lockwood, *The Blackcoated Worker: A Study in Class Consciousness* (London, 1958).

17 Richard Busacca and Patrick O'Donnell, "The State, Redistribution and the System of Social Reproduction" (Paper delivered at the American Political Science Association, Washington, D.C., 1979); M. E. Giminez, "Structural Marxism on the Woman Question," in *Science and Society*, Fall 1978, 301–24.

18 Conrad M. Arensberg, quoted in Colin Bell, *Middle Class Families: Social and Geographical Mobility* (London, 1968), 9.

1. Family, community, and the frontier generation

1   William White, "Genealogy of the White Family," in *Oneida Historical Society Transactions, 1881–84*, 25–30.

2 Philip Greven, *Four Generations* (Ithaca, N.Y., 1970); Lutz Berkner, "The Stem Family and the Developmental Cycle of the Peasant Household," in *American Historical Review 77* (1972), 398–419; John Waters, "The Traditional World of the New England Peasants: A View from Seventeenth-Century Barnstable," in *New England Historical and Genealogical Register*, January 1976, pp. 19–32.

3 Greven, *Four Generations*; Daniel Scott Smith, "Population, Family, and Society in Hingham, Massachusetts, 1650–1880," doctoral dissertation (University of California at Berkeley, 1973).

4 Robert Frederick Berkhofer, Jr., "Industrial History of Oneida County, New York, to 1850," master's thesis (Cornell University, 1955), Chap. 1.

5 Pomeroy Jones, *Annals and Recollections of Oneida County* (Rome, N.Y., 1851), 497.

6 *Columbian Gazette*, March 12, 1804, Oct. 8, 1822; *The Utica Patriot*, July 18, 1803.

7 "Confession of Faith, 1800," First Baptist Church, Deerfield, N.Y., held by Deacon Frederick Krommiller, Utica, N.Y.; "Records of the Session Meetings of the First Presbyterian Church, Utica, New York," Vol. 2, Oct. 24, 1821; hereafter cited as "Session Records, Utica," "Records of Whitesboro Baptist Church," Oct. 4, 1828, Oneida Historical Society, hereafter cited as OHS.

8 "Session Records, Utica," Vol. 2, Oct. 7, 1823.

9 "Minute Book, Court of General Sessions," June 1827, OHS.

10 Berkhofer, "Industrial History," Chap. 1; "Minute Books of the Oneida County Agricultural Society," 1818–1824, OHS; Tench Coxe, *A Series of Tables of the Several Branches of American Manufacture* (Philadelphia, 1810), 32; *Statistics of the Census of the United States as Collected and Returned by the Marshals of the Several Judicial Districts* (Washington, 1841), 12.

11 The Reverend John Frost, "Families Within the Boundaries of the United Society of Whitestown, April 1813–July 1816," First Presbyterian Church, Whitesboro.

12 Anne Taylor and Ann F. Gilberts, *Rhymes for the Nursery* (Utica, 1815), 36–37.

13 *Utica Observer*, Sept. 23, 1834.

14 *Utica Temperance Advocate*, Aug. 25, 1847.

15 "Diary of Hannah M. Gilbert," Aug. 13, 1816, OHS.

16 *Utica Patriot and Patrol*, Oct. 27, 1818.

17 "Session Records, Utica," Vol. 2, Dec. 28, 1824.

18 Will of Frederick Bowman, 1824, Vol. 2, Will books of Oneida County, Oneida County Court House, Utica. Hereafter cited as WBOC.

19 Will of Septa Barnard, 1802, Vol. 5, WBOC.

20 Will of Orre Hovey, 1843, Vol. 7, WBOC.

21 Will of Eli Butler, 1803, Vol. 1, WBOC.

22 Will of Amos Miller, 1806, Vol. 1, WBOC.

23 Will of Thomas Thornton, 1826, Vol. 3; Will of Elisha Newell, 1800, Vol. 1, WBOC.

24 See Berkner, "The Stem Family," 398–419.

25 Taylor and Gilberts, *Rhymes*, 68–9.

26 Isaac Watts, *Divine Songs Attempted in Easy Language for the Use of Children* (Utica, 1810), 28.

27 *Methodist Magazine*, June 1826, 201–09.

28 *Utica Patriot*, April 18, 1815; *Utica Observer*, April 9, 1833.

29 *Young Christian's Guide Containing Important Scriptural Answers* (Utica, 1819), 87.

30 *Methodist Magazine*, December 1821, 468–75.

31 "A Dialogue Between a Missionary and a Man and His Wife Upon the Duty of Prayer" (n.p., n.d.), OHS.

32 *Young Christian's Guide*, 87.

33 Noah Webster, *An American Selection of Lessons in Reading and Speaking* (Utica, 1806), 85–99.

34 *Methodist Magazine*, February 1822, 63; Watts, *Divine Songs*, 20.

35 "Records of the Oneida Conference of the Methodist Church," Aug. 26, 1844, George Arendts Research Library, Syracuse University; hereafter cited as "Records, Oneida Conference."

36 "Records of the Session of the Church of Whitesboro," Vol. 1: Sept. 18, 1800, May 3, 1809; Vol. 2: April 10, 1811, April 13, 1815, Aug. 20, 1821, Parish House, First Presbyterian Church, Whitesboro, N.Y.; hereafter cited as "Session Records, Whitesboro."

37 "Immorality Trials," "Records, Oneida Conference," 1827, 1830, and 1844.

38 Ibid.; "Session Records, Whitesboro," Vol. 1, May 3, 1809; "Session Records, Utica," Vol. 2, July 28, 1825.

39 "Session Records, Whitesboro," Vol. 1, May 3, 1809; Vol. 2, March 11, 1828.

40 Ibid., Vol. 2, July 3, 1818.

41 "Session Records, Utica," Vol. 3, Nov. 10–28, 1834.

42 "Church Covenant, 1800," First Baptist Church, Deerfield, N.Y.

43 George W. Bethune, "The Cross of Christ, the Only Theme of the Preacher of the Faith" (Utica, 1831), 20–1.

44 "Confession of Faith, 1800" 7; P. H. Fowler, *Historical Sketch of Presbyterianism* (Utica, 1877), 105.

45 *Utica Christian Magazine*, November 1814, 183–4; *Utica Christian Repository*, January 1823, 1; *Western Recorder*, March 10, 1829.

46 A. D. Eddy, "A Sermon Occasioned by the Death of Mrs. Beulah Clarke, Wife of William Clarke, Esq. of Utica" (New York, 1827), 28; *Young Christian's Guide*, 87.

47 *Utica Christian Repository*, January 1823, 15.

48 "Session Records, Whitesboro," Vol. 1, Oct. 29, 1807.

49 *Utica Christian Magazine*, March-April 1816, 207–15.

50 *Young Christian's Guide*, 66.

51 M. M. Bagg, "The Earliest Factories of Oneida and Their Projectors," *Oneida Historical Society Transactions*, 1881, 112–24; for an excellent analysis of family and gender in mill towns, see Thomas Dublin, *Women at Work: The Transformation of Work and Community in Lowell, Massachusetts, 1826–1860* (New York, 1979).

52 Isaac Briggs, "An Address Delivered before the Oneida Society for the Promotion of American Manufactures" (Utica, 1817), 5.

53 Berkhofer, "Industrial History," Chap. 1.

54 Bagg, "Earliest Factories," 112–24.

55 "Work Ledger 1827–1829," New York Mills Co. Collection, OHS.

56 Charles Giles, *Pioneer* (New York, 1844), 308.

57 Bernard Farber, *Guardians of Virtue* (New York, 1972), 9.

58 Will of Joseph Harter, 1863, Vol. 14, WBOC.

59 Quoted in Jones, *Annals and Recollections*, 548.

60 Carroll T. Waldron, "A Hundred Years of Amusement in Utica 1806–1906," MS, p. 5, OHS.

61 *An Act to Incorporate the Village of Utica* (Utica, 1817), 20.

62 *The Utica Almanac* (Utica, 1810). For additional information on female benevolent societies in the early nineteenth century, see Keith E. Melder, *Beginnings of Sisterhood: The American Women's Rights Movement, 1800–1850* (New York, 1977).

63 Charles Ray Keller, *The Second Great Awakening in Connecticut* (New Haven, Conn., 1942), 163.

64 "Records of the Female Charitable Society of Whitestown," 1806–14, OHS; "Constitution of the Female Missionary Society of Oneida" (Utica, 1814); "The Report of the Trustees Made to the Female Oneida Missionary Society" (Utica, 1816, 1817–23, 1824, 1825, 1826, and 1827); "Annual Report and Circular of the Female Missionary Society of the Western District of the State of New York" (Utica, 1829, 1831).

65 *Western New York Baptist Magazine*, Sept. 10, 1816, 296–7.

66 John Demos, *A Little Commonwealth: Family Life in Plymouth Colony* (New York, 1970), 194; Alan McFarlane, *The Family Life of Ralph Josselin, A Seventeenth Century Clergyman: An Essay in Historical Anthropology* (Cambridge, England, 1970), 205–10.

67 Richard A. Easterlin, "Factors in the Decline of Farm Family Fertility in the United States: Some Preliminary Research Results," in *Journal of American History* 63 (1976), 600–14.

68 "Journal of John S. Coleman," 1829–43, OHS.

69 A. C. Kendrick, *The Life and Letters of Emily Chubbuck Judson* (New York, 1861), 16–36; Fanny Forrester [Emily Chubbuck Judson], *Trippings in Authorland* (New York, 1846), 41–60, 91–160, 250–72.

2. Family in transition

1 Whitney Cross, *The Burned-Over District: The Social and Intellectual History of Enthusiastic Religion in Western New York* (Ithaca, N.Y., 1950);

Charles Finney, *Memoirs of Reverend Charles G. Finney* (New York, 1876); John Frost, Moses Gillet, and Noah Cole, *A Narrative of the Revival of Religion* (Utica, 1826), 17–25; "The Eighth Annual Report of the Trustees of the Female Missionary Society of the Western District" (Utica, 1824), 24.

2 *Statistics of the Census of the United States as Collected and Returned by the Marshals of the Several Judicial Districts* (Washington, 1841), 121; *Census of the State of New York for 1845* (Albany, 1846).

3 "Assessment List, 1835," MS, OHS.

4 Will of Abraham Miller, 1837, Vol. 5, WBOC.

5 "Work Ledgers of the New York Mills Company," 1827–29, 1836–39, New York Mills Co. Collection, OHS; Robert Frederick Berkhofer, Jr., "The Industrial History of Oneida County, New York to 1850," master's thesis (Cornell University, 1955), 22.

6 "Census of the State of New York, 1821," Appendix, *New York State Assembly Journal* (Albany, 1822); *Census of the State of New York for 1845* (Albany, 1846).

7 *Sabbath School Visitant* (Utica, 1826).

8 John Camp Williams, *An Oneida County Printer* (New York, 1906).

9 "A Vindication of Infant Baptism. In Four Numbers. Including the Rise and Progress of a Dispute Carried on Between Certain Members of the Congregational and Baptist Churches in Sangerfield in the Year 1803" (Utica, 1803), 22, 38; Jabez Chadwick, "Four Sermons on the Mode and Subject of Christian Baptism" (Utica, 1811), 10; John Truair, "Plain Truth on Christian Baptism and Communion" (Utica, 1920), Preface.

10 "Vindication of Infant Baptism," 43; "Baptism Not One of the Plainest Things in the World" (Utica, 1811), 30; Thomas Baldwin, "Christian Baptism as Delivered to the Churches, by the Evangelists and Apostles in the New Testament in a Letter to a Friend" (Utica, 1817), 22.

11 Elijah Norton, "The Methodist System and Church Annihilated by the Scripture of Truth" (Utica, 1812), 15, 22, 54–55.

12 Joshua Leonard, "The Relationship of Children of Christians to the Church Considered in Four Sermons" (Utica, 1808), 20, 51, 83.

13 P. H. Fowler, *Historical Sketch of Presbyterianism* (Utica, 1877), 110.

14 Chadwick, "Four Sermons," 89; "Baptism Not One of the Plainest Things," 49.

15 David Harrowar, "A Sermon on the Total Depravity of Infants and Their Entire Dependence on Sovereign Grace, for Eternal Salvation" (Utica, 1815), 13; *Utica Christian Magazine*, October 1813, 235, 236.

16 Leonard, "Relationship of Children," 74–5; *Utica Christian Repository*, February 1823, 58.

17 *Utica Christian Magazine*, March, 1815, 107–215; *Western Recorder*, Jan. 6, 1824, 1; Baldwin, "Christian Baptism," 33.

18 James Carnahan, "Christianity Defended Against the Cavils of Infidels and the Weakness of Enthusiasts" (Utica, 1808), 17 and 29.

19 Deborah Pierce, "A Scriptural Vindication of Female Preaching, Prophesying, or Exhortation" (Utica, 1817), 19.

20 Elias Lee, "A Letter to the Rev. James Carnahan Pastor of the Presbyterian Church in Utica and Whitesborough Being a Defense of Martha Howell and the Baptists Against the Misrepresentations and Aspersions of that Gentleman" (Utica, 1808), 22–3.

21 Pierce, "Scriptural Vindication," 17.

22 George Coler, *Heroines of Methodism or Pen and Ink Sketches of the Mothers and Daughters of the Church* (New York, 1857).

23 "Female Influence" (Utica, circa 1823), 6.

24 Ibid., 8 and 9.

25 The Reverend John Frost, "Families Within the Boundaries of the United Society of Whitestown, April 1813–July 1816." See Table C.1.

26 Frost, Gillet, and Cole, *Revival of Religion*.

27 "Pastoral Letter of the Ministers of the Oneida Association to the Churches Under Their Care on the Subject of Revivals of Religion" (Utica, 1827), 13, 14, 20.

28 *Utica Magazine*, March 24, 1827, 5; *Evangelical Magazine and Gospel Advocate*, Oct. 15, 1831, 331. See Nancy F. Cott, "Young Women in the Second Great Awakening in New England," in *Feminist Studies 3* (Fall 1975), 14–20, for a recent interpretation of gender, age, and evangelism.

29 The Records of the First Presbyterian Church, Utica, and the First Presbyterian Church, Whitesboro, were transcribed from the original by the New York Genealogical and Biographical Society in 1920, edited by Royden Woodward Vosburgh; these typescripts along with the original records from the Second Presbyterian Church and the Whitesboro Baptist Church are found at the Oneida Historical Society and the Utica Public Library. Church records are unavailable for the local Methodist congregation, which reportedly played a small role in Utica's revivals. The records of Trinity Episcopal Church revealed no significant increase in membership during revival years.

30 "First Annual Report of the Trustees of the Female Oneida Missionary Society" (Utica, 1816); "Eighth Annual Report of the Trustees of the Female Oneida Missionary Society" (Utica, 1824).

31 "A Memorial of the Semi-Centennial Celebration of the Founding of the Sunday School of the First Presbyterian Church, Utica, New York" (Utica, 1867); Fowler, *Historical Sketch of Presbyterianism*, 131.

32 "The Third Annual Report of the Trustees of the Female Oneida Missionary Society" (Utica, 1818), 26; "The Report of the Trustees Made to the Female Oneida Missionary Society" (Utica, 1816), 16.

33 "First Annual Report, Female Oneida Missionary Society," 19; "Annual Report and Circular of the Female Missionary Society of the Western District of the State of New York" (Utica, 1829), 3–5.

34 Amos Glover Baldwin, *Memoirs of Miss Huldah Ann Baldwin* (Utica, 1814), 109.

35 *Methodist Magazine*, February-March 1818, 103–9; July 1810, 265; Emily Chubbuck Judson, *My Two Sisters: A Sketch From Memory* (Boston, 1854), 75.
36 "Session Records, Utica," Vol. 2, July 10–August 1, 1822; "Eighth Annual Report, Female Missionary Society," 3; Rev. James H. Hotchkin, *A History of the Purchase and Settlement of Western New York and of the Rise, Progress, and Present State of the Presbyterian Church in That Section* (New York, 1848), 38–9.
37 "Constitution of the Maternal Association of Utica, adopted June 30, 1824," printed pamphlet, New York State Library, Albany, N.Y.
38 "Session Records, Utica," Vol. 3, April 1833.
39 Finney, *Memoirs*, 176–7.
40 Ibid.; Charles Giles, *Pioneer* (New York, 1844), 310–17.
41 Charles Beecher, ed., *Autobiography, Correspondence, etc. of Lyman Beecher, D.D.* (New York, 1865), Vol. 2, 310–12.
42 "Second Annual Report of the Trustees of the Western Domestic Missionary Society" (Utica, 1831), 13.
43 "Annual Report and Circular of the Female Missionary Society (1829), 3–7.
44 *Evangelical Magazine and Gospel Advocate*, Oct. 15, 1831, 329–31.
45 *Mother's Magazine*, June 1833, 93–5.
46 Beriah Green, "The Savior's Arms Open to Little Children: A Discourse" (Utica, 1836), 12.
47 Ibid., 5–6, 12.
48 Ibid., 13.
49 *Sabbath School Visitant*, June 1824, 5; September 1824, 4.
50 "To Every Mother in Oneida County" (n.d.) 4, OHS; "An Address to Mothers," printed with the "Constitution of the Maternal Association of Utica," 5; *Mother's Magazine*, May 1833, 79.
51 *Mother's Monthly Journal*, January 1836, 10.

3. The era of association

1 *Sabbath School Visitant and Juvenile Magazine*, Aug. 1, 1829, 270.
2 *Genesee St., Utica, N.Y.*, lithograph, *Ladies' Companion* (February 1842), Exhibit: "Made in Utica," April–September 1976, Museum of Art, Munson-Williams-Proctor Institute, Utica.
3 Calculations based on the Manuscript Schedules, *United States Census of Manufacturers, 1850*.
4 "Constitution of the Oneida Bible Society" (Utica, 1812), 7.
5 *Sabbath School Visitant*, March 1825, 3.
6 Ibid., Aug., 1829, 253–4.
7 "Third Annual Report of the American Branch Tract Society of Utica" (Utica, 1829).
8 "First Report of the Directors of the Western Education Society" (Utica, 1819).

9   "Report of the Directors of the Western Education Society of the State of New York" (Utica, 1824), 7.

10 "Resolutions and Membership List, The Society for the Promotion of Temperance," July 21, 1828, MS, OHS.

11 "A Brief Statement of the Proceedings of the Citizens of Utica Touching Certain Measures for Enforcing the Observance of the Sabbath" (Utica, 1828), 9.

12 *Evangelical Magazine and Gospel Advocate*, Dec. 17, 1831, 406.

13 "Circular of the Executive Committee of the Whitestown and Oneida Institute Anti-Slavery Society" (n.p., n.d.), 5; "Second Annual Report of the American Anti-Slavery Society" (New York, 1835).

14 *Quarterly Anti-Slavery Magazine*, October 1835, 34–68; *The Friend of Man*, June 21, 1837.

15 Beriah Green to James Birney, Dec. 30, 1835, *The Letters of James G. Birney*, Dwight L. Dumond, ed. (New York, 1938), 291.

16 [H. M. Howes], "The Enemies of the Constitution Discovered or An Inquiry into the Origin and Tendency of Popular Violence Containing a Complete and Circumstantial Account of the Unlawful Proceedings of the City of Utica, October 21st, 1835 " (New York and Utica, 1835), 61.

17 Ibid., 69.

18 Leonard L. Richards, *Gentlemen of Property and Standing* (London and New York, 1970, 1971), 130–50.

19 "Session Records, Utica," Vol. 3, Dec. 4, 1834.

20 Ibid.

21 Ibid., Vol. 3, Dec. 3 and 17, 1834; January 2 and July 2, 1835.

22 "Session Records, Whitestown," Vol. 3, Oct. 27 and Nov. 21, 1837.

23 A. T. Hopkins, *The Evils and Remedy of Lewdness* (Utica, 1834), 16.

24 *MacDowall's Journal*, March 1834, 34.

25 Only thirty-four female moral reformers could be identified by name. Of this group, six were married to merchants or shopkeepers, five to professionals, two to artisans; two were seamstresses and four had neither occupations nor employed husbands. Seven single women were also identified as moral reformers. For a more detailed treatment of female moral reform, see Barbara J. Berg, *The Remembered Gate: Origins of American Feminism* (New York, 1978); Carroll Smith-Rosenberg, "Beauty and the Beast and the Militant Woman: A Case Study in Sex Roles and Social Stress in Jacksonian America," in *American Quarterly* 23 (October 1971), 562–84; Mary P. Ryan, "The Power of Women's Networks: A Case Study of Female Moral Reform in Antebellum America," in *Feminist Studies* 5 (Spring 1979), 66–86.

26 "First Annual Report of the Female Moral Reform Society of the City of New York" (New York, 1835); *MacDowall's Journal*, Sept. 9, 1833; *Advocate of Moral Reform*, Nov. 1, 1835, June 11, 1836, July 15, 1837.

27 *Advocate of Moral Reform*, July 15, 1837, 294.

28 Ibid., March 1, 1833, 39.

29 Ibid., July 1, 1833; Feb. 7 and Feb. 22, 1836.

30   Ibid., Feb. 1, 1838, 85, 119.
31   Ibid., Sept. 15, 1840, 143.
32   Ibid., Sept. 15, 1842.
33   Ibid., Sept. 15, July 1, 1842.
34   Ibid., Dec. 15, 1841, 191; April 1, 1844, 87.
35   *MacDowall's Journal*, Aug. 8, 1833.
36   *Advocate of Moral Reform*, Aug. 20, 1837; July 30, 1840.
37   See Daniel Scott Smith and Michael Hindus, "Premarital Pregnancy in
     America, 1640–1971: An Overview and Interpretation," in *Journal of
     Interdisciplinary History 5* (1974–75), 537–70. In 1830, for example, one-
     fourth of Utica residents were between the ages of twenty and thirty,
     the largest proportion in the area's history.
38   *Evangelical Magazine and Gospel Advocate*, Oct. 31, 1835.
39   Alice Felt Tyler, "Paulina Wright Davis," *Notable American Women
     1607–1950: A Biographical Dictionary*, Edward T. James, ed. (Cam-
     bridge, Mass., 1974), Vol. 1, 444–5. Information on Clarke and Skinner
     is drawn from scattered references in church and reform society re-
     cords and local histories.
40   Peggy A. Rabkin, "The Silent Feminist Revolution: Women and the
     Law in New York from Blackstone to the Beginnings of the American
     Women's Rights Movement," doctoral dissertation (State University of
     New York at Buffalo, 1975).
41   Fanny Skinner to Mrs. A. G. Weld, June 15, 1838, *Letters to Theodore
     Dwight Weld, Angelina Grimké Weld, and Sarah Grimké, 1822–1844*, Gil-
     bert H. Barnes and Dwight L. Dumond, eds. (New York, 1934), 682–3.
42   *Oneida Whig*, Dec. 27, 1836, Jan. 27, Feb. 7, and Feb. 14, 1837.
43   Ibid.
44   Ibid., Feb. 7, 1837.
45   "Proceedings and Address of the Republican Young Men of the State
     of New York assembled at Utica on the 12th day of August, 1828"
     (Utica, 1828), 24.
46   *Utica City Directory, 1834* (Utica), 40–1.
47   "Literary Club Journal," Nov. 15, 1832, MS, Uticana Collection, OHS.
48   Some Former Utica Residents to the Young Men's Association, June 20,
     1834, James Watson Williams Collection, OHS.
49   "Literary Club Journal," Sept. 29, 1832.
50   *Utica Democrat*, Sept. 28, 1841.
51   Of the nineteen leaders of the protest, sixteen were traced to the *City
     Directory*. All were clerks and all were boarders. Only one boarded
     with a relative and only one with his employer.
52   *Utica City Directory, 1832*, 156–57; for more information on working-
     men's associations and mechanics institutes, see Edward Pesen, *Most
     Uncommon Jacksonians* (New York, 1967), Bruce Sinclair, *Philadelphia's
     Philosopher Mechanics* (Baltimore, 1974).
53   "Charters, Constitutions and By-Laws of the Utica Mechanics Associa-
     tion with a Short History" (Utica, 1864).

54 "Proceedings of the State Convention of Mechanics Held at Utica, Aug, 21, 22, 1834" (Utica, 1834), 8.

55 Ibid., 11.

56 "By Two of the Fraternity," in *Washingtonian Pocket Companion* (Utica, 1842), 88; "Minutes and Memberships, 1842," New York Mills Washingtonian Total Abstinence Society, July 11, 1842, MS, OHS.

57 "Minutes and Memberships, 1842," New York Mills Abstinence Society, July 11, 1842.

58 "Proceedings of the Grand Division of the Sons of Temperance of Western New York" (Utica, 1851), 80; *Washingtonian Pocket Companion*, 59, 61.

59 "Minutes and Memberships, 1842," New York Mills Abstinence Society, Sept. 18, 1842.

60 Scattered issues of the *Utica Teetotaler*, the *Washingtonian*, and the *Temperance Advocate* are available at the Oneida Historical Society, the Utica Public Library, and the New York Historical Society; for more information on artisan culture and its relation to temperance, see Bruce Laurie, "'Nothing on Compulsion': Life Styles of Philadelphia Artisans 1820–1850," in *Labor History* 15 (Summer 1974), 337–66, and Paul Faler, "Cultural Aspects of the Industrial Revolution: Lynn, Massachusetts, Shoemakers and Industrial Morality, 1826–1860, in *Labor History* 15 (Summer 1974), 366–94.

61 *Utica Teetotaler*, March 27, 1852.

62 A. B. Johnson, "An Address to the Utica Temperance Society" (Utica, 1829).

63 *Utica Teetotaler*, Oct. 19, 1850.

64 Ibid., Sept. 28, 1850.

65 Ibid., Aug. 30, 1850.

66 *Utica City Directory, 1817*, 3–19.

67 "Payroll Books," 1841–49, New York Mills Co. Collection, OHS.

68 D. C. Lansing, "Remedy for Intemperance, a Sermon" (Utica, 1832), 5; *Washingtonian Pocket Companion*, 37, 89.

69 *Washingtonian Pocket Companion*, 37, 89.

70 Thomas H. Flandreau, "An Address Delivered at a Meeting of the Female Washingtonian and other Temperance Societies of the City of Utica" (Utica, 1842), 7–8.

71 Will of Ebenezer Ames, Vol. 12 (1854); Will of Joseph Seaton, Vol. 9 (1845), WBOC.

72 F. W. Marchisi, Mercantile Agency Records, 1858, and J. H. Read and Sons, Grocers, Mercantile Agency Records, 1862, in "Early Handwritten Credit Reporting Ledgers of the Mercantile Agency" (Utica), Vol. 476, R. G. Dun and Company Ledgers, Baker Library, Harvard Business School.

73 *Evangelical Magazine and Gospel Advocate*, April 14, 1843, 120.

74 *Mother's Monthly Journal*, January 1836, 10.

75 "Proceedings of the Grand Division of the Sons of Temperance of Western New York" (Utica, 1853), 10.

4. Privacy and the making of the self-made man

1 *Utica Morning Herald*, July 28, 1865.
2 Lavinia Johnson, "Diary," Aug. 8 and Aug. 17, 1859, OHS.
3 See Nancy F. Cott, *The Bonds of Womanhood* (New Haven, Conn., 1977); Kathryn Kish Sklar, *Catharine Beecher* (New Haven, Conn., 1973); Mary P. Ryan "American Society and the Cult of Domesticity, 1830–1860," doctoral dissertation (University of California at Santa Barbara, 1971).
4 *Young Ladies' Miscellany*, August 1842, 2.
5 John Mather Austin, *A Voice to the Married* (Utica, 1841), 38.
6 John Mather Austin, *A Voice to Youth* (Utica, 1838), 61, 64.
7 Johnson, "Diary," Dec. 15, 1859.
8 *Utica Morning Herald*, Jan. 16, 1861.
9 "Court Warrants," 1849, Uticana Collection, OHS.
10 Johnson, "Diary," Aug. 15, 1859.
11 *United States Census of Manufacturers*, Manuscript Schedules (Utica, 1860).
12 "Ordinances of the City of Utica, 1863" (Utica, 1863), 40–1.
13 Lewis Bradley, *Sketch of Utica, 1850*, Munson-Williams-Proctor Institute, Utica.
14 *United States Census of Manufacturers*, Manuscript Schedules (Utica, 1850, 1860, 1870). Clyde Griffen and Sally Griffen, *Natives and Newcomers* (Cambridge, Mass., 1978); Bruce Laurie, Theodore Hershberg, George Alter, "Immigrants and Industry: The Philadelphia Experience 1850–1880," in *Journal of Social History*, Winter 1975, 219–26.
15 Murdock and Andrews, Mercantile Agency Records, 1859; Spencer Kellogg, Mercantile Agency Records, 1857.
16 James Stocking, Mercantile Agency Records, 1851.
17 James Mohr, *Abortion in America: The Origins and Evolution of Public Policy* (New York, 1978), 34–5.
18 *Utica Observer*, Jan. 1, 1833; *Utica Daily Gazette*, Sept. 27, 1856.
19 Linda Gordon, *Woman's Body, Woman's Right: A Social History of Birth Control in America* (New York, 1976); Daniel Scott Smith, "Family Limitation, Sexual Control, and Domestic Feminism in Victorian America," in *Feminist Studies 1*, No. 3-4 (1973), 40–57.
20 Johnson, "Diary," April 2, 1859.
21 J. H. Shroder, Mercantile Agency Records, 1864; Michael McQuade, Mercantile Agency Records, 1854.
22 *Utica Magazine*, Sept. 23, 1827, 101; *Mother's Magazine*, March 1833, 36; Ann Kuhn, *The Mother's Role in Childhood Education: New England Concepts, 1830–1860* (New Haven, Conn., 1947).
23 *Mother's Magazine*, October 1833, 151–7.

24 *Mother's Monthly Journal,* February 1838, 26–7; *Mother's Magazine,* February 1833, 22–6.

25 *Mother's Monthly Journal,* February 1838, 26–7; *Utica Patriot and Patrol,* Oct. 10, 1820; *Mother's Magazine,* April 14, 1833, 95; "Maxims for Mothers," "Maxims for Children," unbound leaflets, 1840, Maternal Association of Utica.

26 *Evangelical Magazine and Gospel Advocate,* Sept. 26, 1829, 97–8.

27 *Mother's Monthly Journal,* April 1838, 30.

28 Ibid., 49–52; March 1838, 425; September 1842, 129–31.

29 "Proceedings of a General Convention of Friends of Education Held at Utica" (n.p., n.d.), 7, 8, 17.

30 Calculations based on the *New York State Census of 1845; Oneida Whig,* Sept. 20, 1842.

31 See, for example, the *Utica Morning Herald,* Nov. 5, 1860.

32 Copies of the boys' newspapers have been preserved in the local history collection of the Utica Public Library.

33 *Oneida Whig,* March 28, 1839.

34 [Emily Chubbuck Judson] *Allen Lucas, the Self-Made Man or Life as It Is* (Utica, 1843), 100–03.

35 *Utica Daily Gazette,* Dec. 14, 1848; *Utica Evening Telegraph,* Sept. 16, 1859.

36 [Judson], *Allen Lucas,* 12, passim.

37 Ibid., 149–50, 174, passim.

38 *Mother's Monthly Journal,* April 1838, 449–52; August 1839: The census measurement of residence in the parental home fails to account for all the Utica natives who left the city entirely. A comparison of the population born in Oneida County with the number of teen-agers of local birth in subsequent census reports suggests that such migration was not excessive, perhaps accounting for only 1 in 5 sons.

39 Will of Charles A. Mann, 1860, Vol. 16; Will of Sophia Clarke, 1855, Vol. 14, WBOC.

40 "First Report of the Trustees of the Oneida Institute of Science and Industry" (Utica, 1828), 8–9; "A Voice From the Oneida Institute," July 1843, 5–12; "Third Report of the Trustees of the Oneida Institute of Science and Industry" (Utica, 1831).

41 "Catalogue of the Officers and Students of Whitestown Seminary for the Year Ending March, 1855" (Utica, 1855), 16; "By-Laws of the Utica Academy" (Utica, 1838); *Utica Daily Observer,* May 18, 1858.

42 "Catalogue of the Officers and Students of Whitestown Seminary, 1865" (Utica, 1865), 32; *New York State Census of 1845.*

43 *Daboll's Schoolmaster's Assistant Being a Plain Practical System of Arithmetic Adapted to the United States* (Utica, 1829), 138, 140; Lyman Preston, *Preston's Manual on Book-Keeping or, Arbitrary Rules Made Plain* (New York, 1829).

44 The earliest available figures (1890s) indicate that white-collar workers earned twice the wages of manual workers; see Robert Burns, "The

Comparative Economic Position of Manual and White Collar Employees," *Journal of Business* 27 (1954): 257–68.

45 Horatio Dryer to Harriet Dryer, April 10, 1856, Dryer Family Papers, New York Historical Society.

46 Hugh White, Jr., to William F. White, May 23, Oct. 17, Oct. 27, 1857, William Manfield White Papers, OHS.

47 Hugh White, Jr., to William F. White, Feb. 16, 1852, Oct. 15, 1854, Sept. 25, 1858.

48 Hugh White, Jr., to William F. White, March 2 and July 30, 1855.

49 Mary Perry to Winifield Perry (n.d.), Winifield Perry Papers, OHS; Mrs. Eliza Baker to Mrs. Ellen Gridley, June 1, 1862, Gridley Family Papers, OHS.

50 *Mother's Monthly Journal*, August 1837, 127; Bradford Merrill, Mercantile Agency Records, 1844.

51 Will of Lewis Bailey, Vol. 12, 1857, WBOC.

52 Anson J. Upson, "An Address delivered at the First Anniversary of the Young Men's Christian Association of Utica New York" (Utica, 1859), 24, 25; Allen S. Horlick, *Country Boys and Merchant Princes: The Social Control of Young Men in New York* (Lewisburg, Pa., 1975); Paul Boyer, *Urban Masses and Moral Order in America 1820–1920* (Cambridge, Mass., 1978), 109–20.

53 A. B. Grosh, "Odd-Fellowship: Its Character and Tendency" (Utica, 1843), 17.

54 "Records of the Whitestown Seminary Phoenix Society," Ms, April 25, May 9, May 25, June 14, June 27, Oct. 3, 1856; May 1, 1857; June 4, 1858; May 20, 1859, Whitestown Collection, OHS.

55 Hiram Denio to Ann Pitkin, Nov. 17, 1827, Oct. 5, 1828; Denio Collection, OHS.

56 Ann Pitkin to Hiram Denio, April 12, 1828, Denio Family Papers, OHS.

57 *A Book for the Millions: The Home Miscellany or Book of Gems, Original and Selected* (Utica, 1857), 19.

58 Sayre and Tucker, Mercantile Agency Records, 1855.

59 Urial Kellogg, Mercantile Agency Records, 1849.

60 Jason Davis, Mercantile Agency Records, 1871; John Turnbridge, Mercantile Agency Records, 1870; Edward B. Paine, Mercantile Agency Records, 1869.

61 Ezekiel Bacon, *Vacant Hours* (Utica, 1845), 60.

5. A sphere is not a home

1 P. H. Fowler, "Women's Sphere of Influence; a Discourse Delivered at the First Occasion of the Death of Mrs. Mary E. Ostrom" (Utica, 1859), 23, 40.

2 Ibid., 40–1.

3 Ibid., 6–8, 34–5.

4   Ibid., 6–8.

5   Ibid., 34–5.

6   Barbara Welter, "The Cult of True Womanhood 1820–1860," in *American Quarterly 18* (1966), 151–74; Mary P. Ryan, "American Society and the Cult of Domesticity, 1830–1860," doctoral dissertation (University of California at Santa Barbara, 1971).

7   John Mather Austin, *A Voice to the Married* (Utica, 1841), 38, 222; *Record of Genius* (Utica, 1832), 36.

8   John Mather Austin, *A Voice to Youth* (Utica, 1838), 272; *A Book for the Millions: The Home Miscellany or Book of Gems, Original and Selected* (Utica, 1857), 16–7.

9   Eliza Coxe, *Memorial Poems of the late Eliza Coxe* (Utica, 1868), 49.

10 *Mother's Magazine,* November 1838, 68.

11 Rachel Munson Williams, "Her Diary," January 11, 1864, Ms, Munson-Williams-Proctor Family Papers, OHS; *Mother's Monthly Journal,* October 1842, 156.

12 Nancy Chodorow, *The Reproduction of Mothering: Psychoanalysis and the Sociology of Gender* (Berkeley, Calif., 1978).

13 *Utica Observer,* April 30, 1833.

14 *Evangelical Magazine and Gospel Advocate,* April 12, 1839.

15 A. C. Kendrick, *The Life and Letters of Emily Chubbuck Judson* (New York, 1861), 245.

16 Mrs. R. Howland to Desire May, Oct. 3, 1847; J. G. May to Desire Babcock May, April to August 1847.

17 Lavinia Johnson, "Diary," July 4, Nov. 23, Dec. 18, Dec. 31,1859, OHS.

18 For a more extensive and pathbreaking treatment of female bonding, see Carroll Smith-Rosenberg, "The Female World of Love and Ritual: Relations between Women in Nineteenth-Century America," in *Signs 1* (Autumn 1975), 1–29.

19 Johnson, "Diary," April 2, Feb. 3, 1859.

20 Ibid., May 20, June 18, 1859.

21 Ibid., Aug. 2, 6, 18, 1860.

22 *Eagle,* May 2, 1850; *Book for the Millions,* 104.

23 Isabel V. Sawhill, "Economic Perspectives on the Family," in *Daedalus 106,* No. 2 (Spring 1977), 115–25; Wally Seccomb, "The Housewife and Her Labour Under Capitalism," in *New Left Review,* January-February 1974, 3–24; Ira Gerstein, "Domestic Work and Capitalism", in *Radical America 7* (July-October 1973), 101–28; Branka Magas, Margaret Coulson, and Hilary Wainwright, "The Housewife and Her Labour Under Capitalism – A Critique," *New Left Review 89* (January-February 1975), 59–71.

24 Laura Tucker, "Essay Book," OHS.

25 *Young Ladies' Miscellany,* September 1842, 25; *Utica Evening Telegraph,* Dec. 8, 1859.

26 Daniel Perry to his father, July 26, 1861, Jan. 20, 1862, Perry Family Papers, OHS.

27 *Utica Morning Herald,* April 25, 1860; *Utica Evening Telegraph,* Oct. 26, 1859.

28 Austin, *Voice to the Married,* 238; *Utica Daily Gazette,* Sept. 8, 1856; E. P. Thompson, "Time, Work-Discipline and Industrial Capitalism," in *Past and Present* (December 1967), 56–97.

29 *Utica Morning Herald,* Sept. 12, 1859. In the 1855 census sample there were 773 native-born male workers as opposed to 334 females.

30 *Utica Observer,* April 29, 1834; *Utica Daily Gazette,* April 15, 1844.

31 Mrs. A. Pullam, Mercantile Agency Records, 1858; Miss R. B. Lumbard, Mercantile Agency Records, 1856–70; Mrs. King, Mercantile Agency Records, 1858–71; Mrs. Eli Maynard, Mercantile Agency Records, 1844–65; Mrs. E. Meyers, Mercantile Agency Records, 1847–69.

32 *United States Census of Manufacturers,* Manuscript Schedules (Utica, 1850, 1860, 1870).

33 *Columbian Gazette,* Feb. 15, 1802; *Oneida Whig,* Oct. 28, 1845; *Utica Daily Gazette,* Feb. 13, 1851; *Utica Evening Telegraph,* Dec. 8, 1860.

34 Helen E. M. Munson, "Servants Instructions," Munson-Williams-Proctor Family Papers, OHS. I am indebted to Fran Cunningham, cataloguer of this voluminous collection, for calling this document to my attention.

35 *Evangelical Magazine and Gospel Advocate,* Oct. 4, 1834; *Utica Evening Telegraph,* Sept. 27, 1859; Fanny Forrester [Emily Chubbuck Judson], *Trippings in Authorland* (New York, 1846), 250–72.

36 *Evangelical Magazine and Gospel Advocate,* April 2, 1831.

37 *Utica Daily Gazette,* Dec. 18, 1852.

38 *Utica Daily Observer,* Nov. 17, 1858.

39 Fanny A. Goodale, "Records of Female Authors of the Counties of Oneida, Jefferson, Herkimer, Madison, and Lewis, prepared for the Columbia Exposition," 1893, OHS.

40 Edmund Hudson, *An American Woman's Life and Work, A Memorial of Mary Clemner Ames* (Boston, 1886).

41 "Westminster Session Records," Feb. 25, 1866, held in Bethany Presbyterian Church, Utica.

42 Calculations based on "Westminster Session Records," May 14, 17, 21, 24, 1863.

43 "The Benevolent Association of the First Presbyterian Church, Utica, New York" (Utica, 1865), 9–11.

44 Ibid., 12–15.

45 Moses M. Bagg, "Historical Sketch of the Utica Orphan Asylum" (Utica, 1880), 4, 11; "Constitution and By-Laws of the Utica Orphan Asylum" (Utica, 1857), 8, 11, 15; Anson J. Upson, "An Address Delivered at the Laying of the Corner Stone of the Utica Orphan Asylum" (Utica, 1860).

46 "Fourth Annual Report of St. Elizabeth's Hospital and Home" (Utica, 1872), 3; "Charter of the Home for the Homeless of the City of Utica" (Utica, 1871), 8.

47 "Ladies Soldiers' Relief Association of Utica and the U.S. Sanitary Commission, A Plea for Continuous Aid and Support" (Utica, 1863), 6–9.
48 *Utica Morning Herald,* May 24, 1864, May 27, 1865.
49 *Oneida Whig,* April 16 and July 20, 1841, June 14, 1842.
50 *Utica Daily Gazette,* June 11, 1842, May 29, 1843.
51 Ibid., March 24, 1849, Nov. 12, 1850, Dec. 15, 1851.
52 *Utica Morning Herald,* April 3, 1860.
53 Fourteen of the twenty-three officers of 1860 were located in the federal census manuscript schedules. The mean value of their family property was $37,863. Of all identifiable officers between 1840 and 1860, 28.6% (12) were wives of merchants and 50% (21) were wives of lawyers or doctors.
54 Based on the tracing of thirty-seven members of the Presbyterian Benevolent Association in the federal census manuscript schedules for 1860.
55 Frances Miriam Berry, *The Widow Bedott Papers* (New York, 1856), 283–4.
56 "Constitution, Utica Orphan Asylum," 11.
57 *Utica Morning Herald,* May 27, 1865. The history of female charity in nineteenth-century cities is illuminated in Susan Porter Benson, "Business Heads and Sympathizing Hearts: The Women of the Providence Employment Society," in *Journal of Social History* 12 (1978), 302–14, and Carroll Smith-Rosenberg, *Religion and the Rise of the American City* (Ithaca, N.Y., 1971).
58 Johnson, "Diary," May 20, June 18, 1859.
59 Ibid., Feb. 16, 1860.
60 *Western Recorder,* July 14, 1829.
61 Mary Clemner Ames, *Eirene; or A Woman's Right* (New York, 1871), 193.
62 Fanny Forrester [Emily Chubbuck Judson], *Trippings in Authorland* (New York, 1846), 200.
63 A. C. Kendrick, *The Life and Letters of Emily Chubbuck Judson* (New York, 1861), 150, 155–6, 184.
64 Ibid., 205–6, 320.
65 Mary Clemner Ames, *Victoire* (New York, 1865), 36, and *Eirene,* 122.
66 Edmund Hudson, *An American Woman's Life and Work, a Memorial of Mary Clemner Ames* (Boston, 1886), 56, 75.
67 Samuel Beardsley to Thomas H. Hubbard, April 16, 1842, New York State Lunatic Asylum Collection, OHS.
68 *Utica Morning Herald,* Aug. 15, 1859.
69 *United States Census of Manufacturers,* Manuscript Schedules (Utica, 1850, 1860).
70 Ames, *Victoire,* 197, and *Eirene,* 132. In the census sample for 1855 there were 613 native-born males as opposed to 840 females in the age group fifteen to thirty.

71   Ames, *Eirene*, 201.
72   See Alice Felt Tyler, "Paulina Wright Davis," *Notable American Women 1607–1950: A Biographical Dictionary*, Edward T. James, ed. (Cambridge, Mass., 1974), Vol. 1, 444–5; Elizabeth Cady Stanton, Susan B. Anthony, and Matilda Joslyn Gage, eds., *History of Woman Suffrage* (Rochester, N.Y., 1889), Vol. 1, 283–9.
73   *New York Herald Tribune*, May 21, 1871, quoted in Nelson Manfred Blake, *The Road to Reno* (New York, 1960), 108–9: Stanton, Anthony, and Gage, *History of Woman Suffrage*, 283–5.
74   Stanton, Anthony, and Gage, *History of Woman Suffrage*, 283–9.

Sources and select bibliography

The social patterns and historical narrative delineated in this book were pieced together from a wide array of documents. My research strategy was simply to examine any historical source ascribed to antebellum Utica and Oneida County, New York, that dealt even tangentially with matters of family and gender. This method uncovered a vast body of documents and artifacts, everything from court warrants to crockery and quilts, all of which were found in profusion in local archives. I relied most heavily on collections of written documents held by the Oneida Historical Society, the Utica Public Library, the New York Historical Society, and the New York Public Library. Among the richest manuscript materials were more than a dozen collections of family correspondence, five diaries, and the records of sundry local institutions, ranging from the Utica Female Academy to the New York State Lunatic Asylum. Utica's churches housed a plentitude of useful documents, including membership lists, proceedings of church trials, and records of benevolent societies. My research strategy also identified an array of serial records that were especially susceptible to social-historical analysis – among them annual city directories, sixteen volumes of wills, credit records for more than six hundred local businesses, and the employment records of the New York Mills Company.

The relatively narrow geographical boundaries of my research also brought into focus a wealth of published documents that often elude historians who choose a larger unit of analysis. I was directed to this local literature by the Historical Records Survey, financed by the Works Progress Administration in the 1930s, which issued an extensive catalogue of Utica imprints. Hundreds of these titles were located at the Utica Public Library; others were found at the American Antiquarian Society in Worcester, Massachusetts, the New York Historical Society, the New York Public Library, and the New York State Library in Albany. These same archives hold scattered copies of some fifteen local newspapers published in Utica between 1796 and 1865, as well as scores of evangelical and reform periodicals.

293

Listed below are those items of published ltierature that were found most useful to the investigation of family and gender, along with the secondary historical literature that influenced my thinking on the subject. This bibliography is far from complete. It is impossible to acknowledge the countless ways in which the ideas of others have seeped into my own perceptions. The historical literature on family and gender has continued to grow exponentially since this manuscript was completed. One example of this recent scholarship, the translation from the French of Jacques Donzelot's *The Policing of Families*, can stand, despite some discrepancies and disagreements, as a fitting comparative and theoretical addendum to this volume.

Records of local churches and associations

Church records

Deerfield, N.Y. The First Baptist Church. "Confession of Faith, 1880"; "Church Covenant, 1800"; scattered records of trustees and deacons, 1800–25.

Oneida Conference of the Methodist Church. George Arendts Research Library, Syracuse University, Syracuse, N.Y. "Immorality Trials" and miscellaneous records, 1827–65.

Utica, N.Y. First Presbyterian Church, Parish House, and Oneida Historical Society. "Records of the Session Meetings," Vols. 1–4, 1821–65; Church Register, 1813–46; marriage records, 1813–50; baptismal records, 1813–50.

Utica, N.Y. Grace Episcopal Church, The Rectory. "Minutes of the Vestry," 1838–89.

Utica, N.Y. Second Presbyterian Church. Uticana Collection, Oneida Historical Society, Utica. Roll Book, 1824–1840.

Utica, N.Y. Westminster Presbyterian Church, Parish Office, Westminster Church. Records of the Session, 1859–67.

Whitesboro, N.Y. First Baptist Church. Oneida Historical Society, Utica. "Records of the Whitesboro Baptist Church," 1803–47.

Whitesboro, N.Y. First Presbyterian Church, the Parish House, Whitesboro. Frost, Reverend John, "Families Within the Boundaries of the United Society of Whitesboro," April 1813–July 1816. "Records of the Sessions," Vols. 1–3, 1815–59. Marriage records, 1795–1850. Registry of Church Members, 1795–1850.

Anti-slavery records

"Circular of the Executive Committee of the Whitestown and Oneida Institute Anti-Slavery Society," n.p., n.d.

[Howes, H. M.], "The Enemies of the Constitution Discovered or An Inquiry into the Origin and Tendency of Popular Violence Containing a Complete and Circumstantial Account of the Unlawful Proceedings at the City of Utica, October 21st, 1835." New York and Utica, 1835.
The Friend of Man, 1836–42.
The Liberty Press, 1845.
"Petition to the Senate and House of Representatives of the United States." Manuscript distributed by Sophia Clarke. Washington, D.C. The National Archives.
"Proceedings at the First Annual Meeting of the New York State Anti-Slavery Society Held at Utica," October 19, 1836. Utica, 1836.
"Proceedings of the Anti-Slavery Convention of American Women, Held in the City of New York." New York, 1837.
"Proceedings of the Anti-Slavery Convention of American Women, Held in Philadelphia, May 15–18, 1838." Philadelphia, 1838.
"Proceedings of the Third Anti-Slavery Convention of American Women, Held in Philadelphia." Philadelphia, 1859.
Quarterly Anti-Slavery Magazine, 1835.
"Second Annual Report of the American Anti-Slavery Society." New York, 1835.

Records of charitable associations

"Annual Reports, St. Luke Home, Hospital and Mission." Utica, 1873.
"The Benevolent Association of the First Presbyterian Church, Utica, New York." Utica, 1865.
"Charter of the Home for the Homeless of the City of Utica." Utica, 1871.
"Constitution and By-Laws of the Utica Orphan Asylum." Utica, 1857.
"Fourth Annual Report of St. Elizabeth's Hospital and Home." Utica, 1872.
"Ladies Soldiers' Relief Association of Utica and the U.S. Sanitary Commission, A Plea for Continuous Aid and Support." Utica, 1863.
"Records of the Female Charitable Society of Whitestown." 1806–14. Utica, Oneida Historical Society.
"Scrapbook." St. Elizabeth's Hospital. Utica, n.d.
"St. John's Home and School." Sisters of Charity. DePaul Provincial House. Albany, n.d.

Education and mutual improvement societies

"Charters, Constitution and By-Laws of the Utica Mechanics Association with a Short History." Utica, 1864.
"The Constitution of the Washington Benevolent Society." Albany, 1812.
"First Report of the Trustees of the Oneida Institute of Science and Industry." Utica, 1828.

"Literary Club Journal." March 12, 1835; May 16, 1833. Utica, Oneida
    Historical Society. Uticana Collection.
"Minute Books of the Oneida County Agricultural Society." 1818–24.
    Utica, Oneida Historical Society.
"Proceedings and Address of the Republican Young Men of the State of
    New York Assembled at Utica on the 12th Day of August, 1828."
    Utica, 1828.
"Proceedings of a General Convention of Friends of Education Held at
    Utica." n.p., n.d.
"Proceedings of a Meeting Held at the Masonic Hall on the Subject of
    Manual Labor in Connection with Literary Institutions." New York,
    1831.
"Proceedings of the Oneida County Teachers' Institute Held in the Court
    House in the Village of Rome." Utica, 1862.
"Proceedings of the State Convention of Mechanics Held at Utica, Au-
    gust 21, 22, 1834." Utica, 1834.
"Records of the Whitestown Seminary Phoenix Society." Utica, Oneida
    Historical Society, Whitestown Collection.
"Third Report of the Trustees of the Oneida Institute of Science and In-
    dustry." Utica, 1831.
"A Voice from the Oneida Institute." July 1843.

                    Evangelical associations and periodicals

Advocate of Moral Reform, 1835–45.
American Branch Tract Society of Utica, Third Annual Report. Utica,
    1829.
"A Brief Statement of the Proceedings of the Citizens of Utica Touching
    Certain Measures for Enforcing the Observance of the Sabbath."
    Utica, 1828.
Evangelical Magazine and Gospel Advocate.
The Female Missionary Society of Oneida. "Constitution." Utica, 1814.
Female Moral Reform Society. "First Annual Report of the Female Moral
    Reform Society of the City of New York." New York, 1835.
Female Moral Reform Society. "Annual Report of the American Female
    Moral Reform Society." New York, 1848, 1849, 1860.
The Female Oneida Missionary Society Reports of the Trustees. Utica,
    1816–27.
Juvenile Magazine, 1827–28.
MacDowall's Journal, 1833–34.
Maternal Association. "An Address to Mothers." Printed with the "Con-
    stitution of the Maternal Association of Utica." Albany, New York
    State Library.
Maternal Association. "Constitution of the Maternal Association of
    Utica, adopted June 30, 1824." Albany, New York State Library.

Maternal Association. "To Every Mother in Oneida County." Utica, Oneida Historical Society, n.d.

Maternal Association. "Maxims for Mothers." "Maxims for Children." Bound with the Maternal Association Membership List, 1840. Albany, New York State Library.

Methodist Magazine, 1818–38.

Mother's Magazine, 1833–38.

Mother's Monthly Journal, 1836–42.

New York Baptist Register, 1826–45.

Oneida Bible Society. "Constitution of the Oneida Bible Society and Circular Letter of the Directors." Utica, 1812.

Sabbath School Visitant and Juvenile Magazine, 1824–29.

Utica Christian Magazine, 1813–16.

Utica Christian Repository, 1823–25.

Utica Evangelical Magazine, 1829.

Utica Magazine, 1829.

Western Education Society. "First Report of the Directors of the Western Education Society." Utica, 1819.

Western Education Society. "Report of the Directors of the Western Education Society of the State of New York." Utica, 1824.

Western New York Baptist Magazine, 1814–23.

Western Recorder, 1824–32.

Western Sunday School Union. "First Report of the Western Sunday School Union of the State of New York," 1826.

Western Sunday School Visitant, 1826.

Temperance associations – records and literature

Flandreau, Thomas H. "An Address Delivered at a Meeting of the Female Washingtonian and Other Temperance Societies of the City of Utica." Utica, 1842.

Galusha, the Reverend Elon. "Address Delivered Before the Rome Temperance Society." Utica, 1830.

New York Mills Washingtonian Total Abstinence Society. "Minutes and Memberships, 1842." Utica, Oneida Historical Society.

The Society for the Promotion of Temperance. "Resolutions and Membership List," July 21, 1828. Utica, Oneida Historical Society.

Sons of Temperance. "Proceedings of the Grand Division of the Sons of Temperance of Western New York." Utica, 1851.

Sons of Temperance. "Proceedings of the Grand Division of the Sons of Temperance of Western New York." Utica, 1853.

Utica Teetotaler, 1850–52.

Utica Temperance Advocate, 1847–48.

Utica Temperance Society. Johnson, A. B., "An Address to the Utica Temperance Society." Utica, 1829.

The Washingtonian, 1842.
Washingtonian Pocket Companion. "By Two of the Fraternity." Utica, 1842.

Published primary sources and Utica imprints

An Act to Incorporate the Village of Utica. Utica, 1817.
Aiken, Samuel C. "Moral Reform." Utica, 1834.
Ames, Mary Clemner. *Eirene; or a Woman's Right*. New York, 1871.
    Victoire, New York, 1864.
Austin, John Mather. *A Voice to Youth*. Utica, 1838.
    A Voice to the Married. Utica, 1841.
Bacon, Ezekiel. *Vacant Hours*. Utica, 1845.
Bagg, Moses. *Pioneers of Utica*. Utica, 1877.
Baldwin, Amos Glover. *Memoirs of Miss Huldah Ann Baldwin*. Utica, 1814.
Baldwin, Thomas. "Christian Baptism as Delivered to the Churches, by
    the Evangelists and Apostles in the New Testament in a Letter to a
    Friend." Utica, 1817.
"Baptism Not One of the Plainest Things in the World." Utica, 1811.
Berry, Frances Miriam. *The Widow Bedott Papers*. New York, 1856.
Bethune, George W. "The Cross of Christ, the Only Theme of the
    Preacher of the Faith." Utica, 1831.
*A Book for the Millions: The Home Miscellany or Book of Gems, Original and
    Selected*. Utica, 1857.
Briggs, Isaac. "An Address Delivered Before the Oneida Society for the
    Promotion of American Manufactures." Utica, 1817.
"Bye-Laws of the Utica Academy" (sic). Utica, 1838.
Carnahan, James. "Christianity Defended Against the Cavils of Infidels
    and the Weakness of Enthusiasts." Utica, 1808.
"Census of the State of New York, 1821." *New York State Assembly Jour-
    nal*, Albany, 1822.
Census of the State of New York for 1835. Albany, 1836.
Census of the State of New York for 1845. Albany, 1846.
Census of the State of New York for 1855. Albany, 1856.
Census of the State of New York for 1865. Albany, 1867.
Chadwick, Jabez. "Four Sermons on the Mode and Subject of Christian
    Baptism." Utica, 1811.
Coler, George. *Heroines of Methodism or Pen and Ink Sketches of the
    Mothers and Daughters of the Church*. New York, 1857.
*Daboll's Schoolmaster's Assistant Being a Plain Practical System of
    Arithmetic Adapted to the United States*. Utica, 1829.
"A Dialogue Between a Missionary and a Man and His Wife." N.p., n.d.
    Utica, Oneida Historical Society.
Davis, Henry. *A Narrative of the Embarrassments and Decline of Hamilton
    College*. Utica, 1829.
Eddy, A. D. "A Sermon Occasioned by the Death of Mrs. Beulah Clarke,
    Wife of William Clarke, Esq. of Utica." New York, 1827.

Essays of the Young Ladies' School. Utica, 1848.

The Evils of Hastening to Be Rich and the Bitter Fruits of Departing From the Path of Virtue. Utica, 1835.

"Female Influence." Utica, circa 1823.

Finney, Charles. *Memoirs of Reverend Charles G. Finney*. New York, 1876.

Fowler, P. H. *Historical Sketch of Presbyterianism Within the Bounds of the Synod of Central New York*. Utica, 1877.

"Reminiscences of First Presbyterian Church, Utica, New York." Utica, 1866.

"Sermon on the Occasion of the Death of Mrs. Harriet Kilburn Brace." Utica, 1859.

"Women's Sphere of Influence; a Discourse Delivered at the First Occasion of the Death of Mrs. Mary E. Ostrom." Utica, 1859.

Frost, John; Gillet, Moses; and Cole, Noah. *A Narrative of the Revival of Religion, Particularly in the Bounds of the Presbytery of Oneida in the Year 1826*. Utica, 1826.

Giles, Charles. *Pioneer*. New York, 1844.

Green, Beriah. "The Savior's Arms Open to Little Children: A Discourse." Utica, 1836.

Grosh, A. B. "Odd-Fellowship: Its Character and Tendency." Utica, 1843.

Harrowar, David. "A Sermon on the Doctrine of Disinterested Benevolence." Utica, 1816.

"A Sermon on the Total Depravity of Infants and Their Entire Dependence on Sovereign Grace for Eternal Salvation." Utica, 1815.

Hopkins, A. T. "The Evils and Remedy of Lewdness." Utica, 1834.

Hotchkin, the Reverend James H. *A History of the Purchase and Settlement of Western New York and of the Rise, Progress, and Present State of the Presbyterian Church in That Section*. New York, 1848.

Hudson, Edmund. *An American Woman's Life and Work, a Memorial of Mary Clemmer Ames*. Boston, 1886.

Jarvis, Edward. "On the Comparative Liability of Males and Females to Insanity." Utica, 1850.

Jay, William. *An Essay on Marriage or the Duty of Christians to Marry Religious*. Utica, 1814.

Jones. Pomeroy. *Annals and Recollections of Oneida County*. Rome, N.Y.: 1851.

Judson, Emily Chubbuck. *Allen Lucas, the Self-made Man or Life as It Is*. Utica, 1843.

My Two Sisters: A Sketch From Memory. Boston, 1854.

[Fanny Forrester]. *Trippings in Authorland*. New York, 1846.

Kendrick, A. C. *The Life and Letters of Emily Chubbuck Judson*. New York, 1861.

Lansing, D. C. "Remedy for Intemperance, a Sermon." Utica, 1832.

Laws and Ordinances of the Common Council of the City of Utica. Utica, 1832.

Lee, Elias. "A Letter to the Rev. James Carnahan Pastor of the Presbyterian Church in Utica and Whitesborough Being a Defense of Martha Howell and the Baptists Against the Misrepresentations and Aspersions of that Gentleman." Utica, 1808.

Leonard, Joshua. "The Relationship of Children of Christians to the Church Considered in Four Sermons." Utica, 1808.

Maynard's Sabbath School Echo, 6th ed. Utica, 1861.

"A Memorial of the Semi-Centennial Celebration of the Founding of the Sunday School of the First Presbyterian Church, Utica, New York." Utica, 1867.

Norton, Elijah. "The Methodist System and Church Annihilated by the Scripture of Truth." Utica, 1812.

"Ordinances of the City of Utica, 1863." Utica, 1863.

"Pastoral Letter of the Ministers of the Oneida Association to the Churches Under Their Care on the Subject of Revivals of Religion." Utica, 1827.

Pierce, Deborah. "A Scriptural Vindication of Female Preaching, Prophesying, or Exhortation." Utica, 1817.

Pomeroy, M.D., T. *Female Complaints: A Brief Examination of the Pathology of Uterine Diseases Together with an Exposition of the Principles and Method of Their Treatment.* Utica, 1851.

Porter, the Reverend Charles S. "Abandonment of God Deprecated by the Aged." Utica, 1842.

Preston, Lyman. *Preston's Manual on Book-Keeping or, Arbitrary Rules Made Plain.* New York, 1829.

Record of Genius. Utica, 1832.

Sherburne, Andrew. *Memoirs of Andrew Sherburne.* Utica, 1828.

Stanton, Elizabeth Cady; Anthony, Susan B.; and Gage, Matilda Joslyn, eds. *History of Woman Suffrage.* Vol. 1. Rochester, N.Y., 1889.

Taylor, Anne, and Gilberts, Ann F. *Rhymes for the Nursery.* Utica, 1815.

Truair, John. "Plain Truth on Christian Baptism and Communion." Utica, 1920.

Upson, Anson J. "An Address Delivered at the First Anniversary of the Young Men's Christian Association of Utica New York." Utica, 1859.
"An Address Delivered at the Laying of the Corner Stone of the Utica Orphan Asylum." Utica, 1860.

The Utica Almanac. Utica, 1810.

Utica City Directory, 1817, 1828, 1832, 1834, 1837, 1838, 1839–65.

"A Vindication of Infant Baptism. In Four Numbers. Including the Rise and Progress of a Dispute Carried on Between Certain Members of the Congregational and Baptist Churches in Sangerfield in the Year 1803." Utica, 1803.

The Wanderer, or Horatio and Laetitia: A Poem. Utica, 1811.

Watts, Isaac. *Divine Songs Attempted in Easy Language for the Use of Children.* Utica, 1810.

Webster, Noah. *An American Selection of Lessons in Reading and Speaking.* Utica, 1806.

Weeks, Raymond. "A Letter on Protracted Meetings Addressed to the Church in Paris." Utica, 1832.

Willson, Mrs. Arabella M. *The Lives of the Three Mrs. Judsons: Mrs. Ann H. Judson, Mrs. Sara B. Judson, Mrs. Emily C. Judson, Missionaries to Burma.* New York, 1856.

Young Christian's Guide Containing Important Scriptural Answers. Utica, 1819.

Secondary sources

Anderson, Michael. *Family Structure in Nineteenth-Century Lancashire.* Cambridge, England, 1971.

Arensberg, Conrad M., and Kimball, Solon T. *Family and Community in Ireland.* Cambridge, Mass., 1968.

Ariès, Philippe. *Centuries of Childhood: A Social History of Family Life.* Translated by Robert Baldick. New York, 1962.

Bagg, Moses M. "The Earliest Factories of Oneida and Their Projectors." In *Oneida Historical Society Transactions.* 1881.

"Historical Sketch of the Utica Orphan Asylum." Utica, 1880.

Bales, Robert F., and Parsons, Talcott. *Family Socialization and Interaction Process.* Glencoe, Ill., 1955.

Berg, Barbara J. *The Remembered Gate: Origins of American Feminism: The Woman and the City.* New York, 1978.

Berkhofer, Robert Frederick, Jr. "The Industrial History of Oneida County, New York, to 1850." Master's thesis. Cornell University, 1955.

Berkner, Lutz. "The Stem Family and the Developmental Cycle of the Peasant Household: An Eighteenth Century Austrian Example." *American Historical Review* 77 (1972), 398–419.

"The Use and Misuse of Census Data for the Historical Analysis of Family Structure." *Journal of Interdisciplinary History* 5 (1974–75), 721–38.

Bledstein, Burton J. *The Culture of Professionalism: The Middle Class and the Development of Higher Education in America.* New York, 1976.

Blumin, Stuart M. *The Urban Threshold: Growth and Change in a Nineteenth-Century American Community.* Chicago, 1976.

Boyer, Paul S. *Urban Masses and Moral Order in America, 1820–1920.* Cambridge, Mass., 1978.

Boyer, Paul S., and Nissenbaum, Stephen. *Salem Possessed: The Social Origins of Witchcraft.* Cambridge, Mass., 1974.

Branca, Patricia. *Silent Sisterhood: Middle Class Women in the Victorian Home.* London, 1975.

Brown, Richard D. "Modernization and the Modern Personality in Early America 1600–1864: A Sketch of a Synthesis." *Journal of Interdisciplinary History* 2 (1972), 201–28.

Busacca, Richard, and O'Donnell, Patrick. "The State, Redistribution and the System of Social Reproduction." Paper delivered before the American Political Science Association, 1979.

Chodorow, Nancy. "Family Structure and Feminine Personality." In *Women, Culture and Society.* Edited by Michelle Zimbalist Rosaldo and Louise Lamphere. Stanford, Calif., 1974.

The Reproduction of Mothering: Psychoanalysis and the Sociology of Gender. Berkeley, Calif., 1978.

Cott, Nancy F. "Young Women in the Second Great Awakening in New England." *Feminist Studies 3* (Fall 1975), 14–20.

The Bonds of Womanhood: "Woman's Sphere" in New England, 1780–1835. New Haven, Conn., 1977.

Cross, Whitney. *The Burned-Over District: The Social and Intellectual History of Enthusiastic Religion in Western New York.* Ithaca, N.Y., 1950.

Decker, Peter R. *Fortunes and Failures: White-Collar Mobility in Nineteenth-Century San Francisco.* Cambridge, Mass., 1978.

Demos, John. *A Little Commonwealth: Family Life in Plymouth Colony.* New York, 1970.

Demos, John, and Boocock, Sarane Spence, eds. *Turning Points: Historical and Sociological Essays on the Family.* Chicago, 1978.

Donzelot, Jacques. *The Policing of Families.* Translated by Robert Hurley. New York, 1979.

Dowd, Douglas. *The Twisted Dream: Capitalist Development in the United States Since 1776.* Cambridge, Mass., 1974.

Dublin, Thomas. *Women at Work: The Transformation of Work and Community in Lowell, Massachusetts, 1826–1860.* New York, 1979.

Dubnoff, Steven. "Gender, the Family and the Problems of Work Motivation in a Transition to Industrial Capitalism." *Journal of Family History 4,* No. 2 (Summer 1979), 121–37.

DuBois, Ellen Carol. *Feminism and Suffrage: The Emergence of an Independent Women's Movement in America, 1848–1869.* Ithaca, N.Y., 1978.

Easterlin, Richard A. "Factors in the Decline of Farm Family Fertility in the United States: Some Preliminary Research Results." *Journal of American History 63* (1976), 600–14.

Faler, Paul. "Cultural Aspects of the Industrial Revolution: Lynn, Massachusetts, Shoemakers and Industrial Morality, 1826–1860. "*Labor History 15* (Summer 1974), 367–94.

Farber, Bernard. *Guardians of Virtue: Salem Families in 1800.* New York, 1972.

Fischer, David Hacket. *Growing Old in America.* New York, 1978.

Flaherty, David H. *Privacy in Colonial New England.* Charlottesville, Va., 1972.

Forster, Colin, and Tucker, G. S. L. *Economic Opportunity and White Fertility Ratios, 1800–1860.* New Haven, Conn., 1972.

Foucault, Michel. *The History of Sexuality,* Vol. 1, *An Introduction.* Translated by Robert Hurley. New York, 1978.

Frisch, Michael H. *Town into City: Springfield, Massachusetts, and the Meaning of Community, 1840–1880.* Cambridge, Mass., 1972.

Fulton, John, and Osterud, Nancy. "Family Limitation and Age at Marriage: Fertility Decline in Sturbridge, Massachusetts, 1730–1850." *Population Studies 30* (November 1976), 481–94.

Galpin, W. Freeman. *Central New York, an Inland Empire.* New York, 1941.

Gerstein, Ira. "Domestic Work and Capitalism." *Radical America 7* (July-October 1973), 101–28.

Giminez, M. E. "Structural Marxism on the Woman Question." *Science and Society,* Fall 1978, 301–24.

Glasco, Laurence. "The Life Cycle and Household Cycle of American Ethnic Groups: Irish, German and Native-Born Whites in Buffalo, New York, 1855. *Journal of Urban History 1* (May 1975), 339–64.

Glick, Paul C. "Updating the Life Cycle of the Family." *Journal of Marriage and Family 39* (1977), 5–13.

Goody, Jack; Thirsk, Joan; and Thompson, E. P., eds. *Family and Inheritance: Rural Society in Western Europe, 1200–1800.* New York and Cambridge, England, 1976.

Gordon, Linda. *Woman's Body, Woman's Right: A Social History of Birth Control in America.* New York, 1976.

Gordon, Michael, ed. *The American Family in Social-Historical Perspective,* 2nd ed. New York, 1978.

Greven, Philip J. *Four Generations: Population, Land and Family in Colonial Andover, Massachusetts.* Ithaca, N.Y., 1970.

Griffen, Clyde, and Griffen, Sally. *Natives and Newcomers: The Ordering of Opportunity in Mid-Nineteenth Century Poughkeepsie.* Cambridge, Mass., 1978.

Gutman, Herbert G. *The Black Family in Slavery and Freedom, 1750–1925.* New York, 1976.

Hareven, Tamara. "The Family as Process: The Historical Study of the Family Cycle." *Journal of Social History 7* (1973–74), 322–9.

"Modernization and Family History, Perspectives on Social Change." *Signs: Journal of Women in Culture and Society 2* (1976), 190–207.

"Cycles, Courses and Cohorts: Reflections on Theoretical and Methodological Approaches to the Historical Study of Family Development." *Journal of Social History 12* (Fall 1978), 97–109.

Hareven, Tamara, and Vinovskis Maris, eds. *Family and Population in 19th-Century America.* Princeton, N.J., 1978.

Hersch, Blanche Glassman. *The Slavery of Sex: Feminist-Abolitionists in America.* Urbana, Ill., 1978.

Horlick, Allan S. *Country Boys and Merchant Princes: The Social Control of Young Men in New York.* Lewisburg, Pa., 1975.

Jareckie, Stephen Barlow. "An Architectural Survey of New York Mills from 1808–1908." Master's thesis. Syracuse University, 1961.

Johnson, Paul E. *A Shopkeeper's Millennium: Society and Revivals in Rochester, New York, 1815–1837.* New York, 1978.

Katz, Michael. *The People of Hamilton, Canada West: Family and Class in a Mid-Nineteenth-Century City.* Cambridge, Mass., 1975.

"Migration and Social Order in Erie County, New York, 1855." *Journal of Interdisciplinary History 8*, No. 4 (Spring 1978), 669–701.

"Origins of the Institutional State." *Marxist Perspectives 1*, No. 4 (Winter 1978), 6–24.

Keller, Charles Ray. *The Second Great Awakening in Connecticut.* New Haven, Conn., 1942.

Kelley, Virginia B.; O'Connel, Merrilyn R.; Olney, Stephen S.; and Reig, Johanna R. *Wood and Stone: Landmarks of the Upper Mohawk Region.* Utica, N.Y., 1972.

Kett, Joseph. *Rites of Passage: Adolescence in America.* New York, 1977.

Kuhn, Ann. *The Mother's Role in Childhood Education: New England Concepts, 1830–1860.* New Haven, Conn., 1947.

Laslett, Peter, and Wall, Richard. *Household and Family in Past Time.* Cambridge, England, 1972.

Laurie, Bruce, "'Nothing on Compulsion': Life Styles of Philadelphia Artisans 1820–1850." *Labor History 15* (Summer 1974), 337–66.

Laurie, Bruce; Hershberg, Theodore; and Alter, George. "Immigrants and Industry: The Philadelphia Experience 1850–1880." *Journal of Social History*, Winter 1975, 219–67.

Lebsock, Suzanne Dee. "Women and Economics in Virginia: Petersburg, 1784–1820." Doctoral dissertation. University of Virginia, 1977.

Levine, David. *Family Formations in an Age of Nascent Capitalism.* New York, 1977.

Lindstrom, Diane. *Economic Development in the Philadelphia Region 1810–1850.* New York, 1978.

Lockridge, Kenneth A. *A New England Town: The First Hundred Years, Dedham, Massachusetts, 1636–1736.* New York, 1970.

Lockwood, David. *The Blackcoated Worker: A Study in Class Consciousness.* London, 1958.

Macfarlane, Alan. *The Family Life of Ralph Josselin, A Seventeenth-Century Clergyman: An Essay in Historical Anthropology.* Cambridge, England, 1970.

McKendrick, Neil. "Home Demand and Economic Growth: A New View of the Role of Women and Children in the Industrial Revolution." In *Historical Perspectives: Studies in English Thought and Society, in Honour of J. H. Plumb.* Edited by Neil McKendrick. London, 1974.

Magas, Branka; Coulson, Margaret; and Wainwright, Hilary. "The Housewife and Her Labour Under Capitalism – A Critique." *New Left Review 89* (January-February 1975), 59–71.

Melder, Keith E. *Beginnings of Sisterhood: The American Women's Rights Movement, 1800–1850.* New York, 1977.

Mills, C. Wright. *White Collar: The American Middle Classes.* New York, 1951.

Modell, John; Furstenberg, Frank; and Herchberg, Theodore. "Social Change and Transitions to Adulthood in Historical Perspective." *Journal of Family History 1*, No. 1 (Autumn 1976), 7–32.

Mohr, James C. *Abortion in America: The Origins and Evolutions of National Policy, 1800–1900.* New York, 1978.

Morgan, Edmund Sears. *The Puritan Family: Religion and Domestic Relations in Seventeenth-Century New England.* New York, 1966.

North, Douglass. *The Economic Growth of the United States 1790–1860.* Englewood Cliffs, N.J., 1961.

Parsons, Talcott, and Bales, Robert F. *Family, Socialization and Interaction Process.* Glencoe, Ill., 1955.

Pessen, Edward. *Most Uncommon Jacksonians; The Radical Leaders of the Early Labor Movement.* Albany, N.Y., 1967.

Pleck, Elizabeth. "Two Worlds in One." *Journal of Social History 10* (Winter 1977), 178–95.

Przybycien, Frank E. *Utica: A City Worth Saving.* Utica, N.Y., 1976.

Rabkin, Peggy A. "The Silent Feminist Revolution: Women and the Law in New York from Blackstone to the Beginnings of the American Women's Rights Movement." Doctoral dissertation. State University of New York at Buffalo, 1975.

Reiter, Rayna R. "Men and Women in the South of France: Public and Private Domains." In *Toward an Anthropology of Women.* Edited by Rayna R. Reiter. New York, 1975.

ed., *Toward an Anthropology of Women.* New York, 1975.

Richards, Leonard L. *Gentlemen of Property and Standing: Anti-Abolition Mobs in Jacksonian America.* London and New York, 1970, 1971.

Roberts, John Martin. "The Social Dimensions of Urban-Industrial Structure: Evangelical Religion, Reform and Economic Growth in Oneida County, New York." Paper, n.d.

Rosaldo, Michelle Zimbalist, and Lamphere, Louise, eds. *Woman, Culture and Society.* Stanford, Calif., 1974.

Rothman, David. *The Discovery of the Asylum: Social Order and Disorder in the New Republic.* Boston, 1971.

Rubin, Gayle. "The Traffic in Women: Notes on the 'Political Economy' of Sex." In *Toward an Anthropology of Women.* Edited by Rayna R. Reiter. New York, 1975

Ryan, Mary P. "American Society and the Cult of Domesticity, 1830–1860." Doctoral dissertation. University of California at Santa Barbara, 1971.

"The Power of Women's Networks: A Case Study of Female Moral Reform in Antebellum America." *Feminist Studies 5* (Spring 1979), 66–86.

Womanhood in America from Colonial Times to the Present. New York, 1975; 2nd rev. ed., 1979.

Sawhill, Isabel V. "Economic Perspectives on the Family." *Daedalus 106*, No. 2 (Spring 1977), 115–25.

Scott, Joan W., and Tilly, Louise A. *Women, Work, and Family*. New York, 1978.

Seccomb, Wally. "The Housewife and Her Labour Under Capitalism." *New Left Review* (January-February 1974), 3–24.

Sennett, Richard. *Families Against the City: Middle Class Homes of Industrial Chicago, 1872–1890*. Cambridge, Mass., 1970.

Shorter, Edward. *The Making of the Modern Family*. New York, 1977.

Sinclair, Bruce. *Philadelphia's Philosopher Mechanics: A History of the Franklin Institute, 1824–1865*. Baltimore, 1974.

Sklar, Kathryn Kish. *Catharine Beecher*. New Haven, Conn., 1973.

Smith, Daniel Scott. "Family Limitation, Sexual Control, and Domestic Feminism in Victorian America." *Feminist Studies 1*, No. 3-4 (1973), 40–57.

"Population, Family, and Society in Hingham, Massachusetts, 1650–1880." Doctoral dissertation. University of California at Berkeley, 1973.

Smith, Daniel Scott, and Hindus, Michael. "Premarital Pregnancy in America, 1640–1971: An Overview and Interpretation." *Journal of Interdisciplinary History 5* (1974–75), 537–70.

Smith-Rosenberg, Carroll. "Beauty, the Beast and the Militant Woman: A Case Study in Sex Roles and Social Stress in Jacksonian America." *American Quarterly 23* (October 1971), 562–84.

"The Female World of Love and Ritual: Relations between Woman in Nineteenth-Century America." *Signs: Journal of Women in Culture and Society 1* (Autumn 1975), 1–29.

Stone, Lawrence J. *The Family, Sex and Marriage in England, 1500–1800*. London, 1977.

Tryon, Rolla Milton. *Household Manufactures in the United States, 1640–1860: Reprints of Economic Classics*. New York, 1966. Reprint of the 1917 edition.

Vinovskis, Maris. "Socioeconomic Determinants of Interstate Fertility Differentials in the United States in 1850 and 1860." *Journal of Interdisciplinary History 6* (Winter 1976), 375–95.

Waldron, Carroll T. "A Hundred Years of Amusement in Utica 1806–1906." Paper, Oneida Historical Society, Utica, N.Y., n.d.

Wallace, Anthony F. C. *Rockdale: The Growth of an American Village in the Early Industrial Revolution*. New York, 1978.

Waters, John. "The Traditional World of the New England Peasants: A View from Seventeenth-Century Barnstable." *New England Historical and Genealogical Register*, January 1976, pp. 19–32.

Wells, Robert V. "Family History and Demographic Transition." *Journal of Social History 9* (Fall 1975), 1–19.

Welter, Barbara. "The Cult of True Womanhood 1820–1860." *American Quarterly 18* (1966), 151–74.

White, William. "Genealogy of the White Family." *Oneida Historical Society Transactions* (1881–84), 25–30.

Williams, John Camp. *An Oneida County Printer.* New York, 1906.
Wrigley, E. A. "The Process of Modernization and Industrial Revolution in England." *Journal of Interdisciplinary History* 3 (1972–73), 225–59.
Yasuba, Yasukichi. *Birth Rates of the White Populations in the U.S., 1800– 1860: An Economic Study.* Baltimore, 1962.

Index

and demography of revivalism, 76–83

discontent, frontier generation, 58–9

and domestication of religion, 98–104

domestic work, midcentury, 198–203

employment, 172–3

family, and associations, 140–1

and family size, 155–7

and feminism, 225–9

fertility, 55–6, 155–7

and hierarchy of sexes, revival era, 71–4

in labor force, 173, 203–9

and leadership of revivalism, 83–98

and marriage, 179–85

and moral reform, association era, 116–27

in patriarchal frontier economy, 33–4

patriarchy, religion, and, 71–5

and preparation of youth for work, 175–6

prospects for, 58

and public welfare, 210–18

and revivalism, 60–1, 79–80, 83–98

and sexual discrimination in wills, 27–8, 29, 80

social isolation and religion, 76–7

sphere, midcentury, 186–91, 218–25

and temperance, 135, 140

"Women's Sphere of Influence," 187

work
boyhood preparation for, 165–79
household, midcentury, 198–210
indentured farm workers, 25–6

working class, and associations, 130–1

Workingmen's Temperance Union, 133

Wright, Francis, 113, 114, 226

Wright, Paulina, *see* Davis, Paulina Kellogg Wright

writers, women, 209–10, 221–2

Yates Clothing, 206

Young Christian's Guide, 33, 34, 41

Young Ladies' Miscellany, 146–7

Young Ladies' Relief Society, 214–15

Young Ladies' Sewing Circle, 197

Young Men's Association, 111–12, 128, 129, 176

Young Men's Christian Association (YMCA), 176–7

Young Men's Literary Club, 128, 129–30, 132

youth
associations, 127–30, 176–7
family, associations, and, 140–1
and moral reform, 122–3
preparation for employment, midcentury, 165–79
and revivalism, 77, 78, 80
and temperance, 135

Youth Abstinence Society, 132